AF522225

AGRICULTURE AND FOOD SECURITY

Contemporary Issues

AGRICULTURE AND FOOD SECURITY

Contemporary Issues

Edited by

DALIP KUMAR

and

ASMI RAZA

Published on behalf of
THE INDIAN ECONOMIC ASSOCIATION

DEEP & DEEP PUBLICATIONS PVT. LTD.
F-159, RAJOURI GARDEN, NEW DELHI-110027

AGRICULTURE AND FOOD SECURITY

ISBN 978-81-8450-360-9

Typeset by S.S. COMPOSERS
3190, Mohindra Park, Shakur Basti, Delhi-110034.

Printed in India at MAYUR ENTERPRISES
WZ Plot No. 3, Gujjar Market, Tihar Village, New Delhi-110018.

Published by DEEP & DEEP PUBLICATIONS PVT. LTD.
F-159, Rajouri Garden, New Delhi-110027.
Phones: 25435369, 25440916
E-mail: ddpbooks@yahoo.co.in • ddpubs@gmail.com
Showroom:
2/13, Ansari Road, Daryaganj, New Delhi-110002 • Telefax: 23245122

Contents

Preface ix

List of Contributors xi

Abbreviations xv

Dalip Kumar and Asmi Raza
Introduction xix

PART A

STRUCTURAL REFORMS AND AGRICULTURAL GROWTH

1. *Ram Naresh Thakur and Satendra Narayan Singh*
Structural Reform, Agricultural Diversification and Economic Growth 1

2. *S.S. Somra and Kuldeep Singh*
Structural Changes and Agriculture in India 44

3. *Dhirendran Nath Konar*
Structural Change in India and Rural Poverty 63

4. *Angrej Singh*
Structural Reforms and Sustaining Growth in Indian Agriculture: The Emerging Trade Order 80

5. *Purushottam Sahu and Babilata Shroff*
Structural Changes in Agriculture: An Empirical Analysis 91

6. *Sanjeev Bhardwaj, Pratibha Misra and Deepak Jain*
WTO and Indian Agriculture:
Task and Challenges 101

7. *Rajendra Prasad Singh and Pankaj Kumar Mishra*
Investment in Agriculture and Structural
Adjustment in Indian Economy 111

8. *Ramakant Pd. Singh and Kumar Gaurav*
Agricultural Reforms and Institutional Finance:
Problems and Prospects 120

9. *Bharti Pandey*
Post-Reform Indian Agriculture: A Survey 132

10. *Satyendra Prajapti and Poonam Kumari*
Structural Reforms in Agriculture 144

11. *Asmi Raza*
Impact of Globalization on Agriculture
in Developing Countries 153

PART B

ALLIED AGRICULTURE WITH REGIONAL PERSPECTIVES

12. *N.P. Singh, B.V. Singh and G.P. Singh*
Developing Milk Producing Units as a Farmer's
Enterprise: Need of Multidimensional Assail 165

13. *Krishna Nand Yadav and Upendra Pd. Singh*
An Analysis of Performance of Dairying Practice in
Bihar: With Special Reference to Patna Dairy Project 174

14. *Ratnesh Kumar*
Review of Returns on Investment in Agro-Processing
Units: A Case Study of Central Public Sector Agro-
Processing Industries 188

15. *Anjana Kumari*
Economic Security against Rising Risks in
Agriculture and Allied Sectors 201

16. *Rajini Kumari and Veena Kumari*
An Analysis of Agro-Economic Condition in Jharkhand 210

17. *Rajnath Upadhyay and Sriman Pandey*
Agricultural Diversification in North-Eastern Region in India 216

18. *Devna Sharma and Rachna Dixit*
Agriculture in Uttarakhand: Problems and Prospects 232

PART C

AGRICULTURAL CREDIT AND POLICY ISSUES

19. *Amarjit Singh Sethi*
Growth and Transformations in Agricultural Output and Inputs in India: Need for Structural Adjustments 239

20. *Samir R. Samantara and B.B. Sahoo*
Rural Credit: Trend, Issues and Challenges in India 259

21. *Vinod Kumar and Ram Bharat Thakur*
Agricultural Credit Flow in Bihar 272

22. *Bharat Bhushan and Kabita Kumari*
Agrarian Structure in India 280

23. *G. Savaraiah, G. Chandrasekhara Rao and M. Devarajulu*
Policy for Land Acquisition for Non-Agriculture Uses and Compensation for Land: An Analysis 290

24. *Dhiren Vandra*
Land Reforms and its Impact on Agriculture in India 297

Part D

FOOD SECURITY ISSUES

25. *Dalip Kumar and Abha Mittal*
Achieving Food Security in India: Issues and Challenges 304

26. *Dastgir Alam, Firdos Ahmad and Jamil Ahmad*
Environmental Resources and their Impact on Foodgrains Production and Productivity 322

27. *R. Raj Kumar and A. Gnanavelan*
WTO and Food Security in India 342

28. *M. Pandiyan*
Globalisation and Food Security in India 351

29. *N.K. Thakur and Alpana Sharma*
Globalization, WTO and Food Security Availability, Access and Affordability of Food PDS and Food Subsidy 360

30. *Ashwini Kant Jha, Bhavna Jha and Dilip Kumar*
Economic Reforms, Agriculture and Food Security in India 380

Index 392

Preface

This book 'Agriculture and Food Security: Contemporary Issues' is an outcome of the 92nd Annual Conference of Indian Economic Association, which was organised by the School of Management, KIIT University, Bhubaneswar, Orissa during December 27-29, 2009. We are thankful to Professor C.H. Hanumantha Rao, the Conference President of the Indian Economic Association for his valuable guidance and immense cooperation. Most of the papers in this book were presented at the conference organized by Indian Economic Association.

The success of the conference was reflected in the lively debate among all the paper writers and discussants. We are also grateful to all the paper writers for incorporating the desired comments and revising their papers.

We extend our heartfelt thanks to Dr. Achyuta Samantha, Founder KIIT and KISS, Bhubaneswar and his colleagues, and all the teaching and administrative staff of the College for their active support in organising and making this conference a success. Thanks are also due to the Dr. Anil Kumar Thakur, General Secretary and Treasurer, Indian Economic Association who spent enormous time and energy for organising the conference and facilitating the publication of this book.

Our special appreciation is due to Dr. Anjani Kumar Jha, the Chairman, Development of Indian Society and Culture (DISC), Dr. Rajesh Jaiswal, Associate Fellow, National Council of Applied Economic Research, New Delhi for a helping hand in bringing out this publication. We are indebted to many friends, colleagues, and teachers for their careful guidance and constant support.

We would like to acknowledge Mr. G.S. Bhatia and his staff of M/s Deep and Deep Publications Pvt. Ltd., Delhi deserve thanks for all the designing, typesetting and printing work to bring out this book. We would like to confess that despite the maximum possible efforts against all odds, we have tried to give the best quality and outlook to the book upto the desired level. We are thankful to all of them.

DALIP KUMAR
ASMI RAZA

List of Contributors

A. Gnanavelan, Research Scholar, IDE, University of Madras, Madras.

Abha Mittal, Associate Professor, Maharaja Ugrasen College, University of Delhi, Delhi.

Alpana Sharma, City Union Bank, Kolakata, West Bengal.

Amarjit Singh Sethi, Guru Nanak Dev University, Amritsar (Punjab).

Angrej Singh, Department of Economic Upadhi (P.G.) College, Pilibhit (U.P.).

Anjana Kumari, L.S. College Campus, Muzaffarpur, Bihar.

Ashwini Kant Jha, Department of Economics, B.N.M. University (W.C), Saharsa

Asmi Raza, Associate Professor, Department of Economics, University of Delhi, Delhi.

B.B. Sahoo, Assistant General Manager in National Bank for Agriculture and Rural Development (NABARD), Head Office, Mumbai.

B.V. Singh, Professor, Department of Economics, Faculty of Social Sciences, Banaras Hindu University, Varanasi (U.P.).

Babilata Shroff, Lecturer, Department of Economics, D.A.V. College, Titilagarh, District: Bolangir, Orissa.

Bharat Bhushan, Lecturer in Economics, T.S. College, Hisua (Nawada)

Bharti Pandey, Reader, Department of Economics, JNPG College, University of Lucknow, Lucknow.

Bhavna Jha, Department of IRPM, M.A.M. College, Naugachia, Bhagalpur.

Dalip Kumar, Project Officer, National Council of Applied Economic Research, New Delhi.

Dastgir Alam, Department of Economics, A.M.U., Aligarh.

Deepak Jain, Lecturer, Economics, M.D. Jain Inter College, Sirsaganj.

Devna Sharma, Department of Economics, D.A.V. (P.G.) College, Dehradun.

Dhiren Vandra, Professor, College of Rural Studies, Shardagram, Mangrol, Dist. Junagadh, Gujarat.

Dhirendran Nath Konar, Professor, Department of Commerce, University of Kalyani, Kalyani, WB.

Dilip Kumar, Department of History, M.L.J. College, Bhagalpur.

Firdos Ahmad, Department of Economics, A.M.U., Aligarh.

G. Chandrasekhara Rao, Dean, Faculty of Arts, Department of Economics, S.V. University, Tirupati.

G. Savaraiah, UGC Nominee, BOM, K.L.E. University, Belgaumm, UGC-Nominee, Governing Body, Siddartha Institute of Technology, Vijayawada, Department of Economics, S.V. University, Tirupati.

G.P. Singh, Reader, Department of AH and D, Institute of Agricultural Sciences, Banaras Hindu University, Varanasi (U.P.).

Jamil Ahmad, Department of Economics, A.M.U., Aligarh.

Kabita Kumari, Research Scholar, M.U. Bodh Gaya.

Krishna Nand Yadav, Department of Economics, R.L.S.Y. College, Aurangabad (Bihar).

Kuldeep Singh, Lecturer of Economics, Wilfred P.G. College, Jaipur.

Kumar Gaurav, Research Scholar (Ecomomics), T.M. Bhagalpur University, Bhagalpur.

M. Devarajulu, Professor, Department of Economics, S.V. University, Tirupati.

M. Pandiyan, Reader, PG and Research Department of Economics, Sir Theagaraya College, Chennai, Tamil Nadu.

N.K. Thakur, Sr. Marketing Manager, 2/175, Vishwas Khand, Gomtinagar, Lucknow (U.P.) G.N.F.C. Ltd., Lucknow (U.P.).

N.P. Singh, Lecturer in Economics, CSN, Faculty of Social Sciences, Banaras Hindu University, Varanasi (U.P.).

Pankaj Kumar Mishra, Research Scholar, Department of Economics, M.G. Kashi Vidyapith, Varanasi (U.P.).

Poonam Kumari, Lecturer, Department of Economics, M.S.Y. College, Gaya, Magadh University, Bodh-Gaya (Bihar).

Pratibha Misra, Research Scholar.

Purushottam Sahu, Department of Economics, Gopalpur College, Gopalpur-on-sea, Berhampur, Ganjam.

R. Raj Kumar, IDE, University of Madras, Madras.

Rachna Dixit, Department of Economics, D.A.V. (P.G.) College, Dehradun.

Rajendra Prasad Singh, Associate Professor, Department of Economics, M.G. Kashi Vidyapith, Varanasi (U.P.).

Rajini Kumari, Department of Economics, Sita Ram Sah College, Nawada, Bihar.

Rajnath Upadhyay, Professor of Economics, MG Kashi Vidyapeeth, Varanasi (U.P.).

Ram Bharat Thakur, Professor of Economics, Dalsingsarai, Samastipur.

Ram Naresh Thakur, H.O.D., P.G. Dept. of Economics and Director, Gandhian Studies Centre, Samastipur College, Samastipur.

Ramakant Pd. Singh, University Professor, Department of Economics, R.D. College, Sheikhpura, T.M. Bhagalpur University, Bhagalpur.

Ratnesh Kumar, Research Scholar, Department of History, B.R.A. Bihar University, Muzaffarpur.

S.S. Somra, Assistant Professor, Department of Economics, University of Rajasthan, Jaipur.

Samir R. Samantara, Assistant General Manager in National Bank for Agriculture and Rural Development (NABARD), Head Office, Mumbai.

Sanjeev Bhardwaj, Reader, Department of Economics, Government Girls P.G. College, Sirsaganj (Firozabad), U.P.

Satendra Narayan Singh, Lecturer, Gandhi Plus Two School, Prabhat Nagar, Jehanabad.

Satyendra Prajapti, Principal, S.N.S. College, Tekari, Gaya, Magadh University, Bodh-Gaya (Bihar).

Sriman Pandey, Professor of Economics, MG Kashi Vidyapeeth, Varanasi (U.P.).

Upendra Pd. Singh, Dept of Economics, S.G.G. College, Patna City.

Veena Kumari, Research Scholar, Dept of Economics, Magadh University, Bodh-Gaya, Bihar.

Vinod Kumar, Dholi, Sakya, Muzaffarpur, Bihar.

Abbreviations

AFTA	: Asian Free Trade Area
AI	: Artificial Insemination
AICIL	: Agricultural Insurance Company of India limited
ANIFPDC	: Andaman and Nicobar Islands Forest and Plantation Development Corporation Limited
APEC	: Asia Pacific Economic Cooperation
APMC	: Agricultural Product Marketing Committee
ATC	: Agreement on Textile and Clothing
ATMA	: Agricultural Technology Management Agency
BDO	: Block Development Officer
BPL	: Below Poverty Line
BWDP	: Bihar Women Dairy Project
CACP	: Commission for Agriculture Costs and Prices
CBD	: Convention on Biological Diversity
CCID	: Central Crop Insurance Department
CDA	: Controller of Defence Accounts
CDR	: Cash Deposit Ratio
CFTRI	: Central Food Technological Research Institute
CMIE	: Centre for Monitoring of Indian Economy
CoMFED	: Co-operative Milk Producers' Federation
CPSE	: Centre for Polymer Science and Engineering
CRAFICARD	: Committee of Review Arrangement for Institutional Credit for Agriculture and Rural Development
CV	: Coefficient Variance
DCS	: Dairy Cooperative Societies

DM	:	District Magistrate
DRG	:	Development Research Group
DSM	:	Dispute Settlement Mechanism
EU	:	European Union
FAO	:	Food and Agricultural Organisation
FCI	:	Food Corporation of India
FIIS	:	Farmer Income Insurance Scheme
FIPs	:	Five Interested Parties
FPS	:	Fair Price Shop
GATT	:	General Agreement of Trade and Tariff
GCA	:	Gross Cropped Area
GCF	:	Gross Capital Formation
GDP	:	Gross Domestic Product
GPs	:	Gram Panchayats
HCR	:	Head Count Ratio
HVCs	:	High Value Commodities
HYV	:	High-yielding Variety
IAP	:	Index of Agricultural Production
IBRD	:	International Bank of Reconstruction and Development
ICOR	:	Incremental Capital Output Ratio
IDA	:	Indian Dairy Association
ILO	:	International Labour Organisation
KBK	:	Kalahandi-Balangir-Koraput
KCC	:	Kisan Credit Card
KVK	:	Krishi Vigyan Kendra
LAA	:	Land Acquisition Act
LDB	:	Land Development Bank
LLPD	:	Lakhs Litre Per Day
MOA	:	Memorandum of Agreement
MSP	:	Minimum Support Price
NABARD	:	National Bank for Agriculture and Rural Development
NACS	:	Network and Academic Computing Services
NAIS	:	National Agricultural Insurance Scheme
NAREGA	:	National Rural Employment Guarantee Act
NCAEPR	:	National Centre for Agricultural Economics and

NDC	:	National Development Council
NDDB	:	National Dairy Development Board
NDP	:	Net Domestic Product
NDRI	:	National Dairy Research Institute
NERAMAC	:	North East Region Agricultural Marketing Corporation
NFSM	:	National Food Security Mission
NGOs	:	Non-government Organisations
NHM	:	National Horticulture Mission
NIPFP	:	National Institute of Public Finance and Policy
NIRD	:	National Institute of Rural Development
NPA	:	Non-performing Assets
NSC	:	National Seeds Corporation
NSSO	:	National Sample Survey Organisation
OECD	:	Organisation for Economic Cooperation and Development
OS	:	Oil Seeds
OTS	:	One Time Settlement
PACS	:	Primary Agricultural Cooperative Societies
PAP	:	Poverty Alleviation Programme
PDS	:	Public Distribution System
PRI	:	Panchayati Raj Institutions
RGR	:	Relative Growth Rates
RKVY	:	Rastriya Krishi Vikash Yojana
SAA	:	Service Area Approach
SAFTA	:	South Asian Free Trade Area
SEZs	:	Special Economic Zones
SFCI	:	State Farm Corporation of India Limited
SHGs	:	Self Help Groups
TAD	:	Titilagrah Agriculture District
TERI	:	The Energy and Resources Institute
TKPD	:	Thousand Kilograms Per Day
TNCs	:	Transactional Corporations
TPDS	:	Targeted Public Distribution System
TRIPS	:	Trade Related Intellectual Property Right
URAA	:	Uruguay Round Agreement on Agriculture

VPMU	:	Vaishaili Patliputra Dughda Sahkari Sangh
VRS	:	Voluntary Retirement from Services
WBCIS	:	Weather Based Crop Insurance Scheme
WCED	:	World Commission on Environment and Development

Introduction

The book Agriculture and Food Security: Contemporary Issues contains thirty chapters elaborating on various aspects of agricultural issues and its impact on food security. Articles in this book are organized in following sections: **Section A**—is going to discuss the issues related to structural reforms and its impact on agricultural growth, **Section B**—analyses allied agricultural activities with regional perspectives, **Section C**—discusses agricultural credit and policy issues, and **Section D**—describes the issues related to food security.

A. Structural Reforms and Agricultural Growth

It is rightly said that in India true culture is agriculture as it is the backbone of Indian economy. Still agriculture is the largest employer of work force and a significant contributor to GDP besides giving support to many agro-based industries as well as non-farm activities. No doubt, after independence India has travelled a long journey from being the food deficient to a surplus producing country. All this could happen due to the green revolution. But again the time has come to think differently in order to make agriculture sustainable. Presently it is faced with several burning issues which need to be addressed without further delay. With this is related the serious issues of food security which is expected to be more serious in future. Agricultural scientists and planners have to address the issue of availability, accessibility and affordability of food to more than one billion population. There is a need to usher the second green revolution by changing our perception and strategies. There is need to encourage organic farming, diversification and more sustainable agriculture.

Indian agriculture needs a set of structural reforms, to

improve the performance of agricultural sector and in particular the agricultural productivity. This section explains the status of agricultural growth during the reform era. Structural reform introduced in 1991 to changes in the areas of trade policies, monetary and financial policies, fiscal and budgetary policies, and pricing and institutional reforms. India became the founder member of WTO in 1994. The salient features of this Reform-1991 are: (i) liberalization (internal and external), (ii) extending privatization, (iii) redirecting scarce Public Sector Resources to areas where the private sector is unlikely to enter, (iv) globalization of economy, and (v) market-friendly state. Indian Agriculture is one of the most important sector in the economy of the country. Agriculture in itself produces more than 18.5 percent of the Gross Domestic product of the country and more than 60 percent people out of Indian population are involved in this sector. This economic reform policy has far reaching effects on: (i) agricultural exports and imports, (ii) investment in new technologies and on rural infrastructure, (iii) patterns of agricultural growth, (iv) agriculture income and employment, (v) agricultural prices, and (vi) food security.

The major factors behind these trends in food production are well-known: long-term investments in infrastructure, education and agricultural research, coupled with rapid labour-intensive growth and productivity increases in non-agricultural sectors often associated with outward-oriented development strategies. There are three goals of agricultural development. These are: (a) to achieve 4 per cent growth in agriculture and raise incomes by increasing productivity (land, labour), diversification to high value agriculture and rural non-farm by maintaining food security, (b) sharing growth by focusing on small and marginal farmers, lagging regions, women, etc., (c) third is to maintain sustainability of agriculture by focusing on environmental concerns. (Mahendra Dev, 2009).

Main issues in Agricultural Development is the necessity to increase productivity, employment, and income of poor segments of the agricultural population. Due to rising input prices and falling output prices coupled with frequent crop failures resulting from unfavourable weather, real income of farmers have shown a declining trend. Majority of the farmers especially those having tiny and marginal land holdings seem to be badly trapped in utter poverty and indebtedness. The situation is becoming worse also because of poor participation of farmers in high value and non-crop enterprises as there is no adequate institutional credit, farmers-friendly technology and marketing support to enable them to undertake such enterprises. When India signed WTO agreement, it was hoped that Indian farmers would greatly benefit from it due to increased global market access. But the volatility of international prices has affected farmers adversely. Export of agricultural commodities have shown a declining trend whereas there is substantial increase in the import of oilseeds and pulses. There is a need for diversification and change in the cropping pattern in order to make agriculture more profitable and sustainable.

On the other issue of Agricultural Trade in the post-reform era, exports as well as imports have increased and balance of trade has also improved. In the process of economic reforms, the term of trade in agriculture have favourable impacts due to exchange rate devaluation. Gulati and Kelley (1999) estimate that if India completely liberalized trade in agriculture, both agricultural imports and exports would increase the value of agricultural production would increase and rural incomes would increase. The total foodgrains production for the year 2008-09 was 2,33,088 million tonnes and stands out as record production. Production of cotton increased from 99.97 lakh bales in 2000-01 to 258.84 lakh bales in 2007-08. Some of the lagging regions like Bihar, showed relatively high growth in recent years. Gujarat recorded high growth of 9 per cent per annum during 2001-02 to 2007-08 (Gulati, 2009).

The chapter is contributed by **Ram Naresh Thakur and Satendra Narayan Singh**. Adequate agricultural production and even distribution of food is high priority global concern. Introduction of structural reform followed by India becoming founder member of WTO after signing the GATT agreement have affected Indian Agriculture in many ways. Agricultural growth rate decelerated from over 3.5 per cent during 1981-82 and 1996-97 to only around 2 per cent during 1997-98 and 2004-05. It was more in context to horticulture, live stock and fisheries. Beside some adverse consequences, these reforms have opened up new opportunities also for possible benefits from trade and specialization, increased private investment in infrastructure and widening choices of new technology like bio-technology. The chapter discusses the diversification of crops especially in eastern region of India. It has been substantiated by several tables containing some relevant data. It refers to several constraints pertaining to land resources, water resources, bio-resources, cropping pattern, horticulture and animal husbandry.

The chapter jointly written by **S.S. Somra and Kuldip Singh** analyses the "Structural Changes and Agriculture in India in the Post-Reform Period". There has been transformation from traditional agricultural economy to the modern industrial economy in which the most striking feature is the strength of the service sector which grew at an average rate of 7.5 per cent. There has been a drastic policy reform in last two decades in the wake of liberalisation and WTO Agreement on Agriculture (AoA). These reforms have mixed effects varying from state to state; region to region and crop to crop. Diversification of agriculture in favour of commercial and high value crops is recognized as a powerful strategy to counter the emerging challenges. The free trade in agriculture mandated under WTO has posed a constant threat to the developing countries in the form of high market induced risk and fall in global prices for farm products which have affected traditional crops and families depending on them. Globalization is a fact of life and so it is not possible to insulate from global developments. The need of the hour is to accelerate agricultural growth which will determine the future of majority of working population.

Dhirendran Nath Konar's paper "Structural Changes in India and Rural Poverty" has tried to show the great structural changes in GDP of country during last two decades. The contribution of GDP in agriculture sector has been coming down but the situation of manufacturing sector has been slowly increasing , while the GDP of tertiary sector has been increasing rapidly. In the recent decade service sector is a major contributor to growth in national income but this sector provides employment only around 21 per cent of labour force. So we can say that the service sector is a major dominant sector but a minor contributor to employment. Author has also discussed some development experiences of Asian countries. A comparative study among Asian countries reveals that the highest contribution to the GDP emerging from service sector has been attained by the Republic of Korea. Korea had observed 62 per cent of labour in service sector.

The paper "Structural Reforms and Sustaining Growth in Indian Agriculture: the Emerging Trade Order," is written by **Angrej Singh**. The author's opinion that agricultural development in overall economic development and in eliminating poverty is key to accelerate economic development and poverty reduction. Furthermore a large number of industries depend on agriculture for raw materials. A high growth in agriculture is an essential condition for reaping advantages from WTO regime. In order to tape huge potential in agriculture, some steps are very imperatives like increase in public sector investment for agricultural infrastructure development, farm electrification, crop diversification, organic farming, good quality seeds, irrigation facilities, etc. Liberalisation of farm inputs, development of warehouses, cold storage, rural godowns, special cargo terminals at air and sea ports, etc. There is need for agricultural export liberalisation and development of agricultural output market. There is a need to regulate unfair trade practices.

The paper "Structural Changes in Agriculture: An Empirical Analysis" is written by authors **Purshotam Sahu and Babilata Shroff**. It begins with PM's emphasis to double annual foodgrain production by 2015 in order to achieve the UN millennium goal of reducing the number of hungry persons by 2015. This paper is based on the findings in all the empirical study on Titaligrah Agriculture district in the State of Orissa, which is considered as mini India due to its diverse agro-climatic condition, enormous natural resources and vast untapped human resources. This paper also refers to the impact of climate change on agricultural productivity. Authors conclude that in the wake of opening of economy, agriculture must transform from diversification by encouraging the farmers towards more integrated approach.

The paper "WTO and Indian Agriculture: Task and Challenges" is the contribution of authors **Sanjay Bhardwaj, Prativa Mishra and Deepak Jain**. The paper discusses the emerging trend in Agriculture after India signing the Agreement on Agriculture (AoA) which provide framework for the long-term reform of agriculture. The provisions and agreements made under GATT and WTO will speed up the process of globalization and allow free companies in India. To protect Indian agriculture and Indian farmers from foreign competition, it is imperative for the government to lay down priority for action by creating level playing field, and distortion-free trade. Indian agriculture needs safety-nets to protect the interest of crops, people and regions which are likely to be adversely affected by globalization.

The paper on "Investment in Agriculture and Social Adjustment in Indian Economy" is written by **Rajendra Prasad Singh and Pankaj Kumar Mishra**. Development economists consider investment as the single most important factor in the process of growth. It determines the level and pace of economic growth. There was sharp deceleration in agricultural investment after 1970s due to sharp decline in public investment in agriculture. The declining trend in investment continued till the end of the 20th Century. There was marginal improvement in agricultural investment growth rate during 2005-06 due to private investment. There is a need of both the public and private investment which is complementary to each other.

"Agricultural Reform and Institutional Finance: Problems and Prospects" is authored by **Ramakant Pd. Singh and Kumar Gaurav**. India is endowed with vast natural, physical and biological resources but due to lack of technology and capital hardly 25 per cent of resources has been put to use. Due to tremendous growth of population and increase in foodgrains demands as well as demand of agricultural raw materials for industrial development, there have been severe problems for agriculture. The paper refers to national policy for farmers, and various schemes and also the role of Panchayati Raj Institutions (PRI). PRI can help in mobilising deposits, disbursement of loans and its proper utilization repayment and recovery of loans.

The paper "Post-Reform Indian Agriculture: A Survey" is authored by **Bharati Pandey**. The slowdown in agricultural growth rate since 1990s has adverse impact on the farming community. The most important cause for decline is the reducing developmental role of state in investment in irrigation, flood control, research extension and institution capacity buildings. Investment in agricultural research and rural infrastructure are the main drivers for agricultural growth. To ensure food security on a sustainable manner, agriculture sector needs to be radically reformed by improving incentives, reforming institutions and increasing investment so that agricultural production may be increased more efficiently. After analyzing various factors for decline and its impacts, the paper concludes with a few suggestions for ushering the evergreen revolution. Evergreen revolution can help us to improve farm productivity without ecological harm.

The chapter on "Structural Reforms in Agriculture" is written by **Satendra Prajapati and Poonam Kumari** jointly. The paper discusses main aims of economic liberalisation and various changes brought in agricultural policy to strengthen Indian agriculture and to make it more export-oriented in the future. The paper elaborates economic liberalisation and emerging trends in agriculture like free trade, increase in production of foodgrains, agricultural exports, diversification of agriculture, increase in floriculture production, food processing, development of agriculture in backward regions, increasing trend of unemployment and its solution, development of new biological techniques, increase in subsidies and investment, etc. It also refers to institutionalization of agricultural credit, setting up of special boards, setting up of national level community exchange programmes and also e-trading.

The paper on "Impact of Globalisation on Agriculture in Developing Countries" is written by **Asmi Raza**. In this paper author has discussed the benefits of globalization for developing countries. Agricultural products, particularly in the agro-based exports are still away from the target mainly because the Uruguay Round Agreement, accompanying Doha Round and Geneva Meet of the Five Interested Parties (FIPs) have thus far been unable to resolve some of the knotty issues, particularly those dealing with subsidies. The intransigent attitude of the developed countries, particularly the EU and the United States on export subsidies in their case and linking this issue with other issues is creating a stalemate. Comprehensive negotiations are called for on these issues in order to pave way for the effective implementation of the URAA and subsequent agreements to the satisfaction of all the concerned parties, particularly the developing countries.

Structural reforms have positive and negative effects on agricultural growth. There has been positive effects on agriculture in terms of improvements in terms of trade, private investments and improved technology. The negative effects can be reduced with the supply side factors in agriculture.

B. Allied Agriculture with Regional Perspectives

Eleventh Five Year Plan (2007-12) targeted four per cent per annum annual growth in GDP from Agriculture and Allied Agricultural sectors. In year 2007-08 this growth rate was 4.9 per cent. But agricultural growth fell to 1.6 per cent in 2008-09, due to severe flood and drought. Major production losses was noticed in Kharif crops. Agricultural growth has accelerated compared to the period 1996-97 to 2003-04. The three year moving average growth in Agriculture was 2.6 per cent from 2004-05 to 2009-10, it has averaged 3.4 per cent. The allocation to agricultural and allied sectors in central plan has been increased from Rs. 21,068 crore in the Tenth Plan to Rs. 50,924 crore in Eleventh Plan. Budgetary allocation of Rs. 8054 crore was sanctioned for Department of Animal Husbandry, Dairying and Fisheries during the 11th Five Year Plan. The utilization during the first four year of Eleventh Plan was only 47 per cent of total allocation for the Department of Animal Husbandry, Dairying and Fisheries. There is a large shortfall in utilization of expenditure in Department of Animal Husbandry, Dairying and Fisheries.

The small farmers produce milk, meat, wool, etc., for the community, with virtually no capital, resource, training and at a cost that no modern technology in the world had ever produced. Food and Fodder Resources will be crucial to the future development of "livestock resources" in the Country. Allied agricultural activities also depend on one of the important factors, this is water management. Water Resources of India contain diverse group of flora and fauna. Agriculture is the greatest user of Water accounting for about 80 per cent of all consumption. Animal Husbandry and Fisheries require abundant water. Development of Water Resources, since Independence, has been undertaken for specific purposes like irrigation, flood control, hydro-power generation, drinking water supply, industrial and various miscellaneous uses

The Chapter "Developing Milk Producing Units as a Farmer's Enterprise : Need of Multi-dimensional Assail" is jointly written by **N.P. Singh, B.V. Singh and G.P. Singh**. Presently India produces 90 million tonnes of annual milk but still the country is short of per capita milk availability of 214 grams as against recommended requirement of 250 grams per person per day. rural milk producers have to face several problems like small herd strength, small landholdings, shortage of fodder, low productivity of milk, lack of training for new viable and sustainable technology, inadequate finance, lack of infrastructure and marketing network, etc. Authors have made sincere efforts to deal with the problems at multi-dimensional levels and suggested some pragmatic steps to ameliorate the condition of small milk producers in the country. The chapter recognizes the fact that milk production is a major non-farm activity which can provide income, livelihood and employment to the rural masses and which can provide fruitful combination of agriculture and industry. Hence milk production activities should be carried on with the approach of integrated rural development.

An analysis of performance of "Dairying Practices in Bihar: with Special Reference to Patna Dairy Project" is contributed by authors **Krishnanand Yadav and Upendra Prasad Singh**. Dairying is an ancient profession and it remained confined to one caste for long. But in changing economic scenario and with changing food habits the demand of milk and milk products has increased many folds. The present growth rate in dairy sector is 4.5% which is faster than just 2% in agriculture sector. This increase was witnessed only after the 'Operation Flood' initiated in 1970s. Bihar state milk Cooperative Federation, popularly known as COMFED has commendable achievements to its credit. The Patna Dairy Project known as Vaishali-Pataliputra Dugdha Utpadak Sangh Ltd. (VPMU) has expanded its business so far as its membership is concerned. The number of its members increased from 56.7 thousand in 1996-97 to 94 thousands in 2007-08. There has been consistent increase in terms of procurement of milk, paneer, ice-cream, dahi, lassi and almost all milk products. The paper concludes that Dairy Practices in Bihar has made marvelous progress in terms of catering the needs of the people, employment of rural work force, income generation and empowerment of weaker sections, but still there is a lot to be done and that needs more proactive policies of the government.

The Chapter "Review of Returns on investment in Agro-processing units : A Case Study of Central Public Sector Agro-Processing Industries" authored by **Ratnesh Kumar** recognizes the interdependence and integration of agriculture and industry as an adjunct for prosperity. Our growth strategy must aim at integrating rural and urban economies by reducing economic disparity and regional imbalances. Though the plan documents and Industrial Policy Resolutions have laid stress on decentralization of industries by promoting agro-processing industries, but there have not been rapid strides on this front. The author concludes that there is a need of not only the appropriate scheme for crop diversification but also of development of industries which will strengthen agricultural base.

The Chapter on "Economic Security against Rising Risk in Agriculture and Allied Sectors" is written by **Anjana Kumari.** Agriculture and allied sectors are considered to be the mainstay of Indian economy contributing 18 per cent to GDP and 65 per cent of livelihood to entire workforce. The author has tried to present clear picture of various sectors like Dairy, Sericulture and Piggery. Author has found out some hurdles in economic security through credit flow like lack of technical knowledge regarding bank schemes, inadequate credit to farmers, delay in loan processing by banks, diversion of credit, etc. She suggests for area specific credit by banks. Beside that private credit agencies may also be allowed to play a supplementary role to the institutional credit for at least some sections of the cultivators and certain types of needs.

The paper "An Analysis of Agro-Economic Condition in Jharkhand" is written by **Rajini Kumari and Veena Kumari**. While the country has been able to achieve the required household food security, Jharkhand is lagging behind by producing around 23.67 lakh tonnes of foodgrains for its huge 30 million population and an average of 80 kg per capita per annum against 170 kg of minimum food requirement. It means there is more than 50 percent food shortage in this newly created state which is rich in forest and minerals. It cannot be denied that the level of food and nutrition security in Jharkhand is alarming and there is need of immediate attention. The major impediments to agricultural development in the state are poor soil condition, low level of irrigation, existence of a large number of small and marginal farmers, massive rural poverty, indifference of youths to agriculture, declining public investment and weak linkage between research, extension and farmers. Hence there is need to begin the process of dynamism and optimism in the farm sector through technology upgradation.

"Agricultural Diversification in North-Eastern Region in India" is written jointly by **Rajnath Upadhyay and Sriman Pandey**. Authors think that low levels of productivity and entrepreneurship contrast the huge potential of the eastern region in the fields of agriculture, horticulture and animal husbandry and fisheries. The time has come to fill the field gaps and to capitalize on the opportunities offered by the region. Major parts of Eastern region lay behind rest of India in terms of many social indicators. The paper discusses the availability of natural resources in eastern region like land, water, bio-resources, fish resources, horticulture, livestock resources, etc. Major issues and concerns of the eastern regions are low productivity, low per capita land availability, weak post-harvest management promoting marketing and value addition, inadequate infrastructure, inefficient marketing, very poor research and transfer of technology and lack of credit facilities. Authors give some pragmatic suggestions for reducing disparity in income, and faster growth and development in the eastern region which has potential but constraints.

The Chapter on "Agriculture in Uttrakhand : Problems and Prospects" is an attempt by **Devna Sharma and Rachna Dixit** to underline some problems and prospects in the newly carved out state. The state witnesses low agricultural productivity due to small size and scattered land-holdings, difficult terrain, unfavourable climatic condition for some crops, lack of improved inputs and technology and inadequate credit and marketing facilities. Some problems have been pin-pointed and a few suggestions have been rendered in this chapter.

C. Agricultural Credit and Policy Issues

C.H. Hanumantha Rao (2003) found that farmers meet 60 per cent of their credit requirements from formal financial institutions and 40 per cent from informal sources including money lenders, traders, friends and relatives. Marginal and small farmers heavily depend on the informal sources of credit. Farmers committing suicide incurs large debts and rely proportionately more on informal sources of credit. Prof. Rao suggests contract farming for relaxing the credit constraint.

The existing price policy of the government is not in tune with the need of agricultural diversification. Non-availability of adequate institutional credit at affordable rate of interest is also one issue of concern. The present rate of interest on crop-loans continue to be high from the prospective of small farmers. Farmers do not have easy access to institutional credit. There is earnest need that the government reviews the Farmer Income Insurance Scheme (FIIS) after concurrent evaluation of the working of the schemes. Agriculture Credit is a crucial input for increasing agricultural production and productivity. Institutional finance for Agricultural credit is disbursed mainly by Commercial Banks, Regional Rural Banks, Land Development Banks, and Cooperative banks. Share of commercial banks in total institutional credit to agriculture is about 48 per cent, that of Cooperative banks is about 46 per cent, and Regional Rural Banks account for 6per cent only. Short-term Credit accounts for 2/3rd of the total institutional lending to the Agriculture. Reduction in Commercial Bank credit to agriculture, in lieu of this reforms process and recommendations of Khusrao Committee and Narasingham Committee, might lead to a fall in farm investment and impaired agricultural growth (Panda, 1996). Price fluctuations is also one important issue in front of farmers. There is a big gap between the producer price and consumer prices. Small and marginal farmers are really facing more problems. Intermediaries and middle men are taking more benefits of these price fluctuations. Vyas Committee Report offers a number of suggestions for ensuring adequate and cost-effective delivery of institutional credit to the Farmers (RBI, 2004). Prof. V.S. Vyas has also suggested that RBI should advise banks to waive margin/ security norms for agricultural loans up to Rs. 50,000 and in case of agri-business and agri-clinics, the limit can be pegged at Rs. 5 lakh. This Committee has also recommended that banks should provide a separate flexible revolving credit limit to the small borrowers of production or investment loans for meeting their temporary shortfalls in family cash flow.

The paper on "Growth and Transformation in Agricultural Output and Input in India: Need for Structural Adjustment" is written by **Amarjit Singh Sethi**. Compiled in four sections the paper summarizes the main findings with the help of some tables, graphs and also used some mathematical tools. Data used in the present paper were compiled for last 57 years period (1950 to 2006-07). For examining long term behavioural growth path, author used 14 different trend paths were estimated for each of the components of agricultural output on which the time series were compiled. The author opines that pace and pattern of agricultural growth plays vital role in socio-economic development. It also contains various policy implications. Keeping in view the observations on structural shifts, non-farming activities like dairying/livestock need be promoted so as to make available organic manure at cheaper rates and shed-off, at least partly, heavy dependence on chemical fertilizers. Water saving cropping pattern and techniques need to be adopted so as to bring down the low input cost on irrigation.

The paper "Rural Credit: Trends, Issues and Challenges in India" is written jointly by **Samir R. Samantara and B.B. Sahoo**. Functioning of Commercial Banks came to be regulated after interventions by the Government of India and the Reserve Bank of India. Financial sector reforms gave thrust on efficiency and visibility of the banks in 1990s. The paper discusses changing trend in rural credit and challenges in the field of rural credit. Since efforts have been made to make the things understood with the help of many relevant table and data.

The paper "Agricultural Flow in Bihar" is presented jointly by **Vinod Kumar and Ram Bharat Thakur**. On the one hand agriculture is a major sector in Bihar's economy but its growth has remained stagnant or declined during the last 15 years. The proportion of indebted farmers increased but the institutional indebtedness has declined and non-institutional indebtedness has increased. This is due to inadequate savings and poor access to institutional credit institutions. The performance of Commercial banks is not only poor but their performance in granting loan to the sectors in Bihar has been very poor. The condition of cooperative societies and banks are also far behind from satisfactory.

"Agrarian Structure in India" is written by authors **Bharat Bhushan and Kabita Kumari**. As per the paper, there is no change in two prominent features of Indian economy—overwhelming dependence of rural population on agriculture and no significant diversification of rural economy in Bihar. Some prominent factors affecting changes in agrarian structure are land market, land reform, demographic pressure, etc. Asian experience suggests that agriculture can absorb additional labour if appropriate technological and organizational interventions are carried out. At last some suggestions are also given in order to accelerate the rural transformation.

The paper "Policy for Land Acquisition for Non-Agriculture Uses and Compensation of Land: An Analysis" is authored by **G. Savaraiah, G. Chandrasekhara Rao and M. Deverajulu**. With population growth in India, the per capita land availability has declined from 0.89 hectares in 1951 to 0.3 hectares in 2001. But more than 65 per cent population still depends on agriculture for livelihood. It is expected that the per capita land availability will further decline to 0.2 hectare by 2050. Government uses Land Acquisition Act, 1984 to acquire land for private business projects. Farmers have been ruthlessly exploited. Due to it rapid industrialization and development of Special Economic Zones (SEZs) have been instrumental in displacing the people, making them homeless, jobless and detritus. The land Acquisition Policy which is a legacy of the British raj has its adverse impacts on all stakeholders, women, tribal on food security and human rights.

The paper "Land Reforms and its Impact on Agriculture in India" was authored by **Dhiren Vandra**. Structural reforms were introduced after 1991 and after India became member of WTO and signed GATT. Since then a lot of importance was given to Privatisation of agriculture-related activities. Many restrictions were removed and domestic intellectual property right was amended. Today, land reforms in India are at the cross-road. Land reforms are not a sufficient but a necessary condition for poverty eradiation. Without it there can be no significant change in the lives of rural poor.

D. Food Security Issues

The agricultural development strategy for the Ninth Five Year Plan is essentially based on the policy on food security announced by the Government, to double the food production and make India hunger free in ten years. The Strategy to ensure food security is as follows:

Doubling food production, Increase in employment and incomes, Supplementary/sustained employment and creation of rural infrastructure through Poverty Alleviation Programmes (PAP), Distribution of foodgrains to the people Below Poverty Line (BPL).

In India, agricultural production, especially rice and wheat production, have increased dramatically since the Green Revolution, which involved improved seeds, fertilizer use and irrigation. Reforms in rice and wheat have focused mainly on liberalization of the export trade as surpluses have emerged. Achieving food security is an important issue for the developing countries like India, where millions of people are suffering from hunger and nutritional deficiency. Food availability and stability are considered good measures of food security. Dr. Amartya Sen, the eminent economist, in his work on the Great Bengal Famine, has attributed the death of millions to the inadequacy, or rather non-existence of an official policy, to cope with the food supply crisis. Poverty and the lack of purchasing power, therefore becomes the crucial consideration in attainment of food security. As most of the poor people in developing countries including India dwell in the country sides so the policies relating to rural development in its comprehensive form encompassing development of agriculture, health, nutrition, education literacy, etc. would alone lead to enduring solution to the problem of food insecurity, poverty, unemployment and social tension in the region. There are three goals of agricultural development. These are: (a) achieve 4 per cent growth in agriculture and raise incomes by increasing productivity (land, labour), diversification to high value agriculture and rural non-farm by maintaining food security; (b) sharing growth by focusing on small and marginal farmers, lagging regions, women, etc., (c) third is to maintain sustainability of agriculture by focusing on environmental concerns.

The paper "Achieving Food Security in India: Issues and Challenges" written by **Dalip Kumar and Abha Mittal** has highlighted the actual picture of Indian Agriculture and situation of food security in India. Authors have also discussed the various techniques to measure the food security. Food Security issues depend on availability, accessibility and affordability of food to all the people round the year. In this paper authors explain the indicators which effected the status of food availability, accessibility and affordability. Authors explain the important challenges to achieve the food security and lastly they introduced some extension of institutions and initiative such as Krishi Vigyan Kendra, Agri Clinics, Kisan Call Centres and Agricultural

Technology Management Agency (ATMA). Food availability must be improved to provide the irrigational facilities and lastly increase the agricultural productivity. Accessibility will improve by the policies for enhancing minimum agricultural wages and absorption of food by the better health facility.

The paper "Environmental Recources and their Impact on Foodgrains Production and Productivity" is written by **Dastgir Alam, Firdos Ahamad and Jasmil Ahmad**. Authors divided this paper in two parts. First they analyzed the impact of area under cultivation and irrigated areas on the level of production and productivity in different states and second type of soil is considered as a factor which influences the level of production and productivity of land. Authors used mathematical tools (regression equation) to validate the result. They used the data of ten major states.

The paper "WTO and Food Security in India" is jointly written by **R. Raj Kumar and A. Gnanavelan**. Main objective of this paper is to study International food security measures and along with indicators of food security. Authors also try to analyse Indian food security policies and WTO during the India's Five Year Plans. Explaining the importance of agriculture in Indian economy, the paper discusses several issues like individual and family food security, food security and agricultural trade, policy reforms, indicators of food security, International food security, etc. At last the paper gives some suggestions in the light of M.S. Swaminathan Committees.

The Chapter on "Globalisation and Food Security in India" is written by **M. Pandyan**. It explains the growing importance of food security and its four components. There has been tremendous progress in food security in India in the period between 1950-51 to 2001-02. When the food production increased from 51 million tonnes to 184 million tonnes. Share of two main cereals has increased but share of coarse cereals has declined from 30 to 18 per cent. This paper has also discussed the status of food security in Ninth Plan as well as Tenth Five Year Plan period.

The Chapter on "Globalisation, WTO and Food Security Availability, Access and Affordability of Food, PDS and Food Subsidy" is jointly written by **N.K. Thakur and Alpana Sharma**. Being an integral part of recent economic process, globalization plays major role in export led growth resulting into enlargement of job market in India This paper points out some advantages as well as disadvantages of globalization and its linkage to WTO and effect on agriculture threatening the food security. It also points out the poor performance of Public Distribution System (PDS) especially in Delhi. In the concluding part, there are some suggestions to revamp the PDS. Government should encourage farmers to produce more by enhancing MSP so that the interests of farmers are to be kept for the welfare of the society. There is a need of nation-wide campaign to enhance food production so that food security may be available as "food for all'.

The paper "Economic Reforms, Agriculture and Food Security in India" is the contribution of **Ashwani Kant Jha, Bhawana Jha and Dilip Kumar**. India is entering into second phase of reforms which is very difficult as hard decisions have to be taken with regards to policies of global competition, labour, disinvestment and privatization. There is earnest need for comprehensive review of government policies in agriculture because of changing external environment especially after India becoming the member of WTO. With the help of a few tables, authors give some suggestions and conclude that the foodgrain production scenario is far from satisfactory. Although India posses sufficient food stock to feed her people but mass poverty and inequality resulting from uneven growth has led to massive entitlement failure. Hence there is urgent need for public action to remedy the situation in context of inaccessibility and unaffordability.

There is a need to focus more on poverty alleviation programmes and employment generation schemes. There is no denying the fact that even more than six decades after independence, food insecurity and starvation are big blots on the face of mother India which is moving on the path of achieving the goal of status of the developed country. This could be attributed to failure of our governance and developmental approach. It is contrary to the committed objective of welfare state and inclusive growth. Some Government programmes like aṣ NFSM, RKVY, NHM and ATMA are very useful for farmers, and farmers will be benefited, if these programmes are properly monitored and effectively implemented under the right policies.. The present UPA government has brought legislations to ensure Right to

Information, Right to Work and is planning to ensure Right to Food to provide safety nets to the teeming millions. But recent study on the implementation of Right to Education reveals that despite this right large number of children are still out of school and the rate of drop-outs is high. If this is the outcome of such ambitious programmes then how can food security be achieved just by ensuring it as a right? Need of the hour is honest and sincere implementation of the right by strict monitoring and efficient governance otherwise the Right to Food will meet the same fate.

References

Gulati, A. and Kelley, T. (1999), Trade Liberalization and Indian Agriculture: Cropping Pattern Changes and Efficiency Gains in Semi-Arid Tropics. Delhi: Oxford University Press.

Gulati, Ashok (2009), "Emerging Trends in Indian Agriculture: What can we learn from these?", 2nd Prof. Dayanath Jha Memorial Lecture, National Centre for Agricultural Economics and Policy Research, New Delhi.

Mahendra Dev, S. (2009), "Structural Reforms and Agriculture: Issues and Policies", Keynote paper presented in 92nd Annual Conference of Indian Economic Association, 27-29 December, 2009 at KIIT, Bhubaneswar, Orissa.

Panda, R.K. (1996), "Possible Impact of New Economic Policy on Agricultural Credit, Farm Investment, and Productivity", Agricultural Situation in India, Vol. 53, No. 6, 1996, p. 391.

Rao, C.H. Hanumantha (2003), Reforms Agenda for Agriculture, *Economic and Political Weekly*, 38(7), February 15-21, pp. 615-20.

RBI (2004), Report of Advisory Committee on Flow of Credit to Agriculture and Related Activities, Reserve Bank of India, Mumbai.

Structural Reform, Agricultural Diversification and Economic Growth

Ram Naresh Thakur and Satendra Narayan Singh

India is an agricultural country where one-third population depends on agriculture sector directly or indirectly. Agriculture continues to be the backbone of the Indian economy. Indian agriculture contributes to the Gross Domestic Product by about 19 per cent. With food being the growing need of the mankind, much emphasis has been on commercializing of agricultural production. Hence, adequate production and even distribution of food has lately become a high priority global concern. With the changing agricultural scenario and global competition, there is a need of exploiting the available resources at maximum level. In Indian agriculture the factors like high soil productivity, supply of balanced crop nutrients, efficient water management, improved crops, better plant protection, post-production management for value-addition and marketing are responsible for higher yield as compared to most of the other countries. Achievements of Indian agriculture like development of HYVs, new hybrids of different crops, research in the area of vaccine production, varietal development through somoclonal variations, developing better quality products and transgenic in crops such as brinjal, tomato, cauliflower and cabbage have strengthened the field. In 21st Century agriculture, application of modern biotechnologies like DNA, finger printing, tissue culture, terminator gene technology and genetic cloning will hold the key in raising the productivity. In the new millennium, the challenges in Indian agricultural sector are quite different from those met in the previous decades. The enormous pressure to produce more food from less land with shrinking natural resources is a tough task for the farmers. To keep up the momentum of growth a careful economic evaluation of inputs like seeds, fertilizers, irrigation sources, etc. are of considerable importance.

Structural reforms in Indian economy were introduced in a big way in 1991, which were followed by India becoming founder member of WTO after signing of GATT agreements in December 1994. Structural reforms and obligations of WTO have affected Indian agriculture in a variety of ways. In structural reforms major emphasis was given on fiscal management, which led to cutbacks in public investment in agriculture and squeeze on agricultural research and extension services. A lot of stress was given to privatization of activities earlier provided by public agencies. A thinking developed that private agri-business companies, especially Transactional Corporations (TNCs), can play significant role in agricultural research and extension and could fill in the gap created by withdrawal of public sector agencies. In view of WTO obligations agricultural trade was liberalized, quantitative restrictions were replaced by tariff barriers and domestic intellectual property rights were amended and extended to agricultural research. Agricultural Produce Marketing (Regulation) Acts were amended to allow private companies to trade in agricultural produce. The banking sector reforms resulted in public and private sector banks reducing priority sector lending in order to ensure their profitability. This led to decline in flow of credit to agriculture. Besides, the scope of priority sector lending was enlarged to cover several activities including lending/contribution to Rural Infrastructural Development and Khadi Village Industries Commission. This led to decline in flow of credit to the farmers. In the wake of huge of stocks of foodgrains with FCI after 1997-98, the terms of trade turned against agriculture partly due to fall and instability in the global agricultural prices.

As a consequence agricultural growth rate decelerated from over 3.5 per cent during 1981-82 and 1996-97 to only around 2 per cent during 1997-98 and 2004-05. The deceleration occurred in almost in all states and covered all sub-sectors such as crops, horticulture, livestock and fisheries. As quite a few input prices rose and output prices stagnated or declined, a large section of farming community came under stress. The Situation Assessment Survey of farmers (2003) brought out that 40 per cent farmers did not wish continue in their profession if alternative employment was available as majority of them found it not profitable. Nearly half of the farmers (48.5%) were under debt with a large proportion of non-institutional debt. The uncertainty of earnings, small and tiny size of the holdings, rising input prices and falling returns with degradation of soil and environment led to the unfortunate phenomenon of suicides among farmers in the areas of commercialized agriculture, especially in rain-fed areas. The farmers' suicides are often accompanied by decline in the absolute number of holdings and area under cultivation. There is growing pressure from non-agricultural sectors for land acquisition especially by corporate sector for Special Economic Zones (SEZs). These developments are occurring in the context of stagnation in the area under irrigation, extensive soil degradation and depletion of ground water resources and climate changes with adverse potential for the future of agriculture in the country.

While these are some of the adverse consequences from the manner in which economic reforms were implemented in the country. These reforms have, nevertheless, opened up new opportunities for agriculture such as possible benefits from trade and specialization, increased private investment, including in marketing infrastructure like storage and transport, and widening the choices in respect of new technologies like biotechnology. But these benefits can be realized only if supply-side constraints for agriculture are eased through increase in public investment in agriculture like irrigation, roads, agricultural research and extension and reforms in the institutions for management of resources. The acceleration in GDP growth and rise in tax-GDP ratio following economic reforms indeed hold encouraging prospects for raising public investment in agriculture. It would, therefore, be useful to examine reforms needed in agriculture in the vital sectors to enable agriculture both to benefit from overall economic reforms introduced in the economy as well as to cope with the emerging challenges in the post-reforms era.

W.T.O.—DOHA ROUND AND INDIAN AGRICULTURE

W.T.O. has opened the door of devastation for Indian agriculture. Agriculture sector is the greatest issue of controversy and deadlock (Obstacle) in 'Doha Trade Talk'. Developed nations are not ready to decrease subsidy on agriculture. To the contrary they has invented ways and opened many back-doors like green box, blue box, etc. Through those measures they do not decrease subsidies but always increase subsidies by several ways. In which way the trade talks of Doha Round has reached in such juncture, which will result into the heavy loss for the developing and poor African and Caribbean countries like India. They cannot gain anything out of it. This has happened due to aggressive policies of the developed countries in the leadership of U.S.A. and the European Union (E.U.). The 'Doha round of trade talk', which is officially known as 'Development round trade talk', has become 'Devastation round trade talk', for developing poor countries. W.T.O. under its 'Doha round trade talk', which started in 2001 with a vision, slogan and objective of helping and giving priorities in the development needs to developing and poor countries, had become 'Killer of development' of the developing countries including India in last eight years in deed.

Indian agriculture has been diversifying during the last two decades towards High-Value Commodities (HVCs), i.e., fruits, vegetables, milk, meat, and fish products. The pace has been accelerated during the decade of 1990s. HVCs account for a large share in the total value of agricultural production. Supply and demand side factors coupled with infrastructural development and innovative institutions drive these changes.

Till the 'fifties, the Eastern Region was reputedly the most prosperous region in the country, maintaining a lead over the other regions with highest foodgrain yield of 644 kg/ha as against 608, 554 and 390 kg/ha in northern, southern and western regions respectively.[1] However, it lost its leading position thereafter, particularly with the advent of the Green Revolution, which ushered in the 'western' model based on large scale adoption of HYV seeds, chemical fertilizers and supplemental irrigation along with plant protection measures. This model, most successful in North Western India, has not been widely replicated in the Eastern region because of a variety of constraints rooted to socio-economic features, fragmented and smaller land holdings as well as institutional, organizational, technological and developmental inadequacies.

The Eastern Region comprising of Eastern UP (85,844 sq km), Bihar including Jharkhand (1,73,877 sq km), West Bengal (88,752 sq km), Assam (78,438 sq km), Orissa (1,55,707 sq km), and Chhattisgarh (1,44,422 sq km) occupies about 28 per cent of the country's geographical area with foodgrain production of 58 million tonnes (34.6% of the total), is inhabited by about 35 per cent of the country's population. The region has 1.24 times higher population density than the national average (318/sq.km against 257/sq km national average: 1991 census).[2] Agricultural development is much below its potential in this region, with the result that employment in the agriculture sector is limited and a large proportion of the population still remains below the poverty line and suffers from malnutrition. For example, Bihar possessed about 3 per cent of the total cultivated area of the country and 8 per cent of the country's population, and produced about 6.9 per cent (14.56 M tonnes) of the total foodgrains in 1999-2000. The average yield of foodgrains in the state was 1620 kg/ha as against the national average of 1697kg/ha. The yield of rice in Bihar was 15.40 q/ha as against national average of 19.90 q/ha.[3] Similarly, the yield of wheat was 20.61 q/ha as against the National average of 27.55 q/ha per capita availability of total land/net cultivated land in the Eastern Region is lowest in the country. In view of the highest percentage of net sown area to geographical area, there is hardly any scope of enlarging the area under cultivation in this region. Most of the farm holdings are marginal to small, and highly fragmented, hampering the adoption of high-tech agriculture. The need of the hour is tenurial reform and consolidation of holdings, the progress achieved in West Bengal in this direction is reflected in the significant growth in production in that State. The soils of the region are relatively fertile and do not have many inherent limitations; however, efforts are required to build up and sustain soil productivity, particularly for intensified agriculture which has to be practiced for faster economic growth. The progress of creation of irrigation potential under major and medium irrigation systems is very slow in all the Eastern Indian states. The irrigation scenario in Bihar, Orissa and West Bengal is revealing. In the case of minor irrigation systems based on surface water, the rate of progress is higher in Orissa followed by West Bengal and Bihar. But in the case of minor irrigation systems based on ground water, the progress is highest in Bihar and lowest in Orissa. This indicates that Government spending on irrigation development is sluggish in all states but private investment in ground water exploitation is fairly significant. The per cent annual growth rate in State financed irrigation systems is just 0.8, 2.1 and 1.8 for major and medium systems, and 1.3, 2.78, and 2.45 for surface flow based minor systems compared to 7.09, 2.79, and 13.5 per cent in privately financed minor irrigation systems, (i.e. based on ground water) of Bihar, Orissa and West Bengal respectively.[4] The percentage of irrigation potential created is satisfactory in Bihar (62%) and West Bengal (65%), but low in Orissa (33%). The major cause is meager exploitation of ground water in Orissa. The number of major and medium irrigation projects is highest in Jharkhand (117) followed by Bihar (98), Orissa (87) and West Bengal (37). The least number in West Bengal may be attributed to the plain topography. The distribution according to source of irrigation shows that canals and wells are the major source of irrigation in Orissa and West Bengal. In Bihar and Eastern U.P.; wells outclass canals, while in Chhattisgarh canals are the major source of irrigation. In Orissa and West Bengal, tanks irrigate a significant area. This factor needs to be remembered while developing technologies for irrigating rainfed/dry land areas. Distribution of crops in irrigated areas shows that rice occupies the major chunk in all the States. While in Chhattisgarh rice occupies as much as 95 per cent, in Orissa it is 77 per cent. However in Eastern U.P., irrigated rice occupies less area than the national average.[5] While water resources are inadequately developed, the developed resources are poorly utilized. Canal water for crop production is available in a relatively uncontrolled manner. It is excessive and uneven during the wet season, and too little during the dry season. In most cases, irrigation is practiced from field to field rather than through field channels which results in inefficient water use.

Ground water is developed to a smaller extent and that too is not fully utilized due to inadequate and erratic supply of electric power or non-availability of diesel and maintenance infrastructure. Rice-based farming systems, involving pisci-culture and rearing of animals/small ruminants, poultry, piggery and goat should be introduced as an integral part of the integrated farming system. With the advent of WTO regime and opening of agriculture to external competition, the prices of rice and other cereal crops may experience downward market trends. This calls for diversification of agriculture for better economic gains to farmers by exploiting the abundant water resources and climate. Research on farming systems approach in the Eastern region, having a predominance of small farmers, should be strengthened to come up with the best possible alternatives for positive economic benefits. Sporadic, market driven developmental efforts are seen in many places through introduction of sweet oranges in Midnapur district of West Bengal, growing of flowers like marigold, rose, tuber rose, gladiolus, jasmine in Midnapur and Hooghly districts of West Bengal. These are some market-oriented viable farming systems for the Indo-Gangetic plain areas of Eastern region. However, this needs to be studied and viable financial and institutional arrangements, including marketing facilities, post-harvest management need to be incorporated for large scale adoption of these alternative systems of diversified agriculture. Other examples of substitution of rice cultivation by market-oriented entrepreneurs are groundnut cultivation in Jajpur, Kendra Para and Balasore districts of Orissa, growing of winter season vegetables like cabbage, cauliflower, French bean, carrot in the coastal districts of Bhubaneswar and Cuttack in Orissa. Water logging is a difficult problem in all the plain areas of Eastern region and persist as wet land ecologies. Such land can be economically utilized for growing suitable crops like Makhana in Dharbhanga District, spices in Samastipur District and Litchi in Muzaffarpur District in Bihar and Water Chestnut in Eastern UP. Similarly, *Swamp Taro* in West Bengal and *Singhara* (Pani Phal) can be popularized, outside traditional growing areas. The Eastern and North-Eastern regions hold enormous potential for development of agriculture, horticulture, animal husbandry and fisheries. The gaps between actual and potential yields are such that huge production increases can be achieved in the region, and for the country as a whole, simply by using available and accessible technologies.

CROPS AND CROPPING PATTERN

Presently due to its high rainfall and waterlogged conditions, rice is the predominant Kharif crop occupying 70-90 per cent of the entire region under irrigation/rainfed. At some places pulses and oil seeds are also grown as Kharif crop Wheat, potato, sugarcane, pulses and oilseeds are the major Rabi crops while jute is also grown as premonsoon crop. The detailed agro-ecological sub-region wise distribution of existing crops and cropping pattern is presented below:

Productivity

West Bengal is the leading producer of rice (13.95 million tonne) in the country, accounting for 15.59 per cent of total production. In the production of maize, Bihar is a close second to Karnataka, with 1.61 million tonne and 14 per cent of overall production. In total production of foodgrains, West Bengal and Bihar stand fourth and fifth respectively in the country. In terms of productivity too, West Bengal had an average yield per hectare of 2192 kg against the national average of 1697 kg. The other States, however, lagged below the national average yield: Bihar 1620 kg., Orissa 1022 kg., Assam 1427 kg. West Bengal has recorded remarkable success in raising productivity levels of rice to 2259 kg./ha, against the national average of 1990 kg/ha. However, this is still well below the productivity levels of Punjab, Tamil Nadu and even Karnataka. In Orissa and Bihar the yield gaps are wide in the case of most crops. The following tables give State-wise details relating to the major crops.

Horticulture

Horticulture, which includes fruits, vegetables including root and tuber corps, mushroom, floriculture, medicinal and aromatic plants, plantation crops, spices and bee-keeping has traditionally been an important activity in the Eastern and North-Eastern regions. Horticultural crops grown in these regions include mango, banana, pineapple, guava, litchi among fruits;

TABLE 1

Agro-Ecological Sub-region-wise Major Crops Cropping Sequences[6]

Sub-region	*Crops*	*Crop sequence*
Hot, dry sub-humid BIHAR	Kharif, Rice, Maize Rabi: Wheat, barley, gram lentil, peas Kharif: Maize, millet (upland) Rabi: Maize, short duration paddy, millet, pulse (mid-land) paddy (low land) sugarcane	Rice-wheat Rice-rice Rice-potato Rice-sugarcane Rice-pulse (residual moisture)
Hot moist sub-humid ORISSA	Kharif: Groundnut, horsegram, maize (laterite soil), rice til, finger millet, cotton, groundnut, sugarcane (other soils) Rabi: Potato, groundnut, vegetables, sugarcane	Predominantly monocropping with cotton/groundnut/maizerice-pulse (residual moisture) Millet-maize, maize-mustard, rice-groundnut, Rice-vegetable Rice-sugarcane, rice-rice rice- wheat, rice-potatomainly monocropped
Hot, dry moist sub-humid JHARKHAND	Kharif: Rice, maize, ragi, pigeonpea Rabi: Wheat, vegetables, potato	Rice-wheat, rice-potato, Vegetables (in irrigated pocket)
Hot, dry, moist sub-humid BIHAR	Kharif: sugarcane, chillies Rabi: Potato, turmeric	Wheat-rice-wheat, rice-sugarcane, rice-potato, rice-pulses, rice-mustard, rice-linseed (residual moisture)
Hot sub-humid to humid WEST BENGAL	Kharif: Rice Rabi: Pulse, oilseed (residual moisture), sugar-cane, potato, vegetables, jute (pre-moonsoon)	Jute-rice Rice-pulse, oilseeds (residual moisture) Rice-sugarcane, rice-potato, rice vegetables
Hot moist sub-humid ORISSA	Kharif: Rice Rabi: Potato (in pockets) sweet potato (new introduction) lentil, coconut	Rice-lentil (relay cropping), Jute-rice-pulse Rice-rice-mung/vegetables

TABLE 2

Average Yield of Major Crops in Assam[7]

S. No.	Crop	Area (M ha)	Irrigated area (%)	Average yield of the state (Q/ha)
1.	Rice	2.42	21.0	13.45
2.	Total Oilseed	0.33	NA	4.74
3.	Mustard	0.29	NA	4.70
4.	Jute and Mesta	0.08	NA	15.29
5.	Sugarcane	0.03	NA	399.9
6.	Potato	0.08	NA	79.86

Source: Agricultural Statistics at a Glance, 2000, DOA, MOA.

TABLE 3

Average Yield of Major Crops in West Bengal[8]

S. No.	Crop	Area (M ha)	Irrigated area (%)	Average yield of the state (Q/ha)
1.	Rice	5.9	26.4	22.25
2.	Wheat	0.37	16.4	21.17
3.	Coarse Cereal	0.06	NA	23.14
4.	Maize	0.04	NA	31.48
5.	Gram	6.02	10.3	8.15
6.	Oilseeds	0.49	68.1	7.787
7.	Jute and Mesta	0.62	NA	21.11
8.	Sugarcane	0.03	32.0	744.20
9.	Potato	0.32	NA	10.32

Source: Agricultural Statistics at a Glance, 2000, DOA, MOA.

potato, onion, tomato, cauliflower among vegetables; chrysanthemum, rose, orchids, etc. in flowers; ginger, turmeric large cardamom, coriander, cumin among spices and coconut, areca nut and tea among plantation crops. The productivity of many of the horticultural crops in this region is much below the National level. This weakness of the region can be converted into

TABLE 4

Average Yield of Major Crops In Orissa[9]

S. No.	Crop	Area (M ha)	Irrigated area (%)	Average yield of the state (Q/ha)
1.	Rice	4.45	37.0	12.12
2.	Coarse Cereals	0.19	9.0	7.75
3.	Maize	0.05	13.3	13.02
4.	Gram	0.03	–	5.94
5.	Arhar	0.14	1.6	6.12
6.	Groundnut	0.08	16.6	9.46
7.	Jute and Mesta	0.03	NA	9.64
8.	Sugarcane	0.02	100	658.97
9.	Potato	0.01	NA	115.75

Source: Agricultural Statistics at a Glance, 2000, DOA, MOA.

TABLE 5

Average Yield of Major Crops in Bihar[10]

S. No.	Crop	Area (M ha)	Irrigated area (%)	Average yield of the state (Q/ha)
1.	Rice	5.2	40.80	13.01
2.	Wheat	2.10	88.40	19.92
3.	Coarse Cereals	0.85	36.40	16.50
4.	Maize (Kharif)	0.69	42.80	18.53
5.	Gram	0.13	3.2	7.66
6.	Arhar	0.07	—	14.99
7.	Mustard	0.10	36.9	8.00
8.	Sugarcane	0.11	25.4	485.47
9.	Jute and Mesta	0.16	—	7.71
10.	Potato	0.19	NA	87.51
11.	Onion	0.02	NA	96.43
12.	Tobacco	0.02	82.4	5.00

Source: Agricultural Statistics at a Glance, 2000, DOA, MOA.

opportunity, and productivity and production levels can be increased significantly to enhance the total production at national level to meet the ever-growing demand for horticulture produce. Since horticulture provides higher return per unit of land and generates higher employment, development of horticulture also helps in alleviating the economic conditions of people below the poverty line whose number is large in the Eastern and North-Eastern region. An important trend observed in the country is that horticulture development has gradually moved out of its rural confines, resulting in adoption of improved technologies and greater commercialization. But in the Eastern and North-Eastern region traditional practices continue to result in low productivity. The gap between actual yield and potential yield is comparatively high in the region, which is attributed to production problems related to use of technology and incidence of diseases; poor infrastructure for post-harvest management and marketing; knowledge gaps and inadequacy of trained human resources; poor institutional support for dissemination of technologies and information; inadequacy of credit support for investment, etc. One of the major problems being faced in planning for horticulture development in the country is the absence of reliable database on production. State-wise data on production of only a few important horticulture crops is available and that only for important producer states. This problem is more pronounced for North-Eastern states for which available database is very sketchy. The problem has been compounded recently by bifurcation of the states of Bihar, UP and Madhya Pradesh. Separate data on horticulture production in eastern part of U.P., Jharkhand and Chhattisgarh are not available. Eastern India contributes significantly to the production of banana, mango, guava, jack fruit and annona. Litchi, makhana and many minor fruits are unique to the region. Mandarin and pineapple produced in the region have excellent quality. Wide variability exists in mango and banana. However, productivity of most fruits continues to be low compared to national average. An interesting feature in the region is the climatic variability, which provides opportunity for harvest of the crop over an extended period.

Vegetables

Eastern states contribute significantly to production of

potato, and productivity is highest in West Bengal. Hills of North-Eastern states and plateau region of Jharkhand, Chhattisgarh also produce potato during September, much before the usual harvesting period. In major production areas, tomato, capsicum, brinjal, cauliflower, cabbage are also important vegetables. Cucurbits like cucumber, melons, parwal contribute significantly to production of vegetables in Eastern India. Parwal is a unique vegetable in Eastern India, which is also used for sweetmeats. Among the tuber crops, sweet potato has been an important crop but area and production has declined in the last few years. Besides, there are various species of tubers which are important components of horticulture produce of this region.

Floriculture

India has diverse agro-climatic conditions which permit growing of different varieties of flowers throughout the year. Besides traditional flowers such as jasmine, marigold, chrysanthemum, tuberose, crossandras and aster, cut flowers such as rose, orchids, gladiolus, carnation, anthurium, gerbera and lilies have become popular for commercial floriculture. Total area under floriculture in the country is 73971 ha. with an estimated production of 4.6 lakh MT of loose flowers and 1156.13 lakh MT of cut flowers. India is home to about 1300 species of orchids, of which about 800 are found in the North-Eastern region of the country.[11] Eastern Himalayas are not only rich in terms of number of species, but more importantly many of them rank at the top of the list of ornamentally important ones. Besides, many cut flowers like carnation, chrysanthemum, aster, rose, etc. are successfully grown in all the states of North-Eastern region. West Bengal has exploited floriculture to some extent, but lags behind in recent technological developments. Potential of floriculture remains largely unexploited in Eastern region. Ranchi of Jharkhand state is known to grow excellent quality of roses and chrysanthemum, but their commercial exploitation is negligible. There exists ample opportunity for the development of floriculture in the region. The strength of the region in floriculture is there to be exploited through well planned strategies.

Spices

India is known for its wealth in spices, producing more

than 50 varieties. Almost all the states grow one or more spices. The area covered under various spices in the country is estimated to be 2.5 million ha with an annual production of 2.87 million tonnes. More than 90 per cent of the spices produced in the country is used for domestic consumption and the rest are exported as raw as well as value-added products. India produces a wide variety of spices like black pepper, cardamom, ginger, turmeric, chillies, etc. and spices occupy an important place among the agro-products exported. North-Eastern region has significant share in the production of spices especially ginger, turmeric, chillies, garlic and coriander. Introduction of black pepper in the region has been highly successful. Small scale production of organically grown spices in Orissa has also been quite successful. There is wide scope for growing of organic spices in the region. In the growing of ginger, improvement of cultivars and production technology coupled with post-harvest management and processing would not only improve the productivity but enhance economic viability. Large cardamom is unique to the region. Demand for this spice is increasing. Full exploitation of its potential should be attempted. Other spices and herbal spices also hold considerable potential.

Plantation Crops

Among plantation crops coconut, arecanut, cocoa and cashewnut find place in the region. Coconut is grown in Orissa, West Bengal, Assam and during the last decade there has been substantial increase in area and production of coconut in Bihar. Arecanut is a traditional crop of Assam and Northern parts of West Bengal. Cocoa, although not grown in the region at present, has good potential considering the favourable climatic conditions. Similarly, cashewnut is an important crop in Orissa and has expanded to the plateau region of Bengal, Jharkhand and Chhattisgarh. Cashewnut is also successfully grown in Meghalaya, Tripura and Manipur. What would be needed is to improve the profitability of these crops through improved production technology and cultivars coupled with good system of marketing. Betel vine is an important commercial crop in the region, and the region has excellent cultivars for commerce exploration. The crop provides livelihood to a large number of small and marginal farmers, as it has potential to give higher income per unit of land. However, in the traditional system of cultivation, yield is low and the problem is faced of incidence of a number of diseases. Export of this crop from the country is estimated to be over Rs. 1,000 crores and area under production in the country is about 45,000 hectare. Among plantation crops, tea is well established but is capable of expansion and requires rejuvenation in certain areas. The small-grower movement has spread and could be the wave of the future. These smallholders either sell their produce to established large producers for processing in their factories, as Arunachal foothill-growers are doing across the border in Assam, or could be cooperativised and supported by apex organizations with the necessary processing and marketing facilities of which there is a good example in Tripura. Upland teas in Meghalaya, Arunachal and the other hill regions have a potential that awaits exploitation. They could provide special varieties and flavours to add both to quantity and quality in tea production. Rubber is doing well in Tripura which now ranks second only to Kerala in production. Here again the small holder must lead the way. The Rubber Board is doing good work in the States and has adopted farmers who have pooled their lands for rubber cultivation under its supervision. This is an interesting model that could be replicated elsewhere and in respect of other plantation crops. It is necessary to develop processing facilities and encourage manufacture of a variety of rubber products which could be marketed in the eastern region and would, in turn, stimulate demand and expansion of acreage. Some 50,000 Jhumia families in Tripura face acute problems of poverty and under-employment. Of all the resettlement projects taken up, tribal rehabilitation in rubber plantations has been found to be possibly the most effective, as it provides continuous employment till the plant attains maturity and subsequently on a long-term basis through tapping of rubber. About 5,000 hectares have been brought under rubber for tribal rehabilitation so far.[12]

Medicinal and Aromatic Plants

Medicinal and aromatic plants form another important component of horticultural commodities. There is a wide gap in demand and production for industrial use. Besides, medicinal plants are also used by a large proportion of rural and urban population. With growing awareness of health care using herbal products, there is renewed interest in exploitation of traditional medicine. The principal plants are: aloe, ammi, majnis, digitalis, ginseng, guggul, isabgol, liquorice, poduphyllum, rauwolfia, aonla, etc. Important aromatic plants are lemon grass, vitevar, patcholi, Palma Rosa, citronella, mint, geremum, lavender, baris, jasmine, etc. Medicinal plants have received national focus and a Medicinal Plants Board has been established under the Department of Indian System of Medicines and Homeopathy. North-Eastern states and Eastern states provide excellent opportunity for the development of medicinal plants. The demand for organically grown medicinal plants can be met from this region. The immediate problem in the context of horticultural produce is of infrastructure, especially road and transport facilities, availability of power, input support systems like seeds, credit, etc. Power supply is erratic and costly, which is an impediment in promotion of processing facilities. Departmental support systems are also very weak. In Bengal, Department of Food Processing has been created but there is no ground level staff. Same is the situation in Bihar and Eastern Uttar Pradesh. This would need to be reviewed so that State Governments can meet the growing needs for horticulture development.

Animal Husbandry

The Livestock and Fishery Sectors provide fish, milk, egg, wool and meat and much needed employment, especially of women, landless, small and marginal farmers, etc., and also cater to several needs of the economy, such as agricultural operations, transport, income generation, fuel and fertilizers, utilization of agricultural by-products and wastelands. India today ranks first in cattle and buffalo, second in goats, third in sheep and seventh in poultry population in the world. About 56 per cent of the world's buffalo population is in India. Livestock production is an integral part of crop farming and contributes substantially to household nutritional security and poverty alleviation through increased household incomes. The returns from livestock especially dairying and mixed farming in small and medium holdings can be highly balanced development of the rural economy and improvement in the economic status of poor people associated with livestock. The production of milk, egg and fish rose from 17.0 million tonnes, 1832 million nos., 0.75 million tonnes in 1950-51 to 74.7 million tonnes, 30.2 billion nos., and 5.26 million tonnes respectively in 1998-99, is a major leap forward. The contribution of Livestock and Fishery sector to total GDP was 7.39 per cent (6.01% from Livestock and 1.39% from Fisheries) in 1998-99 at current prices. The value of output of livestock and fisheries sectors was estimated to be Rs. 1,48,954 crores during 1998-99 which is about 27 per centof the total value of output of Rs. 5,53,175 crores from the Agricultural andAllied sector. This does not include Draught Animal Power which has been valued between Rs. 40 and 95 billion. The contribution of milk alone (Rs. 82,624 crores) was higher than paddy (Rs. 68,230 crores), wheat (Rs. 40,323 crores) and sugarcane (Rs. 23,314 crores). The overall labour investment in livestock farming in small and medium holdings is high (around 73%) compared to crop farming (23%). Women constitute 71 per cent of the labour force in the livestock sector as against 33 per centin crop farming. It is estimated that about 9.8 million people are directly involved in the livestock sector in principal status and another 8.6 million are involved in the subsidiary status. Looking to the contribution of the livestock and fisheries sectors to the GDP, the higher growth rates of between 4 and 5 per cent for milk, meat, egg and fish, the need for increasing animal protein in the food basket and the potential of livestock in rural transformation and employment, it is essential that the Livestock and Fisheries sectors receive higher focus in coming years. Due to reasons of history, the Eastern and North-Eastern regions of the country have not been able to keep pace in agricultural production including animal husbandry and dairying, as compared to other regions of the country. The main stumbling block is the lack of basic infrastructure including road communication, marketing and input supplies. This region has about 320 lakh human population, 86 per cent of whom live in the rural areas (India--73%). The region's 39 lakh milch bovine (92% cow) produce some 26 lakh litres of milk per day, while 21 per cent (India—7%) of the breedable bovine have either never calved or are kept for non-milk purposes. Milk availability per capita (except for Sikkim) is generally much lower than the Indian average. Estimated productivity of the region per lactating animal (1.03 lit/day) is much lower than India's (2.91 lit/day), though the number of milch animals per household are comparable (0.69 and 0.65 animals, respectively). This region also has the largest number of non-descript animals in the country among the population predominantly of tribals and other socially and economically deprived groups, who are landless, small and marginal farmers. The Government of India, through the Centrally Sponsored Schemes, have been supplementing the State Governments' efforts in livestock development. During the Ninth Plan, cattle breed improvement programmes like Extension of Frozen Semen Technology, National Bull Production Programme, Progeny Testing, Ram and Duck production, piggery and poultry development, Integrated Dairy Development have been implemented. However, the capacity of absorption of funds released by the Government of India has been found to be wanting in various respects. In fact, many of the States have not even availed the schemes, though it is on hundred per cent grant basis, which is so vital for enhancing the per capita income of the poor farmers.[13]

Dairy Development

The successful implementation of "Operation Flood" between 1970-96 has brought India to the forefront of milk production in the world. Milk production which was about 17 million tonnes in 1950-51, has risen to 78.1 million tonnes in 1999-2000. The growth rate for the past three decades has been around 4 per cent as against the growth rate of about 2 per cent in our population. The per capita availability of milk, which was 124 grams per capita per day in 1950-51, decreased to 112 grams per day before the advent of Operation Flood in 1970. The per capita availability has now increased to 217 grams per day, which is slightly less than 220 grams minimum nutritional requirement suggested by Indian Council of Medical Research. The benefits of "Operation Flood" by and large could not reach Eastern and the North-East India primarily due to the reason that "Operation Flood" was confined to those regions which were better endowed and relatively higher in productivity, with easy access to urban and peri-urban markets. The state of dairying in the Eastern and North-Eastern regions is clearly reflected by the fact that there are only 6,748 village dairy cooperatives in Eastern region as against the total of 84,289 in the entire country. Further, analysis indicates that the States of Bihar, Orissa and West Bengal constitute about 95 per cent of the dairy cooperatives in this region. In other words, dairying in other States of the region is almost nil. There are only 398,000 farmer members as against 10.6 million farmer members in the whole country.[14]

Development of Poultry and Small Ruminants

One of the emerging areas is the market acceptability of goat meat and its growth potential. The North-Eastern and Eastern states have immense potential to exploit this sector. The advent of stall feeding technology for production of goats provide scope to generate employment opportunities to the educated rural poor. A central program needs to be initiated to popularize the technology in location specific areas. In the North-Eastern states pig breeding and the popularity of pork provides an instrument for social upliftment in this area. It is essential that this sector be exploited fully by providing appropriate inputs in terms of genetic material, health coverage, value addition and marketing. Given the right incentives and programmes this sector can transform the social scenario. Poultry development in the country has taken a quantum leap in the last three decades emerging from a mere backyard practice to a venture of industrial proportions. In spite of commercialization of the poultry sector, unorganized rural poultry production still contributes around 30 to 40 per cent of eggs and broiler production. This sector still needs to be serviced by State interventions as the possibility of private sector extending their services to the rural sector is limited in this region. In order to support rural poultry production, poultry establishments of the Government need to concentrate on programs to support rural poultry production and other avian species till the private sector ensures availability and marketing in the rural areas. The problem of poultry development in the Eastern and North-Eastern regions, basically hinges on non-availability of proper feed and hatcheries. In fact, the cost of production of poultry products in this region is prohibitive, due to high cost of feed, especially maize. Impetus, therefore, needs to be on production of cereals, especially maize, so that the farmer is able to earn profit on the poultry products.

Piggery Development

Piggery is an important activity among weaker sections of society. It is a major animal husbandry activity in the North-Eastern region, where pork is an important food. Indigenous pig breeds need to be improved through crossbreeding with exotic breeds. Nagaland and Mizoram have done quite well in piggery development. More than 80 per cent of the population in the North-East rear pigs. The Government of India is implementing a scheme "Assistance to States for Integrated Piggery Development" to strengthen State Pig Breeding Farms and to assist them in genetic improvement. It is aimed that in next 20 years all the Government Pig Breeding Farms will be able to supply to the farmers the number of the exotic pigs required for crossbreeding.

The vision for agricultural development in Eastern India should comprise of the following elements:[15]

(A) Providing Multiple Livelihood Opportunities

The first priority in agricultural strategies and programmes should be income enhancement of the farmer through provision of multiple livelihood opportunities by increasing non-agricultural employment from utilization of local strengths and resources.

(B) Sustainable Agricultural Development through Farming Systems Approach

Precision farming methods must be adopted to attain optimum income and yield per drop of water and per unit of land and time, through an area specific farming systems approach, combining crop and animal husbandry, horticulture and agro-forestry.

(C) Harnessing the Gains of Frontier Technologies

Innovative extension delivery systems should be evolved to survey the knowledge revolution to the farmers so as to promote higher productivity and sustainable livelihoods.

(D) Sustainable Agro-Forestry Systems

The North-Eastern region as well as parts of the Eastern region can be used profitably for agro-forestry, given good quality planting material, extension support, micro-credit and post-harvest linkages.

(E) Organic Farming

The low input intensity of the region gives it a natural

advantage in production of organic food, bio-products, etc. The region can be promoted as a centre for organically produced eco-friendly goods.

(F) Special Thrust on Fruit and Vegetables

The Eastern region can become a key center for production of a variety of fruit and vegetables. The Technology Mission for Integrated Development of Horticulture in the North-Eastern region may be strengthened to achieve all the required linkages, including credit, in order to make horticulture the basis of economic growth of the region. Synergy between the activities of various agencies involved in this sector needs special attention.

(G) Strategy for Medicinal and Aromatic Plants

Mission mode approach needs to be adopted to develop this sector covering all linkages from research and development of planting material, cultivation, post-harvest technology, processing and manufacturing, patenting and marketing. Given the unique advantages of the Eastern and North-Eastern Regions, this can be an area of high trajectory growth.

(H) Potential for Fisheries

Keeping in view the vast and varied aquatic resources available in the region for fish production, greater attention is required for both utilization of the resources and fish yield optimization from them. The present fish production of the region of about 23 lakh tonnes is just sufficient to provide about 6 kg per capita of fish to its present population against the standard nutritional requirement of 11 kg per capita. To provide the same, the region needs 4 lakh tonnes of fish for its populace. To partially offset the demand, substantial quantity of fish is imported daily into the region from different parts of the country (Andhra Pradesh, Uttar Pradesh, Bihar, etc). These result in draining of funds from the region for a commodity, which could have been produced in the region itself. This is a sector which, integrated with the intensive farming systems approach, can significantly enhance rural income and livelihood security. In Eastern India the abundance of water and the generous monsoons can provide additional income to farmers through fish cultivation in paddy fields, besides the innumerable tanks, ponds, etc. It is ironical that this region, which consumes large quantities of fish in the natural diet is dependent on import of fish from other States. A concerted effort is required to focus on the linkages needed to develop fish farming in the Eastern as well as North-Eastern Region. Vast water bodies situated in reserve forests of the North-Eastern States are lying untapped as the Forest Department does not have the wherewithal to develop such resources. Development of these resources should either be transferred to the Fisheries Department, or the Forests Department could develop the same in consultation with Fisheries Department and by involving local forest dwellers.

(l) Post-harvest Management, Storage and Marketing

These are critical areas that are essential to enhancing the income of producers and for revitalizing the rural economy. In view of the conditions prevailing in the North-Eastern and Eastern regions and the long distances between production centers and the main market, post-harvest losses of the produce of this region is inordinately high and the shelf life of perishables is low. If these regions are to become major production centers of fruit, vegetables and other perishable commodities the aspect of post-harvest management, storage and transportation assume prime importance. The lack of cold chain has been sorely felt in the region. The required infrastructure must necessarily be established, involving linkages from the collection centers to the retail outlets through retaining chambers, reefer vans, value addition centers, etc. State support, in this context, would be unavoidable in view of the difficulty in obtaining private participation of the required scale. The capital subsidy scheme in operation at present may be restructured in the context of the North-Eastern region in order to facilitate the required large-scale expansion of post-harvest and storage infrastructure. The Eastern and North-Eastern regions are characterized by the poorly developed marketing infrastructure, as a consequence of which producers receive much less than the optimum price for their produce. In the absence of an efficient and responsive marketing system, production programmes too are not able to achieve expected returns. The approach should, therefore, be to promote a competitive marketing system by reviewing the existing legal framework, dismantling redundant controls and restrictions, creating the requisite infrastructure, and empowering producers through quality delivery and support systems and promotion of self-help groups. In view of the potential of the region to produce unique products, the importance of marketing becomes all the more critical. Innovative approaches are needed in this context, for which the region provides wide opportunities on account of the weakness of the existing mechanism.

(J) Development of Animal Husbandry

Livestock and dairy development programmes have received scant importance in the Eastern and North-Eastern regions. By and large, the benefits of 'Operation Flood' have also not reached this region, perhaps due to the fact that this is not a major occupation of the inhabitants. However, in Bihar, Orissa, Chhattisgarh and West Bengal, the potential for dairy development is substantial. The rest of the region, particularly, the North East, due to reasons of geography and tradition, is best suited for development of mono-gastric animals, backyard poultry and piggery. Rearing of small ruminants also has great potential in this region. The critical factor, however, will be an efficient delivery and marketing system for reaching consumption centers. An integrated programme is required for promotion of animal husbandry-related occupations in the context of the farming systems approach, covering of linkages from animal breeding and animal health to procurement of produce, processing, transportation and marketing. An important fact to be borne in mind with regard to development programmes in the North-Eastern region is that compartmentalization within States should be avoided for reasons of economies of scale. An original approach needs to be adopted and common infrastructure created with linkages in all the States. In view of the importance of development of the animal husbandry sector in the North East, Government sponsored infrastructure would need to be created either through the North-Eastern Councilor independently. It may be necessary to set-up a Livestock Development Agency/ Corporation for the region with equity participation from the Stake-holders. The proposed organization may be modeled on the lines of National Dairy Development Board with full autonomy and managed by professionals with the following mandate: Supply of essential inputs for livestock development, in terms of liquid nitrogen, frozen semen, straws, feed and fodder, etc., production and supply of piglets/sows, hatching eggs, poultry layers and broilers, and supply to State level hatcheries, establishment of a marketing network and provision of credit at reasonable rates, provision of technical inputs for HRD, extension and training programmes. It has been observed that the State Governments of this region have created large infrastructure in terms of cattle breeding farms, hatcheries, liquid nitrogen plants, semen banks, etc. Without an effective delivery system. These assets may be transferred to the proposed Corporation/Authority, so as to enable optimum utilisation of resources. The proposed body will initially have to be provided a corpus fund by the Central Government with a mandate that it should achieve self-sufficiency in a given time frame.

(K) Marketing

Marketing is the key instrument in the development of the agriculture sector. The success story of dairy development in the country through the cooperatives was largely due to an effective marketing network created by the National Dairy Development Board. Unfortunately, marketing seems to have taken the back seat in the context of Eastern and North-Eastern States, though the States have been implementing Programmes to increase agriculture, horticulture and livestock productivity, for the last several Five Year Plans. The reason why poultry products and milk is flowing into this region from outside points to the inadequacies of marketing infrastructure in the region. The region seems to be caught in a 'Catch-22' situation; though there is excellent demand for products of the region, the farmers are not able to produce and receive fair remuneration due to the high cost of input supplies and a Non-existent marketing network. Due to the small size of the North-Eastern States, many of the institutions set-up for economic development by the respective State Governments, have proved to be unviable. State Governments tend to think and plan in the framework of their geographical boundaries only. Though the Eastern and North-Eastern region has great potential in the animal husbandry sector, the same has not been exploited to the extent it should have been due to reasons of inaccessibility, lack of marketing network, poor infrastructure and delivery system. Though some infrastructure has been created by each of the States in the region, for instance in terms of AI centres, breeding farms, liquid semen banks, hatcheries, liquid nitrogen plant, etc. in the livestock sector, most of these are lying in disuse due to sheer lack of budgetary support and unsupportable burden on the meager resources of the respective Governments. The reason for the non-utilization of infrastructure is largely due to prohibitive cost of inputs, non-availability of effective transportation and delivery system. Most parts of the Eastern region lag behind rest of India with respect to several social indicators. For instance, Bihar and Orissa rank lowest in poverty ratio and infant mortality is highest in Orissa among all major states of India. Development levels vary greatly within the Eastern region. Even within states like Orissa, the coastal and Northern regions have rural poverty head-count ratios of 45 to 46 per cent, but the Southern districts have 69 per cent of rural population below the poverty line making this the poorest area in rural India. Agriculture dominates the economy, accounting for 33 per cent, 32.8 per cent and 26.7 per cent of Gross State Domestic Product respectively in Assam, Uttar Pradesh and Bihar in 1990-2000 as compared to the all India average of 25.2 per cent (at 1993-94 prices).

TABLE 6

Social Development Indicators: Selected States (mid-1990s)

Indicators unit	*Orissa*	*All India*	*Best State*	*Worst State*
Poverty ratio/per cent	48.70	36.1 (Punjab)	11.5	55.2 (Bihar)
Infant mortality/000	105.0	72.0 (Kerala)	16.0	105.0 (Orissa)
Overall literacy/per cent	51.20	56.5 (Kerala)	91.6	42.0 (Bihar)
Female literacy/per cent	38.90	43.9 (Kerala)	88.5	22.0 (Rajasthan)

Source: CMIE, Profile of states of various years and Economic Survey, GoI, various years.[16]

In terms of average per capita Gross State Domestic Product, the Eastern Region lags way behind the rest of India. For instance, in the mid-1990s, Orissa's per capita GSDP was only Rs.1830 as compared to the national average of Rs. 3171. Average per capita income of Bihar and Orissa was the lowest among major Indian states. Growth in GSDP too in Eastern States has been below the national average for major States. For the overall period (1980-97), Bihar and Orissa recorded the slowest growth. The main reason for slow income growth in Eastern States has been slow agricultural growth in all time-periods as compared to the all India level, and indeed, at or below population growth rate.[17]

TABLE 7

Growth in GSDP and Agriculture Sector in Eastern States in 1980-97

States	*1980-85*	*1985-90*	*1990-96*	*1980-97*
Annual average growth rate in GSDP (%)				
Orissa	4.0	3.6	3.7	3.5
ER States (Orissa, MP, UP and Bihar)	4.2	5.1	3.0	3.9
All India	5.0	6.4	6.0	5.5
Annual average growth rate in Agriculture sector (%)				
Orissa	3.1	-1.4	0.2	1.8@
ER States (Orissa, MP, UP and Bihar)	3.2	1.7	1.0	1.5
All India	3.2	4.6	2.7	3.0

@ For the period ending 1995-96 since 1996-97 was a drought year for Orissa. If this year is included, growth rate becomes zero.

Source: Agricultural Statistics at a Glance, 2000, DOA, MOA.

Dependence on Traditional Agriculture

Sluggish growth of the agriculture sector in the Eastern region is mainly due to low irrigation coverage, erratic climate with deviations in rainfall of 20 per cent or more every third year for the last thirty years or so, and, most strikingly, a very high degree of dependence on a single crop, namely rice, which occupies 93.5 per cent of the foodgrains grown. Given the water intensive nature of rice, such reliance on it, where neither nature nor irrigation can be depended on for water, is risky indeed. Agricultural growth in the Eastern states averaged just over 1 per cent per annum over the last two decades. Irrigation water management, excess water management, rain water management, watershed management and ground water management assume greater significance now than ever before for aiding future agricultural growth in the Eastern Region while evolving agro-climatic region specific production and resource management technologies. The Eastern region, which was one of the most developed and prosperous regions of the country prior to independence, is presently prone to a number of biophysical, institutional and socio-economic constraints. This has resulted in a peculiar subsistence agriculture with low input, low yield, low risk technology. Average farm size, irrigation coverage, average fertilizer consumption and power consumption in agriculture are all below the National average. Average fertilizer consumption in Orissa is lowest of any Indian state. The cumulative result of these factors is low productivity and near stagnation or marginal growth in agriculture sector during the recent years.[18]

TABLE 8

Agricultural Indications in Eastern States (Mid-1990s)

Indicators	*Unit*	*All India*	*Orissa*	*Bihar*	*Chhattisgarh*
Average size of operational holding	Ha	1.6	1.3	0.9	2.6
Marginal holding as a per cent of total	%	59.0	53.6	76.6	37.3
Net irrigated area as a per cent of new sown area	%	35.1	32.8	46.7	24.4
Fertilizer consumption Kg/ha	74.8	25.2	77.0	34.7	
Power consumption in agriculture	KWH/ 000ha	379	35	142	228
Yield of foodgrains	Kg/ha	1547	1250	1480	1080
Rice production as a % of foodgrains	%	42.8	93.5	52.5	25.8

Source: CMIE, Profile of states for various years: Economic Survey and Agricultural Statistics at a Glance, Govt. of India.

Inadequate Infrastructure

The Eastern region faces a serious constraint in terms of infrastructure. On most criteria, Eastern States lag behind the all India average. Orissa, for instance, suffers from poor railway and telecommunication infrastructure. Orissa does well in terms of roads, but only for unpaved roads. With weak rural infrastructure, farmers concentrate over whelmingly on rice cultivation, aided by canal irrigation-based supply-led cropping pattern further confounded by lack of adequate drainage network. Water management technologies in conjunction with rural infrastructure development would wean the farmers away from rice monocropping towards crop/farm diversification. Reforms in the irrigation sector have been initiated only in Orissa within the Eastern region. Decentralization of the management of irrigation systems at various levels is happening now with the formation of water users' associations at minor, distributory and project level. Surface irrigation systems are getting rehabilitated and consolidated for facilitating the take over of system maintenance and water distribution responsibilities to the water users themselves.[19]

TABLE 9

Infrastructure in India and Eastern States in mid-1990s

Infrastructure	*Unit*	*All India*	*Orissa*	*Bihar*	*M.P.*
Railways	Km/000	19.1	14.1	30.2	13.3
Road Length	Km/000				
	Vehicle density/ Sq.km				
	Per cent surfaced roads	55.5	19.9	38.5	44.1
Telecommunication	Lines per 100 persons	0.9	0.4	0.2	0.7
Post-offices	Per 10 sq. km.	0.5	0.5	0.7	0.3
Petroleum consumption	As % of requirement kg/person	68.1	38.4	31.5	39.7

Source: CMIE, Profile of states for various years and Economic Survey, GoI, Various years.

High Rainfall and Humidity

The high rainfall and humidity of the region not only creates favourable environment for a wide range of pests, diseases and weeds, but also creates problems in application of current prevalent technological approaches based on inorganic fertilizer application and chemical control measures through spraying and dusting.

Subsistence Cultivation

Both agricultural and horticultural operations in the region are largely subsistence cultivation. Technological advancement has improved the productivity in many parts of the country, but improved inputs, advanced technologies and high tech practices have been adopted in the eastern and North-Eastern region on a very limited scale. The situation is accentuated by lack of awareness about technology, poor capacity of farmers to invest and poor credit support coupled with weak infrastructure.

Post-harvest Management

Horticultural crops being highly perishable suffer heavy losses due to poor post-harvest management, which makes the investment in these crops risky. In the absence of infrastructure facilities, production of these crops suffer from the crippling uncertainty and instability of market conditions. In view of poor risk bearing capacity of marginal farmers, the productivity is adversely affected. Absence of grading, sorting and packing facilities, storages, pre-cooling and cold-storage infrastructure are a severe constraint particularly with regard to horticultural produce.

Marketing

Marketing of produce is a major component of the total production system and has a major role to play in making this system viable. As witnessed in the recent past, farmers even in Bihar and parts of Orissa are generating marketable surpluses, but in the absence of marketing infrastructure they are unable to get remunerative prices for their produce. Co-operative marketing is very weak in the Eastern and North-Eastern region. The entire marketing system is handled by commission agents. Fruits are mostly auctioned by the orchard owner to pre-harvest contractors resulting in low returns, which do not encourage investment to achieve higher productivity. By and large, the marketing system is oriented neither to the producer nor consumer, but to the middle man, who earns exploitative margins. Moreover, the long distances between production and consumption centres is also a disincentive to the producer.

The concept of diversification conveys different meaning. According to R.L. Cohen the term diversification of farm refers to raise product on farm with a variety of products so that the loss of a single crop would not affect him so seriously.[20] Hopkins and Murray says, "by diversification we shall mean that several things are produced for market so that the farmer depends on several sources of income".[21] D.S. Chauhan has opined that diversification in agriculture is a shift from cropping with poor returns to cropping cash crops and other income generating farming like dairy, poultry, fishery, meat production: and vegetables.[22] All these concepts generally convey the movement of resources, especially labour out of agriculture, to industry and service sector a sort of structural transformation. Within agriculture, however diversification is considered as shift of resources from one (or livestock) to a large mix of crops and livestock. Keeping in view the varying nature of risk and expected returns from each crop (livestock) activity and adjusting in such a way that it leads to optimum portfolio of income.

Thus, the diversification of agriculture seeks to actualise the vast untapped growth potential of agriculture and strengthens agricultural development and promotes value addition. There will be better utilisation of land with satisfactory rotation of crops. It reduces the business risk. There are two phases of risks: Crop failure because of unfavourable weather and loss due to unfavourable prices. In both cases, insurance, against loss by diversification is only parties.

Losses may be reduced by selecting rotation of crops which make most of their growth during different part of the season. The risk from unfavourable prices is reduced by diversification. There are year to year variations in price from the corresponding, fluctuation in size of each crop over the entire country an advance in price may offset a decrease in the yield. An individual farmer may have a poor crop when the crop for the country as a whole is large. He then not only has a small crop to market but gets a low price for it. Therefore, a farmer would be likely to gain by having more than one crop to sell.

Unfortunately diversification of cash crops does not safeguard against the most serious type of price decline. In major business depressions all farm price decline together. During such periods the problem is to try to select those crops which fall more slowly during the decline they try to shift to those which respond most quickly during the recovery. For instance, prices of dairy products fall more slowly than grain prices during the decline, but grain prices usually rise more rapidly during recovery. In this case a small amount of flexibility in farming enterprise is worth working for.

Indian agriculture is at cross roads and the path of development is not smooth. The agricultural sector is facing a serious problem like unemployment and poverty. Though, the foodgrains production has been more than comfortable and even reached embarrassingly high levels, but yet the people in rural areas are moaning under the pressure of poverty and unemployment.

The architect of the Green Revolution such as M.S. Swaminathan warned us[23] way back in 1968 to move cautiously, lest we should end up turning an era of agricultural prosperity to an era of agricultural disaster. Similarly, our planning fathers, such as Mahalanobis had cautioned as that mere growth of foodgrains would not bring prosperity to all and hence special efforts are needed to bring equity and social justice.[24] The policy-makers who failed to steer the course of agricultural development overlooked these crucial aspects of diversification which should be able to put agriculture as well as agriculture-related industry on fast track to provide jobs with higher wage income. The recent model of agricultural development stresses on farm diversification for sustainable development.

In favour of agricultural diversification it is said that the green revolution essentially the seed after fertilizer technology benefited all the farmers who adopted it in the earlier period, but intensive use of technologies became unsustainable. The fatigue of Green Revolution is left. The contribution of technology to productivity has been declining. Land degradation occurred in the lands used for Mono-cultures and soil depleting crops. Excess use of chemical fertilizers and pesticides polluted water bodies.

Pesticides residues remained in the food and fodder produced. Over exploitation of ground water to falling water tables and caused permanent damage to aquifers. Lack of legumes in the cropping systems eroded soil replenishment mechanisms. Water and wind erosion depleted the top soil. Lack of vegetative cover and tree cover resulted in larger run-off and less water collected into water bodies. Denuded hills and land sides in the hills reduced the water flows into the rivers and other surface water bodies.

All these natural resources degradation need to be reserved. Arable land which is about 51 per cent of geographical area should be taken into cultivation for horticulture development. The largest area is to be used for livestock and fisheries. These products will not be able for food security only but environmental sustainability will be maintained with agricultural prosperity.

Through the agricultural diversification, we can achieve the growth targets of plan against the constraints of diminishing land resources, increasing biotic and abiotic stress, threatened loss of bio-diversify, striking natural resources, intensifying competition in the world trade, etc. Therefore, producing food and to generate employment and income remain our biggest challenge in the years to come. Thus, for agricultural sustainability a road map is being prepared which will focus on horticulture crops, dairy, poultry, fisheries, pulses, and oilseeds, etc.

The horticulture sector which includes a wide variety of crops such as fruits, vegetable spices, plantation crops, floriculture, medicinal and aromatic plants, cashew, etc. is nowadays recognised as an important sector for potential diversification and value addition in agriculture, horticulture crops, particularly now fruits are receiving increasing attention in view of its commercial importance accentuated by quick transportation to vast internal market. India, accounts for 10 per cent of world production of fruit crops, Mango, Banana, Citrus, Apple, Guava, Papayas, Pineapple, and Grapes account for the bulk of fruit production. In dry land areas, ber and amla have become popular. India grows a wide variety of species like black pepper, ginger, cardamom, turmeric, garlic. chillies, etc. The area under spices in expanding and North-Eastern region is also becoming an important area for production of spices. The groundnut, coconut and cashew occupy a premier position in the

TABLE 10

Estimated Production of Principal Horticulture Crops

(Million Tonnes)

Crops	*1997-98*	*1998-99*	*1999-00*	*2001-02*
Fruits	43.3	44.0	45.5	46.60
Vegetables	72.7	87.5	90.8	96.54
Spices	2.2	2.9	2.9	3.08
Cashew	0.4	0.5	0.5	0.46
Arecanut	0.3	0.4	0.33	0.33
Coconut	13.1	14.6	12.25	8.80
Others	1.5	1.6	1.75	0.17

Source: Economic Survey, India, 2002-03, p. 162.

world. The estimated production of main horticultural products and their exports have been proved as a means of diversification for making agriculture more profitable through efficient land use.[25]

Now, horticulture crops production has begun to move from rural confines to commercial ventures and has attracted

TABLE 11

Exports of Horticulture

(In Million $)

Year	*Spices and Vegetables*	*Fruits and Processed Food*
1990-91	133	120
1995-96	237	240
1997-98	379	287
1998-99	388	221
1999-2000	408	288
2000-01	354	352
2001-02	314	327

Source: Economic Survey, 2000-01 to 2002-03, Govt. of India, Ministry of Finance, New Delhi.

young entrepreneurs, since it has proved to be intellectually satisfying and economically rewarding. The export demand for some of the horticulture products is increasing.[26]

Next to horticulture, the floriculture is occupying a prime position under diversification scheme of agriculture for generation of income and employment opportunities.

Fisheries sector plays an important role in the socio-economic development of the country. It has been recognised as an important income and employment generator and export earner. The following table shows the volume of fish production and its export in India.

TABLE 12

Production and Export of Fish in India

Year	*Fish Production (lakh tonnes)*			*Export of Marine Product*	
	Marine	*Inland*	*Total*	*Quantity (lakh tonnes)*	*Value (Rs. Crore)*
1990-91	23.0	15.4	38.4	1.4	893
1996-97	29.7	23.8	53.5	3.8	4121
1998-99	27.0	26.0	53.0	3.0	4627
1999-2000	29.0	28.3	57.0	3.0	5116
2000-01	28.0	28.0	56.0	5.03	6296
2001-02	29.0	31.0	60.0	4.58	5815

Source: Economic Survey, India, 2002-03, p. 164.

The total production of fish in India has increased from 38.4 lakh tonnes in 1990-91 to 60.0 lakh tonnes in 2001-02. Again, the total value of exports has also increased from Rs. 893 crore in 1990-91 to Rs. 5815 crore in 2001-02.[27]

India is quite rich in respect of livestock resources. It provides regular employment to about 11 million in principal and 8 million in subsidiary status. The contribution of milk alone (Rs. 1,03,804 crore) was higher than paddy (Rs. 73,965 crore), wheat (Rs. 43,816 crore) and sugar cane (Rs. 28,592 crore) in 2001-02, besides 84.6 million tonnes of milk, the livestock sector contributed 34 billion eggs, 50.7 million kgs of wool, 4.92 million tonnes of meat and 5.8 million tonnes of fish. India has the large livestock population accounting for 57 per cent of the world buffalo, 16 per cent of cattle population. Much of the livestock is reared under sub-optional conditions due to the low income status of livestock owners. Despite all these constraints, India has

TABLE 13

Production and Per Capita Availability of Milk in India

Year	*Production (in MT)*	*Per Capita Availability (gm/day)*
1990-91	53.5	176
1998-99	75.0	211
1999-00	78.0	214
2000-01	81.4	223
2001-02	84.6	226

Source: Annual Report, 2002-03, Department of Animal Husbandry, Govt. of India, Economic Survey, 2002-03, Ministry of Finance, Govt. of India.

become the largest producer of milk in the world. Both the production and per capita availability of milk have been increasing over the years.[28]

Thus, diversification of agriculture as a panacea for promoting agri-business sustainability, has become a dire need of the day. Agriculture policy of the country of mostly designed by the government for agricultural diversification to raise the level of income and standard of living of farmer within a definite time frame. This policy is being framed for all round and comprehensive development for the agricultural sector. The main objective of agricultural policy is to increase per hectare value-added rather than raising physical output by raising the productivity of agriculture in general and productivity of small and marginal holdings in particular.

The Indian states, which traditionally dependent on agriculture for a higher growth in state domestic product, have witnessed a sharp decline in agriculture's share in SDP in recent years. The share in SDP has declined in all the major states between 1993-94 and 2001-02, as shown in Table 14.

The best examples probably are eastern states such as Assam, Bihar, Jharkhand, Manipur, Meghalaya, Nagaland,

TABLE 1.14

Share of Agriculture in State Domestic Product

(In Percentage)

Year	*1993-94*	*1994-95*	*1995-96*	*1996-97*	*1997-98*	*1998-99*	*1999-2000*	*2000-01*	*2001-02*
Andhra Pradesh	33.3	31.1	31.1	31.0	26.2	29.2	27.3	28.8	27.6
Assam	39.4	38.7	38.3	37.1	38.0	36.5	35.2	33.6	32.8
Bihar	48.6	51.0	46.4	50.0	41.7	45.6	40.7	39.8	38.5
Chhattisgarh	31.1	32.1	29.6	29.1	22.4	23.4	22.4	18.7	23.8
Goa	14.8	13.5	12.5	11.3	10.9	9.30	8.9	9.8	8.0
Gujarat	22.4	26.6	22.1	25.9	23.3	23.0	15.7	13.6	17.3
Haryana	42.2	42.2	39.3	38.9	35.4	34.7	33.7	32.6	31.1
Himachal Pradesh	32.2	29.6	28.3	26.9	25.4	23.9	21.2	22.0	—
J & K	32.9	35.6	34.6	35.2	24.1	18.9	18.3	21.7	—
Jharkhand	22.7	24.0	22.4	24.1	18.9	18.3	21.7	—	—
Karnataka	35.6	35.5	32.2	31.0	28.8	28.2	30.0	29.9	26.2
Kerala	30.3	30.7	29.1	28.8	26.5	25.4	24.3	23.7	23.2
MP	39.8	39.9	36.7	36.4	35.4	33.9	325.5	26.7	28.9
Maharashtra	19.5	18.7	17.5	19.3	15.1	16.1	16.1	15.6	15.1
Manipur	35.5	33.9	32.6	30.3	30.9	31.2	27.3	28.3	27.5
Meghalaya	25.3	25.0	26.1	26.9	25.5	24.1	25.5	24.6	23.6
Nagaland	24.4	25.3	29.9	23.1	24.6	27.1	30.5	—	—
Orissa	39.8	37.4	35.1	33.5	36.6	34.2	30.1	28.1	30.5
Punjab	46.1	45.7	32.9	43.8	40.6	39.8	40.5	40.3	39.3
Rajasthan	34.0	36.2	33.6	36.4	34.0	32.8	27.9	35.8	29.5
Tamil Nadu	24.1	23.8	20.1	19.0	19.1	19.9	17.8	17.3	16.4
Tripura	35.3	33.1	33.0	32.1	29.5	28.9	28.1	23.3	27.7
Uttar Pradesh	39.0	38.0	37.2	36.7	34.7	35.1	36.0	35.2	35.1
West Bengal	32.4	32.7	31.2	30.9	30.9	28.2	27.2	26.1	26.2

Source: *Kurukshetra*, Vol. 53, No. 8, June 2005, Table 5, p. 6.

Tripura and West Bengal. Agriculture production in these states has grown rapidly throughout the last decade but agriculture share in SDP has declined continuously. Therefore, these states are economically backward, and ecological frangible region of the country which constitutes one-fifth of area but one-third of human population of the country. Per capita net sown area in eastern India is less due to high population density. Small and marginal holdings constitute more than 80 per cent of total number of holdings in Eastern India. Cropping pattern in the region is dominated by traditional and low productivity crops coupled with low availability of per capita net sown area. The income and employment at small farms are inadequate.

The region is endowed with rich soil and good climatic condition for production of a variety of high value horticultural crops like Mango, Litchi, Papaya, Banana, Pineapple, etc. and commercial crops like tea, raw jute, sugarcane, potato, chilly, tobacco, with livestock to augment income and employment. Although, Assam, Bihar and Bengal grow a large variety of crops. Rice is the most important among the cereals maize occupies the second place. Another crops are Jawar, Bazara, Maroa have got special importance in Bihar, Jharkhand and in hilly areas of Assam. Mixed cropping is largely practised in the state of Bihar in respect of the rabi crops viz. wheat, gram and barley, the area under these three crops mixtures forming 40 per cent of the total area devoted to these crops. The main sugarcane growing area is found in Champaran and Saran in Bihar state, which claim between them 50 per cent of the total area under this crop. Among the oilseeds, the most important varieties grown in Bihar region are linseed, rape and mustard. Bihar is only second in importance to West Bengal in the production 'of Jute whereas Assam is famous for tea plantation.[29]

But compared with all-India rates of yield, the Eastern region is lower in the case of most of the crops except some of the pulses (such as Arhar, Masoor and Khesari) and Jute and Tea. The tragedy of the Eastern region lies in the fact that while containing one-third of the human population of India, it posses only slightly more than 6 per cent of all-India net sown area; and although, the region tries to make up for this handicap by 70 per cent more cultivators, 120 per cent more agricultural labourers and 60 per cent more animal power in cultivating an acre of land than the all India averages and also by wider use of double cropping and irrigation than all India, yet in spite of this intensive cultivation, the rate of return per acre is generally lower than other regions of India.[30] The only redeeming feature is that a large portion of crops is not receiving high price than India as a whole. Therefore, diversification in agriculture is necessary to shift from cropping foodgrains and other cereals with poor return to cropping high' priced crops with livestock. In Eastern region, judiciously exploits water, human resource and agro-climatic condition, it will become a developed region. If farmers of this region start producing horticulture and floriculture crops alongwith fisheries and livestock, it would not create more man days, but also will bring a good returns.

The issue of agricultural diversification as an engine of development has to play a decisive role in rising GDP growth rate of India in general and Eastern region of the country in particular. Farm diversification is quite essential in Eastern region for promotion of agri-trade, agri-exports, agri-business, agro-industries, eradication of poverty and unemployment. The higher productivity can boost the promotional areas which will come from hightech agriculture and cultivation of high value items (fruits, vegetables, seeds, animal husbandry). The impact of such farming will be not indirect farm employment but increasing the demand for non-farm labour. The key to poverty alleviation lies in rural growth based on higher productivity in a varieties of crops and livestock in the eastern region of India.

Indian agriculture has made remarkable progress since independence. While the rate of growth of Indian agriculture has been slackening, the speed of agricultural growth in the Eastern region has been slower than the rest of the country. Till the fifties, the Eastern Region was reputedly the most prosperous region in the country, maintaining a lead over the other region with highest foodgrain yield of 644 kg/ha. However, it lost its leading position thereafter, particularly with the advent of the Green Revolution. The Green Revolution was especially successful in North-Western parts of the country and for a variety of reasons such as fragmented and smaller land holdings as well as institutional, organizational, technological and developmental inadequacies, etc. could not get success in Eastern and North-Eastern states. However, the Eastern Region holds enormous potential for development of agriculture, horticulture, animal husbandry and fisheries. The gap between actual and potential yields is such that huge production increases can be achieved in the region, and for the country as a whole, simply by using available and accessible technologies.

The Eastern Region comprising of Eastern UP, Bihar including Jharkhand, West Bengal, Assam, Orissa and Chhattisgarh occupies about 28 per cent of the country's geographical area with foodgrain production of 58 million tonnes (34.6% of the total), is inhabited by about 35 per cent of country's population.[31]

Agriculture development is much below its potential in this region, with the result that employment in the agriculture sector is limited and a large proportion of population still remains below the poverty line and suffers from malnutrition. Hence, the highest priority must be accorded to exploiting the available potential in the region.

Land Resources

Land is a very important factor of production. Per capita availability of total land/net cultivated land in the Eastern India is lowest in the country. Most of the farm holdings are marginal to small, and highly fragmented, hampering the adoption of hightech agriculture. The soil of the region are relatively fertile and do not have many inherent limitations, however, efforts are required to build up and sustain soil productivity, particularly for intensified and diversified agriculture which have to be practiced for faster economic growth. In all the Eastern states more than 30 per cent of the total geographical area suffers from one or the other soil degradation problem such as soil erosion problem, salinity and solicity problem, soil acidity problem, etc.

Water Resources

Water is the most essential element of agriculture. The Eastern region is rich in rain, surface and ground water resources. The average annual rainfall ranges from 1100 to 2000 mm, which is sufficient to meet the agricultural water requirement. Annual surface water flow is abundant (117 m ha-m), but much less is utilizable (36 M ha-m) of which only about one-third has been actually utilized. Ground water potential is also high (30 m ha-m) of which less than 20 per cent is being utilized. The Eastern region is also rich in regard to river. There are seven major rivers which have catchments area larger than 20,000 sq km and four medium rivers which have catchments area larger than 5000 sq km. However, the Eastern region generally faces the problem of drought and flood which cause immense uncertainty and instability in agricultural productivity and production.[32]

In spite of all the abundance of water resources the

progress of creation of irrigation potential under major and medium irrigation systems is very slow in the entire Eastern region. The government spending on irrigation development is sluggish in all states but private investment in ground water exploitation is fairly significant. Generally the canals, wells are the major source of irrigation in Eastern states of India. Distribution of crops in irrigated area shows that rice occupies the major chunk in all the states in Eastern region, the water resources inadequately developed as well as developed resources are poorly utilized. Canal water for crop production is available in a relatively uncontrolled manner. It is excessive and uneven during the wet season, and too little during the dry season. Ground water is developed to a smaller extent and that too is not fully utilized due to inadequate and erratic supply of electrical power or non-availability of diesel and maintenance infrastructure.

Bio-Resources

Eastern region of India is also rich in regard to bio-resources. It possesses a distinct identity, not only because of its geography, history and culture but also because of the great diversity in its natural ecosystem. Its climate varies from dry winter and hot summer to tropical savannah. Physiographically, the entire eastern region could be divided into three regions with different geographical nature and distribution of flora and fauna: Plateau and Hills, Coastal plains, and Gangetic plains. Large area in this region can be brought under crop diversification. The coastal region of Eastern India (such as Sundarbans, West Bengal and Chilka Lake, Orissa) is the site of great biodiversity of both flora and fauna. Coconut is an important plantation tree of Eastern states of India. Besides, among plantation crops arecanut, cocoa, cashewnut, tea and rubber find place in the region.

Crops and Cropping Pattern

In Eastern region, due to its high rainfall and water logged conditions, rice is the predominant Kharif crop occupying 70-90 per cent of the entire region under irrigation/rain fed. Wheat, potato, sugarcane, pulses and oilseeds are the major Rabi crops. West Bengal is the leading producer of rice in the country, accounting for 15.59 per cent of total production. In total production of foodgrains, West Bengal and Bihar stand fourth and fifth position respectively in the country.[33]

Horticulture

Horticulture, which includes fruit, vegetable, floriculture, medicinal and aromatic plants, plantation crops, spices and bee-keeping has traditionally been an important activity in the Eastern states of India. The productivity of many of the horticultural crops in this region is much below the national level. An important trend observed in the country is that the horticulture development has gradually moved out of its rural confines, resulting in adoption of improved technologies and greater commercialization. But in the Eastern region traditional practices continue to result in low productivity. However, an interesting feature in the region is the climatic variability, which provides opportunities for harvest of the crop over an extended period. Since horticulture provides higher return per unit of land and generates higher employment, development of horticulture also helps in alleviating the economic condition of people below the poverty line whose number is large in the Eastern region.

Eastern states contribute significantly to production of different vegetables as such, potato, tomato, capsicum, brinjal, cauliflower, cabbage, cucumber, melons and parwal, etc. The climatic condition of India is also favourable for floriculture. India has diverse agro-climatic condition which permit growing of different varieties of flowers throughout the year. Potential of floriculture remains largely unexploited in Eastern region. Furthermore, Eastern states provide excellent opportunities for the development of medicinal plants.

Apart from the above favourable condition of horticulture in Eastern India, horticulture faces some problems. The immediate problem in the context of horticulture produce is of infrastructure like road, transport, power, etc. Input support system like seats, credit, etc. and departmental support systems are also not in a good position. One of the major problems being faced in planning for horticulture development in the country is the absence of reliable database on production. Horticulture development is currently constrained by marketing arrangements.

Animal Husbandry

It comprises livestock and fishery sectors which provide fish, milk, egg, wool, meat and much needed employment and many more. Eastern states have immense potential to exploit these sectors. There are various constraints faced by the animal husbandry in Eastern states; such as, low productivity of animals, inadequate veterinary services, non-availability of improved breeds, shortage of feed and fodder, poor dissemination of technical know-how, absence of backward and forward linkages for processing and marketing.

Notes and References

1. India: 1951.
2. India, Census: 1991.
3. Bihar Through Figures: Government of Bihar.
4. Second Bihar State Irrigation Report.
5. Saikia, P.D.: Changes in Pattern of Land Holding and its Use in Assam: Raifore, Batori: Directorate of Information and Public Relation, Government of Assam, 1996.
6. Saha, N.: Economics of Shifting Cultivation of North-Eastern India, Agro-Economic Research Centre, Jorhat, 1973.
7. Agricultural Statistics at a Glance, 2000, DOA, MOA.
8. *Ibid.*
9. *Ibid.*
10. *Ibid.*
11. Government of India: Agriculture in Brief. Ed.-14, Directorate of Economics and Statistics, Ministry of Agriculture and Irrigation, Government of India, New Delhi.
12. NEC Secretariate: Basic Statistics, North-Eastern Council (NEC), Shillong.
13. Planning Commission: Ninth Five Year Plan Document.
14. Government of Assam: World Agricultural Census, Assam, 1970-71, Directorate of Economics and Statistics, Government of Assam.
15. NEC Secretariate: Basic Statistics, North-Eastern Council (NEC), Shillong.
16. CMIE: Profile of States of Various years and Economic Survey, GoI, Various years.
17. Agricultural Statistics at a Glance, 2000, DOA, MOA.
18. CMIE: *op. cit.*
19. CMIE: *op. cit.*
20. Cohen, R.L.: Quoted from Mohanty, B.K.: Regional Approach with Farm Diversity; *Kurukshetra*, Vol. 53, No. 8, June 2005.
21. Hopkins and Murray: Farm Management.
22. Chankan, D.S.: Agricultural Economics.
23. Srivastava, M.P. and S.R. Singh: Prospects of Second Green Revolution; *Kurukshetra*, Vol. 53, No. 3, Jan. 2005.
24. Mahalanovis, P.C. Quoted in VEPA: Second Green Revolution: A Catalyst for Rural Uplift, *Yojana*, Vol. 48, Aug. 2004.

25. Economic Survey, India 2000-03, p. 162.
26. Economic Survey, 2000-01 and 2002-03, Government of India, Ministry of Finance, New Delhi.
27. *Ibid.*, p. 164.
28. Annual Report, 2002-03, Department of Animal Husbandry, Government of India, Economic Survey, 2002-03, Ministry of Finance, Government of India.
29. *Kurukshetra*, Vol. 53, No. 8, June 2005, Tab. 5, p. 6.
30. Bhanu, B.: Transforming Indian Agriculture: The New Indian Express, May 2, 2004.
31. Mohanty, B.K.: Regional Approach with Farm Diversity, *Kurukshetra*, Vol. 53, No. 8, June 2005.
32. Goswami, S.N., Chatterjee, S. Sen, Others and Bhalla: Crop Concentration and Diversification in India—"A Spatio-Temporal Analysis Geographical Review of India", Vol. 66, pp. 50-62.
33. *Ibid.*

References

Thakur, R.N. (2004), 'North Bihar Regional Planning', 'Decentralised Planning and Development—New Directions', Ed. Amalesh Banerjee, Kanishka Publisher, New Delhi.

Thakur, R.N. (2006), 'Planning Cash-Crops and Diversification of Agriculture—A Micro Study', National Seminar Organised by the Indian Economic Association (IEA) at Indira Gandhi Science Complex (Planetorium), Patna, March 26-28.

Thakur, R.N. (2008), 'Regional Planning for Cash-Crops in North, Bihar—A case study of Samastipur District', 'Growth and Diversification of Agriculture', Eds. A.K. Thakur, K.B. Padamadeo, Deep and Deep Publisher, New Delhi.

Thakur, R.N. (2009), 'Nature and Pattern of Agricultural Diversification in Bihar and Estern India', Paper presented in 12th Annual Conference, Economic Association of Bihar (EAB), Conference Volume, T.M. Bhagalpur University, Bhagalpur, July 4-6.

Thakur, R.N. (20010), 'Nature and Pattern of Agricultural Diversification in Bihar and Eastern India,' 'Globalisation and Diversification of Agriculture in India,' Eds. A.K. Thakur and Roy, Regal Publication, New Delhi.

Structural Changes and Agriculture in India

S.S. Somra and Kuldeep Singh

INTRODUCTION

The generation and sustenance of economic growth, especially in the early stages of most developing countries, are to a large extent, determined by the performance of agricultural sector (Rennis and Fei, 1961). In India, an agricultural sector unresponsive to stimuli or unstable in nature may substantially impede steady growth of the economy. The present government is cautious about to provide strength to agricultural sector and presently there were made several provisions in the Eleventh Plan for this purpose but their performances is now awaited.

Basically, under the structural changes process we have considered the transformation of a traditional agricultural economy to a modern industrial economy. In India the structural changes received potential attention in recent years (since 1991). India has a strong, vibrant and fast-growing economy which is rapidly integrating with the global economy (Ernst and Young, 2006). India is forecast to become the third largest economy in the world, after China and the US, by the year 2050 overtaking all other developed economies (Wilson and Purushothaman, 2003). Now the policy challenge for India is not to raise growth from 8 to 10 per cent. Rather the primary challenge is to sustain rapid growth while extending rapid growth and its benefits to more regions, sectors and people. Rapid growth is not a 'natural' state for an economy keeping rapid growth requires continuous effort. In recent years the empirical literature on structural changes and convergence has devoted increasing attention to inter-regional analysis. The established results on inter-regional convergence appeared to be quite robust for different regions/countries, with most reporting a trend of convergence although at different degrees of significance. The neoclassical growth theory as proposed by Solow-Swan and the 'catching-up' theory maintain that there will be convergence in levels of per capita income across countries.

A striking feature of India's structural reforms over the past decade has been the strength of the services sector. Average services grew more slowly than industry between 1951 and 1990. Growth of services picked up in the 1980s, and accelerated in the 1990s when it averaged 7.5 per cent per annum, thus providing a valuable prop into industry and agriculture which grew on average by 5.8 per cent and 3.1 per cent respectively. The growth of GDP during 2002-06 is 7.2 per cent. Here the growth of the agriculture sector is 1.7 per cent, growth of industry sector is 8.3 per cent and growth of services is 9.0 per cent, these figures slightly change in later phase 2006-09.

In recent debate on agricultural development, efforts from every part of economy have been made to improve the agricultural performance through the instruments of technological innovation and institutional innovation. One of the major challenges in the 11th Five Year Plan is to reverse the deceleration in agricultural growth. The two major sources of growth in agriculture, viz., area expansion and productivity growth, which served well in the past, are now plagued with some limitations. It is argued that any significant technological breakthrough cannot be expected in the near future and hence, one has to depend on the exploitation of the potential of the existing technology. Therefore, another alternative which may prove to be very useful in this context, at least in the short-run, is to move towards diversification into high value crops (Government of India, 2006).

Literatures on modern agriculture technology adoption studies reveal that several subjective and objective factors are responsible for the incomplete adoption of High Yielding Varieties (HYV). In a study by (Goyari, 2005), it was observed that majority of sample farmers were found adopting new paddy seeds because of above mentioned advantages of new seeds. Along with such advantages, HYV seeds have been found to exhibit higher fluctuations in yields and profits across plots and across farm households than traditional seeds. So, to avoid risk, a rational farmer may like to allocate his available land between two technologies (between new and local varieties) rather than completely switching to the former. This argument, as pointed out by (Saha, 2001), is based on two things; one, farmers are risk averse and two, the HYV cultivation involves greater risk compared to traditional paddy cultivation. Farmers' considerations of higher risk associated with HYV paddy cultivation has been considered as an important factor among many socio-economic factors acting on the incomplete adoption of HYV (Feder, etc.,1985).

STRUCTURAL REFORMS AT GLOBAL LEVEL AND IN INDIA

The concept of structural changes at global level basically came in existence with Kuznets, Chenary, Denison, etc. around sixth decade of last century. Under Structural changes generally we have considered the overall changes in the economy or different sectors for rapid development/growth. The general scenario of world development during last four-five decades remained very changing. Several studies showed different views. However, there is a causal relationship among development, globalisation and structural changes. (Stiglitz, 1998, Hurroll and Woods, 2000) argued that globalisation leads to increase in disparities as trade openness increases differentials in returns to education and skills. Globalisation marginalizes certain groups of people or geographic reasons and opening up lags behind development of adequate institutions and governance. (Agenor, 2003) found U-shaped relationship between globalisation and poverty indicating that globalisation at low (high) levels tends to increase (decrease) poverty. He used trade and financial openness to compute a simple globalisation index based on principal component analysis using data of 62 countries during 1995-2001 and computed regression equation between Gini coefficient and globalisation index and found negative relation. Over the last 100 years, global disparities by most measures have been increasing. The ratio of average income of the richest to the poorest country in the world increased from 9:1 at the end of the 19th century to about 30:1 in 1960 to more than 60:1 today. (Birdsall, 2002) remarked that asymmetric globalisation widens the disparities. Moreover, (Pritchett, 1995) found that the ratio of GDP per capita of the richest to the poorest country rose from 8.7 in 1870 to 38.1 in 1960 and 51.6 in 1985. The standard deviation of log per capita income which was between 0.513 and 0.636 in 1970, it rose from 0.867 in 1960 to 1.025 in 1985.

The neo-classical growth theory predicts convergence whereas endogenous theory predicts less convergence or divergence. The empirical evidence showed that during the first wave of globalisation, convergence in per capita income and real wage took place within the Atlantic economy due to an increase in international trade and massive international migration. The deglobalisation period is characterized as widening disparities between richest and poorest regions and among Atlantic economy. The golden age period was a 25 years period of rapid growth, relative stability and declining disparities. There was a considerable convergence among Western Europe and OECD and a decline in the GDP gap in per capita income between the poorest and the richest regions. Similarly, (Lindert and Williamson, 2001) found that a significant globalisation disparities relationship does not exist. On the contrary, the Human Development Report (2005) showed that the decomposition of disparities using Gini and Theil index proved that world disparity enhanced up to 1990s, then declines. The disparities in OECD and Latin American Countries were gradually stipulated but reverse was seen in South Asian countries. Disparities in the Africans, East and Central European countries rose till 2000, and then declined till 2015. The report also observed that out of 73 countries, 53 have seen disparities rise and political influence were found in those researches which do not support in conclusion that "globalisation is good for the poor" or that anti-inflationary policies are "pro-poor". In every region, during 1960-80 and 1980-1998, except East Asia and South Asia, the later period showed remarkably slower growth. Their regression did not show the relationship between openness of the economy and the income of the poor.

The World Bank—a sparing critic of growth, arrived at the following conclusion in one of the recent world development report (1990), "Many developing countries have not merely failed to keep pace with the industiral countries; they have seen their incomes fall in absolute terms." Equally emphatically, declares the world resources (1992-93) report over the past twenty years, "clearly, there has been no narrowing of the gap between rich and poor countries. Economically the gap is widening." After same four decades of energetic growth efforts, more people than ever before, 1.1 billion, now live in poverty. There has been a gradual decline or marginalisation of third world countries in the world economy. Between 1950 and 1973, the Third-World share in world exports dropped from 31.1 per cent to just 18.4 per cent. Again, between 1980 and 1989, the average per capita income in Africa declined by 2.2 per cent. "Development options" are rarely even considered in regard to Africa any longer—an entire continent seems to be slipping into the "role of an international welfare case." A majority of the "role of an international welfare case." A majority of the "hopeful looking" countries of the 70s, the newly industrialising countries, also became bogged down in crisis and poverty, where there has been some economic progress, mounting empirical evidence shows that it has been largely to the benefit of the already better off social groups. "For many of world's poor, the 1980s was a 'lost decade'—a disaster indeed." (WDR, 1990, p. 7) Only a few export oriented NICs from the Asian region (the four tigers—South Korea, Taiwan, Singapore and Hong Kong, as well as Malaysia and Thailand) have improved their position in the world economy. (Marmora and Massner, 1989) Thus, then, economic growth viewed globally, has certainly not trickled down. And whatever economic growth that has happened in the third world, it has been "growth without development," (regardless of how development is defined). (Braun, 1990, p. 56)

STRUCTURAL REFORM IN INDIA

In India the aforesaid topic became the matter of discussion since 1991, when the intensive phase of globalization was started. The review of some studies on development and globalization (structural changes) in India shows very different type of reflection for different sectors and segments of the economy but in the present paper there is focus on agriculture. In a research (Jha, 2000) found that change of Gini coefficient was -4.73 in rural area and -0.6 in urban area during 1957-63, but the change of head-count ratio was -6.63 in rural area and 2.92 in urban area having the average growth rate of 3.94 per cent. On the other hand, change of Gini were -0.73 in rural area and -0.95 in urban area and the change of rural and urban head-count ratios were –14.23 and –11.43 respectively during 1963-64 to 1989-90 with the GDP growth rate of 4.03 per cent. But, during the period of 1990-91 to 1996-97 the change of Gini coefficients were 2.40 in rural area and 2.17 in urban area but the change of head-count ratios were –2.21 in rural area and –4.18 in urban area with the growth rate of 5.63 per cent. Therefore, globalization increase growth rate, decreased poverty ratio but increased disparities in India. Surjit S. Bhalla (2003), calculated shape of distribution elasticity for India as 0.8 and change in Gini was -1.6 and Head-Count Ratio was 48.2 and 29.4 in 1999 and the elasticity of poverty growth was –2.4 and hence net impact of growth on poverty reduction is 1.92, i.e. growth diminished poverty and disparities during 1983-99. It is too low in Bihar and too high in Kerala and West Bengal. Bhowmik, D. (2000), calculated regression equation between Gini coefficient and growth rate of GDP during 1956-57 to 1990-91 and found that one per cent increase in growth rate diminished Gini by 0.01598 per cent per year although the test is insignificant. Similarly, the regression equation between the two during 1991-92 to 1999-2000 showed that one per cent rise in growth rate stipulated the Gini coefficient by 0.05368 per cent per year. But the estimate is insignificant. It means that growth enlarged disparities in the reform period. Moreover, the disparities widens among the Indian states since Gini of the State Domestic Product during 1980-81 to 1990-91 increased at the rate of 0.149 per cent per year but it increased at the rate of 0.412 per cent per year during 1991-92 to 2001-02 which asserted that the degree of disparities rose or accelerated in the reform period among the States or it can be said that the disparity widens among the Indian states. This can also be verified by the Poverty Disparity Index which showed that the index in rural area was 23.19 per cent in 1973-74 that enhanced to 40.96 per cent in 1987-88 and further to 67.93 per cent in 1999-00. In urban area the index was 27.75 per cent in 1973-74 which stepped up to 67.75 per cent in 1999-2000. This means that disparity widens in rural and urban area. That is, rich states became richer and the poor became poorer (Pal, 2003). Even, the coefficient of variation of average growth rates among the states jumped from 0.14 in the 1980s to 0.29 in the 1990s which showed the uneven development where southern states performed better than the eastern and central states. Again, the growth, inflation and trade off do not exist in the development of states. (Bhattacharya and Sakthivel, 2004).

As per NSS (National Sample Survey) data, found that the growth rate of employment came down from 2.7 per cent per annum during 1983-94 to 1.07 per cent during 1993-2000 when GDP growth rate went up from 5.2 per cent to 6 per cent and the employment rate further accelerated to 2.8 per cent during 2000-05, on the other hand, unemployment rate also increased from 7.3 per cent in 1999-2000 to 8.3 per cent in 2004-05. Even, the employment elasticity has fallen from 0.41 to 0.15 during the period from 1983-84 to 1993-94 and 1993-94 to 1999-2000 which showed that the employment growth decelerated while GDP growth rate accelerated. More convincing evidence is that 50th and 60th Round NSS data asserted that the male unemployment increased from 5.6 per cent to 9 per cent in rural areas and from 6.7 per cent to 8.1 per cent in urban areas during 1993-94—2004. Again, the female unemployment increased from 5.6 per cent in 1993-94 to 9.3 per cent in 2004 in rural areas and from 10.5 per cent to 11.7 per cent in urban areas (ET, 2006). The sectoral GDP growth rates are asymmetric where tertiary sector growth rate is accelerating but primary and secondary sectors are stagnant in the 90s including the deceleration of employment growth rate. Hence, there is a weak linkage between sectors in the growth process/development (Bathla, 2005).

Agriculture Development

Agriculture sector in India underwent drastic policy reforms during the almost last two decades on account of liberalization and WTO agreement on agriculture (AoA). These reforms have had mixed effect on the agriculture sector in India and this effect vary from state to state, region to region and crops to crops. An analysis of the impact of reforms on the nature and extent of integration between the world and domestic commodity markets over the years has shown the empirical evidence to suggest that the extent of integration between commodity markets in Haryana with that of world market increases during in post-reform period. More specifically, the short-run elasticity estimates using error-correction model have shown a turnaround during liberalization indicating faster transmission of world prices to the domestic market than that they did prior to liberalization period which in turn has significant effect on the trend and variation of domestic commodity prices (Brigit, 2003).

The agriculture performance in India during 1950-51 to 1964-65 was mostly, an account of the expansion in cultivated area and on account of regional specialization requiring little investment resources. The trend of rate of growth of output was high with fluctuations (Vaidyanathan and Minhas, 1988; Chakaravarty, 1986). The faster growth during the First Five Year Plan had led to relative de-emphasizing of agriculture in terms of public investment in the Second Five Year Plan. This suggests that the planners considered agriculture sector as the bargain sector with large unexploited potential and the one which could provide the requisite agricultural surplus with a relatively short time lag, after putting a certain minimum infrastructure in place (Chakaravarty, 1984). However, subsequently, there was a fall in the agricultural output level and also there was greater output instability. It was increasingly being felt at that time that agricultural sector's unsatisfactory performance is operating as the binding constraint on the smooth growth of the industrial sector as well as the rest of the economy. This led to adoption of the green revolution technology.

During the period 1967-68 to 2004-05 the green revolution strategy aimed at rapid technology modernization of Indian agriculture by deliberately concentrating investments in crops and regions where returns were expected to be relatively higher and certain. As the exclusive emphasis of this strategy was on rising yield per-cropped hectare through the intensification of inputs, the focus of agricultural development inevitably shifted to the developed regions and to the resources of rich farmers (Rao, 1994). The bulk of the increase in agricultural output as a result of application of new technology has been concentrated in a small geographic area of Punjab, Haryana, parts of Uttar Pradesh, Maharashtra, Gujarat, West Bengal, and Karnataka. The spread of new technology consisting of water seed-fertilizer was to be achieved through a policy package. This was done with the dual objectives of maintaining farm prices at affordable levels while ensuring that producers did not suffer on account of volatility in output prices and/or high input prices. However, the growth of output was a result of mainly; the increase in yield per hectare; change in the composition of gross-cropped area (GCA) in favour of commercial crops and the regional technologically dynamic changes in the eighties to the eastern and central regions of the country. The period 1967-68 to 1979-80 was characterized by a slow down in the growth rates of GDP primarily as a result of reduced public and private investment. During this period, GDP grew at only 3.45 per cent per annum and the per capita income growth 1.11 per cent as compared with growth rates 4.00 per cent and 1.69 per cent per annum respectively during 1950-51 to 1964-65. There was a slow down in the growth rates of all the major sectors of the economy.

Again during 1980-85 to 1990-91 compared in the growth rates of 4.5 per cent per annum and after 1991-92 to 1996-97 the annual growth was probably near to earlier situation. However, during 1997-98 to 2004-05 there emerged a critical situation of agriculture sector and the annual growth rates decline from earlier level or may be negative. This period is probably stagnant phase or there slight decline in agriculture sector is remains concern. In this direction the government in 11th Plan Document put special stress on agricultural sector development to maintain the earlier record of growth rates.

Table 1, which gives levels and growth of aggregate crop output at the state level during 1962-65 to 2004-05, brings out several interesting features of the regional pattern of agricultural development in India since the mid-1960s. The 1962-2005 period has been divided into four sub-periods, namely, 1962-65 over 1970-73 (1st Period), 1970-73 over 1980-83 (IInd Period), 1980-83 over 1992-95 (IIIrd Period) and 1996-99 over 2003-05 (IV period). Levels and growth rates have been worked out by taking triennium averages for 1962-65, 1970-73, 1980-83, 1990-93, 1996-99 and 2003-05.

The new agricultural technology introduced during the mid-1960s led to significant growth in agricultural output. Despite considerable interstate variations, most states shared the gains of the new technology. Taking the entire period 1962-65 to 2003-05, total agricultural output in India at constant 1993-94 prices increased at a compound annual growth rate of 2.11 per cent. During this period, the highest output growth rate of 2.19 per cent per annum was recorded by the north-western region of India, followed by the central and southern regions. The lowest growth rate of 1.6 per cent was registered by the highly populated eastern region. There were important changes during the various sub-periods in the pattern of agricultural development. During the first phase of the Green Revolution, that is from 1962-65 to 1970-73, the new technology was confined to wheat and the main beneficiaries were the irrigated north-western states of India, in particular Punjab, Haryana and Western Uttar Pradesh. Another state that benefited from the wheat revolution was West Bengal. The new technology had hardly any impact on rice. The main foodgrain crop (rice) growing eastern and southern states were not able to derive appreciable gains from the new technology. The southern states of Karnataka, Kerala and Tamil Nadu also registered medium to high growth, but in their case the new technology made appreciable contributions only in limited areas. Crop output in the dry rainfed states in the central region was hardly influenced by new technology and agricultural production in that region was characterised by sharp weather induced year-to-year fluctuations. While Rajasthan recorded a very high growth rate of 4.29 per cent, Maharashtra recorded a negative growth rate of 3.64 per cent with Gujarat and Madhya Pradesh recording a positive but low growth rate of nearly 2 per cent per annum.

Since only a few states were able to derive substantial gains from the new technology, regional inequalities were accentuated during this period. During the IInd period 1970-73 over 1980-83 and IIIrd period 1980-83 over 1992-95 the agricultural development and output growth rate shown overall and improvement probably in all states as per Table 1. In the IVth period from 1996-99 over 2003-05, the agriculture development situation and growth rates in different states is probably stagnant or slight decline. This is an unsatisfactory picture of agriculture development while the government has started the IInd phase of liberalization and globalization. Thus the new economic policy benefits not occur up to now in the pocket of agriculture sector. No doubt, in 11th Plan government made special efforts to development of agriculture sector to achieve the target overall higher growth rate of Indian economy.

Factors Affecting

Area under irrigation and use of fertiliser and electric power show a moderate to high increase in various states during the first period (1985-86 to 1995-96). The only exception to this was the use of power in agriculture in Himachal Pradesh. Net sown area in all the states either showed an increase or stagnation, except in Bihar and Himachal Pradesh, which showed a slight decline during 1985-86 to 1995-96. During the second period, i.e. 1995-96 to 2003-04 input use in most of the states either declined or increased at a slower rate as compared to the first period, with a few exceptions (Table 1).

After 1995-96, net sown area showed a decline in all the states except Bihar, Jammu and Kashmir and Punjab. The decline was more than 2 per cent per annum in Tamil Nadu and more than half a per cent in Orissa, Andhra Pradesh, Madhya Pradesh, Kamataka and Kerala. Net sown area remained stagnant in Uttar Pradesh and in West Bengal. Area under irrigation followed a sharp decline in Andhra Pradesh, Tamil Nadu, Orissa, and Rajasthan Expansion of irrigation slowed down in all the states.

Use of fertiliser declined at more than 4.6 per cent in Madhya Pradesh. Other states which recorded a decline in fertiliser use were Rajasthan, Tamil Nadu and Gujarat. Only four states, namely, Assam, Himachal Pradesh, Jammu and Kashmir and Punjab showed higher growth in fertiliser after 1995-96 as compared to the period between 1985-86 and 1995-96. All the remaining states show lower growth in fertiliser after 1995-96 as compared to the previous decade. Power supply to agriculture witnessed a setback after 1995-96 in all the states except Himachal Pradesh which showed close to 9 per cent growth rate in power supplied to agriculture. States like Bihar, Jammu and Kashmir, Kerala, Madhya Pradesh, Maharashtra, Orissa, Rajasthan, Uttar Pradesh and West Bengal experienced a decline in power supply to:

TABLE I

Growth Rate of Factors Affecting to Agricultural Development

State	*Period*	*Net sown area*	*Irri-gated area (%)*	*NPK (Ferti-lizer)*	*Power consum-ption in agri-culture*	*Change in crop pattern (%)*
Andhra Pradesh	1985-86 to 1995-96	0.11	1.85	7.01	15.52	16.4
	1995-96 to 2003-04	-0.71	-1.70	0.03	4.18	9.9
Assam	1985-86 to 1995-96	0.22	0.00	10.36	16.99	5.3
	1995-96 to 2003-04	-0.03	0.00	'19.92	NAC	4.8
Bihar	1985-86 to 1995-96	-0.54	1.37	2.40	4.44	5.7
	1995-96 to 2003-04	0.26	0.58	0.79	-4.33	3.2
Gujarat	1985-86 to 1995-96	-0.01	3.62	6.84	17.92	14.3
	1995-96 to 2003-04	-0.19	0.63	-0.74	5.36	8.7
Haryana	1985-86 to 1995-96	0.06	2.30	7.18	11.41	15.9
	1995-96 to 2003-04	-0.37	1.67	3.37	4.26	9.4
Himachal Pradesh	1985-86 to 1995-96	-0.26	0.23	1.76	-6.83	4.0
	1995-96 to 2003-04	-0.31	0.51	5.31	8.75	3,0
Jammu and Kashmir	1985-86 to 1995-96	0.14	0.71	2.95	17.83	3.8
	1995-96 to 2003-04	0.29	0.14	4.14	-16.68	5.2
Karnataka	1985-86 to 1995-96	0.13	3.51	4.89	18.00	15.0
	1995-96 to 2003-04	-0.68	0.28	3.22	1.74	11.0
Kerala	1985-86 to 1995-96	0.27	1.31	2.52	10,48	8.5
	1995-96 to 2003-04	-0.50	-0.57	-0.26	-8,16	8.0
Madhya Pradesh	1985-86 to 1995-96	0.30	7.46	6.93	28.49	13.1
	1995-96 to 2003-04	-0.67	1.50	-4.66	-7.72	7.3
Maha-rashtra	1985-86 to 1995-96	-0.11	3.36	8.11	13.62	10.4
	1995-96 to 2003-04	-0.28	2.43	2.48	-5.73	11.1
Orissa	1985-86 to 1995-96	0.10	2.08	5.10	16.92	23.1
	1995-96 to 2003-04	-0.80	-1.06	2.84	-7.03	7.7
Punjab	1985-86 to 1995-96	-0.05	1.26	1.58	7.66	10.3
	1995-96 to 2003-04	0.30	0.65	1.82	-0.73	6.6
Rajasthan	1985-86 to 1995-96	1.68	4.92	12.29	11.56	10.7
	1995-96 to 2003-04	-0.23	-0.89	-2.35	-1.19	10.5
Tamil Nadu	1985-86 to 1995-96	0.02	1.64	2.04	9.63	12.5
	1995-96 to 2003-04	-2.09	-3.01	-0.41	4.92	18.0
Uttar Pradesh	1985-86 to 1995-96	0.08	3.16	3.45	9.09	8.1
	1995-96 to 2003-04	0.05	1.41	2.65	-10.06	7.7
West Bengal	1985-86 to 1995-96	0.11	2.93	4.99	27.35	9.5
	1995-96 to 2003-04	0.00	NAC	4.38	-7.05	4.7
All-India	1985-86 to 1995-96	0.29	2.91	5.20	13.36	7.9
	1995-96 to 2003-04	-0.46	0.68	2.10	-0.46	5.1

NAC: Not available or not comparable.

Sources: Various issues.

(1) Land Use Statistics at a Glance, Directorate of Economics and Statistics, Department of Agriculture and Cooperation, Ministry of Agriculture, Government of India, New Delhi.

(2) Agricultural Statistics at a Glance, Ministry of Agriculture, Government of India, New Delhi. Agriculture while the remaining states witnessed lower growth rate of power supply in the second period.

Pace of crop diversification slowed down in all the states except Tamil Nadu and Maharashtra. The pace of diversification remained high in Rajasthan and Andhra Pradesh though it was lower compared to 1985-86 to 1995-96. It is interesting to observe that even high level of diversification in Tamil Nadu, Maharashtra and Rajasthan did not help in maintaining the tempo of growth in these states. We tried to explore this further, and from the secondary data, it seems as if farmers in these states are shifting crop pattern away from cash crops to low value crops. The reason for this could be a stress on water resources and high level of market risk associated with high value crops. However, this needs further probing.

Options for Revival

Some of the important causes for slowdown and poor growth of agriculture are obvious from the results discussed above. In order to find pragmatic options to revive agricultural growth, it is pertinent to explore the possibilities of raising level of factors associated with growth from their current level, which is presented in Table 2.

Despite progress in irrigation, the level of crop intensity continues to be quiet low in most of the states. In Andhra Pradesh, Karnataka, Tamil Nadu, Madhya Pradesh, Maharashtra, Gujarat and Rajasthan more than one crop is taken on less than 30 per cent of area under cultivation. This shows that there is considerable scope to raise output through an expansion of area under double cropping.

Fertiliser use in the recent years is as low as 28 kg per hectare in Assam and as high as 328 kg per hectare of net sown area in Punjab. Similarly, fertiliser use is below 40 kg per hectare in Rajasthan and Madhya Pradesh, and 55 kg in Orissa.

Increasing fertiliser use is a significant option for raising agricultural output in most of the states. Elasticity of crop output with respect to fertiliser use is estimated to vary between 0.134 and 0.700 in various states. Consumption of electric power per hectare was just 9 kwh in Assam, 30 kwh in Orissa and only 34 kwh in Himachal Pradesh. Electric power used in agriculture varies between 80 and 300 kwh in Kerala, Jammu and Kashmir, Bihar, Madhya Pradesh, West Bengal, UP and Rajasthan, whereas it exceeded 1,000 kwh in Andhra Pradesh, Gujarat, Haryana, Punjab and Tamil Nadu. Increase in electric supply to agriculture is important for promoting irrigation and thus raising output.

The coverage of irrigation in various states varies from 14-97 per cent. There is a large gap between the current level and the ultimate irrigation potential except in the case of Punjab, Haryana and Rajasthan which have already exceeded the potential irrigation level.

Bihar has water resources to extend irrigation to entire gross cropped area, with a further scope to provide irrigation to expansion in gross cropped area through an increased cropping intensity. Similarly, Uttar Pradesh has the potential to raise the level of irrigation to 95 per cent from the present level of 68.4 per cent. In Orissa and Assam irrigation can be extended to more than two-thirds of cropped area, whereas at present this facility is available to less than 27 per cent area. Elasticity of crop output with respect to irrigation is estimated to vary between 0.303 and 1.004 in various states. Because of low use of inputs, level of productivity of most of the crops is quite low in most of the states. There are several reasons for this; poor network of input distribution; lack of resources and non-availability of adequate credit for purchase of modern inputs; decline or stagnation in public investments in irrigation and other infrastructure during the 8th and 9th and up to mid-10th Five Year Plans in real terms.

Improved technology is most important for the growth of output. Available evidence shows that there is a big gap between the level of yield with improved farm practices in farmers' fields and the yield with practices followed by the farmers. Besides the need for extension to transfer improved technology to farmers, the critical factor in this is the availability of quality seed. Most of the farmers do not distinguish between "seed and grain" and use common grain as seed. Research

TABLE 2

Level of Cropping Intensity, Irrigation, Fertiliser and Power Used in Agriculture during 2001-02 and 2003-04

State	*Cropping intensity (%)*	*NPK Kg/ Hectare*	*Power Cons/ha KWh*	*Irrigated Area Actual (%)*	*Irri-gation Poten-tial as per cent of Current GCA*
Andhra Pradesh	122	176	1240	41.1	75.6
Assam	146	28	9	14.3	66.8
Bihar	135	105	123	47.6	123.5
Gujarat	114	89	1577	35.9	44.6
Haryana	180	270	1415	83.2	71.7
Himachal Pradesh	173	80	34	19.3	35.0
Jammu and Kashmir	148	91	160	40.5	72.4
Karnataka	116	118	832	25.0	39.7
Kerala	135	87	85	14.9	70.8
Madhya Pradesh	127	38	274	26.1	44.7
Maharashtra	127	95	549	17.1	32.7
Orissa	150	55	30	26.6	69.9
Punjab	186	328	1374	96.6	82.5
Rajasthan	128	40	244	29.5	25.2
Tamil Nadu	117	171	1927	51.0	72.7
Uttar Pradesh	154	188	292	68.4	94.8
West Bengal	176	213	178	50.8	62.7
All-India	135	121	598	39.9	60.7

Source: Calculated from various issues of statistical abstract of India.

institutes have very limited capacity for seed multiplication and they can supply only quality seeds in small quantity. So far production and supply of quality seed were mainly entrusted to public sector agencies, namely, the National Seeds Corporation and the state level seed corporations. Compared to the need for quality seed in the country, these corporations as such are serving a limited purpose. India needs to develop a competitive market for seeds by expanding the role of public sector and by encouraging private sector in seed business in a big way. This feels that transferring some of the subsidies from other inputs to seed would be more paying.

CONCLUSION

In conclusion, there are several points discussed in structural change in the agricultural development scenario of India. No doubt, these all things are needed collectively to face the present changing situation of the world. The structural change process should move in the right direction to include all segments of society/nation or it is necessary to fulfil the requirement of recently popular concept of inclusive growth. Diversification of agriculture in favour of commercial and high value crops is in fact recognised as a powerful strategy to counter the emerging challenges. As a risk management device crop diversification towards the crops in which a country has comparative advantage as compared to imports was traditionally assumed to be efficient in facing international competition. But now it has become inevitable as free trade in agriculture mandated under WTO has posed a constant threat to the developing countries in the form of high market induced risks and fall in global prices for farm products that have adversely affected traditional crops and families depending upon them. The main reasons for deceleration and stagnation in agricultural output after 1995-96 are a slowdown in growth of fertiliser use, irrigation, and energy (electric power) in some cases, stagnation or even a decline in other cases. Crop intensity and area under cultivation have also shown either a poor growth or a decline. Diversification towards high-value crops has also slowed down and in some cases farmers have been diversifying away from the high-value crops towards low-value, less risky and less input-demanding crops. Low level of input use and low productivity in most of the states offer some ray of hope to revive agricultural growth, but this would require simultaneous efforts on several fronts include; stepping up investments and putting in place suitable institutional mechanisms to exploit irrigation potential that exists in most of the states; increasing power supply to the sector; promoting fertilizer use by expanding the distribution network and improving credit facilities for farmers; establishing competitive seed markets and ensuring attractive prices for seeds; improvement in terms of trade for agriculture; and measures to mitigate risk in farming. Thus, the present scenario and growth rate of agriculture is witness to stress more and more on agricultural development in 11th Plan.

As we know, globalization is a fact of life and India is taking serious measures to get ready to operate in a new liberalized framework where foreign direct investment and capital inflows are expected to play a major role in accelerating investment and in promoting growth through the application of improved technology. In this context, it is impossible to keep insulated from global developments. The clear lesson is that India should learn to walk on two legs. While liberalization the economy, policy-makers should remember that it is only agricultural growth which is going to determine the fortunes of a vast majority of working people in India and that it is only agricultural growth that makes a dent in their poverty. There need of effective research and development to evolve cost saving technology, improved infrastructure, efficient markets and several other bold initiatives to improve competitive edge of Indian agriculture.

References

Agenor, Pierre Richard (2003), 'Does Globalisation Hurt the Poor?' The World Bank.

Barro, R.J. and Sala-i-Martin, X. (1995), Economic Growth, Singapore: McGraw-Hill International Edition.

Bathla, S. (2005), 'Intersectoral Growth Linkages in India: Implications for Policy and Liberalized Reforms', Institute of Economic Growth, New Delhi.

Bhalla, Surjit S. (2003), 'Recounting the Poor', 1993-99, *EPW*, Jan. 25, 2003, pp. 338-49.

Bhattacharya, B.B. and Sakthivel, S. (2004), 'Regional Growth and Disparities in India: Comparison of Pre- and Post- Reforms Decades', *Economic and Political Weekly*, March 6, pp. 1071-77.

Bhowmik, D. (2000), 'A Decade of India's Economic Reforms', Article Published in S. Murty (Ed.), *Economic Reforms Today: Pros and Cons* (RBSA, Jaipur) pp. 28-63.

Birdsall, Nancy (2002), 'A Symmetric Globalisation: Global Markets Require Good Global Politics', Center for Global Development Paper No. 12, October.

Brigit, Joseph (2003), 'Trade Libaralization and Primary Commodity Prices: Empirical Evidence from Select Tropical Crops in Kerela, India; GTAP Resource # 1537 7th Annual Conference on Global Economic Analysis http//wwwgtab: ageron produce edu/conference/2004/ program.asp.

Chakarvarty, S. (1984), 'Power Structure and Agricultural Productivity', in Desai (ed.), Vol. 'Agrarian Power and Agricultural Productivity in South Asia', New Delhi.

Chakarvarty, S. (1986), 'Development Planning: The Indian Experience', Oxford University Press, Delhi.

Economic Times (ET), (2006), dated 28.2.06.

Ernst and Young (2006), Doing Business in India, Ernst and Young Private Limited, New Delhi.

Feder, G., Just, R.E. and Zilberman, D. (1985), 'Adoption of Agricultural Innovation in Developing Countries: A Survey', *Economic Development and Cultural Change,* 33(2).

Goyari, P. (2005), 'Flood Damages and Sustainability of Agriculture in Assam', *Economic and Political Weekly,* Vol. XL (26), June 25, pp. 2723-29.

Government of India (2006), Towards Faster and More Inclusive Growth An Approach to the 11th Five Year Plan (2007-2012), Planning Commission, Yojana Bhavan, New Delhi, December.

Hurroll, A. and Woods, N. (2000), 'Globalisation and Inequality in R. Hoggott' (Ed) *The New Political Econometrics,* Wiley.

Jha, Raghabendra (2000), 'Reducing Poverty and Inequality in India—Has Liberalisation Helped?', WIDER, WP-204, November.

Kuznets, S. (1961), 'Economic Growth and Contribution of Agriculture Notes on Measurement,' *International Journal of Agricultural Affairs,* Vol. 3, No. 2, pp. 56-57.

Lindert, P.H. and Williamson, J.G. (2001), 'Does Globalization make the World Unequal', University of California, Davis and Harvard University.

Mankiew, N.G., Romer, D. and Weil, D.N. (1992), 'A Contribution to the Empirics of Economic Growth', *Quarterly Journal of Economics,* 107 (May): 407-37.

Metha, S.J., Crihfield, J.B. and Giertz, F. (1992), 'Economic growth in American States: The end of Convergence', Working Paper No. 20, The Institute of Governments and Public Affair, University of Illinois.

Pal, P.K. (2003), 'Dimension of poverty of India: Measurement and Determinant', 86th IEA Conference Volume, Kolhapur, pp. 126-42.

Pritchett, L. (1995), 'Livergence, Big Time,' Policy Research Working Paper No. 1522. (Washington DC., World Bank).

Rao, Hanumantha C.H. (1995), 'Liberalization of Agriculture in India: Some Major Issues, *Indian Journal of Agricultural Economics,* Vol. 50, No. 3, pp. 450-72.

Rao, C.H.H. (1994), 'Agricultural Growth, Rural Poverty and Environmental Sustainability, Oxford University Press, New Delhi.

Rao, Hanumantha C.H. (2005), 'Essay on Development Strategy, Regional Disparities and Centre-State Financial Relations in India', New Delhi: Academic Foundation.

Rennis, G. and H. Fei (1961), 'A Theory of Economic Development' *The American Economic Review*, Vol. IV (LI), No. 4.

Saha, A. (2001), 'Risk in HYN and Traditional Rice Cultivation: An Enquiry in West Bengal Agriculture', *Indian Journal of Agricultural Economics*, Vol. 56(1).

Somra, S.S. (2001), "Agriculture Development of Rajasthan, *Political Economics Journal of India*, Vol. 10, Issues 1 and 2, January-June.

Somra, S.S. (2003), "Inter-State Imbalances and Economic Reforms in India" in the *Journal of Sardar Patel Institute of Economic and Social Research*, Ahmedabad, '*Anvesak*', July-Dec. 2002, Volume 32, No. 2, pp. 77-88.

Stiglitz, J.E. (1998), More Instruments and Broader Goals: Moving towards the post-Washington Consensus.

Vaidyanathan, A. (1988), India's Agricultural Development in a Regional Perspective, Delhi.

Wilson, D. and Purushothaman, R. (2003), Dreaming with BRICs: The Path to 2050, Goldman Sachs Global Economics, Paper No. 99, New York.

Structural Change in India and Rural Poverty

DHIRENDRAN NATH KONAR

INTRODUCTION

The purpose of this paper is to show that with the passage of time, especially in the second half of the last century, the path of development (as has been revealed through the sectoral composition of the gross domestic product, GDP) that has been followed in India is quite inconsistence with the pattern followed by other developing countries of Asia, namely China, Indonesia, Thailand, Philippines, Malaysia, Republic of Korea and Pakistan. This means that over time the contribution of agriculture to the GDP has, radically, been coming down, that of industry to the GDP has been slowly increasing while that of the service sector has been increasing at a quick speed. However, the occupational classification of workers in India fails to corroborate the pattern revealed in most of those countries. In India the primary sector still absorbs the bulk (around 67%) of the labour force, the secondary sector provides the least employment (about 13%) while the service sector provides employment not exceeding 21 per cent. It is a fact that the share of services to the GDP in each and every country mentioned above has increased. But the increase has been much larger in the case of India than most others. Consequently, the service sector has emerged as the dominant sector; industry is a poor third sector contributing only about one-fourth of the GDP. Though the service sector is the major dominant sector but a minor contributor to employment. Without entering into the reason behind it we may, at ease, say that its consequence has been very unsatisfactory in the sense that it has given rise to massive poverty across the countryside.

THEORETICAL PERSPECTIVES ON STRUCTURAL CHANGES

Economic development has, historically, been associated with structural changes in the national economies. It has, in fact, most often been defined as a process combining economic growth with changing share of different sectors in the national product and labour force. The most general structural changes that have been observed over a long period of time have followed a sequence of shift from agriculture to industry and then to services. Thus, an underdeveloped economy is characterized by (a) a predominant share of agriculture, (b) with development the share of industry increases and that of agriculture declines, and (c) subsequently, after reaching a reasonably high level of development, the services sector increases in importance and it becomes a major component of the economy. This pattern has not only been observed historically but also holds across the countries with various levels of development. Structural shifts and changing sectoral shares are found to hold for both the national product and the work force. Some structural economists like Kuznets have empirically demonstrated that growth is brought about by changes in sectoral composition.

SECTORAL SHARES (IN PER CENT) OF GDP IN INDIA IN THE SECOND HALF OF THE LAST CENTURY

Three basic components of GDP of a country are: (a) primary sector (agriculture and allied activities), (b) secondary sector or industry, and (c) tertiary sector or service sector. The contribution of each of these sectors to the GDP of our country has been furnished in Table 1.

TABLE I

Sectoral Share in GDP (in percentage) in India Between 1950-51 and 2006-07 at 1993-94 Prices

Sectors Years	*1950 -51*	*1960 -61*	*1970 -71*	*1980 -81*	*1990 -91*	*2000 -01*	*2006 -07*
Agriculture and Allied	55.4	50.9	44.5	38.1	30.9	26.6	18.5
Industry	16.1	20.0	23.6	25.9	30.0	25.0	26.4
Services	28.5	29.1	31.9	36.0	39.1	48.4	59.5
Total	100.0	100.0	100.0	100.0	100.0	100.0	100.0

Source: Statistical Outline of India, 2002-03, Page14, Tata Services Limited, Department of Economics and Statistics and RBI, Handbook (latest).

The above Table illustrates that at the time of initiation of planning in India the percentage contribution of agriculture and allied activities to the GDP was about 55, that of industry being about 15 and finally, that of services being about 29. Since then there has, however, been radical change in the percentage contributions of these sectors in 2000-01, that is, within a time span of just five decades. The percentage share of agriculture had, significantly, fallen from 55.4 to 26.6, that is, a fall of more than 50 per cent; that of industry had increased from 16.1 to 25.0, an enhancement by more than 50 per cent; finally, that for services from 28.5 percentage to 48.4 percentage, an increment of about 70 per cent. This is the scenario of structural changes in the Indian economy as had been observed in the second half of the last century. In the new millennium we notice that the contribution of agriculture to the GDP in 2006-07 had, rapidly, fallen to 18.5 per cent from 26.6 per cent in 2000-01.The contribution of industry increased to 26.4 per cent in 2006-07 from 25.0 per cent in 2000-01 whereas the contribution of the service sector increased to 59.5 per cent in 2006-07 from 48.4 per cent in 2000-01.

Let us now demonstrate the occupational classification of workers in the second half of the twentieth century. This has been presented in Table 2.

An obvious conclusion from Table 2 is that the occupational structure of India clearly reflects the backwardness of the Indian economy. Between 1951 and 2001, that is, within a period of 50 years the proportion of working population engaged in the primary sector consisting of agriculture and allied activities

TABLE 2

Occupational Classification of Workers (in percentage) in India Between 1951 and 2001

Sectors Years	*1951*	*1961*	*1971*	*1981*	*1991*	*2001*
Primary sector	72.1	71.8	72.1	68.8	66.8	60.0
Secondary Sector	10.7	12.2	11.2	13.5	12.7	18.0
Tertiary sector	17.2	16.0	16.7	17.7	20.5	22.0
Total	100.0	100.0	100.0	100.0	100.0	100.0

Source: Complied from CMIE, Basic Statistics Relating to the Indian Economy, Vol. 1, All India, August 1993 and Economic Survey, Government of India, Relevant Issues.

indicated only a marginal decline from about 72 per cent in 1951 to about 67 per cent in 1991 and further to 60 per cent in 2001. In 2001 we see that in the tertiary sector only 1.5 per cent more workers have got employment. However, in the secondary sector the percentage of additional employment has been relatively more. This is really significant, since a large percentage of population dependent on the primary sector is a clear indication of the prevalence of large-scale disguised unemployment in agriculture and consequently, of low per capita labour productivity and prevalence of wide-spread poverty.

A comparative study between Tables 1 and 2 is indicative of the fact that in course of just four decades between 1950-51 and 1990-91 the percentage contribution of agriculture and allied activities to our GDP had come down by more than 44 whereas that of employment in this sector had been reduced approximately by 5. During the same time interval the contribution of services to the GDP had increased by more than 37 per cent while that of employment in that sector had increased approximately by 19 per cent. In case of industry the percentage increase to GDP between 1950-51 and 1990-91 had been 86.3 while the percentage increase in the level of employment in this sector was 18.7 only.

Thus the historical view that with the gradually declining contribution of agriculture and allied activities to GDP the level of employment in this sector will, significantly, fall and with the quickly increasing contribution of the Service Sector to the GDP there will be more absorption of labour in this sector have been belied in the experience of development of the Indian Economy during the second half of the twentieth century.

DEVELOPMENT EXPERIENCE OF SOME ASIAN COUNTRIES

At this stage it will be worthwhile to portray the development experience attained by some Asian countries mentioned earlier. Table 3 will give a focus to this direction.

TABLE 3

Sectoral Contribution (in percentage) to GDP in Some Asian Countries Between 1960 and 2002

Sectors	*Agriculture*		*Industry*		*Services*		
Countries	*(1)*	*(2)*	*(3)*	*(4)*	*(5)*	*(6)*	*(7)*
	1960	*2002*	*1960*	*2002*	*1960*	*2002*	*2002***
China	*30	15	49	51	21	34	31
Indonesia	50	18	25	45	25	38	39
Thailand	40	9	19	43	41	48	33
Philippines	26	14	28	33	46	53	47
Malaysia	36	9	18	47	46	44	50
Republic of Korea	37	4	20	41	43	55	62
Pakistan	46	23	16	23	38	54	34
India	55	24	16	25	29	51	22

*Relates to 1980.
**Percentage Share of Employment in Services.
Source: Papola, T.S., pp. 10-11.

A significant difference between the growth patterns of some Asian countries including India has been seen in the shift of labour force with changing sectoral structure of the economy, especially in the employment share of services. A comparative study between columns (6) and (7) of Table 3 reveals that the highest contribution to the GDP emerging from services has been attained by the Republic of Korea. In doing so Korea had absorbed 62 per cent of labour in that sector, a commendable achievement from the standpoint of absorption of labour. In case of Malaysia 50 per cent absorption of labour in services helped it to attain 44 per cent of GDP. That is, a relatively higher percentage of employment in services resulted in a relatively lower percentage of GDP. In Philippines 47 per cent employment of labour in services generated 53 per cent of GDP. In Pakistan 54 per cent contribution by the services to the GDP had been attained by the absorption of 34 per cent employment in services. This may also be analyzed by taking note of the ratios between employment in services and the contribution of these to the GDP attained by the countries we have been referring to. These ratios in order of the countries expressed in Table 3 are 0.91, 1.03, 0.69, 0.89, 1.14, 1.13, 0.63 and 0.43 highlighting the fact that the contribution of services to the GDP has become most employment-friendly in case of Malaysia followed immediately by the Republic of Korea and Indonesia. In case of India the contribution of services to the GDP has become the least employment-friendly as in this country 51 per cent contribution to the GDP emanating from services had resulted from only 22 per cent absorption of labour in the services. What a poor absorption of labour in the service sector!

Perhaps we have by now come to a stage to mention that the basic distinction between the Indian experiences of development from others in this group is the difference in the growth of employment and of GDP in the service sector. In all other countries the share of employment in services has been more or less consistent with that of GDP. In India, however, the employment share has shown much slower increase than the share of GDP. This means that growth of services in India has been much less employment-intensive than in other countries.

BASIC NATURE OF INDIAN ECONOMY

The Indian economy is basically rural in nature. According to the census of 1991, 74.28 per cent of our population lived in rural areas and they contributed about 33.7 per cent of the total Net Domestic Product (NDP) in 1987-88 at 1980-81 prices. In contrast, 25.72 per cent of our total population lived in urban areas and they contributed about 66.3 per cent of the total NDP. In 1960-61 the percentage of total people living in rural areas was 82.03 and they used to contribute 56.6 per cent of the NDP while about 18 per cent of our total population living in urban areas used to contribute 43.4 per cent of our NDP. Just think of the contrast! Within the course of thirty years from 1961 to 1991 the population of rural India decreased only by about 8 per cent, though in the same period the contribution coming to the NDP from the rural India fell by about 23 per cent. According to the census of 2001, 72.2 per cent of our total population live in rural areas and they contribute only about 27.9 per cent of the total NDP(in 2000-01 at 1993-94 prices) while 27.8 per cent of our total population living in urban areas have been contributing 71.1 per cent of the total NDP. Thus between 1991 and 2001 population of rural India increased by 2.1 per cent while the contribution coming to the NDP from the rural areas fell by about 7.2 per cent (from 35.1% in 1993-94 to 27.9 % in 2000-01) (vide Statistical Outline of India, 2002-03, Tata Services Limited). Such a sorry state of affair has resulted in massive poverty in rural India.

In India we have the developed rural India and the underdeveloped rural India. Punjab, Haryana, Tamil Nadu, Andhra Pradesh, Kerala and parts of Maharashtra come under the developed rural India while the rest are underdeveloped where power, infrastructure, etc. are big problems. Rural India is like a pyramid. The top of the pyramid is occupied by the rich farmers and businessmen who constitute 5 per cent of the population. The next of the pyramid belongs to those with a regular income and the base of the pyramid is occupied by the vast majority of the people who are daily wage labourers.

Rural India has been caught in the so-called development trap. Low incomes of the rural households are due to the lack of economic opportunities. Most of the people of rural India are unable to pay for goods and services. As a consequence organizations feel it costly to do business in rural India, which leads to inadequate provision of infrastructure and that, in turn, leads to lack of economic opportunities and so on. Various studies even give the idea that urban poverty is predominantly due to the fact of impoverishment of rural peasantry which forces them to move out of villages to seek some subsistence living in the cities and towns. Though there have been quite a number of schemes and programmes which have been attempted by the Central and State Governments and a few foreign agencies to address the question of rural poverty, most of them have only marginal effects. Maximum percentage of the people in the poorly connected villages live on a low productivity agriculture, cattle rearing and related casual work. Because of the inability of value addition most of the villages are always at the subsistence level. Most of the poor of the villages do always distress sale.

Since industry and services fail to absorb the level of employment commensurate with their contribution to the GDP, the increasing army of labour force is bound to fall back upon agriculture as their means for subsistence. To illustrate this we proceed to the next section.

AGRICULTURE STILL THE LARGEST PROVIDER OF EMPLOYMENT IN INDIA

There can be no denying the fact that India is basically a land of agriculture as it pertinently holds a very important place in our National Economy. It is the mainstay of the vast majority of our population. Even today more than 58 per cent of our working population remains in the field of agriculture (Economic Survey, 2003-04). Still now agriculture accounts for about 22 per cent of our Gross Domestic Product (GDP) and it still provides maximum employment to our ever increasing labour force. It has been known that even now 72 per cent of our population lives in rural areas (Census of India, 2001) spreading over six lakh of villages. A very important aspect of Indian Economy is with regard to the percentage of total workers engaged in agriculture mainly as cultivators and agricultural labourers. The necessary information in this regard taken from the latest census of India, 2001 has been presented in Table 4.

The information contained in Table 4 is the testimony to the fact that the bulk of our economy falls back upon agriculture and allied services.

From Table 4 we get the idea that at the all-India level nearly 38 per cent of total workers are engaged in services and other industries while about 58 per cent of them are engaged in agriculture alone. The corresponding picture across the major states of India can be discerned from the Table itself.

It is a fact that rural economy of India is characterized by the prevalence of large volume of surplus labour in the form of disguised and open employment. It is also a fact that although farming activities are the basic activities of most of the rural people in India, there are relatively few households for which the

TABLE 4

Percentage Share of Total Workers (in 2001)

Industry and States	*Cultivators*	*Agricultural Laborers*	*Employees in Household* Services	*Employees in Other Industries*
Andhra Pradesh	22.67	39.64	4.50	33.19
Assam	39.14	13.51	3.43	43.92
Bihar	29.17	48.18	3.87	18.78
Gujarat	27.56	24.49	1.88	46.08
Haryana	36.34	15.22	2.47	45.96
Himachal Pradesh	65.56	3.11	1.67	29.66
Jammu & Kashmir	43.37	6.72	6.23	43.67
Karnataka	29.49	26.40	3.98	40.13
Kerala	7.19	16.07	3.55	73.19
Madhya Pradesh	42.93	38.66	3.92	24.49
Maharashtra	28.56	26.85	2.49	42.10
Orissa	29.69	35.04	4.83	30.44
Punjab	22.96	16.40	3.36	57.29
Rajasthan	53.37	10.63	2.74	31.26
Tamil Nadu	18.39	31.16	5.24	45.21
Uttar Pradesh	40.92	25.11	5.33	28.64
West Bengal	19.03	24.92	7.30	48.76
All India	58.41*		4.07	37.52

* Combines both cultivators and agricultural labourers.

Source: Necessary arrangements have been made on the data taken from Census of India, 2001.

exclusive source of income is agriculture. Occasionally, these people undertake a variety of other non-farm activities for coping up with their family necessities. It may be mentioned that most of these activities are, normally, related to agriculture.

The plight of labourers coming outside the jurisdiction of the organized sector may be portrayed by mentioning the range of minimum wages presented in Table 5.

It is quite clear from Table 5 what minimum wages prevail in different parts of India. At the same time it is doubtful whether even this minimum wage is paid. The labourers in the unorganized sector have, thus, to bear a very pathetic life and they are hardly in a position to make a square meal a day.

The contribution of agriculture to the GDP in India has, significantly, been declining while the absorption of labour in this sector has not been decreasing to the extent it should have. As a

TABLE 5

Details of Minimum Wages in October 2001

States	*Minimum Wages Day (Rs.)*	*Maximum Wages Day (Rs.)*
Andhra Pradesh	27.0	63.2
Arunachal Pradesh	40.0	42.1
Assam	32.8	50.7
Bihar	38.0	58.6
Delhi	70.7	99.7
Goa	28.0	125.0
Gujarat	64.8	95.4
Haryana	70.3	79.0
Karnataka	49.4	77.4
Kerala	30.0	143.7
Madhya Pradesh	50.4	56.5
Maharashtra	42.5	116.6
Punjab	69.3	151.2
Rajasthan	50.4	63.3
Tamil Nadu	45.0	109.5
Uttar Pradesh	42.0	70.6
West Bengal	59.0	165.8

Source: Statistical Outline of India, 2002-03, Tata Services Limited (p.151).

consequence, poverty has not been diminishing across rural areas all over the country. Such a picture will be brought out in the following section.

INCIDENCE OF RURAL POVERTY ACROSS THE MAJOR STATES OF INDIA

A vivid description of the incidence of rural poverty across the major States of India has been displayed in Table 6.

A critical analysis of Table 6 discloses the fact that between 1993-94 and 1999-2000 there has been a quick fall in rural poverty on all- India basis (from about 37 per cent to 27 per cent). Similar is the case with major States of India, though there are wide fluctuations among these States. The Table reveals that in both the years Punjab headed the States in the reduction of poverty while Haryana improved its position from sixth in 1993-94 to second in 1999-2000. However, in Haryana there was 70.5 per cent

TABLE 6

Change in the Incidence of Rural Poverty Across Major States of India in 1993-94 and 1999-2000

States	*1993-94*	*1993-94*	*1999-2000*	*1999-2000*
	Incidence of rural poverty	*Ranks in increasing order*	*Incidence of rural poverty*	*Ranks in increasing order*
Andhra Pradesh	15.92	2	11.05	4
Assam	45.01	13	40.04	13
Bihar	58.21	15	44.30	14
Gujarat	22.18	3	13.17	5
Haryana	28.02	6	8.27	2
Karnataka	29.88	7	17.38	7
Kerala	25.76	4	9.38	3
Madhya Pradesh	40.64	10	37.06	12
Maharashtra	37.93	9	23.72	9
Orissa	49.72	14	48.01	15
Punjab	11.95	1	6.35	1
Rajasthan	26.46	5	13.74	6
Tamil Nadu	32.48	8	20.55	8
Uttar Pradesh	42.28	12	31.22	10
West Bengal	40.80	11	31.85	11
All-India	37.27	----	27.09	--
Around States*				
(a) Mean	33.82	----	23.74	----
(b) S.D.	135.17	----	103.13	----
(c) C.V.	399.71	----	434.41	

Source: Planning Commission, Government of India.
Taken from Economic Survey, Government of India, 2001-02, Table 10.5 (Page 239). Statistical Measures have, however, been calculated by the author himself.

reduction in rural poverty while in Kerala there was 63.59 per cent reduction in it between these two years. In Rajasthan there had been 48.07 per cent reduction in rural poverty while in Punjab there was 46.86 per cent reduction in rural poverty. However, the Spearman's rank correlation coefficient of the incidence of rural poverty among the States concerned in 1993-94 and 1999-2000 has been found to be +0.94, indicating that with respect to the incidence of rural poverty the ranks of the major

States in India between 1993-94 and 1999-2000 have remained almost undisturbed. This is especially true to the four States belonging to East India, namely, Bihar, Assam, Orissa and West Bengal. Another interesting feature of the incidence of rural poverty in the 90's of the last century is that though there has been a diminution in it across the major States of India, the inter-State disparity in the incidence of rural poverty has been increasing. The relatively higher value of the coefficient of variation in the incidence of rural poverty in 1999-2000 compared to that in 1993-94 is a clear testimony to it. However, an increase of coefficient of variation by about 8 per cent may not mean that the inter-state disparity of rural poverty has increased. To be sure of it we have performed the famous F-test for judging the equality of two standard deviations displayed in the above Table. The F-test relevant in this case is $F=S_2/S_1$ where S_2 is the standard deviation for the year 1993-94 and S_1 is the standard deviation for the year 1999-2000 and its value has been 1.72 (insignificant).This refrains us from making such generalization.

SUGGESTIONS

1. Much more emphasis has to be given for the furtherance of agriculture and rural development. It is heartening to note that the Eleventh Five Year Plan has given due priority to it, where it has been stated, "One of the major challenges of the 11th Plan must be to reverse the deceleration in agricultural growth from 3.2 per cent observed between 1980 and 1996-97 to a trend average of only 1.5 per cent subsequently This deceleration is, undoubtedly, the root of the problem of rural distress that has surfaced in many parts of the country———. A second Green Revolution is urgently needed to raise the growth rate of agricultural GDP to around 4 per cent. This is not an easy task since actual growth of agricultural GDP including forestry and fishing was only 1 per cent per annum in the first three years of the Tenth Plan. This calls for action on both the demand side and supply side."
2. There can be no denying the fact that rapid growth of population, especially in the rural areas, is the key

causal factor that perpetuates poverty in our country. It is also a fact that the population growth is larger among the poor than the all-India rate of growth. It is usually said that low-income families include many victims of temporary bad luck. The faster growth of population among the poor caused partly by poverty aggravates it instead of eliminating the same. This calls for a reduction in the rapid rate of growth of population in the rural areas. For this the modern devices of birth control should reach at the doorsteps of the rural people and they should be convinced of utilizing the same. The best means for doing the same is the spread of education, at least primary education among men and women of all walks of life. We may recall here that at the dawn of the Meiji era in 1869, the King of Japan took the responsibility for the dissemination of the universal primary education alone and no other social welfare program. Again, with the introduction of compulsory primary education in 1870, the Great Britain assured its own ascendancy in the industrial world and paved the way for a sharp decline in the birth rate. These are the obvious lessons from History. It is really a matter of great regret that we have not yet learnt these lessons and applied these to our country even after more than six decades of Independence.

3. Together with reduction in the growth rate of rural population in our country we should keep a watchful eye on the entry of people from neighboring countries. The census data of 2001 reveal that in West Bengal, for example, the natural rate of growth of population between 1991 and 2001 has come to a decline but the districts facing the border have shown a huge growth rate of population and this has led to a rapid growth rate of population, especially in the rural areas. Thus immigration from other countries should be stopped immediately otherwise poverty cannot be eliminated from our country. Not only that the huge pressure of population may eat into the vitality of our country and that will lead to many untoward incidents in the far and wide of the country.

4. The poorer section of our society should be given some minimum amount of land and the means for cultivating and harvesting the same. They have their own labour and energy which they cannot apply productively because of dearth of land. The present debate on industrialization in many States in our country gives the hint that the Governments of these States are highly in favour of industrialization even at the huge cost of agricultural land. In this respect also a hasty decision should not be taken. China's road to industrialization has not solved the unemployment problem to the extent it was expected to. In the present Indian context there will be much chaos and disturbances if the farmers are thrown of the agricultural land and industries are set-up. For example, the proposed Tata's small car factory at Singur in the district of Hooghly in West Bengal will throw many farmers of their land and they will be bound to remain unemployed. Besides, the mere production of cars is not enough. It is also a fact that there will be no dearth of demand for these cars as there are many prospective buyers with sufficiently high purchasing power. But the question is that these cars will not be kept idle in the garage. These must be plied on the road so as to maximize the satisfaction of the owners. Then the natural question is that since the roads are already overcrowded with traffic, will not the plying of the new cars further aggravate this situation? Will not the introduction of the new cars make our speed slower rather than faster? These and similar other questions appear in mind because the width of roads is already stagnant and the roads in important towns in our country have not been following the standard norms. As a consequence, a few wealthy persons will, unhesitatingly, get some pleasure in life but that will be possible only at the cost of many unpleasant incidents. So we should look before we leap and do everything in a judicious manner.

5. The principle of the Gandhiji's idea of "Village self-sufficiency" or "Gram Swaraj" should be adopted as the basis of economic development. India is still now a land of villages whereas per 2001 census about 72 per cent of our total population has been living. Hence, we should pay more attention to the development of villages and for this the technique of decentralized district plan may be adopted.
6. It is high time to rethink the pay structure of the persons associated with the service sector and the mode of payment to employees of this sector through vouchers.

CONCLUSION

Our analysis of the sect oral composition of GDP in Indian economy reveals that there has, in recent decades, been the pre-eminence of service sector as the major contributor to growth, raising its share rather sharply in the national output. As a result we have been able to attain an annual growth rate of GDP to the extent of more than 8 per cent. But such high growth rate has not solved some vital problems the Indian economy has been suffering from.

The higher GDP growth has failed to increase wages of rural labourers. Besides, even as wages of India's industrial workers have been increasing at a record rate; agricultural labourers in the country's backyard have been fighting a grim battle for survival. The real tragedy is that the higher GDP growth, improvement in macro-economic variables and even of higher value of rupee has put little impact on the economic conditions of rural labourers. Yojana Bhawan's high-sounding talks that the economic prosperity would percolate down the landless agricultural labourers have been belied. Economic conditions of rural labourers have, instead of being strong and stout, been weak and poorer. Poor performance of the agricultural sector may, partly, be held responsible for the sorrowful plight of the rural labourers. But there is no guarantee that the higher rate of growth of agricultural output will strengthen the economic status of the workers engaged therein.

In an imperfect market like Indian agriculture where

supply of labour is more than the demand for it, wage rates are bound to be low. More than 50 per cent of the male workforce in India is engaged in the agricultural sector either as agricultural labourers or in agriculture-related activities. The Government realized the gravity of the situation and to come to the rescue of the workers, fixed the minimum wage rate through legislation. But we may recall that legislation alone can not solve this serious problem (like the Child Labour Prohibition Act, etc.). The workers need definite program to improve their marketability outside the agricultural sector.

References

Ahluwalia, M.S. (1978), "Rural Poverty and Agricultural Performance in India", *Journal of Development Studies.*

Bardhan, P.K. (1971), "On the Minimum Level of Living and the Rural Poor—A Further Note", *Indian Economic Review,* Vol. 6.

Bhattacharya, B.B. and Mitra, Arup (1990), "Excess Growth of Tertiary Sector in Indian Economy: Issues and Implications", *Economic and Political Weekly,* November 3.

Census of India 1991, Series 1- India Paper 3 of 1991: Provisional Population Totals—Workers and Their Distribution.

Census of India 2001 and Relevant Issues.

Chenery, Hollis B. and Lance J. Taylor (1968), "Development Pattern Among Countries and Over Time", *Review of Economics and Statistics,* November.

Chenery, Hollis B. and Moshe Syrquin (1975), Pattern of Development, 1950-1970, Oxford University Press.

Clark, Colin (1940), The Conditions of Economic Progress, London, Macmillan.

Dandekar, V.M. (1986), "Agriculture, Employment and Poverty", *Economic and Political Weekly,* September 20-27.

Dandekar, V.M. and Rath, N. (1971), "Poverty in India, Dimensions and Trends", *Economic and Political Weekly,* January, 2nd.

Datta, M. (2001), The Significance and Growth of Tertiary Sector: Indian Economy, 1950-1997, Northern Book Centre, New Delhi.

Dutta, Ruddar and Sundharam, S.K.M. (2005), The Indian Economy, S. Chand & Company, New Delhi.

Fisher, A.G.B. (1939), "Production; Primary, Secondary and Tertiary", *The Economic Journal,* Vol. XV.

Konar, D. N. (1997), "Trend of Indian Agriculture in the Post- Independence Period", *Artha Beekshan,* Vol. 6, No. 2, Dec.

Konar, D.N. (2004), The Scenario of Population Growth in India, Akansha Publishing House, New Delhi

Kuznets, S. (1966), Modern Economic Growth: Rate, Structure and Spread, New Delhi, Oxford and IBH Publishing Co.

Mellor, J.W. and Desai, G.M. (Ed.) (1986), Agricultural Change and Rural Poverty, Oxford University Press.

Minhas, B.S. (1970), "Rural Poverty, Land Distribution and Development", *Indian Economic Review*, Vol. 5.

Mitra, Ashok (1988), "Disproportionality and the Services Sector: A Note", Social Scientist, April.

Panchamukhi, V.R., Nambiar, R.G. and Mehta, R.R. (1986), "Structural Changes and Economic Growth in Developing Countries", New Delhi, Eighth Congress of International Economic Association, Theme 4, Dec.

Papola, T.S. (2004), "Structural Changes in the Indian Economy: Some Implications of the Emerging Pattern", *Artha Beekshan*, Vol. 13, No. 4, March.

Papola, T.S. (2005), Emerging Structure of Indian Economy—Implications of Growing Inter-Sectoral Imbalances, Presidential Address, the 88th Annual Conference of the Indian Economic Association, December 27.

Radhakrishna, R. (2002), "Agricultural Growth, Employment and Poverty: A Policy Perspective", *Economic and Political Weekly*, Vol. 37, No. 3.

Statistical Outline of India, 2001-02, 2002-03 and Other Relevant Issues, Tata Services Limited.

The Economic Survey, Government of India, 2001-02, 2005-06 and Other Relevant Issues.

The Economic Times (2007), 6th June and 6th July, Kolkata.

The World Bank (Relevant Years): The World Development Report, Oxford, Oxford University Press.

Todaro, M.P. and Hariss, J.R. (1970), Migration, Unemployment and Development: A Two-Sector Analysis, *American Economic Review*, Vol. 60, No. 1.

Structural Reforms and Sustaining Growth in Indian Agriculture: The Emerging Trade Order

ANGREJ SINGH

The present study identifies elements of a strategy for action by India to exploit and develop its agricultural potential by strengthening the competitivencess and supply capabilities so as to take full advantage of trading opportunities under the multilateral trading system. The development of agricultural infrastructure, increase in productivity, irrigation facilities, farm electrification, availability of credit at affordable rate, accessibility to good quality seed, crop diversification, organic farming, etc. seem to hold great promises for sustainable development of India agriculture with structural reforms.

Agriculture is the backbone of Indian economy. It is an important source of GDP with 21 per cent of it originates in this sector. It is also the main stay of Indian population. Besides, the agricultural sector plays a crusial role in food security of the country. Being a large country, India's food security is more a function of the harvest than of the food imports. By production of food and raw materials, agriculture provides the bases of subsistence for an overwhelming number of Indians. About 56 per cent of total population directly earns its livelihood from agriculture. In the emerging liberalized farm trade order the sector holds like horticulture, animal husbandry, dairy and fisheries are important in improving the overall economic conditions, health and nutrition of the rural masses. In fact, most of the Indian poor, that is, to be precise 74 per cent are in the rural area. Most of them draw the bulk of their income directly from agriculture, while others rely on it indirectly by providing goods and services to farmers.

The role of agricultural development in over all economic development and in eliminating poverty is also equally important. As a matter of fact, sustained and accelerated development of Indian agriculture is the key to acceleration in economic development and poverty reducation, furthermore a large number of industries like textiles, silk, sugar, rice, flourmills and milk products get raw material from agriculture. Its strong forward and backward linkages within the rural sector and with the other sector of the economy provide added stimulus for growth and income generation significant progress in promoting economic growth, reduction in poverty and enhancing food secutity cannot be achieved without developing more fully the potential human and productive capacity of the agricultural sector and enhancing its contribution to overall economic and social development. A strong and vibrant food and agricultural system thus, constitutes an important factor in the strategy of overall economic growth and development. Any change in agriculture sector has a spill over effect on the entire India economy.

However, the world agricultural trading system experienced a tremendous change during the second half of the 20th Century. The agreement on agriculture (AOA) signed in 1994, and implemented since January 1995, with establishment of the WTO, is an attempt to establish a fair and free market-oriented world trade in agricultural commodities through stage-by-stage reduction in trade distorition domestics support, export subsidies and tariff peaks. By gradual elimination of imperfections in world agricultual trade, the AOA strive to open up new opportunities for leading agricultural producers. The developing countries are expected to gain through increase in their share in world agricultural trade. However, despite the completion of implementation phase (1995-2004), developing countries are still net importers of agricultural commodities (Ramphul, 2006a). Being an agricultural dominating economy, India can hope to achieve substantial growth of agricultural exports in the coming years. However, in the WTO regime, India's share in world agricultural exports has increased but the increase has less than that of for imports. The net terms of trade for agriculture and India's specialization in agricultural trade have worse affected (Ramphul, 2006b). India's agricultural obligations under AOA falls under three boarder areas, namely market access, domestic support and export subsidies. In terms of market access, India has not only maintained the AOA bound rates, but has unilaterally reduced the most favoured nation (MFN) tariff rates substantially compared to AOA final bound rates (Ramphul, 2006b). In terms of domestic support, i.e., Aggregate Measurenment of Support Indian agriculture has net taxed rather than subsidized (Bhatia, 1994; WTO, 1998, 2002; Hoda, 2001; Bhalla, 2004). It reveals that Indian cultivators have not been received the fair prices for their produce. Benefits of imputs subsidies have been totally passed on the consumers of agricultural commodities. Indian cultivators have been still exploited despite the large quantum of inputs subsidies. Finally in terms of export subsidies India is not provided any subsidy to agricultural exporters, which is prohibited by AOA provisions (WTO, 1998, 2002). Thus, to comply with AOA obligations India is completely free to undertake any agricultural development measure, However, increasing global competition in the era of liberalized farm trade under the WTO regime requires Indian agriculture to be competitive in terms of quality as well as price in a more fiercely competitive world market. India has comparative advantage in producing various agricultural commodities (Ramphul and Vedpal, 2006; Gill and Brar, 1996; World Bank, 1997; Jha, 2001; Bhalla, 2004). However, for sustaining this position and alleviate supply-side constraints certain strategies would have to be adopting if India aspires to emerge as an exporter of the agricultural products.

Against this backdrop, it becomes essential to design certain appropriate strategies for enhancing the competitiveness of Indian agriculture in the WTO regime. It will lead to create gainful employment in a self-sustaining basis in rural area, raise standards of living for the farming comunity, preserve environment and serve as vehicle for a resurgent national economy. The present study is a humble attempt in this direction, i.e., it designs some short-run strategies for institutional and organizational changes with a view to grasp opportunity thrown up by the AOA. To that end, an assessment is made of the main constraints facing its agricultural development, including those associated with globalization and the international trading regime for agriculture. Policy lessons of relevance for Indian agriculture are drawn, based on the experience over the past three decades or so and focusing on success stories in agricultural development and the enhancement of competitiveness.

ENHANCING COMPETITIVENESS OF INDIAN AGRICULTURE

The WTO has opened up new opportunities for developing countries. India can hope to achieve substantial growth of exports in the coming years. The following measures may be adopted to harness the opportunity opened by new trade regime.

Agriculture Growth with Efficiency

A high growth in agricultural output is a necessary condition for reaping advantageous opportunities of the WTO regime. Growth in output can take place through three major routes, namely: (i) growth in productivity, (ii) expansion of net cultivated area, and (iii) shift in cropping pattern from low value to high value crops. The productivity in Indian agriculture is much lower as compared to that in other leading crop producing countries. There is also a wide gap in the yield levels among and within states. Thus there is an immense potential for improving agricultural productivity. This requires concerted and simulations efforts on several fronts: (i) increase in use of modern inputs like fertilizer, insecticides/pesticides, modern implements/ machineries, (ii) increase in use of high yielding varieties seeds, i.e., genetically modified seed like Bt cotton, (iii) provision of institutional credit at affordable rate for purchase of modern inputs, (iv) expansion of area under irrigation, (v) improvements in crop and animal germ plasma, (vi) infrastructure for storage and cold storage, and increase in agricultural investment. As far area expansion is considered it can be increased by increase in crop intensity. Out of 328.78 million hectare, an area about 107.4 million hectare is estimated to be degraded (10th Five Year Plan). A sizable area of degraded land needs soil conservation, water harvesting and vegetative cover. This however, requires huge investments in agriculture infrastructure, which is beyond the reach of small and marginal farmers. For this public sector must come forward.

Increase the Public Sector Investment for Agricultural Infrastructure Development

Public sector investment plays a crucial role in the development of agricultural infrastructure like dams, canals, farm electric reticulation, rural roads, agricultural markets and research. Indian farmers are at a disadvantage in respect of agricultural infrastructure compared to other leading countries in farm production from where most of competition comes. Development of infrastructure is a key domestic factor for the efficient production and marketing. But investment in agriculture sector has been declined from 2.1 per cent of gross domestic product (GDP) agriculture in 1993-94 to 0.89 per cent in 2002-03. Public investment fell from Rs. 5369 crore in 1993-94 to Rs. 4950 crore in 2002-03. In fact there has been a continued decline in public investment in agriculture from 1995-96 to 1998-99. There is a misperception that public investment has declined due to increase in agricultural inputs subsidies. But during the last 15 years, inputs subsidies as a percentage of value of agriclutural output have remained constant at their 1990-91 level, i.e., 6.23 per cent, while public sector investment as a percentage of value of agricultural output has declined. The declining trend in public sector investment needs to be checked. Thus, there is a strong case for much higher public investment in agricultural infrastructure.

Farm Electrification

Availability of adequate power at affordable prices is a key to a competitive agriculture. However, the supply of electricity to agriculture sector in India is far from satisfactory. There are several reasons for this. First, the generating capacity in various states is below per their requirement. Secondly, existing capacity in various states in grossly under utilized because of poor electric reticulation and poor distribution and maintenance. There are further hurdles in the way of electrification of tube-wells. These are: (i) high electric reticulation charges, (ii) irregular power cuts, and (iii) lengthy and complex procedures for electric connections. To enhance the competitiveness of Indian agriculture there is a need for huge investment for power generation to supply adequate electricity to agriculture.

Crop Diversification

Recent changing patterns of consumption and demand have instructed to go for greater diversification of farming systems towards commercial crops. In the light of competitiveness of Indian agriculture more emphasis should be given on the production of fruits, vegetables, medicinal and aromatic plants, mushroom, groundnut, flowers, tree farming, animal husbandry, dairying, aqua culture and edible oil seed, etc. To facilitate such diversification adequate infrastructure for post-harvest handling, processing, storage and marketing is needed. Special attention must be paid to reorient our research agenda in the context of diversified agriculture, value-addition, post-production technology and agribusiness. Minimum support price and procurement operation can be used as an instrument for desired crop diversification.

Organic Farming

As has been duly acknowledge in the 10th Five Year Plan that heavy dependence on chemical fertilizer in the past four decades has led to a deficiency of micro-nutrients and matter content in Indian soil. To restore the soil health and increase productivity, organic farm wastage can be converting into vermin compost/manure, which will provide more nutrients to the crop and correct the deficiency of micro-nutrient in soil. To encourage the productivity of agriculture there is a need for adopting the organic farming. The development of organic farming needs to increase in testing and certification facilities for organically produced food. Organic farming should be an economic proposition as well because the cost of inputs in organic farming is less than the chemical fertilizer. Moreover, prices of organic farm products are higher in world market. Thus, organic farming is a good opportunity for India to increase its exports. Therefore, emphasis must be laid on organic farming by using natural manures, bio-fertilizers, bio-pesticides, etc.

Good Quality Seeds

Availability of good quality, i.e., disease-free and high yielding seed is a *sign qua non* for enhancing the productivity of Indian agriculture. Furthermore seed is a vital and basic input for attaining higher yields. To a certain extent, the efficiency of other agricultural inputs likes fertilizers, irrigation pesticides, etc. depends on the quality of seeds. Indian agriculture is facing an acute shortage of good quality seed. On an average, instead of good quality seeds, Indian farmers use 80 per cent home grown seeds. Today, genetically modified seeds like BT-Cotton can raise the Indian agricultural yields to the comparable level with other leading farm producing countries. For this emphasis should be laid on research in economic viable genetic engineering. Adequate efforts should be made for strengthening planting material and seed production systems to meet the growing needs of farmers for diversified agriculture. To meet challenges of TRIPS regime extension services should provided by various central and states agriculture research universities/intuitions to educate farmers for self-production processing and storage of seeds.

Irrigation Facilities

Irrigation is another key factor for improving the agricltural productivity. Expansion of area under intensive agriculture is not possible without increase in area under irrigation. Of 95.4 million hectare of total created irrigation potential only 85.4 million hectares is being utilized (10th Five Years Plan). At present only 38 per cent of net cultivated area is covered under irrigation and the rest of 68 per cent still depends on monsoon (ASAG, 2004). Thus, through an increase in irrigation facilities, India has a large potential for effecient growth of agricultural output. Completion of a number of major and medium irrigation projects which have been started before several years need to be exploited. This once again calls for more public sector investment.

Rain Water Harvesting and Conservation

Water is an essential ingredient of modern high yielding crops. The efficiency of other inputs like seeds, fertilizer, etc.

largely depends on adequate supply of water. However, in the northern states of India, ground water resources are dwindling fast due to poor water harvesting, excessive run-off and poor recharging of ground water. Rain harvesting and water conservation together hold the key to check the steeply rising number of dark blocks. It will also increase the productivity in rain fed areas. There is a misperception that ground water depletion can be checked by increasing user charges, i.e., through decrease in canal irrigation subsidy and power subsidy. But this is not true. In fact, the solution lies in rainwater harvesting, integration of revers, nationalization of water resources and a rational distribution of water. Water harvesting will help in preventing floods and soil erosion. Therefore, both centre and state governments should make adequate budgetary allocation to water shed development programs and conservation measures.

Liberalisation of Farm Inputs

Currently the import of various tradable inputs like fertilizer, seeds, pesticides and machinery, etc. is either restricted through import licensing or by high import tariff. It discourages farmers to use modern implements. Duty free and open import of agricultural inputs will certainly increase the farm mechanization, which will increase the yield level of various crops.

Development of Warehousing, Rural Godowns, Cold Storage and Special Cargo Terminals at Air and Sea Ports

Adequate, well-dispersed and efficient handling, storage and transport facilities for agricultural commodities are essential for reducing post-harvest losses, maintaining food quality thereby increasing exports. At present, the price spread from the farm gate to the consumer is very wide on acount of deficiencies and inadequacy in existing marketing infrastructure. The Food Corporation of India has shortage of foodgrain storage in open shade, which is often contaminated by rain. Even in roof shaded store, grain spoilage because of occurs fungal attack. Thus, there is a need for modernization of handling, storage and transporation system for foodgrain procured by government agencies, Storage facilities are all the more important for high perishable crops like horticulture products and onions, etc. There is need for increase in refrigeration facilities refrigerated vehicle, fast track transport facilities and special cargo terminals at air and sea ports for agricultural products. To generate appropriate product-specific storage capacity huge investment is needed. Keeping in view that public sector funds are limited, private sector participation in the development of storage facilities is highly desirable. Furthermore, to reduce the post-harest losses, primary processing facilities must promoted near the production areas.

Agricultural Export Liberalisation

From Ist April 2001, the quantitative restrictions on imports of agricultural commodities have both removed but restrictions on exports continued. To encourage the agricultural exports, there is a need phasing out all restrictions on movement, stocks, credit, exports and processing of agricultural products. These are impinging on free exports of agcicultural commodities. Besides removing restrictions on the export of agricultural products, there is need for establishing a single window system to deal with the requirements of farmers for promotion of agricultural exports. The incentives for research to deal with plant protection and quarantine regulations in line with the WTO regime are also desirable. A comprehensive strategy for the development of international market intelligence for specific farm products, with a focus on potential in importing countries, quality standards, competitive price scenario, etc. is called for. There is a need to formulate a consistent policy for export of agricultural products and processed agro-products in which the country has comparative advantage.

Development of Agricultural Output Market

In India, because of the dominance of traders current agricultural marketing system is unable to provide proper share to farmers in end consumer prices. The primary rural markets are the first contact point for the rural producers and sellers. There are over 27,000 primary rural markets, which are scattered across the country. However, these are not equipped with basic facilities like platforms for sale and auction, electricity, drinking water, link roads, trader's premises and facilities for post-harvest management, etc. Therefores, these markets require attention for price competitive marketing to attract more buyers. The basic objective of setting up a network of markets should be to ensure reasonable profits to the farmers by creating a conducive environment for the free and fair play of supply and demand forces. It will regulate unfair market practices and ensure transparency in transactions. There is a need to abolish fees, cess, taxes, duties, etc. on procurenment of agricultural or horticultural produce. Expansion of physical markets with good facilities and services would attract farmers and buyers which will create a competitive trade environment and result in offering the best prices to producers and sellers. Public sector can encourage support price to remote areas where infrastructure/trading capablilities are limited and not well structured. For international marketing of agricltural products, there is a need for promoting infrastructure for quality assurance (especially for perishables), standardization and grading. Private sector and joint ventures for developing markets need to be encouraged with suitable policies and incentives for free and competitive trade.

It may be conclude that for the sustainable development of Indian agriculture full support is required from all concerns and in all possible forms. The imperatives discussed above are only indicative. They have one of a tentative nature rather than cut land dry solutions for the problems at hand. There are number of other areas which deserve attention of investigator and researchers in future. For instance, involvement of small and marginal farmers in gain from liberalization of agriculture, transmission of international price volatility to domestic markets in WTO regime, implication of WTO environmental clauses for Indian agriculture, WTO regime and wage productivity ratio into Indian agriculture, agricultural development and spatial dimension, etc. The list is only indicative and not an exhaustive one.

References

Bhalla, G.S. (2004), "Globalization and Indian Agriculture", Academic Foundation Publication, New Delhi.

Bhatia, M.S. (1994), "Agricultural Pricing, Marketing and International Trade under New Economic Environment", *Indian Journal of Agricultural Economics,* Vol. 49, No. 3, July-Sep. 1994.

Gill, S.S. and J.S. Brar (1996), "Global Market and Competitiveness of Indian Agriculture: Some Issues", *Economic and Political Weekly,* Vol. 31, No. 32 (August 10), 2166-77.

Government of India (2002), "Tenth Five Year Plan 2002-07", Planning Commission, New Delhi.

Gulati, Ashok and Sharma, Anil (1994), "Agriculture under GATT: What It Holds for India", *EPW*, July, 16, Vol. 29, No. 29, pp. 1852-67.

Jha, Brajesh (2001), "Indian Agriculture and the Multilateral Trading System", Bookwell Publication, New Delhi.

Ramphul (2006a), "WTO and World Trade in Agricultural Commodities Hopes and Realities", *Asian Economic Review*, Dec., pp. 505-14.

____(2006b), "WTO and India'a Agricultural Trade", *The Indian Journal of Commerce*, Oct-Dec, pp. 62-72.

_____and Ved Pal (2006), "India's Comparative Advantage in Farm Trade in the Emerging Trade Order", *Foreign Trade Review*, July-September, pp. 35-61.

WTO Secretariat's (1998), "Trade Policy Review of India", Geneva.

____(2002), "Trade Policy Review of India", Geneva.

Structural Changes in Agriculture: An Empirical Analysis

PURUSHOTTAM SAHU AND BABILATA SHROFF

INTRODUCTION

To achieve the UN Millennium goal of reducing the number of hungry persons by 2015, Prime Minister's emphasis to double annual foodgrains production by 2015 from 210 m. tonnes to 420 m. tonnes, Eleventh Plan Approach to have GDP growth in agriculture 4 per cent, save India from the Malthusian trap, to face the post-reform challenges and the most important to have sustainable economic development; India must boost its agricultural production applying modern location specific technology. Since land is a shrinking resource for agriculture, the pathway for achieving these goals has to be higher productivity per unit of arable land and irrigated water (Swaminathan, 2006).

Orissa, a mini-India, blessed with a diverse agro-climatic condition, enormous natural resources and untapped human potential, has a great potentiality to keep India in a comfortable position. Due to lack of irrigation facilities (13.8% for Kharif 2005 and 4.5% for Rabi 2005-06) the main occupation agriculture is subject to low productivity resulting in low income and employment insecurity. Marginal returns in traditional crop cultivation have thrown the farmers into the pool of harassment, dislike to the occupation, shift to non-farm sector, indebtedness, suicide and distress migration. The nation is in the threat of food security and gradually derailing from the track of sustainable economic development.

Though agriculture provides livelihood to a majority of the workforce, a vast majority of them (about 80%) are either small and marginal farmers or agricultural labourers. In spite of the efforts of the Government during planning, irrigation is inadequate which made agriculture a seasonal business and gambles of monsoon made the sector weak to provide livelihood security. Agriculture has lost its past glory. Since per unit area productivity in irrigated areas is reaching a plateau, bulk of the future increase in food production has to come from rain fed areas (Ramakrishna and Venkateswarelu, 2006). In face of shrinking natural resources, ever increasing demand for food and other agricultural products and to provide livelihood security to the farming class by sustaining their employment and income; there is a need for structural change in agriculture. Titilagarh Agriculture District of Bolangir Revenue District under the KBK Districts of Orissa has to manage itself under rain fed conditions applying appropriate cultivation technique involving low investment and low risk, fully exploit the vast area of unutilized and underutilized land and replace the low-valued crops by high-valued crops (mainly in upland). To have structural change in agriculture we have to shift from subsistence to commercial farming. Though this trend has been started since a decade or two, there is a need for massive crop diversification, i.e. shifting to high-valued crops and intergrate other primary sector activities and value-added activities to agriculture matching with the dynamic set-up.

THE RESEARCH PROBLEM

The cropping pattern of the Titilagarh Agriculture District is dominated by traditional and low productivity crops. Low production has resulted into low income and employment insecurity. Lack of alternative job opportunities has encouraged out-migration. Being full of natural resources and untapped human power, it has enormous potentiality for sustainable agriculture development through diversification.

OBJECTIVE

Basic objective of this study is to examine the perspectives of structural changes and diversification for sustainable development of agriculture in Titilagarh Agriculture District. Besides, suitable policy measures are also given for ensuring sustainable agriculture and livelihood security of the farmers.

METHODOLOGY

The study is based on both primary and secondary data. The primary data is collected through field survey. The secondary data are collected from Government and non-government organizations.

A PROFILE OF TITILAGARH AGRICULTURE DISTRICT

Titilagarh Agriculture District (TAD) comes under Bolangir Revenue District under the KBK districts of Orissa. The undivided Kalahandi-Bolangir-Koraput (KBK) or the 8 districts Kalahandi, Nuapada, Bolangir, Sonepur, Rayagada, Koraput, Nowrangpur and Malkangiri districts of the state look like the sick children of Orissa. This area has attracted the attention of international media, politicians, and research scholars due to its recurring drought and flood, chronic and transient poverty, hunger and starvation death, underdevelopment and out-migration, distress sale of property and children, and outbreak of epidemics. Though very rich in natural resources this area has a substantial regional disparity in terms of literacy (31.58% which is 63.61% for the state), health and poverty stricken people (74.24% BPL which is 47.17% for the state). This area constitutes a sizeable amount of tribal population (16.7% SC and 38.95% ST). While 85.03% of our state population lives in rural areas, it is 89.89 per cent for KBK. 90.5 per cent of rural population of this region is basically engaged in primary sector activities.

The TAD covers an area of 342,638.86 ha. spreading over 2 sub-divisions (Titilagarh and Patnagarh), 8 Blocks, 167 GPs, 3

NACs and 1088 villages. It has a hot and moist and sub-humid climate. Its broad soil groups are red and yellow, red and black, brown forest and lateritic. Total cultivated area of this district is 227,165 ha out of which high land constitutes 123,419 ha, medium land 47,485 ha. and low land 52,261 ha, i.e. 54.33 per cent of total land is upland. Paddy area is 105,890 ha, i.e. 47 per cent.

121,275 ha, i.e. 53 per cent of land are under non-paddy crops. Rainfall of the TAD is erratic because it is 947.7 mm, 710.8 mm, 1461.1 mm, 697.0 mm, 1444.7 mm, 1140.0 mm and 989.2 mm respectively for 1999, 2000, 2001, 2002, 2003, 2004 and 2005.

For Kharif 2005 only 13.8 per cent of land, i.e. 31,358 ha. of land have irrigation potential. This district has no major IP, 1815 ha medium IP, 250 no. of lift IP covering 4438 ha, 11661 numbers of dug wells covering 9201 ha, 138 minor IP covering 14565 ha and 5830 ha are irrigated by other sources like WHS, nalas, ponds, etc. For Rabi 2005-06 only 4.5 per cent, i.e.10175 ha is under irrigation. Medium irrigation points cover 506 ha, 12 minor irrigation points cover 815 ha, 231 number of lift IP covering 3101 ha, 12004 dug wells for 3814 ha and 1939 ha from other sources like WHS, nalas, ponds, etc.

THE EMPIRICAL ANALYSIS

To study the problems and prospects of crop diversification in TAD, 5 villages Mahada, Shagunamunda, Kumbhari, Nanajhar, and Mahulpara are taken on a random basis where almost all the people depend upon agriculture. Condition of different villages with crop diversification farmers is explained below.

I. Village MAHADA

Located in the Titilagarh Block has 302 ha of land out of which upland is 200 acres, medium land is 150 acres, 250 acres low land and the remaining government land. The village has 20 big, 80 medium and 53 small farmers while 30 are landless agriculturists. This year migration is 23 (seasonal) which occurs during December to May every year. In the absence of irrigation in the upland, before 2003 they were producing short duration paddy and getting 3 quintals of paddy per acre and about 20 acres were used for vegetables. Now they are producing groundnut (from 2003 to 2006 used for vegetables) in 130 acres with inter-cropping urad, paddy in 50 acres and vegetables (mainly cauliflower) in 20 acres.

2. Village SHAGUNAMUNDA

Out of 80ha (200 acres) up, medium and low land are 80, 40 and 80 acres respectively with two lift irrigation points for a little more than 40 acres. Out of 165 households BF, MF, SF and landless are 7, 15, 103 and 40 respectively and migration is 33 (seasonal). Previously, paddy was produced in the upland, but after diversification paddy (5 acres), groundnuts (25 acres), urad (20 acres), tomato (5 acres), brinjal (6 acres), cauliflower (10 acres) and sunflower (9 acres) are produced. Wells and water from 2 small rivers are used for irrigation for which some vegetables are also produced in the low land after paddy.

3. Village KUMBHARI

Out of 135 households (121 BPL) and 200 acres of land (upland 120, medium 20 and low land 60 acres). There are 7 BF and all others are small and marginal farmers. Migration of this village is 50 (to Hyderabad and Vizag). Irrigation is from 6 big dug wells, 15 open wells, 1 *jore* (stream), 2 *nalas*, 3 small tanks and a *munda* (big tank). The last 2 are used if required. In the upland, 80 acres are under cotton (widely produced since the last 3 years with inter cropping bhodei—a wild cowpea), 30 acres are under mango with inter cropping banana and ladies finger, tomato, brinjal, etc., and 10 acres (low quality) used for sweet potato and gurji (a coarse cereal). Since 2001 the farmers started cotton widely, but failure of cotton crop (due to insects) in 2002 forced some farmers to diversify to fruits and vegetables.

4. Village NANAJHAR

This village has 11 BF, 102 MF, 74 SF and 107 landless labourers out of 1408 population. Migration also exists. Out of 431.73 ha geographical area, cultivated area is 358 acres (upland-148 acres, med-149 acres and low land-61 acres). Irrigated area is 22 ha for Kharif and 8 ha for Rabi. Area under different crops in the upland is: paddy+arhar=4 ha; moong+arhar=1 ha; groundnut+arhar=1 ha; fruits like mango, lemon and amla=11.6

ha; vegetables=1 ha and onion=1 ha. rose and gladiolus after digging a well with his family labour. This year he earned Rs. 18000 though mango is not yet produced for market. Now they are in a position to lead a better life and also giving attention towards the education of their children.

5. Village MAHULPARA

This village has a geographical area of 236.13ha out of which 194.35 acres are cultivated area (upland=97, med=65, lowland=32 acres). Area under irrigation is 13 ha in Kharif and 6ha in Rabi. The cropping area is Paddy+Arhar=5 ha, Moong+Arhar=1 ha, Groundnut+Arhar=1 ha, fruits like mango, lemon and amla in 2.7 ha, vegetables in 0.5ha, and onion in 0.5 ha. out of 196 households (958 populations) 38 are SF, 80 are MF, 25 are BF and 53 are landless labourers. This year migration is 36. Under the watershed development land is bonded and gurji (produced previously) is now substituted by fruits, vegetables and flowers.

Big patches of upland at the outskirt of the Titilagarh town which were lying idle are now covered with some patches of flowers (rose, tuberose, marigold and gladiolus), fruits (mango, guava, pomegranate, coconut, sapota, lemon, orange, etc), vegetables and grass (in one big farm for their diary animals). Vermiculture units are also under construction.

All these diversifications are made in the upland and there is an increse in income.

In villages like Ranabandh, Bitabandh, Darlo and other few only one or a countable no. of farmers have gone for diversification and improved their incomes. On the other hand, in villages like Sirul, Tetelkhunti, etc. none of the farmers have gone for diversification rather searched for subsidiary non-farm activities.

FINDINGS

1. Almost all the people in the villages studied depend upon agriculture and most of them are poor. They do not want to take risk in adopting a new crop and/or new technique and follow some (BF) who adopt and succeed. While adopting a new crop they look into the

livelihood security, the BF look at profit (which may be in the long-run). Crop diversification has raised the level of income and standard of living of the small and marginal farmers and provided high profit to the big farmers. Besides, all those who have diverted from their traditional crops have raised their incomes.

2. Crop diversification to fruits assures better returns on investment and provides regular source of employment and income for long period in comparison to the traditional crops.
3. The unused land is now gradually used and high profit induces them to search new 'niche'. In Shagunamunda and Mahada, vegetables were more profitable but oilseeds proved most profitable, while in Kumbhari failure in cotton crop forced some to divert to fruits and vegetables. No farmer is willing for fodder crops.
4. At least some amount of irrigation is required for each crop.
5. With crop diversification the farmers are becoming market-oriented. But they are not in a position to touch the high income earning consumer's market except for onion.
6. Only a few entrepreneurs (big farmers) whose land is at the outskirts of the Titilagarh town have adopted sprinkle and drip irrigation.
7. Crop diversification is made successfully only with the aid of the watershed department and National Horticulture Mission. Area under horticulture crops and organic farming is encouraged. But due to illiteracy and lack of awareness, the poor farmers are not in a position to leave the indiscriminate use of chemical fertilizers. Among a few farmers interest towards organic farming is also increasing.
8. In almost all the villages the upland in close proximity to the village or house are only used while others are not.

PROBLEMS

Agriculture in this area is restricted due to lack of irrigation (rain-fed dry area), temperature (highest in the State), illiteracy, migration (to Hyderabad, Vizag, Raipur, Rajkot...), market insecurity, discouraging rural atmosphere and the most important poverty (avoid taking risk).

CHALLENGES OF CLIMATE CHANGE

This region is also not free from the challenges of climate change. Since the last 20 years this region is experiencing rise in temperature (even touching 50°C, rising period of heat spell, gradually shifting trend of rainfall, untimely and erratic rainfall. In this ever changing climatic regime the farmers face problems in the choice of appropriate crop.

THE NEW DIMENSION

Crop diversification has a bright future to trigger agriculture development and achieve the twin objective of providing livelihood security of the poor and achieve the goal of food and nutritional security of the nation. Adoption of appropriate location-specific crop pattern with lab-land link will remove poverty, check migration, remove dislike to agriculture, beat stagnation and improve the rural economy. As it is a dry area, the fruits and vegetables are very tasteful and nutritious. A wide variety of fruits and vegetables could be produced here, but new market assurance should be given. Establishment of processing units would encourage area under horticulture crops; crops like cotton, oilseed, etc increase employment and check migration. Education and awareness regarding agricultural waste management, organic farming, value addition activities, etc would be very helpful.

It is a vast unexploited area which could draw the attention of the corporate sector subject to the condition that the agriculturists will not be exploited rather feel secure regarding income, employment, marketing, etc.

Here rain water harvesting is a focus area for sustainable agricultural production but attention should be made on efficient management of the available water resources. Recycling of industrial and municipal waste water should be made and channeled for farming and charging the underground water. Using the household surplus and waste water, kitchen gardens should be encouraged. This will also help the pockets. Urban farming should be encouraged, so that no patch of urban land will remain idle. Water should be treated as an economic good. It should be priced and traded. So that economic use of water will be made.

CONCLUSION

With the opening of the economy agriculture must transform from subsistence to commercial and crop diversification mainly in the upland is the best answer to face the post-reform challenges along with sustainable agriculture development and provision of livelihood security to the masses.

Organizing and encouraging the farmers towards the formation of a more integrated approach to agriculture, i.e. linking agriculture to other primary sector activities like forestry, fishery, poultry, diary, goatary, bee-keeping, etc. could provide a sustainable life to the rural masses. It should be of right kind and for right reason otherwise it will be 'Di-worse-ification'. In a dynamic set-up the producers must be encouraged to find a new 'niche'.

REFERENCES

Annual Credit Plan for 2002-03, Bolangir District, Orissa.

Annual Credit Plan for 2003-04, Bolangir District, Orissa.

Boom Time for Fruit farming in Kashmir (2005), p. 48, *Yojana*, June.

Das, B.P., National River Linking Proposal and Its Impact on Orissa, p. 258

Das, Satya P., WTO and India, *Orissa Economic Journal*, Vol. XXXII, Nos. 1 and 2

EU-Common Agricultural Policy: Way to Protect and Compensate Farmers, p. 18, *Chronicle*, Jan. 2006.

Garg, R.B.I., Contract Farming: An Overview, p. 42, *Kurukshetra*, April 2005.

Green Revolution: Right Time to Go for Second Revolution, p. 29, *Chronicle*, May 2006.

Hajra, Nilanjan, Land Reforms are a Crying Need: Orissa VISION 2020, p. 222.

Handbook on Agricultural Finance: Andhra Bank.

Kalam, A.P.J. Abdul, Integrated Water Mission, p. 2, *Yojana*, June 2005.

Kumar, Dinesh and Shivay, Y.S. (2007), Sustainable Crop Production andFood Security in India; p. 11, *Kurukshetra*, July.

Mishra, A.K., Changing Profile of Agriculture in Orissa: Towards a Policy Framework through NATP, Orissa VISION 2020, p. 133.

Nanda, Ambika Prasad, Globalization and Agriculture in Orissa: Search for a Perspective.

Nyack, Amiya R., Bio-Technology Development in Orissa.

Patel, Amrit (2006), Financing Small and Marginal Farmers: Some Policy Issues, p. 24, *The Indian Banker*, April, Vol. 1, No. 4.

Pattnaik, B.K., New Dimensions of Agriculture Reference ORISSA Century Edition, p. 238.

Potential Linked Credit Plan 2008-09, Bolangir; by NABARD, Orissa Regional Office, Bhubaneswar.

Ramakrishna, Y.S. and Venkateswarlu, B. (2006), Dry land Farming: Issues and Strategies, p. 51, *Yojana*, August.

Rath, Sabyasachi (2006), Horticulture in Orissa; Souvenir, National Seminar on Post-Harvest Management and Marketing of Horticultural Crops, Directorate 28, *Chronicle*, April.

Reference ORISSA Century Edition.

Reference ORISSA Century Edition.

Reference ORISSA Century Edition, p. 241.

Reference ORISSA Century Edition, p. 246.

Roy, Sanjoy (2005), Jackfruit Cultivation in Tripura, *Yojana*, July.

Sinha, B.N., Rivers of Orissa and Prospects of Interlinking

Swaminathan, M.S. (2007), Agricultural Renewal and Prosperity, p. 89, *Yojana*, Jan.

WTO and Indian Agriculture: Task and Challenges

Sanjeev Bhardwaj, Pratibha Misra and Deepak Jain

The World Trade Organization is the most powerful legislative and judicial body in the world. By promoting the "free trade" agenda of multinational corporations above the interests of local communities, working families, and the environment, the WTO has systematically undermined democracy around the world.

The World Trade Organization (WTO) is an international organisation designed to supervise and liberalize international trade. The WTO came into being on January 1, 1995, and is successor to the General Agreement on Tariffs and Trade (GATT), which was created in 1947, and continued to operate for almost five decades as a *de facto* international organisation. Ordinarily, the world Trade Organisation (WTO) is an organisation for liberalizing trade. It's a place for them to settle trade disputes. It operates a system of trade rules. It deals with the rules of trade between nations at a global or near-global level. WTO is responsible for negotiating and implementing new trade agreements, and is in charge of policing member-countries, adherence to all the WTO agreements, signed by the bulk of the world's trading nations and ratified in their parliaments.

The WTO is a place where member governments go to try to sort out the trade problems they face with each other. The first step is to talk. The bulk of the WTO's current work comes from the 1986-94 negotiations called the Uruguay Round and earlier negotiations under the General Agreement on Tariffs and Trade (GATT). The WTO is currently the host to new negotiations, under the "Doha Development Agenda" launched in 2001. Where countries have faced trade barriers and wanted them lowered, the negotiations have helped to liberalize trade, and in some circumstances its rules support maintaining trade barriers.

AGREEMENT ON AGRICULTURE (AOA)

The new international economic order that is taking shape under the aegis of WTO is likely to pull down drastically the levels of domestic protection in all areas of economic activity. As far as agriculture is concerned, the Agreement on Agriculture (AoA) provides framework for the long-term reform of agriculture trade and domestic over the years to come, with the objective of introducing increased market orientation in agricultural trade. AoA deals specifically with:

1. providing market access,
2. regulating domestic support, and
3. containing export subsidies.

Providing Market Access

AoA required that the prevailing non-tariff barriers in agriculture, which were considered trade distorting, were to be abolished and converted into tariffs so as to provide the same level of protection and subsequently the tariffs were to be progressively reduced by a simply average of 36 per cent by the developed countries over 6 years (year ending 2004). The minimum market access opportunities were to be provided at 3 per cent of the domestic consumption in 1986-88 (to be established by the year 1995) and rising up to 5 per cent by the end of the implementation period.

Reducing Domestic Support

As far as the question of reducing domestic support is concerned, AoA divides domestic support into two categories—

1. trade distorting, and
2. non-trade distorting (or minimal trade distorting).

All trade distorting domestic support is placed in, what is called, 'Amber Box'. As far as non-trade distorting or minimal trade distorting domestic support measures are concerned, they have been divided into (1) Green Box, (2) Blue Box, and (3) Special and Differential (S & D) Box, the Green Box measures include assistance given through environmental assistance programmes, services such as research training and extension, marketing information, certain types of rural infrastructure, etc. The support under Green Box is excluded from any reduction commitments and is not subject to any upper limit. Subsidies under Blue Box include direct payments given to farmers in the form of deficiency payment, direct payments to farmers under production limiting programmes, as in European Union, etc. Support under Blue Box is also exempted from any reduction commitments but it has an upper limit. The Special and Differential (or S & D) Box measures include measures taken by developing countries, otherwise subject to reductions, such as investment subsidies and various agricultural input subsidies generally available to low income and resource poor producers in a developing country.

Export subsidies and the quantities of exports that receive subsidies. Taking averages for 1986-90 as the base level, developed countries agreed to cut the value of export subsidies by 36 per cent over the six years starting in 1995 (24% over 10 years for developing countries).

Developed countries also agreed to reduce the quantities of subsidized exports by 21 per cent over the six years (14% over 10 years for developing countries). Least-developed countries do not need to make any cuts. During the six year implementation period, developing countries are allowed under certain conditions to use subsidies to reduce the costs of marketing and transporting exports.

THE LEAST-DEVELOPED AND THOSE DEPENDING ON FOOD IMPORTS

Under the agriculture agreement, WTO members have to reduce their subsidized exports. But some importing countries depend on supplies of cheap, subsidized food from the major industrialized nations. They include some of the poorest countries, and although their farming sectors might receive a boost from higher prices caused by reduced export subsidies, they might need temporary assistance to make the necessary adjustments to deal with higher priced imports and eventually to export. A special ministerial decision sets out objectives, and certain measures, for the provision of food aid and aid for agricultural development. It also refers to the possibility of assistance from the International Monetary Fund and the World Bank of finance commercial food imports.

Other Agreements Related to Agriculture

While AoA is directly concerned with agriculture, there are some other WTO agreements that have a close bearing on agriculture and influence free and fair trade in agriculture. In particular, one may mention three agreements: (1) Agreement on Sanitary and Phyto-Sanitary (SPS) measures, and (2) Agreement on Technical Barriers to Trade, (3) Trade Related Intellectual Property Rights (TRIPs). As far as agreement on SPS measures is concerned, section 2 of the Article says that SPS measures conforming to international standards shall be deemed to be necessay for protection of human, animal or plant life or health. Section 3 of the Article allows countries to fix higher standards than international standards if there is a scientific justification or as a consequence of consistent risk decisions based on an appropriate risk assessment. Agreement on TBT aims to encourage the use of International standards and calls for national testing and certifying bodies to avoid discrimination against imports. Agreement on TRIPs covers seven types of intellectual property for protection, namely, patents, copyrights, trademarks, industrial designs, geographical indications, design layouts of integrated circuits and undisclosed information. As far as agriculture is concerned, Article of the agreement requires members to provide for protection of plant varieties either by patent or by an effective *sui generic* system or by any combination thereof.

The Work Progamme of the Future

On the basis of its working and experience ever since its very inception, the WTO has launched work on the so-called 'new issues' which underline its task ahead as well as the Challenges it faces today. Hence, an attempt is made to present an in-depth analysis of its new agenda—the WTO work Programme of the future and the new challenges it faces today and also in the years to come.

An important task facing the World Trade Organisation (WTO) is that of making the new multilateral trading system truly global in scope and application. While the present membership accounts for more than 90 per cent of world trade, a number of nations are still outside. Many of them have requested accession to the WTO. Twenty-eight governments ranging from China, the Russian Fedreation, Ukraine, and Vietnam to the Baltic States, Bulgaria, Mongolia, Panama and Vanuatu are at various stages of a process that has become more involved because of the WTO increased coverage relative to the GATT.

One "new" issue that is already in the WTO work programme is the relationship between trade and the environment. At the heart of the matter how we relate the rules-based multilateral trade system, continued trade liberalization and further development of the global economy to environmental policy, concerns and objectives. It is also not difficult to see how ill-considered international environmental agreements could needlessly frustrate trade and reduce incomes—and even put at risk environmental reform and improvement. WTO will contribute to a better understanding of the issues, and assist governments in developing more coherent policies in this area.

Trade and investment is a leading issue for the new agenda, since one of the consequences of globalization is to lessen the distinctions among different forms of market access. Reducing tariffs and eliminating other trade barriers at the frontier was the recipe for liberalization. Foreign investment was an altogether different matter. Indeed, countries often used to regard tariffs and other trade barriers as convenient mechanisms for inducing foreign investment.

Indeed, the importance of investment was recognized in the General Agreement on Trade in Services negotiated in one of the four modes of services supply in respect of which WTO member undertook market access commitments. The Uruguay Round Agreement on Trade Related Investment Measures calls for an examination by members within five years of the case for developing provisions on investment policy.

Some WTO members would like to see the new agenda including the subject of trade and social standards. This is a highly controversial issue, and in the absence of a consensus there is no possibility that it could be brought into the agenda of the WTO.

The First issue to be clarified is the nature of the subject; are we talking about the computation advantage of developing countries which comes from lower wages levels—as the issue is sometimes presented—or are we talking about human right or labour standards: it is fundamentally important to clear the terms of the debated as relates to trade.

The second point is to identify what are the key issues related to trade; for example, are we talking about child labour or trade union rights in terms of labour standards or in terms of human rights?

Finally, the ILO has recognized the necessity of improving its means of acting on these issues. Let us now talk about reciprocity and growth of regionalism in international trade relations. Let us now talk about reciprocity and growth of regionalism in international trade relations.

There is a need to improve the rules and the procedures under which the WTO's members can assess this crucial relationship. But it is also clear that the legal issues are only part of the story.

The relation between regional and multilateral liberalization in practices has been a different and generally more positive story. For example, successive enlargements of the European Union have been followed by multilateral trade negotiation, which have maintained a *de facto* link between progress at the regional level and at the multilateral level. These links are the reason why most people have seen regional agreements as building blocks for multilateral free trade.

Among WTO members, the dispute settlement mechanism is proving an effective instrument in which both developing and developed countries are participating. The use of anti-dumping and countervailing procedures, which is subject to new disciplines, seems to have been failing in developed countries, although an increasing number of developing countries are using such trade defence mechanism.

In Asia and the Pacific, new members have been added to Asian, and completion of the Asian Free Trade Area (AFTA) has been accelerated from 2008 to 2005, with expansion both of the range of goods covered by the Agreement and in its overall scope to cover services and intellectual property. Negotiations among the members of the South Asian Preferential Trading Arrangement were initiated in 1996, aiming to achieve a South Asian Free Trade Area (SAFTA) by 2001.

Another long-term regional integration project covering Asia and the Pacific zone (including the Americas) is the Asia Pacific Economic Cooperation (APEC) forum, which aims at reaching free and open trade and investment in the region by 2010 for the developed and 2020 for the developing economies.

One of the important tasks of the WTO is to consolidate what we have done. The second is to give substance to our building negotiating agenda, which essentially constitutes unfinished business emanating from the round. The third is to meet the new challenges already gathering on the horizon. Allow me to say a little about each of these.

Another part of the Uruguay Round's unfinished business is the built-in agenda for future work. This comprises several elements. WTO members have already established a mandate to enter into successive round of negotiations in trade in services, with a view to achieving progressively higher levels of liberalization. The first such negotiation must begin within five years. Similarly, in agriculture members are committed to engage in negotiations aimed at further reductions in agricultural support services. These commitments and a number of others in the WTO Agreement clearly reflect recognition of the need for continual, incremental trade liberalization—a virtuous circle of global cooperative efforts that is the basis of an effective multilateral system.

Priority Issues for Indian Agriculture

India had expected that with the dismantling of domestic support in developed countries and widespread reduction in export subsidies by these countries, as a part of their commitments under WTO, market access for Indian agricultural products in developed countries would expand. However, as is clear from the detailed discussion above, the developed countries have played their cards very cleverly and have taken effective steps to block agricultural exports from developing countries including India behind various loopholes in AoA and allied agreements. On the other hand, India has provided increased market access to other countries by effectively dismantling quantitative restrictions during the last few years. To protect the Indian agriculture and Indian farmers from foreign competition, it is therefore imperative for the government to lay down priorities for action. In particular, action is required in the following directions:

1. The principles of the level playing field, distortion free trade and efficiency require that the high level of subsidy and support in developed countries must be brought down.
2. A country which globalizes its agricultural sector cannot achieve self-sufficiency in production because globalization will require specialization in those agricultural commodities in which it has a comparative advantage. For countries like India, with large population and low purchasing power, the impact of globalization on availability of food at relatively lower prices is of concern both politically and ethically.
3. Deepak Nayyar and Abhijit Sen have shown that world market prices are liable to more years-to-year fluctuations than domestic prices. Therefore, dismantaling of trade barriers is likely to increase volatility of domestic prices and farm incomes. Accordingly, adequate steps must be taken to protect farm incomes. Further, domestic prices will be more volatile when there is an incidence of dumping by countries have bumper harvest. Therefore, due precaution has to be taken in case of large scale imports of agricultural commodities.

4. Rao and Jeromi point to the possibility that globalization may adversely affect certain areas, some crops and some groups of people. This is due to the reason that benefits from globalization will largely accrue to some areas which have comparative advantage, and some sections of the population that are engaged in producing the export commodities. Therefore, the Indian agricultural policy needs to build-up adequate 'safety nets' to protect the interests of crops, people and regions which are likely to be adversely affected by globalization.

CONCLUDING REMARKS

This is a fact that with India's signing of GATT and becoming founder member of WTO, globalization of agricultural production will experience global competition and global market forces will play a leading role in determination of investment level, cropping pattern, prices, quality and level of international trade. The provisions and agreements made under GATT and WTO will speed up the process of globalization and allow free companies in India. The increasing international trading opportunities in agricultural sector are bright and favourable for those countries which produce large surplus. Their gains depend on their export competitiveness. That is if they are in a position to supply these commodities in international markets at prices lower than their competitions, only then their exports will be increased. Our analysis, as well as studies, conducted on this issue conclude that they are far off from the expected gains. Their products are comparatively costlier and their socio-economic conditions are not conducive to face the world competition. Besides, the issue of eliminating subsidies as well as imposition of intellectual property rights are also not favourable to Indian agriculture. At least the worst sufferer will be the two-third majority of small and marginal farmers. No doubt, despite various criticism, these proposals and agreements have been signed world over. Hence we can't leave it. The only effort which is sincerely needed at this juncture is to find out a way that could minimize the damages and maximize the benefits. And this need sincere and continuous efforts towards the improvement and upgrading of technology applicable to agriculture and rural development.

References

Bibek Debroy (1996): Beyond the Usuguay Round—The Indian Perspective on GATT, Sage Publications.

Gill, S.S. and Brar, J.S. (1996): Global Markets and Competitiveness of Indian Agriculture, *EPW*, August 10.

Government of India, Economic Survey, 2006-07 (Delhi, 2007), Box 6, 7, p. 125 and Economic Survey, 2007-08 (Dehli, 2008), Box 6, 9, p. 150 IMF: World Economic Outlook, October 1996.

Panchamukhi, V.R. (1996): World Trading system: Challenges for Rural India, T.N. Rai Memorial Lecture at Manipal, January, 1996, Published in *Pigmy Economic Review*, May-July.

Ravishankar and M.V. Arinivasa Gowda: World Trade Organisation.

WTO (1995): The Task Ahead, *Southern Economist*, Vol. 33, No. 21, Bangalore, March 1.

WTO Publication Services, Geneva: WTO Trading into the Future—A Booklet.

Investment in Agriculture and Structural Adjustment in Indian Economy

Rajendra Prasad Singh and Pankaj Kumar Mishra

Agriculture continues to be a prime pulse of the Indian economy. It is at the core of socio-economic development of the country. It accounts for around 19 per cent of GDP and about two-thirds of the population is dependent on the sector. Growth of other sectors and overall economy hinges on the performance of agriculture to a considerable extent through its backward and forward linkages. It is not only a source of livelihood for a large population of India but also has a special significance as source of income, though meager it is, for those dependent on agriculture. Attaining sustainable growth of agriculture is an imperative in order to meet the steadily rising need of food and fiber for the burgeoning population. However, with the beginning of New Economic Reforms the onus on agriculture grew more. It is now expected that agriculture would satisfy not only the domestic demand but also encash on its comparative advantages and contribute substantially to foreign exchange earnings by way of exports. To meet these objectives upgradation and modernization of technology and management practices in agriculture have become a critical importance.

But Indian agriculture notwithstanding its importance, suffers from various constraints such as traditional methods of cultivation, heavy dependence on monsoon, fragmentation of land holdings and low productivity, which entails upon supply of adequate and quality inputs, basic infrastructure related to irrigation, storage, marketing, etc. and development of various institutions that take care of the credit and other emerging needs of the farming community in general and small and marginal farmers in particular. To fulfil these needs it requires that level of investment in agriculture be enhanced in a significant way. The adding aspects to agricultural economy due to globalisation make the investment demand in agriculture not only greater but also urgent.

The investments in any sector generate capital in the form of infrastructure, improvement in quality of natural resources and lead to the creation of production as well as other assets. The importance of capital in a country's economic development is well recognized and documented.

It has been stated and elaborated by the development economists of the first generation that investment is the single most important factor in the process of growth.[1] It is the investment that determines the level and pace of economic growth. The investment in any economy comprises two components—public and private. While public investment is determined largely by government policy which bases upon the availability of funds in its coffer, private investment is influenced by a variety of factors, which differ over time and space. Like in other sectors of the economy investment in agriculture is undertaken by both public as well as by private sectors. While public sector investment in agriculture is undertaken for building up necessary infrastructures, private investment in agriculture made by private corporate and households either for augmenting productivity of natural resources or for undertaking such activities, which supplement income sources of farmers. These investments enable farmers to grow existing crops extensively and intensively and also enable them to take up non-conventional/ high value crops and allied activities.

During the earlier period of planned development efforts in

India there was acute need to develop primarily the basic infrastructures and institutions for agricultural growth and that task could only be performed by the public investment. Farming community at large was poor and therefore it was not in position to take up any sort of investment on its own. That is to say that in the then give circumstances public investment had also to play role that could have been mostly played by the private investments. In due course of time, private investment started to follow the suit of public investment and the total investment in agriculture began to rise. But the need of Indian agriculture for a reasonable growth rate necessitates for a much higher level of investment and for that matter public investment to continue to play the dominant role. But by the mid-1980s it was recognized that public expenditure in India was going beyond its means and becoming one of the main source of imbalances generated in the economy. In view of the policy-makers this trend of public expenditure was not only had to be halted but its level had to be slashed in order to restore balance in the economy. To achieve this end a wide range of macro-economic policy shift started in the economy. It was proclaimed that Indian economy would be put to higher growth path and new set of economic policies with underlying philosophy of *laissez faire* and free play of market forces would be put in the place. These policy changes were comprehensive and were known as New Economic Policy which aimed at structural adjustment of Indian economy. The guiding principle of structural adjustment was to lessen the government role in the economy in substantial way and let the private enterprise and market forces to occupy the dominant position in economic life of the country. In the field of investments it implied that level of public investment had to be cut drastically in the economy as a whole in general and in the agriculture sector in particular.

The architects of structural adjustment argued that so for public investment had created a large stock of capital in agriculture sector and the farming community of the country had come of age. Now it is able to make investment for agricultural growth on its own and face the vagaries of free play of the market forces. However, it was stated that with decline in public investment the government would bring forth a set of macro-policies that would be conducive to increasing private investment and agricultural growth. Critics of this policy were skeptic of this view and argued that given the large proportion of marginal and small farmers and their weak resource base who occupy the significant proportion of agricultural land, private investment in agriculture could not rise to the extent desired to reach the envisaged level of agricultural growth rate and to fulfil various objectives dependant upon it. These macro-policies themselves would not be in a position to raise growth at higher level, unless it is supported by the sufficient public investment. It may be argued that if public investment declines, macro-policies by encouraging private investment may compensate the decline in public investment. This is possible, provided public and private investments are complementary. The fact remains that they are not; the public investment is generally meant for medium and major projects, whereas the private investment is, mostly used in purchasing the farm equipments and minor irrigation.[2]

Despite the critics apprehensions the internal economic conditions and external pressure forced upon the Indian economy to undergo structural adjustment of some specified nature and the associated policies were brought into become the main instruments in shaping the future growth path of Indian economy. Now sufficient time has passed in restructuring the Indian economy. It may be of interest to know the growth trends of investment in Indian agriculture, its composition as well as its performance in terms of agricultural production and productivity.

An analysis of investment trends in Indian agriculture over a span of last five decades and so brings to fore a disquieting scenario especially for the time span that falls under the period of structural adjustment. Table 1 reveals that the share of agriculture investment in the total investment of the Indian economy remained around 14 per cent or somewhat above up to 1970s, it sharply declined in the period that followed thereafter. The decline was particularly rapid in the 1990s wherein this share came down to the level of 7.9 per cent from a level of 11.4 per cent in 1980s. During the period of 2000-06 the share not only remained at the low level but further declined by 0.5 per cent and came to be 7.4 per cent. The reason for this poor figures for the ratios related to agriculture sector was that the annual average growth rate of investment in the economy as a whole was 65.5 per cent in the 1980s and 72.2 per cent in the 1990s while the average for the agriculture sector in respective years was only 17.2 per cent and 20.3 per cent. During 2000-06 the annual average investment in the economy as a whole grew by 40.2 per cent from the level of Rs. 222892 crore in the 1990s to the level of Rs. 312543 crore; agricultural investment in this period grew only by 30.6 per cent from its relatively much lower level of Rs. 17136 crore to the level of Rs. 22387 crore. These data easily suggest that agriculture sector bore the brunt of correction in macro-imbalances and the structural adjustment in the Indian economy has been done so far without paying much attention to the ground reality and requirements of the agriculture sector.

The sharp deceleration in agricultural investment after 1970s was caused basically by sharp decline in public investment in agriculture. While in 1980s both public and private investment decline sharply. The decline was much steeper in private investment in 1980s but in 1990s private investment in agriculture grew up by 59.9 per cent whereas the growth of public investment was became negative by 24.9 per cent. Thus the average annual public investment of Rs. 4837 crore in the 1990s declining from the level of Rs. 6443 crore in 1980s became comparable to annual average of public investment of Rs. 4851 crore in the 1970s. Marginal improvement in agricultural investment growth rate during the period 2000-06 was largely caused by private investment wherein it rose by 39.7 per cent from relatively high level of private investment in the 1990s. However, public investment in this period grew up only by 8.3 per cent from the lower level of 1990s. Though under period of structural adjustment the growth of public investment decelerated for the economy as whole but in agricultural sector the decline was in its absolute level. However, the growth of private investment for the economy as a whole has been far better than that of agriculture sector. That is why the growth of private investment in agriculture sector could not offset to the decline of public investment to a extent to achieve a higher growth rate for agriculture sector.

Due to negative and lower growth of public investment in agriculture sector in 1990s and later period the share of public investment in this sector declined to its total investment sharply in comparison of the economy as a whole. As Table 2 reveals the share of public investment were 45.55 per cent both in agriculture sector as well as for the economy as a whole. In agriculture sector

TABLE I

Trends in Investment in Indian Agriculture and in Overall Economy

(At 1993-94 prices)

Year	Average annual investment in agriculture (Rs. crore)						Average annual investment in economy as a whole (Rs. crore)						Share of agriculture in total investment (per cent)
	Public	Per cent increase	Private	Per cent increase	Total	Per cent increase	Public	Per cent increase	Private	Per cent increase	Total	Per cent increase	
1950s	—	—	—	—	4370	—	—	—	—	—	25508	—	17.9
1960s	2904	—	3929	—	6833	56.4	21281	—	27577	—	48858	91.5	13.9
1970s	4851	67.0	7297	85.7	12149	77.8	33511	57.5	44690	62.1	78201	60.1	15.9
1980s	6443	32.8	7840	7.4	14243	17.2	57539	71.7	71914	60.9	129454	65.5	11.4
1990s	4837	-24.9	12299	56.9	17136	20.3	74265	29.1	148627	106.7	222892	72.2	7.9
2000-06	5237	8.3	17184	39.7	22387	30.6	85327	14.9	227216	52.9	312543	40.2	7.4

Source: Computed from National Account Statistics and Agricultural Statistics at a Glance, Ministry of Agricultural, GoI.

it came sharply down to 28.7 per cent in 1990s and 23.77 per cent in 2000-06. The figures for the economy as a whole remained comparably higher at a level of 34.66 per cent and 28.72 per cent respective periods. Hence, in reducing the public investment in agriculture sector on the name of structural adjustment planners and policy-makers has been more particular. Due to this untoward focus of adjustment process the share of public investment in agriculture to total public investment in the economy declined from the level of 11.6 per cent in 1980s to the level of 6.5 per cent in 1990s and 6.1 per cent in 2000-06. This should be read keeping in view that there has been long felt need of stepping up investment in the agricultural sector of India. The other aspects of structural adjustment of enhancing the private sector investment in agriculture sector was not working to the level desired. The failure of structural adjustment in totality reflected from the facts, as shown in Table 2, that ratio of agricultural gross capital formation to agricultural GDP was 8.0 per cent in 1980s, it came down to 6.5 per cent in 1990s. There was slight improvement in this ratio in 2000-06 wherein it turned back to the level of 7.9 per cent. But this seemingly improvement took place in the background the share of agriculture in total GDP dropped rather sharply, i.e. from the level of 29.1 per cent in 1990s to 21.8 per cent in 2000-06. This implies that agriculture performance in the later period is not comparable to its earlier periods.

However, in view of the need of agriculture growth the ratio of 8.0 per cent of gross capital formation in agriculture to agriculture GDP is far from satisfactory. To fill the various objectives of the agricultural development it has been estimated that this sector should grow at the rate of 4.0 per cent per annum. To achieve this rate of growth it is required that the investment in agriculture should be raised at the level which is 16.0 per cent of the total agriculture GDP.[3] Declining investment over time has emerged as a major binding constraint on the performance of agriculture and remains a cause of concern. Capital formation has slowed the pace and pattern of technological change and the infrastructural development with adverse ramification on agricultural productivity. On the contrary, with the rising private investment in the agriculture there has been a large increase in the capital intensity of agricultural production during 1990s. As a

TABLE: 2

Composition of Investment in Agriculture

Year	*Ratio of public investment*		*Share of public investment in agriculture total public investment*	*Share of agriculture in Total GDP*	*Ratio of GCF to agricultural GDP*
	Agriculture Sector	*Economy as a whole*			
1950s	—	—	—	56.1	5.1
1960s	43.57	44.56	13.7	47.8	6.4
1970s	40.60	43.57	14.3	42.8	9.1
1980s	45.55	45.55	11.6	36.4	8.0
1990s	28.72	34.66	6.5	29.1	6.5
2000-06	23.77	28.72	6.1	21.8	7.9

Source: Computed by Authors from the sources mentioned in the Table 1.

result, the incremental capital-output ratio (ICOR) doubled during this period from about 2 to 4. This implies higher cost of production and lower profitability.[4]

It may also be noted that the macro-policies, like price policy, monetary and credit policies, etc. developed for effective structural adjustment in the agriculture sector, are supposed to create conditions for growth, which may not be achieved at higher level unless there is sufficient allocation of public investment in agriculture. It may be argued that if public investment declines, macro-policies by encouraging private investment may compensate the decline in public investment. This is possible, provided public and private investments are complementary. The fact remains that they are not; the public investment is generally meant for medium and major projects, whereas the private investment is, mostly used in purchasing the farm equipments and minor irrigation.[5] On the basis of these observations it could be concluded that cutting the public investment drastically and trying to compensate and raise the total investment in agriculture by enhancing private investment through various policy measures would not prove to be wise action. However, if private investment in agriculture rose up to certain extent in the 1990s it was well supported by accumulated huge capital stocks[6] over long periods of time. But only that level of accumulated stock and a marginal or lower level of increase in public investment could not be envisaged to play the same role for all times to come. There is still persistent acute need of raising the investment in agriculture on a massive scale. Therefore enhancing the public investment with a proper choice of project portfolio would be crucial for inducing private investment as well as total investment in agriculture. Of course, the government has to create a favourable policy and development support environment for filling the investment gap in agriculture by promoting private investment as well as by ensuring effective utilization of capital stock created by both public and private investment.

Notes and Reference

1. Y.V. Reddy, "Agriculture: Emerging Issues and possible Approaches", 40th Convocation address of the Acharya N.G. Ranga Agriculture University, Hyderabad on June 5, 2008.
2. S.D. Sawant, *et. al.*, "Capital Formation and Growth in Agriculture", *EPW* March 16, 2003.
3. Tenth Five Year Plan, Government of India.
4. V.N. Mishra, "Trade policy, Agricultural Growth and Rural Poor" *EPW*, No. 43, October 25, 2003.
5. Swant, S.D., *et. al., op. cit.*
6. B.R. Pulapre, *et. al.*, "Agriculture Growth in India since 1991", DRG study No. 27, RBI Mumbai, 2008.

Agricultural Reforms and Institutional Finance: Problems and Prospects

RAMAKANT PD. SINGH AND KUMAR GAURAV

INTRODUCTION

A healthy economy requires a strong and Sustainable rural base. While India has been well endowed with natural, physical and biological resources, such as land, water, livestock, fisheries, forestry, vegetation, climate, solar wind energy, etc. with the aid of science, technology and Capital the Country has not exploited even 25 per cent of their potential for agricultural development. Agriculture, apart from providing livelihood and food security, has tremendous potential to fuel Country's economic growth and has maximum careening impact on secondary and tertiary sectors. According to the world Development Report "The GDP growth arising from agriculture is almost four times as effective in reducing poverty as GDP originating outside the Sector." Agriculture development is inevitable as the government is committed to legislate right to food (Guarantee of Safety and Security) Act. Providing for "the physical, economic and social right of all citizens to have access to safe and nutritious food, consistent with, an adequate diet necessary to lead an active and healthy life with dignity" make agricultural development inevitable.

India has often been described as an area of subsistence agriculture. Great advances, however, have been made in the Indian agriculture in the past independence period. The recent improvements as a consequence of land reforms, consolidation of holdings, provision of irrigation facilities, science life advances in agricultural researches, implements, use of fertilizers, manure and pesticides have ushered the green revolution in large segment of country increasing agricultural production by 62 per cent.

With the initiation of economic reforms since 1991 it has the Indian economy on a higher growth trajectory. Annual growth rate in the total gross domestic product (GDP) has from below 6 per cent during the initial year's reforms to more than 8 per cent in recent years. The Planning Commission in its approach paper to the Eleventh Five Year Plan has stated that 9 per cent growth rate in GDP would be feasible during the Eleventh Plan period. However, agriculture that accounted for more than 30 per cent of total GDP at the beginning of reforms, failed to maintain its pre reform growth. On the contrary, it witnessed a sharp deceleration in growth after mid-1990s. This happened despite the fact that agricultural productivity in most of the states was quite low as it were and the potential for the growth of agriculture was high.

The GDP of agriculture increased annually at more than 3 per cent during the 1980, since the Ninth Five Year Plan (1996- to 2001-02), India has been targeting a growth rate of more than 4 per cent in agriculture, but the actual achievement has been much below the target. More than fifty per cent of the workforce of the country still depends upon agriculture and allied sectors can lead to acute stress in the economy because the population dependent upon this sector is still very large. A major cause behind the slow growth in agriculture in the consistent decrease is important in the sector by the state government. While public and private investments are increasing manifold in sectors such as infrastructure, similar investments are not forthcoming in agriculture and sectors, leading to distances in the community of farmers, specially that of the small and marginal segment have the need for increasing states that increase this investment in the agriculture and allied sectors has been felt.

Concerned by the slow growth in the agriculture and allied sectors, the National Development Council (NDC), in its meeting hold on 29th May 2007 resolution that a special additional control assistance scheme (RKVY) be launched.

The NDC resolved that agricultural development strategies must be reoriented to meet the needs of formers and called upon the control and state governments to a strategy to rejuvenate agriculture. They reformed its commitment to achieve 4 per cent annual growth in the agricultural sector during the 11th Plan; the resolution with respect to the additional central assistance reads as below.

Introduce a new additional central assistance scheme to incentives states to draw up plans for their agriculture scheme more comprehensively, taking agro-climatic conditions natural resources issues and technology into account and integrating livestock, poultry and fisheries more fully. This will involve a new scheme for additional central assistance to state plans administered by the union ministry of agriculture over and above its existing sponsored schemes; to supplement the state specifies strategies including special schemes for beneficiaries of land reforms. The newly created national rain fed area authority will on request assist states in planning for rain fed abase.

The department of agriculture, in compliance of the above resolution and in consultation with the Planning Commission has prepaid the guidelines for the RKVY Scheme, to be known as NADP (RKVY), that are contained in this document.

BASIC FEATURES OF THE RKVY

The RKVY aims at achieving 4 per cent annual growth in agriculture sector during the XIth Plan period by in Suring a holistic development of agriculture and allied sectors. The main objectives of the scheme one:

(i) To incentives the states so as to increase public investment in agriculture and allied sectors.
(ii) To provide flexibility and autonomy to states in the process of planning and executing agriculture and allied sector schemes.
(iii) To ensure the preparation of agriculture plans for the

district and the states based on agro-climatic conditions, availability of technology and natural resources.

(iv) To ensure that the local needs/crops/priorities are better reflected in the agricultural plans of the states.

(v) To achieve the goal or reducing the yield gaps in important crops, through focused interventions.

(vi) To maximize returns to the formers in agriculture and allied sectors.

(vii) To bring about quantifiable changes in the production and productivity of various components of agriculture and allied sectors by addressing them in a holistic manner.

The sad port of the unclear agriculture necessarily be discussed because it breaks the momentum far higher rate of agricultural growth. They are as:

(i) *Overcrowding is agriculture*: Overcrowding and the consequent pressure of population on land have led to sub-division and fragmentation of holdings, decline in the area of land per capita, disguised unemployment in agriculture, and marginal productivity of labour which may be zero or even negative. The pressure of population on land has been so heavy that between 1901 and 1998 the area of cultivated land precultivator has declined from 0.43 hectare to 0.20 hectare, despite an expansion in average. It is clear therefore, that not much can be achieve unless: (a) Growth of rural population is checked, and (b) the pressure of population on land is reduced.

(ii) *Discouraging rural atmosphere*: Still the rural atmosphere is not congenial for speedy growth of farm Sectors, because Indian farmers are poor, illiterate ignorant, superstitious, conservative and bound by cast system and joint family. A very small group of production, however, this change is much slower in states like Bihar, Madhya Pradesh, Rajasthan and U.P. All these states suffer from low levels or literacy.

(iii) *Inadequacy of finance*: Due to inadequacy of finance farmers had to depend upon the village moneylender are better in the agricultural plans of the states and had to pay rates of interest so high that once a former had borrowed, he was bound to lose his land and become a landless labourer. Other sources of finance did exist such not sufficient as per their need on time.

(iv) *Size of holding*: In India, not only agricultural holdings are small but they are fragmented too. Since the average agricultural holdings are too small no scientific cultivation with improved implements, seeds, etc. is passable. Small sized holdings lead to great waste of time, labours and cattle pause, difficulty in proper utilization of irrigation facilities, etc.

(v) *Poor techniques of production*: The Indian farmers have not adopted the modern methods which are so widely adopted in the countries of the west and in Japan.

(vi) *Inadequate irrigation facilities*: One of the basic causes for the weakness of Indian agriculture has been that most of the farmers throughout the country have to depend upon rainfall and very few of them can avail the facilities of artificial irrigation.

In recent years the agricultural problems have become much more severe and intense. The tremendous growth of population and increase in demand for foodgrains and agricultural raw materials due to economic growth. According to V.K.R.V. Rao, India requires a minimum growth rate of 4 per cent in foodgrains and 6 per cent in non-food crops during the rest of the century to meet the basic requirements of the economy for food and agricultural raw materials.

A part from the general problems of agriculture in India here it is to discuss the financing problem of Indian agriculture. Financing agriculture is not a single problem but consists of combined problems of a large number of individual farm units. For each unit the financing problems are different: for the welfare of the farmer and his family depends not only on securing the right amount of capital, but also how well this capital is invested in a business of economic size and upon the degree of managerial ability with which the whole frames operated.

Robert's Ross

An introduction to agricultural economies (1951, p. 217) one important factor that weighed almost decisively was the nature of farm credit being fundamentally different from non-farm credit. This fundamental difference between the two should be clearly compared live all produces, producing in anticipation of demand, the farmer also needs credit. He has to bridge the gap between the initiation of production and the final sale of his produce, provide his own working expenses and maintain his family. But the farmer needs credit for a longer period and, untied the manufacturer who would shop both production and borrowing when the prices of his production fell down, the farmer actually needed more credit in the event of the falling prices for his product. The farmers, unlaces other produces did not find themselves in a position to stop production all of a sudden. Thus, the farmers demand for credit to a large extent, was inelastic and this kept farm credit neglected in the hands of commercial banking system.

The peculiarities of agricultural operations added fuel to the fire. The excessive dependence of agriculture upon nature and biological factors, the instability of farm output and prices the small size of holdings, seasonality of operations, large time-lag involved in granting and recovering loans, continuous demand for credit and most of other factors rendered continuous demand for credit and most of other factors rendered economic calculation of farm operations difficult and complicated. Illiteracy on the port of farmers, lack of infrastructural facilities, and reluctance of farmers in adopting new technology and lack of proper accounting proved further stumbling blocks in the way of commercial banks entry in the farm sector. As a result, agriculture whose contribution to national income in 1967-68 amounted to 53.2 per cent accounted for only 2.1 per cent in bank credit up to March end 1967. Whereas industry with a contribution of 18.1 per cent to national income in 1967-68, had an enviable share of 64.3 per cent. Thus commercial banks, prior to nationalization were content with lending a very small proportion of credit to the farm sector. Even this scanty amount of credit was devoted more to agricultural processing and marketing than to agricultural production.

SOURCES OF CREDIT TO AGRICULTURE INSTITUTIONAL SOURCES-NON-INSTITUTIONAL SOURCES

The policy of single agency approach for the provision of institutional credit to agriculture had resulted in inadequate in on all fronts. The rural credit survey committee had pointed out the picture of agriculture credit in 1951-52 with the following words: "agriculture credit as supplied by different agencies falls short of the right quantity in not of the right type and by the criterion of need (not overlooking the credit worthiness) fails to go to the right people. With the nationalization of 14 major Commercial Banks, momentous decision of much wider importance was given effect in the spare of farm credit, i.e. the substitution of multi agency approach in place of single-agency approaches. The multi-agency was born out, deliberate policy to lift agriculture development from low equilibrium trap.

In multi-agency approach RBI, scheduled commercial banks including public sector banks and private sector banks, state co-operative banks, district cooperative banks, on gram Panchayat levels primary agriculture co-operative societies are banking as institutional financing bodies in India.

Policy on agriculture credit aims at progressive institutionalization of credit agencies for providing credit to farmers for raising agricultural production productivity. Agricultural credit is disbursed through a multi-agency network consisting of cooperatives, Commercial Banks and Regional Rural Bank (RRBs).

The farm credit package announced in June 2004 stipulate doubling the flow or institutional credit for agriculture in the ensuing three years. The credit flow to farm sector get doubled during two years as against the stipulated time period of three years. During 2006-07 the total institutional credit flow to agricultural sector was as 203,297 crore having shares of Co-operative Banks, 20.9 per cent, Regional Rural Banks 10.1 per cent and Commercial Banks at 69 per cent.

Government has decided that from kharif 2006-07, farmers would receive crop loan up to a principal amount of Rs. 3 lakh at 7 per cent rate of Interest. This year the government of India is providing interest subvention of 2 per cent per annum to public sector banks, Regional Rural Banks (RRBs) and Co-operative

Banks on account of short-term agriculture credit disbursed out on their own resources.

REVIVAL OF COOPERATIVE CREDIT STRUCTURE

In January 2006, the government announced a package for revival of short-terrn rural cooperative credit structure. Involving financial assistance of Rs. 13596 crore, NABARD has been designated on the implementing agency for the purpose.

A Department for Cooperative Revival and Reform has been set-up in NABARD for facilitating the implementation process. States are required to sign a memorandum of understanding (MoU) with NABARD committing to implement the legal, institutional and other reforms and envisaged in the revival package. So far, 21 states and 3 UTs have agreed to implement the package. The task force has also submitted its report for revival of long-term cooperative credit structure. The report has been forwarded to the state governments for their comments. A financial package for revival of long-term cooperative credit structure would be developed based on the comments.

The government has decided to provide two per cent subsidy to public sector banks and Regional Rural Banks to ensure availability of form loan at 7 per cent interest. This benefit will not be applicable to private sector banks. Union government provided interest subsidy of 2 per cent to ensure that farmers receive short-term production credit at 7 per cent with an upper limit of Rs. 3 lakh on the principal amount for Kharif and Rabbi crop 2006-07. The government has decided to provide this interest subvention to public sector banks and RRBs on lending from their own resources and refinance at concession rate to Cooperative Banks and RRBs on their borrowings from NABARD. Besides, the state governments have been requested to provide interest subsidy to Cooperative Banks on the amount disbursed from their own resources to ensure their disbursement of ground level credit at a rate of 7 per cent per annum. Reserve Bank of India and NABARD have issued instruction to all public sector banks, Regional Rural Banks and Cooperative Banks for their interest subsidy on form loans.

It is evident from Table 1 that institutional credit have been

TABLE 1

Flow of Imitational Credit to Agriculture

Institutions	*2002-03*	*2003-04*	*2004-05*	*2005-06*	*2006-07*	2007-08 *upto Nov.* 2007
Cooperative Bank	23716	26959	31424	39404	42480	33070
Percentage Share	34	31	25.1	21.8	20.9	24.0
Regional Rural Banks	6070	7581	12404	15223	20435	15925
Percentage Share	9	9	9.9	8.4	10.1	11.6
Commercial Banks	39774	52441	81481	125859	140382	88765
Percentage Share	57	60	65	69.8	69.0	64.4
Total	69560	86981	125309	180486	203297	137760

Source: NSSO.

given to agriculture sector from 2002 to 2007-08. It has been also targeted to provide agricultural credit to the tune of Rs. 325000 crores for the year 2009-10. In 2008-09 agricultureal credit flow was at Rs. 2,87,000 crores.

But the governments recents efforts at financial inclusion have so far not with significant success in rural areas. A recent NSSO study shows that only 27 per cent of cultivator households get any institutional credit. Another 22 per cent borrow from money lenders while the remaining 51 per cent have no access at all to credit. This means over half of rural Indians do not borrow because of lack of access or because they do not have the capacity to borrow. They are so poor that lenders do not trust their repaying ability. A large number of them are from unirrigated dry areas.

Rural Credit accounts for only 15 per cent of total bank credit of Rs. 11,24,300 crore lent by Commercial Banks as on 31 March 2005, Only Rs. 1,60,479 crore went to rural India. Five states—Andhra, Karnataka, Uttar Pradesh, Maharashtra, and Tamil Nadu together account for 50 per cent of outstanding rural credit as on 31 March 2005. The entire north-east comprising the seven states—Arunachal Pradesh, Assam, Manipur, Meghalaya, Mizoram, Nagaland and Tripura, account for only 3 per cent of the outstanding loans. Thus the regional disparity in credit delivery to agriculture or rural sector is a challenging task before the financial institutions.

Future Prospects

At the request of the Govt. of India RBI appointed this Agricultural Credit Review Committee under the Chairmanship of Professor A.M. Khusro to go into the entire gamut of rural credit in India. The Committee submitted its report in 1989. The suggestions and recommendations of the Agricultural Credit Review Committee had broadly two objectives. Firstly, the financial viability of the lending agencies in rural areas must be maintain in order to improve and enlarge the flow of credit to the rural areas. Secondly, the rural credit system should be strengthened.

Scheme of Debt Waiver

This scheme of debt waiver and debt relief for farmers proposed in the budget 2008-09 with an amount of 60000 crores under the scheme for marginal formers (in holding up to 1-2 hectares) there had been complete waiver of all loan that unpaid until February 29, 2008. In respect of other farmers there had been one time settlement (OTS) scheme for all loans that were overdue on December 31, 2007 and which remain unpaid until February 29, 2009 under OTS, a rebate of 25 per cent was given against payment of the balance of 75 per cent. This scheme unables these farmers who could not repay their loans in time due to draught, floods and unfavourable circumstances, to get credit afresh and cultivate their land. Time given to the farmers having more than 2 ha of land to pay 75 per cent of their overdue under this scheme extended from 30th June 2009 to 31st December 2009 in 2009-10 budget.

Rehabilitation Package

The Govt. of India has approved rehabilitation package of Rs. 16978.69 crores for 31 suicide prone districts in four states of Andhra Pradesh, Maharashtra, Karnataka and Kerala. The rehabilitation package aims at establishing a sustainable and viable farming and livelihood support system through debt relief to farmers improved supply of institutional credit.

Service Area Approach (SAA)

The concept of service area credit planning has been introduced in 1989 with an emphasis to integrate and coordinate the credit plans with the development plans at the local level. In this approach 10 to 15 villages to each bank branch have been assigned, it is a first step in the direction of planning below village to block to district and then to state levels (Ojha, 1988) the most important objectives of service area approach and to improve the quality of lending and ensure its linkage to production and productivity, and the institutional credit agencies would have their own perception of development potential and constraints of areas under their jurisdiction.

Kisan Credit Card Scheme

To provide adequate and timely support from the banking system to the farmers for their cultivation needs including purchase of all inputs in a flexible and cost effective manner. NABARD had advised banks to extend coverage through expanding their outreach by lending to more farmers including non-wilful defaulters and lessees tenant farmers, share croppers, who may have been outside the fold of the scheme, as also new farmers. About 705.55 lakh KCC have been issued up to Nov. 2007. The scheme has been extended to all types of loan requirements of borrowers of State Cooperative Agriculture Rural Development Banks. It covers short, medium and long-term credit also.

Micro-Finance Institutions

In recent years, a number of micro-finance initiatives have been introduced. Micro-finance is a novel approach to "banking with poor" as they attempt to combine lower transaction costs and high degree of repayments. This is essentially because of the involvement of the potential beneficiaries of rural credit in the credit delivery mechanism. The major thrust of these micro-finance initiatives is through the setting up of Self-Help Groups (SHGs). NABARD has actively promoted these initiatives Self Help Group bank linkage programme and training and also through providing refinance revolving fund assistance and grants.

Insurance Cover

To cover the risks of agriculture in certainties different crop and live stock insurance schemes have been introduced by the Govt. of India. It is necessary to ensure their credit eligibility.

Formation of National Policy for Farmers

The formation of National Commission on Farmers in 2007 by the Commission has been approved by the Govt. of India. The national policy for farmers among other things has provided for a holistic approach to development of the farm sector.

Thus after adoption of new policy in 1991 the potentialities of agriculture sector has increased a lot. Because rural income and agricultural exports are rising, which will increase the demand for rural credit. The growing importance for high value crops, may necessitate involvement of newer financial agencies such as non-banking financial institutional companies.

According to the report of NABARD expert Committee on rural credit under Chairmanship of Dr. V.S. Vyas, more autonomy should be given to institutions and stress should be laid on self-regulation and on accountability. Cooperatives should be revitalized.

In this regard the role of Panchayati Raj Institutions will be effective. PRI can help in mobilizing deposits, disbursement of loans and its proper utilization repayment or recovery of loans. This will be more useful in proper functioning of financial institutions.

References

Dr. Amrit Patel (2009), Rural Infrastructure for Rural Growth, *Kurukshetra*.

Guidelines prepared for the National Agricultural Development Plan, Govt. of India, May, 2007.

Guidelines for National Agricultural Development Plan (RKVY).

Robert, C. Ross (1951), An Introduction to Agricultural Economics, p. 217.

Narayan Swami and Narsimhan (1944), The Economics of Indian Agriculture, Roch-House, Madras, Part I, Second edition, p. 9.

All India Rural Credit Survey, Report of the Committee of Directors, Vol. II, The RBI, Bombay, 3rd, Impression, 1950, p. 245.

Post-Reform Indian Agriculture: A Survey

BHARTI PANDEY

INTRODUCTION

Indian agriculture is facing stagnation in the era of reforms. The economic reforms initiated in early 1990s, not only failed to help agricultural growth but have actually aggravated the situation. In fact, fatigue of green revolution is amply evident. Besides, several environmental and economic factors are hampering agricultural growth. It must be emphasised here that if farm economics and ecology go wrong, nothing else will go right in agriculture.

The rationale of liberalising agriculture was based on the basic premise that the earlier policy deliberately skewed the terms of trade against agriculture through protectionist industrial and trade policy regimes alongwith over-valued exchange rate. Hence, it was advocated that once the prices are set right the incentive structure in agriculture would tend to improve and thereby farmers' willingness and ability to produce more will increase in response to higher prices. Gulati and Sharma (1997) opined that if domestic prices were aligned with world prices, average incomes in agriculture in the early 1990s would have been 16 to 25 per cent higher than what they indeed were. Thus, the argument for liberalisation of agriculture trade was based on imparting efficiency in Indian agriculture.

The period 1985-2000 was characterised by greater emphasis on the production of pulses and oil seeds as well as vegetables, fruits and milk. The launching of Technology Mission resulted in rapid rise in oilseed production. The mission approach involved concurrent attention to conservation, cultivation, consumption and commerce. This period witnessed huge grain reserves with the government. However, the nation experienced a paradoxical situation characterised by 'grain mountains' concomitant with 'hungry millions'. During this period there was a persistent decline in public investment in irrigation and the infrastructure which are prerequisites for agricultural progress alongwith big jolt to the co-operative credit system. Despite various policy efforts made by the government since 2000, the agrarian scenario is characterised by policy fatigue implying sluggishness in technological innovations, extension and production. The deeply rooted agrarian crisis is well reflected in terms of an irony embodying the fact that the farmers who keep others alive are now compelled to take their own lives and quit farming if there is an alternative option. The agricultural deceleration is occurring at a time when international prices of major foodgrains are spiralling. This is partly attributable to the diversion of grains for ethanol production. If the economy does not succeed in raising foodgrains production much faster than the population growth and in strengthening public distribution system with adequate foodgrains reserves, severe foodgrains crisis will be an inevitable implication. The country has reached a situation where grain mountains have dwindled ramifying diminishing grains reserves and escalating prices.

A slowdown in agriculture growth since the mid-1990s has adversely impacted the livelihood base of the farming community at large. The showdown has occurred in all the sub-sectors of agriculture, including livestock and horticultural growth in the immediate past. A large number of proximate and structural factors have contributed to the decline of agriculture. The foremost among them is the reduced developmental role of state in investment in irrigation, flood control, research, extension, and institution building in the context of liberalising agriculture.

The biggest challenges before the policy-makers, therefore, are how to enhance the agricultural productivity and sustain the livelihood of resource poor marginal and small farmers and generate productive jobs for the farm workers. The Eleventh Plan envisages that the agriculture should grow at least by 4 per cent per annum to achieve the targeted GDP growth rate of 10 per cent. One of the challenges for achieving inclusive growth during this Plan relates to the revival of Indian agriculture. Its growth rate was less than 2 per cent in the last decade. Farming is becoming a non-viable activity. Disparities in productivity across regions and crops have persisted.

Against this backdrop the UPA governments' flagship programmes involving Bharat Nirman schemes to accelerate foodgrains, vegetables and fruit production, such as the National Food Security and Horticulture Missions and the Rashtriya Krishi Vikas *Yojana* are efforts in right direction. Moreover, landless labour families are being enabled to earn some income toward-off total deprivation through the National Rural Employment Guarantee Act (NREGA). If all these programmes are implemented properly, will help to reverse the declining and depressing trend seen in our agricultural scenario until 2007.

TRENDS AND TENDENCIES

The period of liberalisation of Indian agriculture has witnessed slow-down in agricultural growth. There has been significant decline in the rate of growth of foodgrains production, especially rice and wheat. The per capita foodgrain availability declined from about 175 kg. in the triennium ending 1992 to 163 in the triennium ending 2001 (U. Patanaik, 2001). The post-reform period has also witnessed decline in per capita availability of pulses and coarse cereals. In fact, over-emphasis on rice and wheat during the green revolution had already led to a decline in the availability of pulses per head in the 1960s and 1970s. This decline was partially reversed in the 1980s. However, the absolute decline in the production of pulses in the 1990s had reduced availability to levels lower than in 1951.

Estimates given in Table 1 show that the Index of Agricultural Production (IAP) posted a growth of 3.1 per cent per annum during the period 1949-50 to 1964-65. This was attributable to high growth rates in both foodgrain and non-foodgrain production. However, the growth rate of IAP declined to 2.3 per cent during 1967-68 to 1980-81. The period between 1981-82 and 1991-92 witnessed a recovery with a 3.4 per cent growth rate of the IAP. Significantly, during the period 1992-93 and 2005-06 there was a sharp decline in the growth rate of IAP when it dipped down to 1.2 per cent. This trend bears testimony to the fact that for the first time since independence the rate of growth of IAP fell behind the rate of growth of population. There has been a moderate kick up in agricultural growth rate between 2005-06 and 2006-07. However, the following observation of the Planning Commission merits special significance: "not only is the period too short to reach firm judgements on trends, the prolonged deceleration over several years has meant that despite the improvements, per capita output of cereals, pulses, oilseeds, and also of some major vegetables and fruits (e.g., potatoes and bananas) in 2006-07 remained below 1996-97 levels." (GoI, 2008, p. 5)

TABLE 1

Growth Rate in Index of Agriculture Production

Period	*Growth rate in Index of Agriculture Production (in per cent).*
1949-50 to 19964-65	3.1
1967-68 to 1980-81	2.3
1981-82 to 1991-92	3.4
1992-93 to 2005-06	1.2*

*Note: Less than the population growth.

Source: Computed from National Accounts Statistics, Central Statistical Organisation.

Estimates presented in Table 2 show that compound growth rates of index of area under rice posted a negative growth of -0.1 per cent per annum during 2001-08 compared to the 1990s. Though the yield has shown an increase during the same period but the growth rate of production of rice declined from 2.0 per cent to 1.9 per cent. Compound growth rates of index of area, production and yield of wheat show a declining trend from 1.7

per cent, 3.6 per cent and 1.8 per cent respectively in 1990s to 1.3 per cent, 1.4 per cent and 0.1 per cent during 2001-08, respectively. Growth rate of index of yield of sugarcane shows a declining trend during 2001-08 as compared to 1990s. In the case of coarse cereals, pulses and nine oilseed, growth in index of area, production and yield during 2001-08 improved as compared to 1990s.

TABLE 2

Compound Growth Rate of Area, Production and Yield of Major Crops in India (in per cent per annum with Base 1981-82 = 100)

Major Crops	*Area*			*Production*			*Yield*		
	1980-81 to 1989-91	*1990-91 to 1999-2000*	*2000-01 to 2007-08*	*1980-81 to 1989-91*	*1990-91 to 1999-2000*	*2000-01 to 2007-08*	*1980-81 to 1989-91*	*1990-91 to 1999-2000*	*2000-01 to 2007-08*
Rice	0.4	0.7	-0.1	3.6	2.0	1.9	3.2	1.3	2.0
Wheat	0.5	1.7	1.3	3.6	3.6	1.4	3.1	1.8	0.1
Coarse cereals	-1.3	-2.1	-0.4	0.4	0.0	3.3	1.6	1.8	4.3
Pulses	-0.1	-0.6	1.9	1.5	0.6	3.4	1.6	0.9	1.7
Sugarcane	1.4	-0.1	1.9	2.7	2.7	2.2	1.2	1.1	0.3
Cotton	-1.3	2.7	1.5	2.8	2.3	17.5	4.1	-0.4	15.8
Nine Oilseeds	2.5	0.2	3.4	5.4	1.4	7.2	2.5	1.4	3.7

Source: Department of Agriculture and Co-operation, Krishi Bhawan, New Delhi.

The deceleration in the rate of growth in the foodgrains has led to a decline in the per capita net availability of cereals and pulses in the country. Table 3 shows that in 1981 per capita net availability of cereals was 417.3 grams per day which increased to 468.3 gram per day in 1991. It declined to 407.4 grams per day in 2007. The per capita net availability of pulses was 37.5 grams per day in 1981, it improved to 41.6 grams per day in 1991. However, it went down to 35.5 grams per day in 2007.

GROSS CAPITAL FORMATION IN AGRICULTURE

The economic reforms in India agriculture intensified the process of public as well as private resource crisis brewing from

TABLE 3

Per Capita Net Availability of Cereals and Pulses

Year	*Per day (grams)*		
	Cereals	*Pulses*	*Total*
1981	417.3	37.5	454.8
1991	468.5	41.6	510.1
2001	386.2	30.0	416.2
2002	458.7	35.4	494.1
2003	408.5	29.1	437.6
2004	426.9	35.8	462.7
2005	390.9	31.5	422.4
2006	412.8	32.5	445.3
2007	407.4	35.5	442.8

Source: Directorate of Economics and Statistics, Department of Agriculture and Cooperation.

the mid-1980s. Gross Capital Formation (GCF) in India agriculture has declined drastically. The public sector GCF in Indian agriculture declined to one-third in 1999-2000 of what it was in 1980-81. Contrary to the expectations, the reform measures did not stimulate much increase in private investment. Estimates given in Table 4 shows that GCF in agriculture as a share of agricultural GDP began to decline from the early 1980s and continued to decline in the 1980s. In the 2000s the share began to rise, settling at 12.5 per cent of the agriculture GDP in 2006-07. Public investment in agriculture, as a share of agriculture GDP, began to decline from the early 1980s and continued to decline in the 1990s upto 2004-05. After that there was a moderate improvement in public investment; in 2006-07, the share was 3.7 per cent which was still considerably lower than the share for the early 1980s. Private investment in agriculture after stagnating in the 1980s rose immediately in the 1990s and more rapidly in the 2000s. While the rise in private investment in the 1990s was insufficient to compensate for the fall in public investment, the rise in total investment in the 2000s was aided significantly by the growth in private investment.

TABLE 4

Gross Capital Formation in Agriculture as a Share of GDP from Agriculture

(in per cent)

Period/Year	*GCF in agriculture on a share of Agricultural GDP*		
	Public Sector	*Private Sector*	*Total GCF*
1980-81 to 1984-85	5.0	5.5	10.5
1985-86 to 1989-90	3.5	5.2	8.7
1990-91 to 1994-95	2.4	5.9	8.4
1995-96 to 1999-00	2.0	5.9	7.9
2000-01	1.8	7.8	9.6
2001-02	2.0	9.1	11.1
2002-03	2.0	9.8	11.8
2003-04	2.1	8.0	10.2
2004-05	2.8	8.3	11.1
2005-06	3.2	8.5	11.7
2006-07	3.7	8.9	12.5

Source: National Accounts Statistics, Central Statistical Organisation.

IRRIGATION IMPERATIVES

The key role of irrigation in the new technology in agriculture has been well recognised. It allows multiple cropping and support changes in cropping pattern. It is found that in most states households with access to irrigation have only about half the poverty incidence compared to households without irrigated land.

C.H. Hanumantha Rao (2003) observes that India has an irrigation potential of 58.5 million hectares from major and medium irrigation projects. The existing schemes exploit only 60 per cent of this potential. The Bharat Nirman Programme proposes to create 10 million hectares additional assured irrigation. The Planning Commission (2006) notes achieving this goal would require accelerating the pace of 1.42 million hectares per year in recent years to 2.5 million hectares per year. A large number of major and medium irrigation projects launched in Ninth and Tenth Five-Year Plans are incomplete. According to the Ministry of Water Resources, 4.2 million hectares of irrigation capacity can be added by simply completing these projects. Furthermore, India is well behind other countries in Asia in the use of participatory irrigation management (Rao: 2002). Planning Commission (2000) estimate that irrigated land transferred to water users associations in India is only 7 per cent, as compared to Indonesia (45%), Thailand (22%), and Philippines (66%).

Panda (2007) attempts to link irrigation and poverty reduction for rural households. It is found that at all India level Head Count Ratio (HCR) is 19.79 for the households which have irrigated facilities and 30.71 HCR without non-irrigated facilities. The effect of irrigation facility even among the ST households is evident from the fact that the HCR declines dramatically from 51 per cent for ST households without irrigation facilities to 29 per cent for ST households with irrigation facility. Moreover, land is the most important asset among rural households. Indeed, the landless and marginal farmers happen to be among the poorest families in different States. Significantly, households with less than one hectare have more than the average incidence of poverty. Hence, the focus should be on capacity-building among small and marginal farmers enabling them to face the pressures of free markets. Also, expansion of irrigational facilities and ensuring excess to these may be a potent tool of poverty reduction in rural areas.

PUBLIC SPENDING ON AGRICULTURE AND RESEARCH

The Green Revolution incorporating high rates of public investment in crop research, infrastructure and market development alongwith suitable policy support resulted in considerable growth in food crop productivity. This occurred despite increasing land scarcity and high land values. However, recent experience demonstrates that the locus of agricultural research and development has largely shifted from the public to the private multi-national sector. There was a significant slowdown of public expenditure on two specific sectors within agriculture: research and extension.

Table 5 shows that in the 1990s and 2000s, there was a decline in the rate of growth of public spending on agricultural research and extension compared to the earlier decade. The growth rate of public spending on agricultural research fell from

6.3 per cent in the 1980s to 4.8 per cent in the 1990s and 2000s. The corresponding figures for agricultural extension were 7 per cent in the 1980s and 2 per cent in the 1990s and 2000s.

TABLE 5

Growth in Real Public Expenditure on Agriculture Research and Extension

Period	*Growth rate of Public Expenditure (in per cent per annum)*	
	Research and Education	*Extension and Training*
1960s	6.5	10.7
1970s	9.5	-0.1
1980s	6.3	7.0
1990-2005	4.8	2.0

CREDIT CONSTRAINTS

C.H. Hanumantha Rao (2003) found that farmers meet 60 per cent of their credit requirements from formal financial institutions and 40 per cent from informal sources including moneylenders, traders who manage the sales of inputs and credits, friends and relatives. Marginal and small farmers heavily depend on the informal sources of credit. It is a well known fact that exceptionally high interest rates are charged by private moneylenders and traders. Furthermore, farmers committing suicide incur large debts and rely proportionately more on informal sources of credit. This implies poor availability of credit to the distress-ridden farmers. It may further be noted that imperfections in the credit market are because of imperfections in land market. In fact, few farmers can use land as collateral to have access to credit from financial institutions; ensuring ownership is costly for this. However, the village money lender is familiar with the ownership of land and has the resources for litigation if dispute arises. Hence, he is willing to accept land as collateral, given the condition that he can earn exorbitant interest rate. Furthermore, a sharecropper has indeed no access to institutional credit in States where land leasing is illegal. This being the case, the grant of state guaranteed land titles and legalisation of land leasing where it is not currently permitted would help relax the credit constraint to some extent. Rao (2003) suggests contract farming for relaxing the credit constraint. High value agriculture involves more working capital and is riskier than the cultivation of traditional crops. Processors and NGOs work closely with the farmers to ensure the specific variety and quality of produce. Hence, their monitoring costs of such loans are low. They may also act as non-banking intermediaries for farmers, as they command a sound position and thereby have easy access to formal financial institutions. It may further be argued that self-help groups (SHGs) of women can play an instrumental role in expanding rural credit. One of the merits of SHGs is that they provide an opportunity for womenfolk amongst marginal and small farmers to enter into non-farm activities such as housing, dairying, water harvesting, marketing of agricultural goods, and health and education programmes.

SUGGESTIONS

There is need of an evergreen revolution which can help us to improve farm productivity without ecological harm. Enhancing small farm productivity and profitability will make a major contribution to reduce hunger and poverty but this will depend on our ability to assure remunerative prices for farmers' produce. Technologies which can help to enhance land, water and labour productivity are urgently needed. Moreover, in order to improve soil quality, the government can restructure the fertilizer subsidies in such way that it would reduce the consumption of nitrogenous and encourage phosphatic and potassic fertilizer. In view of high variability in agro-climatic conditions, particularly in unfavourable areas research has to become increasingly location specific. The strategy for a small farm management revolution will have to be developed by Panchayati Raj Institutions. Agriculture policies have to be gender sensitive. Though the crop sector may not be able to grow at 4 per cent per annum but horticulture and allied activities like dairy, poultry and fisheries have to grow at the rate of 6 to 7 per cent to achieve 4 per cent growth in agriculture. Strengthening of food processing industry in tandem with agriculture may attract larger investment in agriculture and thereby raise its productivity and farmers' income. Domestic and thereafter global integration of food market will immensely spur growth and employability of rural economy.

Investment in agriculture research and agriculture and rural infrastructure are the main drivers for agricultural growth and poverty alleviation. It is known that public investment in agriculture is lower than the requirements needed for achieving 4 per cent growth. Bharat Nirman programme is in the right direction but the progress has to be much faster. The existing anti-poverty programmes may be made more transparent with governance that minimises leakages and benefits the poorest of the poor. Moreover, to ensure food security on a sustainable manner, agriculture sector needs to be radically reformed by improving incentives, reforming institutions and increasing investment so that agricultural production may be increased more efficiently. Enabling production and marketing environment is to be created so that farmers get higher prices for their produces. The farmers need to have a sustainable income, which will give them the incentives to work in fields. These are long-term challenges which have to be addressed at the earliest. Importantly, the funds already earmarked for various programmes need to properly deployed and value realised. State governments have a critical role to play in agriculture development. Finally, there is an imperative need to step up public investment in the infrastructure, i.e., irrigation, research and extension, besides in social development comprising rural health, education and skills.

References

Acharya, S.S. (2000), 'Subsidies in Indian Agriculture and their Beneficiaries', *Agricultural Situation in India*, Vol. 57, No. 5, pp. 251-60.

Bhalla, G.S. and Singh, Gurmail (2001), Indian Agriculture: Four Decades of Development, Sage Publications, New Delhi.

Chand, R., S.S. Raju and L.M. Pandey (2007), 'Growth Crisis in Agriculture: Severity and Options at National State Levels', *Economic and Political Weekly*, Vol. 42, No. 26, 30 June, pp. 2528-34.

Dantwala, M.L. (1986), "Strategy of Agricultural Development since Independence", New Delhi, pp. 1-15.

Datta, Gaurav (1998), 'Poverty in India and Indian States: An Update', *Indian Journal of Labour Economics*, Vol. 41, No. 2, pp. 191-211.

GoI (2000), Mid-Term "Appraisal of Ninth Five Year Plan (1997-2002)", Planning Commission, New Delhi.

GoI (2005), "Agriculture and Food Security", Mid-term Review of the Tenth Five Year Plan, Part-II, Chapter 5, Planning Commission, New Delhi.

GoI (2006), Towards Faster and More Inclusive Growth: An Approach to Eleventh Five Plan, Planning Commission, New Delhi.

GoI (2008), "Agriculture", Chapter in the Eleventh Five Year Plan, Planning Commission, New Delhi.

GoI (2007), Report of the Expert Group on Agricultural Indebtedness, New Delhi, Ministry of Finance, July.

GoI, Economic Survey, New Delhi, Ministry of Finance, various years.

Gulati, Ashok and Bathla, Seema (2001), "Capital Formation in Indian Agriculture: Revisiting the Debate", *Economic and Political Weekly*, 36(2), May.

Gulati, Ashok and Mullen, Kathleen (2003), "Responding to Policy Reform: Indian Agriculture in the 1990s and After", Working Paper No. 189, Stanford Center for International Development, Stanford.

Gulati, Ashok and Sharma, A. (1997), 'Freeding Trade in Agriculture: Implications for Resource Use Efficiency and Cropping Pattern Changes', *Economic and Political Weekly*, December 17.

Hirashima, S. (2000), "Issues in Agricultural Reforms: Public Investment and Agricultural Reforms", *Economic and Political Weekly*, October 28, pp. 3879-84.

International Food Policy Research Institute (IFPRI) (2005), "Indian Agriculture and Rural Development: Strategic Issues and Reform Options", Strategy Paper, Washington.

Structural Reforms in Agriculture

SATYENDRA PRAJAPTI AND POONAM KUMARI

I. INTRODUCTION

After four decades of socialism, public sector industries, bureaucracy, licences, quotas and permit raj, the Indian economy was forced to embrace economic liberalisation in 1991. Economic liberalisation means reducing governmental inferference in economic activities and encouraging privatisation. The following were the main aims of economic liberalisation:

(i) Removing the hindrances in the process of economic development, (ii) increasing productivity, effectiveness and competitiveness of the Indian industry in order to enter the international markets, (iii) ensuring fast development of the agricultural sector, (iv) widening the scope of the private sector, (v) stopping red tapism, inefficiency and misuse of resources, (vi) developing better money and capital markets by making infrastructural changes in the financial sector, (vii) giving utmost priority and attention to research and innovation, and (viii) solving the basic problems of the economy (such as poverty, unemployment, illiteracy, etc.) while maintaining better co-ordination with the global economies.

Keeping the above factors in mind, many changes were made in the agricultural policy also, which include strengthening Indian agriculture and making it more export-oriented in the future.

2. ECONOMIC LIBERALISATION AND EMERGING TRENDS IN AGRICULTURE

Prior to liberalisation, the main aim of the agricultural policy in India was achieving self-sufficiency in food. Due to this reason, the bulk of investment in agriculture and the use of the latest technology were concentrated in the areas of achieving food security and improving irrigation facilities. This was mainly due to the reason that in the states having good irrigation facilities, the results were prompt, better and secure. However, there has been a major change in the emerging trends in agriculture because of liberalisation. This change is providing greater strength to the already achieved food security and moving ahead in the direction of availing the opportunities arising in agri-exports and agro-based-industries. Following are the main emerging trends in Indian agriculture as a result of liberalisation:

(1) Free Trade

There were some restrictions in taking certain agricultural products from one place to another. On the other hand, there has always been full freedom to transfer industrial goods to any part of the country. The industrialists themselves determine the price of their p'oducts as per the conditions prevailing in the market. As a result of liberalisation, the trade in agricultural goods has also been freed from all restrictions. Nowadays, all restrictions on transferring foodgrains from one state to another have been removed and the farmer can sell his produce in any market he wants. This has benefitted both the farmers as well as the consumers.

(2) Increase in the Production of Foodgrains

With liberal import of good quality seeds, fertilizers, pesticides now Indian farmers have increasingly started using them. It has resulted in increase in agriculture production and productivity. Now our agriculture production is sufficient to meet domestic demand of agricultural products. It should also be kept in mind that after sometime the demand for foodgrains is likely to fall. Because many new products are now available in all areas, including rural areas, which is resulting in a shift in tastes and preference of consumers. Now people consume not only foodgrains but also other things like fruits, juices, salads, snacks, etc. It is estimated that, by the year 2010, the demand for foodgrains will increase only at the rate of 2.6 per cent, which includes foodgrains required for feeding animals. This is considerably lower than the current target growth rate of 4 per cent in agriculture production in Eleventh Plan. So, after meeting domestic demand, surplus foodgrain may be exported.

(3) Agricultural Exports

One of the major trends emerging in agriculture as a result of liberalisationis the possibility of growth of agricultural exports. India is favourably placed as compared to other countries as far as agricultural exports are concerned because of the low import requirements of commodities required in agriculture, low cost of labour and diverse climatic conditions which are favourable for agriculture. It is now being felt that agricultural exports play an important role in generating employment opportunities and bringing about diversification in agriculture. The improved quality of agricultural products has further increased the scope of agricultural exports. The Export-Import Policy announced for the period 2004-09 has provided many facilities agricultural exports. In this policy a special export promotion scheme for agricultural products named—Vishesh Krishi Upaj *Yojana* has been started. Previously, the export of certain commodities was prohibited but now these commodities can be exported by acquiring licences. These commodities include oilseeds, edible oils, pulses, coconut, sugarcane, etc. During 2006-07, the value of exports of agricultural products was Rs. 58,959 crore. India has tremendous export potential in the areas of dairy farming, sericulture, floriculture, horticulture and the like.

(4) Diversification of Agriculture

After new economic policy, there is increasing trend of diversification in Indian agriculture. Now apart from traditional crops, many commercial crops like cashewnuts, spices, cocoa, oilseeds, rubber, jute, flowers, fruits, medicinal plants, herbs, etc. are increasingly cultivated. This diversification has helped Indian farmers in increasing their income.

(5) Increase in the Production of Horticulture

The physiography, climate and qualities of the soil enable India to produce a variety of horticultural crops such as fruits, vegetables, spices, cashewnuts, coconuts, cocoa, betel, medicinal and aromatic herbs, etc. India ranks second in the world in the production of fruits and vegetables.

Before liberalisation in 1991-92, the annual production of fruits was only 290 Iakh tonnes, which increased to 576 lakh tonnes in the year 2005-06, with bananas and mangoes forming more than half of the total production. India is largest producer of mango and banana in the world. India's share in world production of mango is 39 per cent and in banana it is 23 per cent. India is the largest producer of coconut, cashewnuts, ginger, turmeric and black pepper. National Horticulture Mission, 2005 seeks to double the horticulture production by 2011-12. Therefore, the production of fruits, vegetables, cashewnuts and horticultural products is showing trends of constant increase, and the exports of these horticultural products are also showing trends of increasing constantly.

(6) Increase in Production of Floriculture

Since liberalisation, floriculture, i.e., production of flowers and the exports of flowers from India are increasing constantly. In 1994-95, flowers worth Rs. 30 crore were exported from India and, by 2005-06, it had increased to Rs. 101 crore.

(7) Food Processing

The food processing industries are also showing trends of growth. Fruits, vegetables and milk are all perishable commodities. It is estimated that goods worth Rs. 3,000 crore are lost in this way every year. Food processing industries such as Cereal based, Meat, Fish, Fruits, Vegetables, Milk, etc. are being developed in order to prevent such losses. The National Horticulture Board is providing the infrastructure for the packaging, storage and transportation of horticultural products. This industry offers great possibilities in providing widespread employment and boosting agricultural exports. Many steps are being taken to attract the private sector to the food processing industry. The products of this industry have been exempted from the central excise duty. In the year 2005-06 government announced 100 per cent tax rebate on profits for first five years of newly set-up food processing industries. Foreign equity participation upto 100 per cent and agreements for foreign technology are given prompt approval and clearance for the food processing industry, and there are no restrictions on entry of foreign companies in this industry. During 1991, non-traditional food items worth Rs. 194 crore were exported, but by 2006-07, their exports had risen to Rs. 1,836 crore. Upto March 2006, 49 Food Parks have been sanctioned in the country. Various fiscal incentives are provided like reduction in import duty on machinery for food processing, exemption of excise duty on food products, etc. The investments being made in this industry are also constantly increasing.

(8) Development of Agriculture in Backward Areas

During the period after Green Revolution, agricultural research and technology were concentrated in certain specific areas and in the field of foodgrains only. However, after liberalisation, with the demand being favourable for exports, many new activities are being stressed upon. In parts of the country which are dependent upon rains for irrigation and dry land areas which are still backward from the point of agricultural production, relatively more emphasis is being laid on animal husbandry, horticulture, floriculture, dry farming, etc. Many new techniques are being developed for these activities and for benefitting the agricultural areas where there is widespread poverty and backwardness.

In 2005-06, 'Bharat Nirman' Programme was launched covering main components of infrastructure development including—improving irrigation, constructing rural roads, rural electrification, etc. to develop agriculture in backward areas.

(9) Increasing Trend of Unemployment and its Solution

In the areas affected by Green Revolution, the opportunities for employment are rapidly decreasing due to increased mechanisation. Many special programmes for employment and rehabilitation are being emphasised to overcome the problem of unemployment. There is wide scope for increasing agricultural exports which will generate additional employment avenues. In areas dependent upon the rains, or having dry land, where labour is cheap, the use of new techniques is increasing. As a result of this, there are greater possibilities for the labourers in these areas to find work. Through research and development, efforts are being made to develop dry farming technology. It will generate more employment opportunities.

(10) Increase in the Productivity of Agricultural Resources

One of the main aims of liberalisation is to increase the productivity of resources utilised in agriculture. Productivity of the resources is being improved through better allocation of resources among various areas and the use of latest technology. The new era of liberalisation has laid emphasis on new plant varieties, improved variety of seeds, using new technologies in processing and marketing and encouraging the farmers to plant crops which are suitable for that area. Farmers are suggested about the crop, they should cultivate keeping in view the climatic conditions and the type of soil of their farms.

(11) Development of New Biological Techniques

The ever-increasing population of India and the ever-increasing demands of the rich class are putting a lot of pressure on the environment. Apart from these, the unlimited exploitation of natural resources is also damaging the environment. The use of chemical fertilizers; pesticides, etc., in agriculture has also raised the possibilities of incidence of serious problems. In order to avoid this and protect the environment, there is a growing tendency in agriculture to give more emphasis to the development of new biological techniques which are environment-firendly.

(12) Increase in Subsidies

The subsidies granted by the government to agriculture, particularly in the areas of fertilisers, electricity, foodgrains and irrigation have been constantly increasing. During 2006-07, the total subsidies granted by the government amounted to Rs. 52,935 crore. Out of these, Rs. 16,127 crore subsidy is given on fertilizers. The government is unable to reduce these subsidies due to political reasons, because some wealthy farmers who have considerable political influence are opposing the decrease in subsidies being granted for electricity, fertilizers and irrigation.

(13) Trends of Investment in Agriculture

The percentage contribution of public sector investment in agriculture is decreasing, whereas the percentage share of private sector investment in agriculture is increasing. The trends in public and private sector investment in agriculture are shown with the help of the following table:

Trends of Investment in Agriculture

Year	*Total Investment (Rs. crore)*	*Public Sector Investment (Rs. crore)*	*Percentage Share of Public Sector Investment*	*Private Sector Investment (Rs. crore)*	*Percentage Share of Private Sector Investment*
1993-94	13,523	4,467	33	9,056	67
2000-01	38,735	7,155	18.5	31,580	81.5
2004-05	48,576	10,267	21.1	38,309	78.9
2005-06	54,539	13,219	24.2	41,320	75.8

Economic Survey, 2006-07.

Above tablet shows that during the period 1993-94, out of the total investment made in the agricultural sector, the share of the public sector was 33 per cent and by 2005-06 it fell to 24.2 per cent. Public sector investment, which was Rs. 4,467 crore in 1993-94, was increased to Rs. 13,219 crore in 2005-06. Thus, public sector investment in agriculture is decreasing in terms of percentage. On the other hand, private investment, which was Rs. 9,056 crore in 1993-94, increased to Rs. 41,320 crore in 2005-06. In the same manner, private investment which was 67 per cent of the total investment in 1993-94 increased to 75.8 per cent of the total investment in 2005-06. The main reasons behind this increase in private investment are the encouragement being given to the development of agriculture and favourable changes being made in trade policies. Total investment in agriculture as a percentage of GDP was 12.5 per cent in 2006-07. In Eleventh Plan, it is targeted to increase this percentage to 16 per cent so as to achieve growth target of 4 per cent per annum in agriculture.

(14) Institutionalisation of Agricultural Credit

After the implementation of liberalisation policies, there has been a growing trend for institutionalisation of agricultural credit. Earlier the Indian farmer had to rely upon unorganised sources, such as money lenders; *Shaukars,* zamindars. Borrowing of money from unorganised sources has many ill-effects, such as high rates of interest, manipulation of accounts, etc. But now, the maximum amount of funds is borrowed from organised sources like—cooperative societies, regional rural banks, commercial banks, etc. Share of organised sources in agriculture credit has increased from 10 per cent in year 1951-52 to 66 per cent in the year 2002-03. On the other hand share of unorganised sources like mahajans, shaukars, etc. has decreased from 90 per cent in 1951-52 to 34 per cent in year 2002-03. In the era of liberalisation, the farmer is also showing an increasing trend of repaying a greater percentage of the loans.

(15) Setting up of Special Boards

The government has set-up special boards for specific commodities like tea board, jute board, tobacco board, cashewnuts board, etc. These boards are working for improving marketing and for boosting exports of specific commodities.

(16) Setting up National Level Commodity Exchange

For introducing future trading in commodities, the government has established National Level Commodity Exchange in 2003-04. The major agricultural commodities traded at this exchange are wheat, cotton, oil, jute, rubber, spices, etc.

(17) E-trading

During 2005-06 a scheme **AGMARKNET** was implemented to provide electronic connectivity to important wholesale agricultural markets in the country. Government has interconnected 993 agricultural markets through internet and started e-trading in year 2005-06 and this number has increased to 2700 in March 2007.

In brief, improving productivity by better allocation of resources among the various areas and crops, and employing the latest technology are the main aims of liberalisation. Emerging trends in agriculture in post-liberalisation era are emphasising exports, use of modern techniques in production, processing and marketing of agricultural produce, diversification of agriculture, institutionalisation of agricultural credit, etc.

References

Economic Survey, Govt. of India.
Indian Economy by Mishra and Puri.
Indian Economy by Dutta and Sundram.
Indian Economy by P.K. Dhar.
Internet.

Impact of Globalization on Agriculture in Developing Countries

Asmi Raza

The ongoing drive for globalization, characterized by immense increase in international trade and flow of foreign direct investment (FDI), entails two significant aspects: the global ideological shift and the spread of new information and communications technology (ICT). Recent years have witnessed a realignment of national policies towards economic liberalization with a dismantling of the State's role in economic management and a greater opening of economies to international trade and investment. The spread of digital technology (Internet, mobile phones, and fax) has contributed to the increase in trade and investment. The multinational enterprises, having plants in several countries and their network of affiliates and partners, now control one-fifth of world manufacturing GDP, and one-third of world trade takes place between globally placed factories of multinationals (World Bank: 1999).

Conceivably, there are three mechanisms for the diffusion of globalization effects - trade, foreign investment, and the dissemination of new ideas. International trade has increased the fastest for manufactured goods. Changes proposed under the Uruguay Round Agreement and the Doha Round are likely to impact on trade in agricultural goods too. Under the Agreement, substantial reduction in tariffs on agricultural products was expected and the subsidization of exports had to be cut by one-third of its 1986-87 levels by 2000. The second promise has been implemented whereas the first one remains unfulfilled. Given the fact that all measures are implemented, agricultural trade, could rise by as much as 50 per cent, making the world better-off by US $ 160 billion (Economist, 27 March 2000: 13). On the other hand, food prices can be expected to rise by 5 per cent over a decade. This is prone to increase the urgency to augment productivity levels in developing countries' agriculture to ensure survival against competition. The net importers of food will have to face up to rising consumer prices.

FDI IN AGRICULTURE

Some impact of foreign direct investment on developing countries' agriculture in the form of the introduction of new export commodities is becoming discernible. Flower growing owes much to cross-border investments in the form of transfers of capital, technology and skilled personnel from developed countries. The transmission of demands by international supermarket chains is another burgeoning avenue. This could even result in multinationals investing directly in the agriculture sector. Such an eventuality could have negative impacts for developing countries' small-scale farmers, who now account for most of the global labour force.

The rapid pace of globalization can affect the agriculture sector in developing countries on three counts: (i) domination of the food trade by a few multinational corporations (MNC); (ii) widening of technology gaps between rich and poor countries; and (iii) agriculture's shrinking role as the sector employing most of the labour force in the poorer countries. The MNCs' penetration of developing countries is bound to increase under the prevailing milieu of liberalization. Small-scale farmers could be the casualties in this process. Moreover, foreign enterprises in agriculture may well attempt to replicate the technology known to them, and this would certainly mean the displacement of vast numbers of workers from the agriculture sector. In countries where the agriculture sector employs three-quarters of the labour force, a decline in employment of just 10 per cent would require modern sector employment to increase by 30 per cent. In that case such countries may indeed have to step in and dictate the pace of globalization and channel its direction.

AGRICULTURAL EXPORTS

World trade in agricultural commodities recorded growth at an annual rate of 5.6 per cent between 1975 and 1998, signifying a 3.5-fold increase in aggregate terms (Table 1). However, the growth was unevenly distributed, with Western Europe and developing Asian countries registering the best performance and sub-Saharan Africa the worst. The final outcome of the underlying trends was a decline in the developing countries' share of world agricultural exports, from 32 per cent in 1975 to 30 per cent in 1998, the gains in Asia being offset by losses in sub-Saharan Africa and Latin America and the Caribbean. For the world as a whole agricultural exports comprised 10.5 per cent of total exports at late 1990s, clearly a minority and on a declining trend for many decades. Latin American and Caribbean countries relied most heavily on agricultural exports, which accounted for 23.8 per cent of total exports, higher even than Africa with 19.5 per cent.

However, worldwide both agricultural and manufacturing export growth in the 1990s continued at the same pace as in the 1980s. Undoubtedly, developing countries' agricultural growth rose, as did manufacturing export growth, but with a difference. Within developing countries' agricultural exports, the growth rate of those to other developing countries grew more than two-fold, while those to developed countries stagnated. Accordingly, the share of developing countries' agricultural exports to other developing countries between 1980-81 and 2000-01 grew from 9.5 per cent to 13.4 per cent, while their share of agricultural exports to developed countries declined from 25.8 per cent to 22.9 per cent during the same period. On the other hand, developing countries' share in manufacturing exports to developed countries increased from 12.7 per cent in 1980-81 to 21.1 per cent in 2000-01 (World Bank: 2003).

While agricultural exports have been growing more slowly than manufacturing exports, they have at least been increasing faster than agricultural output. Thus, between 1950 and 1998, world agricultural output tripled but agricultural exports quintupled. In the meantime, manufacturing output increased nine-fold and manufacturing exports almost 34-fold (WTO: 1999, Table 1). In other words, manufacturing output expanded much faster than agricultural output, thereby relegating agriculture to a smaller share of the world economy. Manufacturing exports totally dominated world merchandise trade by 1998, their share reaching around 90 per cent. While agriculture exports' share of developing countries to developed countries has declined, share of manufacturing exports has increased. This shows that globalization has meant very much a globalization of manufacturing exports.

TABLE 1

Export Performance, 1975-98

	Growth rate 1975-98 (% p.a.)	*Share of region in world agricultural exports (%)*		*Share of agricultural exports in total exports 1998 (%)*
		1975	*1998*	
World	5.6	100.0	100.0	10.5
Developed countries	5.8	67.7	69.7	-
Developing countries	5.3	32.3	30.3	-
Sub-Saharan Africa	2.3	6.3	3.0	19.5
Asia	6.7	11.7	14.7	7.7
Latin America and the Caribbean	5.1	14.0	12.4	23.8
Eastern Europe	2.9	4.3	2.3	11.7
Western Europe	6.9	32.6	43.2	10.1
North America	4.5	21.4	16.6	11.1

Source: FAO Statistics, 1999; WTO: Annual Report, 1999.

AGRICULTURAL GROWTH AND POVERTY REDUCTION

Growth in agricultural sector is a *sine qua non* for alleviating poverty in the developing countries. Bulk of the world's poor population depends directly on agriculture for their livelihoods (Fan, Hazell and Thorat, 1999). Enhanced agricultural productivity also provides cheaper food that constitutes a large share of expenditures of poor households (Fan, 2000). Besides, a modernizing agriculture is helpful in creating jobs in agricultural processing and marketing, input supply, and consumer products and services, and indirectly generating jobs for those leaving farm. The agricultural sector, owing to its relative size and its significant linkages to the rest of the economy, is the primary engine of economic growth in developing countries. In low-income countries, agriculture is thus far the largest employer of in these countries, employing 68 per cent of the labour force and producing 24 per cent of the GDP. In middle-income countries, though the share of agriculture in the GDP falls below 10 per cent, agriculture still accounts for one-fourth of total employment.

Growth in agriculture wields a positive impact on poverty reduction, because poverty is predominantly a rural phenomenon. Abut two-thirds of the poor reside in the rural areas, and the rural poor worldwide will 'outnumber their urban counterparts for at least another generation (Alderman, 2001). Even alleviation of urban poverty can be facilitated through the growth of rural sector, especially agriculture. For instance, in India the general poverty measures have responded more positively to rural economic growth than to urban economic growth (Datt and Ravallion, 1996). Indirect benefits like higher wages, low food prices, increased demand for consumer and intermediate goods and services, augmentation in agro-business, rise in the returns to labour and capital and improvement in the overall allocative efficiency of factor markets etc., accrue to both urban and rural households as a sequel to the agricultural growth. It was demonstrated by a study of 35 representative countries, conducted in 1997, that a one per cent increase in agricultural GDP per capita created a 1.61 per cent gain in the per capita incomes of the poorest 20 per cent of the population (Timmer, 1997).

AGRICULTURE AND TRADE BARRIERS

It is now an established fact that openness and integration with the world economy is instrumental in promoting growth and reduction in poverty. Many individual country studies conducted from the 1970s through the 1990s have concluded that "trade does seem to create, even sustain higher growth" (Srinivasan and Bhagwati, 1999). More particularly, trade liberalization has been shown in a number of studies to be associated with augmented growth in the agricultural sector. In a comparison of episodes of trade policy reform, Michaely, Choksi, and Papageorgiou (1991) discerned that if the liberalization attempts were sustained, then the agriculture sector would grow at an average rate of 5.7 per cent in the four years following the reform, as compared to 2.8 per cent in the years previous to reforms. Reversion of the reform programme partially or fully resulted in the analogous figures of 2.3 per cent and 2.8 per cent.

A detailed study of the effects on agriculture of trade, pricing, and macro-economic policies of 18 developing countries conducted by Schiff and Valdes (1992a, 1992b) revealed that the protectionist, anti-export policies pursued by most of these countries had the effect of reducing both agricultural and general economic growth. The findings of a World Bank (1994) study of 29 Sub-Saharan African countries revealed that when overall macroeconomic policies (including trade policy and related exchange rate policy) are considered, the group of countries that demonstrated a "large improvement" had a weighted agricultural growth rate of 3.5 per cent per year between 1986 and 1993 in contrast to 2.5 per cent for those with a "small improvement" and 0.3 per cent for those with a "deterioration" in macroeconomic policies.

Nevertheless, some progress has been achieved in global agriculture and trade policy reform. However, the pace of progress remains brittle and has not afforded requisite liberalization and technical support that developing countries had expected from the Uruguay Round of Agreement. Implementation of domestic reform and trade liberalization under the terms of the Uruguay Round Agreement on Agriculture (URAA) has been cumbersome in both the OECD and developing countries for four main reasons. In the first instance, domestic policy distortions and support remain high in many OECD countries. Total support in OECD amounted to $311 billion in 2001, which constituted 1.3 per cent of their GDP—an amount equal to the GDP of all countries in the Sub-Saharan Africa region. The current levels of agricultural support in OECD countries are still a prime factor that impacts upon world production, distorting trade and depressing world prices of agricultural products. This support forms a significant burden to both developing country farmers and low-income consumers whose food consumption still forms a bulk part of total household expenditure.

The developing countries are still in dark about the future plans of the OECD countries about the subsidies being provided to agriculture. The Five Interested Parties (FIP)—the US, the EU, India, Brazil and Australia—a group formed in the Post-Doha round to sort out the widening differences between the developed countries and the developing countries on the vexing issues related to agriculture, held some meetings in Geneva but failed to reach amicable accord, just ahead of the forthcoming Hong Kong ministerial conference of the World Trade Organization (WTO). Hopes were pinned on FIP's Geneva talks to pave way for a possible agreement. The United States and the European Union, who could not resolve differences among themselves on increasing market access, sought to interlink various issues provoking strong resistance from developing countries at a recent meeting in Geneva in October 2005 (*Economic Times*, 21 October 2005).

Secondly, there still exist high tariff barriers and tariff escalation on agriculture and agro-industrial products in many countries. Keeping in view the current levels of support, agricultural tariffs remain extremely high, despite the reductions envisaged under the URAA regime. According to recent estimates, average agricultural tariffs were about six times as high as industrial tariffs (Gibson *et al.*, 2001, OECD, 2001b). Though new rate tariff quotas, as a sequel to the URAA, have reportedly replaced non-tariff barriers, out-of-quota tariff rates still remain high and sometimes prohibitive. Tariffs of more than 50 per cent exist for 60 tariff lines in case of Canada, 71 per cent in the European Union, 14 in Japan, and 8 in the United States (McCulloch, Winters, and Cirera, 2001). The developing countries' exports incur a loss of about $5 billion due to such tariff rates that are exclusively focused on agriculture. Tariffs vary from 29 per cent for sugar in the United States to 162 per cent for grains in the European Union.

Thirdly, the upper level of export subsidies, as prevalent in the developed countries, has been instrumental in distorting world markets for prime commodities. The high levels of export subsidies, as available in OECD countries, have remained a key factor in global food markets and wield a substantial impact on world prices and market conditions. International export subsidies between 1995 and 1998 accounted for $27 billion, of which more than 90 per cent was from the European Union. Export subsidies cause reduction in prices and make it cumbersome for potential agricultural exporting countries to compete. Though for importers, export subsidies envisage short-term benefits in terms of lower import prices, but for both developed and developing countries they can be deleterious to agricultural development in the long-term.

Fourthly, policies of many developing countries continue to create a bias against their own agricultural sector as those of other developing countries. However, in recent years, developing countries as a group have improved their macroeconomic and trade policies. However, in many developing countries the practice of continuing protection to manufacture gods, the operation of inefficient state-owned marketing enterprises for primary agricultural exports is still in vogue. Under such circumstances, apart from creating an overall bias against agriculture, the trade policies of developing countries erect barriers to enhance South-South trade in agricultural products.

CONCLUSION

The benefits of globalization for developing countries' agricultural products, particularly in the agro-based exports are still away from the target mainly because the Uruguay Round

Agreement, accompanying Doha Round and Geneva Meet of the Five Interested Parties (FIPs) have thus far been unable to resolve some of the knotty issues, particularly those dealing with subsidies. The intransigent attitude of the developed countries, particularly the EU and the United States on export subsidies in their case and linking this issue with other issues is creating a stalemate. Comprehensive negotiations are called for on these issues in order to pave way for the effective implementation of the URAA and subsequent agreements to the satisfaction of all the concerned parties, particularly the developing countries. The forthcoming ministerial meeting of the WTO at Hong Kong is going to be crucial in this regard. Its outcome is not expected to resolve this deadlock overnight but a positive attitude and willingness for a fresh round of negotiations can help to achieve a breakthrough.

Undeniably, while the impact of globalization on the agricultural sector will certainly augment, it entails certain limitations. Globalization, by definition, is limited to the modern sector, this being conditioned by two external factors—income elasticity of demand and the nature of technological innovations—and one internal factor—the strategic and symbolic importance of agriculture and land. Primarily, income elasticities are prone to dictate higher returns in industry and services compared to agriculture, inducing capital to flow into the non-agricultural sectors. Recent technological innovations too have been faster in the non-agricultural sectors compared to agriculture. In the developed countries such innovations have trickled down to the farms through the spread of information technology—and lately genetic engineering—but even then the gains in productivity *per se* in agriculture have been much more limited than in the rest of the economy. This is all the more true for developing countries, where the productivity gap between agriculture and non-agriculture has always been wide and has increased further under globalization.

For developing countries, it is essential to be selective while choosing the export strategy. The need to diversify the export base is now widely accepted as part of conventional wisdom. The traditional export crops simply do not provide any viable basis for generating the surpluses needed for development, given that demand for them is declining with the availability of substitutes.

It is a happy augury that increasing attention is being focused on the resolute drive towards globalization and agriculture's role in it. 'Marginalization' is perhaps the one cardinal effect perpetually linked with globalization. Undoubtedly, the agriculture sector as a whole is getting marginalized in comparison to the modern sector. The lurking dilemma is that if agriculture is allowed to have foreign direct investment (FDI) as part of the globalization process, the possibility of small-scale farmers being not only marginalized but indeed deprived of their lands as farms attached to multinational procuring companies are established in developing countries to furnish standardized products on the world markets cannot be ruled out. Consequently, it seems imperative to debate the role of agriculture under globalization and to draw lessons for how the process can be transformed to benefit the maximum number of people and countries. As the Director-General of the ILO recently said:

> Globalization as we know it today will not survive unless its benefits reach more people. It has yet to pass [this] test of social legitimacy... Policies have [...] shaped globalization and they can be changed. If the current model of globalization does not change it will not survive. Our joint task is to shape the process so that the power and potential of the global market, the knowledge economy and the network society reaches every nation, every village, every household... The basic test of the global economy will be its capacity to deliver decent work for all (ILO, 2000, 13).

References

"Agriculture and Technology", in *The Economist* (London), 25 Mar. 2000, p. 9.

Alderman, Harold (2001), "What has Changed Regarding Rural Poverty since Vision to Action?", Rural Strategy Background Paper 5, World Bank, Washington, D.C.

Datt, Gaurav, and Martin Ravallion (1996), "Why have Some Indian States

Done Better than Others at Reducing Rural Poverty?", Poverty, Income Distribution, Safety Nets, Micro-Credit Working Papers, 1594, World Bank, Washington, D.C.

Fan, S., P. Hazell and S. Thorat (1999), "Linkages between Government Spending, Growth and Poverty in Rural India", IFPRI Research Report 10, International Food Policy Research Institute, Washington, D.C.

Fan, S. (2000), "Technological Change, Technical and Allocative Efficiency in Chinese Agriculture", *Journal of International Development,* 12: 1-17.

Gibson, P. et al. (2001), Profiles of Tariffs in Global Agricultural Markets, Agricultural Economic Report 796, USDA, Economic Research Service, Washington, D.C.

Harris, Barbara (1990), "Another awkward class: Merchants and agrarian change in India", in Henry Bernstein *et al.* (eds.), The Food Question: Profits *versus* People, New York, Monthly Review Press.

ILO (2000), World of Work, No. 34, April-May, p. 13.

Jamal, Vali and Karel Jansen (1998), Agrarian Transition in Viet Nam, SAP 2.74/WP.128, Geneva, ILO.

McCulloch, N., A. Winters and X. Cirera (2001), Trade Liberalization and Poverty: A Handbook, London, Centre for Policy Research.

Michaely, M., A.M. Choksi and D. Papageorgiou (1991), "The Design of Successful trade Liberalization Policies", in A. Koves and P. Marer (eds.), Foreign Economic Liberalization: Transformation in Socialist and Market Economies, Boulder, Colo., Westview.

OECD (Organization for Economic Cooperation and Development), (2001), OECD Observer, Policy Brief, November, Paris, OECD.

Schiff, M. and A. Valdes (1992a), A Synthesis of the Economics in Developing Countries, Vol. 4, The Political Economy of Agricultural Pricing Policy, Baltimore, the John Hopkins University Press.

———(1992b), "Agriculture and the Macroeconomy", Policy Research Working Paper, 1967, World Bank, Washington, D.C.

Srinivasan, T.N., and Bhagwati, J. (1999), "Outward-Orientation and Development: Are Revisionists Right?", Economic Growth Centre Discussion Paper 806, Yale University, New Haven, Conn.

Timmer, C. Peter (1997), "How Well Do the Poor Connect to the Growth Process?", Consulting Assistance on Economic Reform Discussion Paper 178, Harvard Institute for International Development, Cambridge. Mass.

World Bank (1994), Adjustment in Africa: Reforms, Results and the Road Ahead, New York, Oxford University Press.

World Bank (1997), Bioengineering of Crops: Report of the World Bank Panel on Transgenic Crops, Environmentally and Socially Sustainable Development Series No. 23, Washington, DC, October.

World Bank (1998), Agricultural biotechnology: The next "Green Revolution", Technical Paper No. 133, Washington, DC.

World Bank (1999), Global Economic Prospects and the Developing Countries, 1998/99, Washington, D.C.

World Bank (2003), Global Economic Prospects, 2003. Washington, D.C.: World Bank.

WTO (1999), Annual Report, 1999, Geneva.

Developing Milk Producing Units as a Farmer's Enterprise: Need of Multidimensional Assail

N.P. Singh, B.V. Singh and G.P. Singh

INTRODUCTION

With an estimated 90+ million tonnes of annual milk production from animals managed by nearly 70 million farmers, India is the top-most milk producing country in the world. The average annual growth is about 5.6 per cent. The per capita milk availability is about 214 grams per day as against the recommended requirement of 250 grams. Milk is one of the most important items of common vegetarian diet of Indian people. With rapid industrialization, economic growth and 250 million potential economically strong domestic consumers of milk and milk products, there is a very strong potential for future growth of the industry.

Impressive work has been done under the guidance of the National Dairy Development Board under "Operation Flood" programmes for organizing dairy production, processing and marketing of milk and milk products by the cooperative dairy sector following the well known "Amul" model—a three-tiered cooperative structure of village level dairy cooperative societies, a district level cooperative milk union and a state level cooperative milk marketing federation where the profits are shared by the farmer members.

The small rural milk producers have several problems. The major problems faced by the farmers include small herd strengths, small land holdings, shortages of green and dry fodder, low productivity of animals, non-availability of timely inputs for breeding, feeding and health care of animals, lack of suitable education/training for skill development for new viable and sustainable technology, inadequate finances, poor rural infrastructure facilities and lack of proper marketing support for their produce.

In last 40-50 years, many development programmes have been taken up by the central and state Governments under the five year development plans.

PRESENT SCENARIO

Some important issues of the Dairy industry are as under:

Breeding of Animals

- As per 1992 Livestock Census, India had a very large base of 56.3 million breedable indigenous cows and 42.5 million breedable buffaloes. However, majority were non-descript low producing animals. India also had 6.36 million cross-breed cows that had a good potential for milk production but the same was not fully exploited due to inadequate feeding and management.
- A new breeding programme—"National Cattle and Buffaloes Breeding Programme" has been taken by the Government of India with massive financial assistance to the state Livestock Development Boards.
- Since last several years, massive programmes have been taken up for cross-breeding of local non-descript cattle mainly utilizing semen of two exotic breeds namely Holstein Friesian (for irrigated areas and for

farmers with adequate fodder resources) and Jersey (for dry/hilly areas and farmers having low fodder resources). In case of buffaloes the programme is for upgrading of local buffaloes using semen of better dairy breeds like Murrah, Mehasana, etc. It is observed that the overall field results of cross-breeding with artificial insemination (A.I.) are still not very satisfactory. For example, data of 17 million inseminations done through a large network of about 43782 A.I. centers showed that the number of calves born were only 15 per cent of A.I. done in the field. Only about 10 per cent of the breedable buffaloes were covered by A.I., the rest being covered by natural insemination service from locally available bulls for whom correct pedigree history was not available.

- Buffalo is the major contributor (52.3%) to India's milk production. Therefore, more emphasis is required on buffalo development.

Feed and Fodder Development

- Almost 70 per cent of arable land is dry or rainfed land having an erratic rainfall, and poor productivity of cereal grains resulting into low output of dry fodder.
- As a result of rising human population, there is a tremendous pressure on land for its utilization for construction of human housing, roads and industries.
- The land holdings per farmer-household are getting fragmented and reduced.
- As and when irrigation facilities are available, the farmers tend to take cash crops and value-added crops. The land for fodder cultivation and availability is a last priority.
- The cattle population and therefore the demand for fodder is increasing every year.
- All the above issues have adversely affected the fodder balance for milk production. There is tremendous overall shortage of fodder availability against the nutritional demand for dairy cattle.

Pandey (1995) had estimated that by year 2002, the gap (demand minus availability) of fodder in India will be 606.2 million tonnes for dry fodder, 1018.0 tonnes of green fodder in Kharif (monsoon) season and 1174.36 tonnes of green fodder in Rabi (winter) season.

Dairy Cattle Health

- The work of diagnosis and treatment is mostly done by the State veterinary departments. They have well qualified technical manpower but lack financial resources.
- Most of the important vaccines and medicines are manufactured in the country. However, there is a shortage of diagnostic agents.
- Where farmers have high producing dairy animals, they are willing to pay for the services and private veterinary practice is possible and flourishing. A good networking amongst the veterinary laboratories and teaching institutions.
- Almost every state has a state Agricultural University and a veterinary faculty.

Production and Marketing of Milk

- Most of the milk in India is produced in villages. Quantity of milk produced per household is very small.
- About 56 per cent of milk is available as marketable surplus for urban areas. Fairly large quantity of milk is converted to local milk products (khoa, paneer, butter, ghee, etc.).
- The share of organized sector is small (private—11-12%, Government/cooperative sector—11-12%).There is still a very large portion of milk market in the hands of unorganized sector which has adverse effect on the farm-gate price of the milk.
- In Government/cooperative sector, almost 80 per cent milk is marketed as liquid milk and only 20 per cent

as milk products. While it is reverse in the private sector—only 30 per cent is marketed as liquid milk and 70 per cent as milk products with value addition.

- In absence of properly developed infrastructure for preservation of raw milk in local areas many plants in Government sector collect fresh raw milk from the far-flung rural areas (each producer having very small quantities) twice a day, send it over a long distance to towns for processing, incurring high cost on transportation. This erodes the profitability. As a result, many plants have become uneconomical, non-functional or they are working much below their potential capacities. Alternative strategies need to be developed to store raw milk in bulk coolers in the rural area and transport it in bigger volumes at a longer intervals. There is also a need to use alternative and cheaper energy sources to store cool milk, and develop rural markets so that much of the milk produced in the rural areas finds consumption avenue in the nearby local markets (Arora, Bhogal and Biswas, 1998).
- There is a need to set-up schemes for diversification and preparation of value-added milk products at the production centers instead of sending raw milk over long distances. Depending upon the market demand for a particular product, quantum of raw milk available, and financial position of the milk plant, suitable milk processing and product manufacturing units can be set-up (Royer, 1995).

The dairy products with high demand potential can be largely grouped under following categories:

(a) Prepared by reconstitution of liquid milk e.g. Flavoured milk with different fat content, flavours, etc.

(b) Prepared from culturing methods (microbial fermentation) e.g. Indin milk products Dahi, Mishti Dahi, Lassi, Butter milk (Chhas), Kadhi, Butter (Makhhan), Ghee, Chakka, Shrikhand, etc.

(c) Prepared by condensation of milk e.g. indian milk products, Kheer, Kulfi, Basundi, Rabdi, Burfi, Pedha, Kalakand, Gulab Jamun, etc.

(d) Prepared by acid precipitation eg. Indian milk products e.g. Paneer, Channa, Sandesh, Rasgolla, Rasmalai, etc.
(e) Products such as lactose, casein, etc.

Suitable technologies and model projects for several dairy products have been developed by institutions like NDDB Anand, NDRI Karnal, NDRI Bangalore, CFTRI Mysore, etc. NABARD has prepared and circulated to banks suitable techno-economic model schemes (Suriya, 2001).

THE PROBLEM

Milk producing is a major non-farm activity that can provide income, livelihood and employment to the rural mass *vis-a-vis* can provide fruitful combination of industry and agriculture. Integrated farming system in which milk producing unit is a key component should be considered as a system of rural development. The developmental drives for milk producing units have been limited to animal health keeping by costly modern medicines, breed improvements and analysis of cost and benefits limited to expenditure on animal feed, medicine and maintenance and sale revenues of milk. These disintegrated and short-sighted efforts could not transform the spectrum of milk producing units and made them unviable and unsustainable. On one hand, new diseases, short life and lactation span, high costs have been eating away the basic capital, and eradicating native breeds and system altogether, on the other. A divorce between agriculture and milk producing unit is at the door. The tale of economic success of milk producing units in Gujarat mainly draws from the institutional reforms in form of cooperative movement could teach only to imitate and resorting to cooperatives without having knowledge of local institutions and individual constructs resulting into a failure. For example, in Purvanchal region of Uttar Pradesh cooperatives of any form have been a failure.

Disintegrated efforts such as new breeds that are ecologically misfit, curing of diseases in place of curing and caring of animals and ventures of economic protection in place of promotions may only be a short-term solutions. Clue to success may lie in bringing up of milk producing units as small and medium enterprises and as integrated part of agriculture in particular and the rural social system in general. The solution to the problem of sustainable development of milk producing units is trans-disciplinary and rooted into native system of knowledge that views every aspect to be a part of one great whole.

THE MULTI DIMENSIONAL ASSAIL: THE SOLUTION

The multi-dimensional assail may include four interlinked compartments:

I. The Technical Part

There is a need to research and to improve quality of animal, animal health systems integrating animal production, existing bio-technologies, efficient feeding, resource and product management. In longing of eco-friendly, sustainable and native knowledge-based development, following three propositions, to begin with, could be identified for examination—

(a) Breeding by local high yielding varieties.

(b) Use of indigenous herbal products and knowledge (Ayurvedic treatment of animals) for increasing output and animal health.

(c) Improvements in by-products for the development of subsidiary units

II. Organizational Part

There is a need to research and to improve organizational structure of milk producing units *vis-a-vis* agricultural production. For instance, following areas may be evaluated and improvements may be worked out—

(a) Organizing and collaborating different subsidiary units.

(b) Organizing and collaborating different milk producing units and agriculture by selection of interdependence. Cropping pattern in tune of grains having good quality straw and production of herbals, use of bio-fertilizers, etc.

III. Economic Part

Economic part is an area that is less researched or researched in limited and artificial framework. What is important to note that benefits calculated so far, takes only the net revenue by selling milk and milk products into account. Similarly, on the cost side, direct cost of animal rearing is included. Therefore, they refer to the point gain. Logically, this is not possible to make a long-term policy prescription to undertake a development process. The implicit assumptions of a market economy are seldom taken into account that market is not a smooth sailing episode rather is made to sail. People have been waiting markets to improve rather than riding on it. In this context, three main areas could be identified for cost management and improvements in decision process.

(a) Production cost management that may include short-term and long-term cost considerations in terms of fixed and variable capital, labour and technology, and inter-dependence of subsidiary units and agriculture.
(b) Marketing management that may include order getting (creation of demand, advertisements and introduction of new products, etc.) and order filling costs (transportation, post-sale services, etc.).
(c) Transaction cost managements that may include Vertical integration (interlinking with other small and medium industries), Asset specificity (Site specificity, Physical asset specificity, Human asset specificity, Brand name capital, Dedicated assets, Temporal specificity), and cost of contracts.

IV. Individual Construct and Social Part

In bringing up of milk producing units as small and medium enterprises, study of and improvement upon individual constructs and social frame is very important. Individual has to be developed into an entrepreneur be it an innovator, imitator, Fabian, drone, solo operator, inventor, and challenger or life timer in a particular social context. Following areas are identified:

(a) Study and development of entrepreneurial skills and opportunism by value orientation and personal ideology.

(b) Study and development of institutions in terms of written (law of the land) and unwritten (social practices, customs and taboos) laws.

TO SUM UP

The milk production is one of important non-farm activity that add to farmers' income. The milk production can also be taken as an activity independent of regular agriculture. This offers a link between agriculture and industry. Despite the activity being a profitable one, it is undertaken by specified castes other than the farmers. This is because it is not considered as entrepreneurial activity one at par with the other non-agricultural activity. For the development of milk producing units on the line of small and medium enterprises, a multidimensional attack is required that would include technical, organizational, economic reforms. It would also solicit training of personnel to improve the personal construct of the individual.

REFERENCES

Arora, V.P.S., T.S. Bhogal, P.G. Biswas (1998). Milk Marketing in North-West Uttar Pradesh and the Role of Cooperative: A Temporal Analysis. Author Affiliation: Department of Agricultural Economics, G.B. Pant University of Agriculture and Technology. Indian Cooperative Rev., 36: 70-77.

Ghose, A.K. and K.L. Maharajan (2002). Milk Marketing Channels in Bangladesh: A Case Study of Three Villages from 3 Districts. J. Int. Develop. Cooperat., 8: 87-101.

Hobbs, J.E. (1997). Producers Attitudes towards Marketing Channels for Finished Cattle. *Farm Manage.*, 9: 566-579.

Prabhat (2005). Animal Husbandry and Dairying. *Kurukshetra*, pp. 30-35.

Royer, J.S. (1995). Industry Note—Potential for Cooperative Involvement in Vertical Coordination and Value-added Activities. *Agribusiness* 11: 473-81.

Suriya, M.S. (2001). Milk Marketing Strategies. *Ind. J. Market*, 31: 24-25.

Tsourgiannis, L. and J. Eddison, M. Warren (2008). Factors Affecting the Marketing Channel Choice of Sheep and Goat Farmers in the Region of East Macedonia in Greece regarding the Distribution of their Milk Production. *Small Ruminant Research* 79 (2008) 87–97.

Vijayalakshmi, S. and J. Sitaramaswamy (1995). Rationalization of Milk Procurement, Processing and Marketing in Southern India. *Agric. Syst.*, 48: 297-314.

Hobbs, J.E. (1996). A Transaction Cost Approach to Supply Chain Management. *Supply Chain Manage*, 1:15-27.

An Analysis of Performance of Dairying Practice in Bihar: With Special Reference to Patna Dairy Project

Krishna Nand Yadav and Upendra Pd. Singh

Dairying is taking a shape of noble profession in the country. Though it is an ancient profession and it was limited to one caste or to a limited society. But under changing economic scenario as well as changing food habits the demand of milk and milk products has increased many fold across the country. Though, there is a vast inequality in per capita availability of milk in India but growing production of milk in India has proved a miles stone in the path of development and it has opened many dimensions of development at several fronts.

India has occupied first position in the production of milk in the world followed by America in second position. The contribution of buffalo, cow and she goat is 50 per cent, 46 per cent, and 4 per cent respectively in the production of milk in India. Agriculture contributes to the GDP to an extent of 25 per cent of which one-fourth is through livestock products.

A growth rate of 4.5 per cent has been achieved by the dairy sector during the past decade as compared to the 2 per cent growth recorded by the agriculture sector as a whole in India. Hence, dairying is an important farming which involves both—large-scale employment and income generation. Over 70 per cent of milk produced in our country is by small, marginal and landless farmers. There are about 100 million farm holdings in our country. Medium and large holdings with a holding size of over 4 hectare account for only 8.8 per cent of the total holdings. 77.4 per cent of farm holdings possess land size less than 2 hectares.

In fact India's milk production began to rise after implementation of "Operation Flood" program since 1970 crossing 30 million tonnes mark in 1980 and 50 million tonnes mark in 1990. In 1998 it was 71 million tonnes which accounts 13 per cent of the world milk production and finally India stood first in the world milk production in 1999 with a production of 77 million tonnes. In India, per capita milk availability per day was 112 gm in 1970 which grew upto 232 gm is 2004-05 due to success of operation flood programme. The recommended requirement of milk is 220 gm per day. But, level of par capita consumption rate varies as compared with the developed nations. In USA, per capita consumption is about 900 gm whereas in India, per capita availably of milk in Punjab, Haryana, North-Eastern states is 800 gm, 640 gm and 20 gm respectively. In our country, about 46 per cent of total milk production is used as liquid milk whereas 28 per cent for making ghee and 12.5 per cent in the use of curd as well as khoa, etc. In addition to above, 6.5 per cent milk is converted in to butter, 3.6 per cent powder and only 3.4 per cent is used for manufacturing cottage and processed cheese, ice-cream and other high value products. India has fixed a target to double the production of milk by 2015 but it is possible only when organized farming in dairying is introduced on large scale.

DAIRYING PRACTICE IN BIHAR

Bihar State Milk Co-operative Federation (COMFED) which is popularly known by its short name, i.e. COMFED has accomplished several commendable jobs for the expansion of dairy practices in Bihar by linking farmers to milk unions and milk unions to COMFED. In fact, COMFED came into existence in 1983 as the implementing agency of 'Operation Flood' programme of dairy development on Anand pattern in the state. Consequently, all operations made by erstwhile Bihar state dairy corporation was handed over to COMFED. The products of COMFED is touching the highest peak in the market under its brand name 'SUDHA'. During 2008-09, there were six legally formed milk unions which coverd at least twenty-six districts of the state while there are some other dairies also which cover some other districts of the state as well as a few districts of Jharkhand state, but these dairies could not form their unions. Hence, these dairies work under direct supervision of COMFED. A significant matter which deserves to be mentioned here is that the state of Jharkhand is also being covered by the COMFED of Bihar till date. Presently the COMFED is working in a systemic manner and it works under three tier work system—(a) Primary Dairy Co-operative Societies working at village level, (b) District union at district level which collect milk of farmers from villages level societies and different identified districts falling under the domain of one district union. This district union takes care for the betterment and advancement of farmers of primary co-operatives societies, (c) COMFED itself at state level federation which is the apex administrative body of state level milk co-operative federations headed by an IAS Officer as Managing Director.The COMFD provides a complete supervision and management as well as guidelines to the district level unions and also to the primary co- operative societies at some occasions. COMFED covers the following district unions and dairies and the districts falling under the Zone of different milk unions and dairies. In fact, district milk unions organize the dairy co-operative societies (DCS) network in the districts which fall under their zone.

COMFED deserves all the credits for hiring very talented and devoted officers and staffs to win over the lost confidence of farmers and to expand the dairy co-operative movement in the State of Bihar. The state government signed the "Operation Flood" agreement with the support of National Dairy Development Board. Though the initial progress was very slow during 1985-86 and there were only 1030 Dairy Co-operatives Societies (DCS) and only 25 thousand milk producers could become the members of these Dairy Co-operatives.

The annual turnover was only Rs. 9.57 crore at that time and there were four prominent milk unions in the state, viz., Vaishal Patliputra Milk Union, Patna, Khagaria, Begusarai, Barauni Milk Union, Barauni, Mithila Milk Union; Samastipur and Tirhut Milk Union, Muzaffarpur, which could be formed during 1987 and 1988. But now the number of organized district milk unions have increased along with some other dairies which are discussed below.

Milk Union	Covered Area
1. Vaishal Patiputra Dugdh Utpadak Sahkari Sangh Ltd. (VPMU), Patna	Patna, Vaishali, Nalanda, Saran and Sheikhpur Districts
2. Desharatna Dr. Rajendra Prasad Dugdh Utpadak Sahkari Sangh Ltd. (DRAMU) Barauni	Begusarai, Khagaria, Lakhisarai and part of Patna Districts.
3. Tirhut Dugdh Utpadak Sahkari Sangh Ltd. (TIMUL), Muzaffarpur	Muzaffarpur, Sitamarhi, Sheohar, E. Champaran, Siwan, Gopalganj and West Champaran Districts.
4. Mithila Dugdh Utpadak Sahkari Sangh Ltd. (MMU), Samastipur	Samastipur, Darbhanga and Madhubani Districts.
5. Shahabad Dugdh Utpadak Sahkari Sangh Ltd. (SMU). Arrah	Bhojpur, Buxar, Kaimur and Rohtas Districts.
6. Vikramshila Dugdh Utpadak Sahkari Sangh Ltd. (VIMUL), Bhagalpur	Bhagalpur, Munger, Banka and Jamui Districts.

Dairies of COMFED	Covered Area
I. Magadh Dairy Project, Gaya Dairy, Gaya	Gaya, Jahanabad, Arwal and Nawadah.
II. Kosi Dairy Project, Purnia Dairy, Purnia	Purnia, Araria, Katihar, Kishanganj, Supaul, Saharsa and Madhepura.
III. Jamshedpur Dairy	East-West Singhbhum and Saraikela.
IV. Ranchi Dairy	Ranchi, Gumla, Lohardagga, Hazaribagh, Simdega and Chatra.
V. Bokaro Dairy	Bokaro, Dhanbad and Giridih.

With the continuous efforts of these milk unions and other dairies there became a large expansion in the co-operative societies which are being depicted under Chart 1.

CHART I

Year-wise Progress of Organization of DCS is Depicted

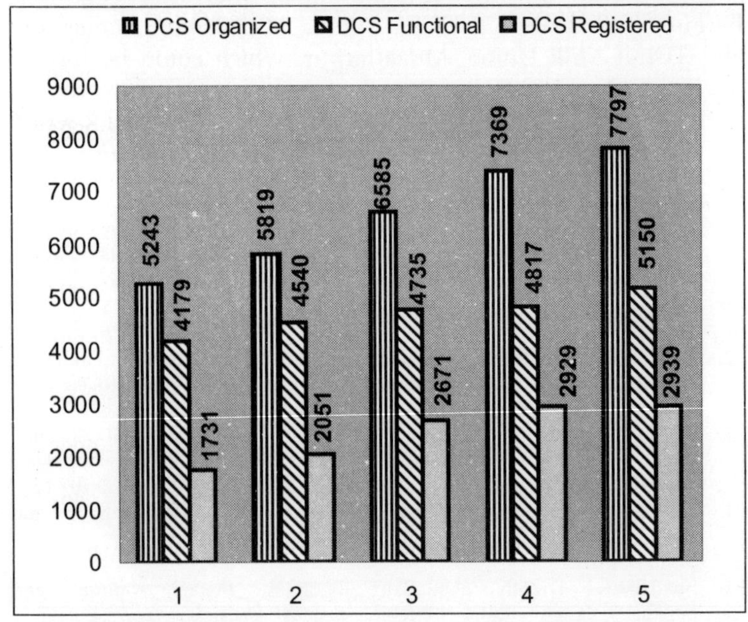

Source: COMFED, Patna.

Till Sept. 2009

The rapid expansion in the organization of DCS involves many important factors which relates to welfare and comfort to the farmers like provision of 100 per cent. Testing of producers milk at DCS, timely and regularly payment to milk producers by every10th day, free supply of milk testing equipment, supervision of DCS by the Field staff and regular visit to DCS even by the bond members of the milk unions, formation of task force for identification of problem areas and subsequently immediate action and timely distribution of fodder seeds as well as cattle feed and finally, overcoming the shortcomings in the delivery system of services to the farmers.

Milk Procurement and COMFED

The COMFED has done a commendable job in procurement of milk since its birth except a few years. The daily average milk procurement during 1994-95 was witnessed an average of 144.33 thousand kgs. per day (TKPD) which has jumped more than 5 times to around 632 TKPD in the year 2008-09. Though the progress was impeded in July-September 2007 and during second half of 2008 due to natural disaster in the form of devastating flood in north Bihar. The flood affected badly to the milk production but with sustained efforts, the milk production has recovered once again and crossed the previous peaks which has been exhibited with the help of Chart 2.

CHART 2

Milk Procurement by COMFED (2008-09)

(Qty. in TKPD)

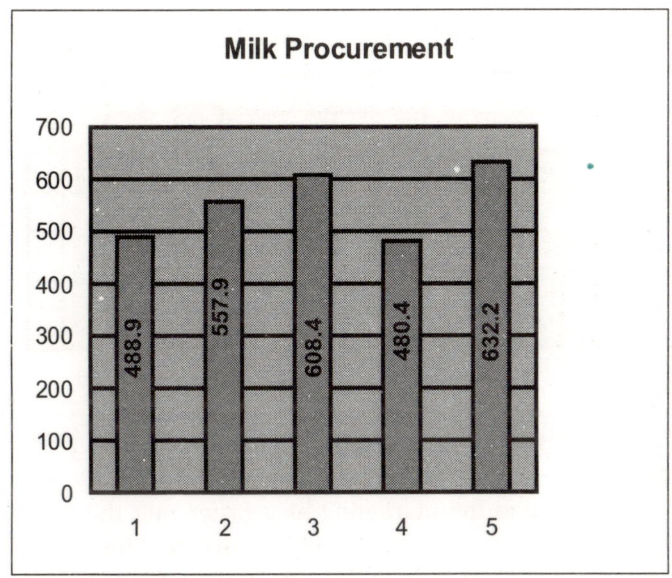

Source: COMFED, Patna.

Till Oct. 2009

Milk Marketing By COMFED

It was experienced during a few years back that liquid milk marketing was one of the neglected areas of business made by COMFED. Progress was very slow during 1987-88 and only

100.55 thousand liters per day sale was observed during this period while there was a slight progress during 1992-93, i.e. 106.54 thousand liters per day (TLPD). However, some strategies for improvement adopted in 1993-94, changed the trend completely in the average marketing of liquid milk and a faster growth rate was observed in the coming years. That is why, year 2003 was celebrated as "market development year" by COMFED and the daily average marketing of liquid milk in 2006-07 was 532.11 TLPD which is a five-fold increase as compared to 1992-93 (106.54 TLPD) This progress of milk marketing can be observed at a glance with help of Chart 3.

CHART 3

Daily Average Milk Marketing

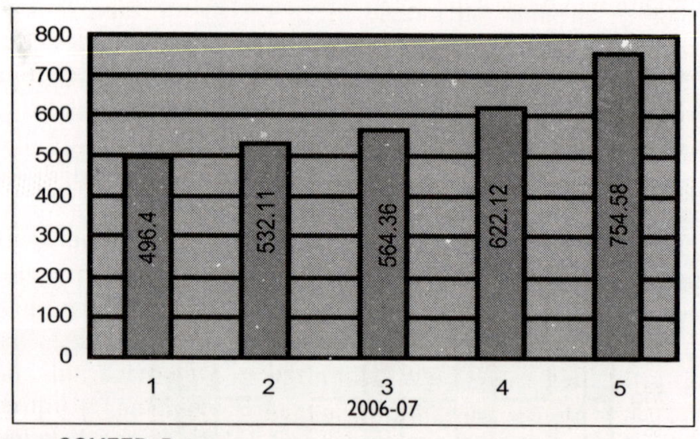

Source: COMFED, Patna.

Till Sept. '09'

To improve the marketing at a faster rate the COMFED adopted certain and steps in form of improvement measure which include strengthening of poor delivery system and reaching close to the consumers by expanding the retail network and establishing new whole day milk booths as well as regular improvement in the quality of milk and milk products, etc.

PERFORMANCE OF PATNA DAIRY PROJECT

Patna Dairy Project is also known as Vaishal Patliputra

Dugdh Utpadak Sahkari Sangh Ltd. (VPMU), Patna which is of one of Milk Union Units of COMFED. There are at present 1257 numbers of functional Dairy Co-operative Societies (DCS) in the areas of PDP covering the district of Patna, Vaishali, Nalanda and fringe areas of Saran with a total membership of 94222. The daily average procurement has reached upto 92824 litre during the year 2008-09. It is being expected that the Project shall collect above one and half lakh litres of milk per day in commencing year. The Patna Dairy Project is proud of 173 number of Women Co-operative Societies exclusively managed and run by women folk. Emphasis is being given to consolidate the functioning of the primary societies by increasing the members' participation and Patna Dairy Project is also trying to increase number of farmers is DSC under its domain.

Different graphs are being presented to show the number of functional societies, number of members, yearly daily average milk procurement and selling and production of different milk product materials at local level by Patna Dairy Project.

PATNA DAIRY PROJECT

FIGURE I

Total No. of Members (In Thousand Number)

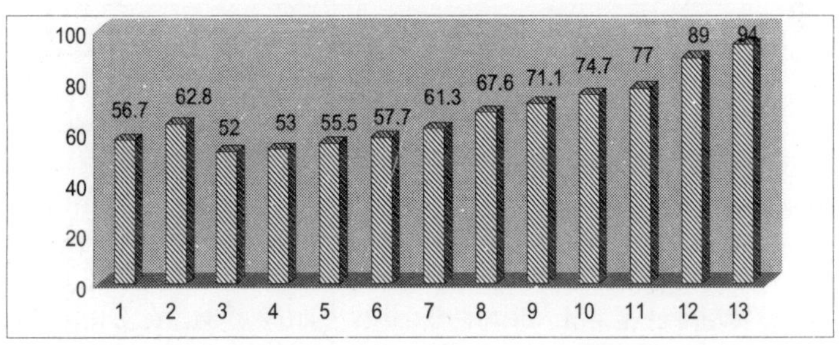

'96 – 97 '97 – 98 '98-99 '99-00 '00-01 '01-02 '02-03 '03-04 '04-05 '05-06 '06 -07 '07-08 '08 -09

Figure 1 clearly shows that total no. of members of Patna City Project was 56.7 thousand in 1996-97 and 55.5 thousand during 2000-01 which grew up to 94 thousand during 2008-09.

Figure 2 gives clear impression that there was 53.16 thousand kilo of milk procurement per day during 1998-99 and 159 thousand kilo during 2006-07 which declined to 92-82 during

PATNA DAIRY PROJECT

FIGURE 2

Milk Procurement (Avg./Day) (In Thousand Kgs.)

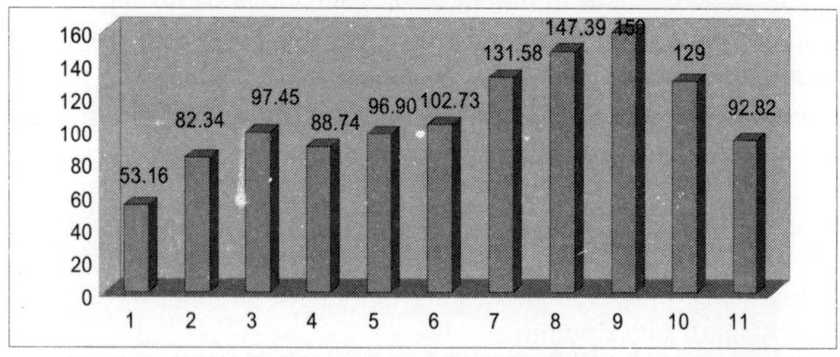

'96 – 97 '97 – 98 '98-99 '99-00 '00-01 '01-02 '02-03 '03-04 '04-05 '05-06 '06 -07 '07-08 '08 -09

2008-09 that clearly shows that Patna Dairy Project could not supply the milk as per demand of people at local level and due to natural disaster the procurement of milk reduced during 2008-09.

PATNA DAIRY PROJECT

FIGURE 3

Local Milk (Avg./Day) (In Thousand Lts.)

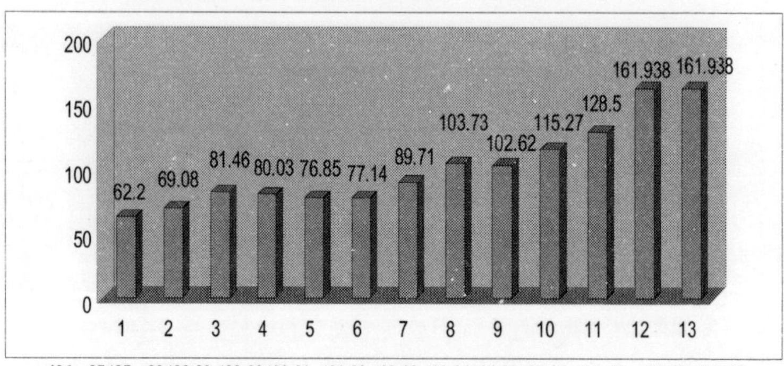

'96 – 97 '97 – 98 '98-99 '99-00 '00-01 '01-02 '02-03 '03-04 '04-05 '05-06 '06 -07 '07-08 '08 -09

Under Figure 3 local milk sell as recorded as 62.2 thousand litres in 1996-97 and 1976-85 thousand during 2000-01 which rose upto 161.938 thousand litres per day during 2000-09. The production and sales of *paneer* has been shows.

PATNA DAIRY PROJECT

FIGURE 4

PANEER (In MTs)

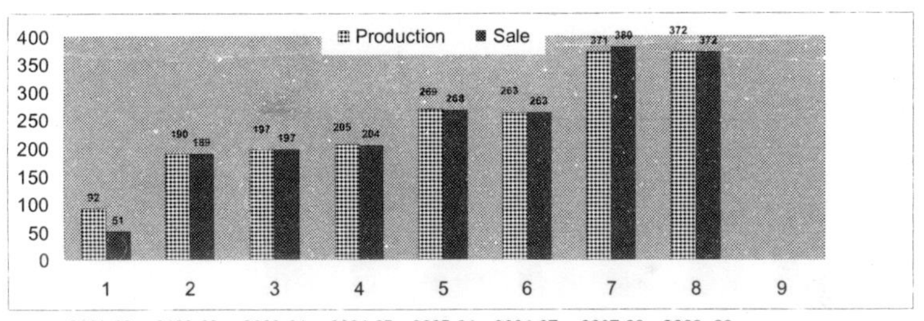

2001-02 2002-03 2003-04 2004-05 2005-06 2006-07 2007-08 2008 -09

Under Figure 4 which is more than three-fold production and sale in 2008-09 compared to 2001-02. During 2001-02, 151 MTs sale was made which grew up to 355 MTs during 2008-09.

PATNA DAIRY PROJECT

FIGURE 5

ICE-CREAM

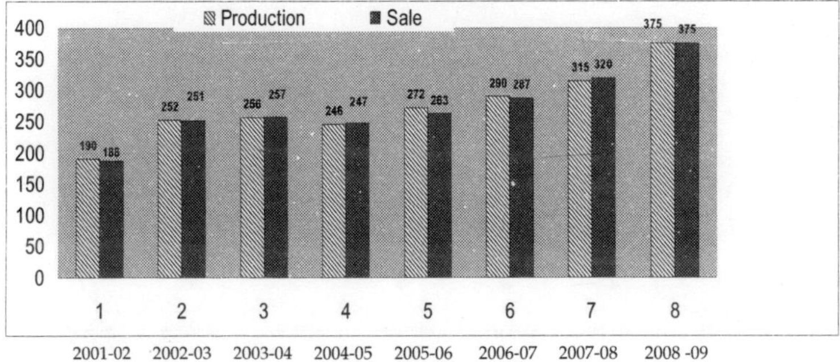

2001-02 2002-03 2003-04 2004-05 2005-06 2006-07 2007-08 2008 -09

Figure 5 shows sale of 188 MTs ice-cream which grew upto 375 MTs during 2008-09. While the sale of Misti Dahi was 68 MTs during 2002-03 which increased to 192 MTs during 2008-09 as has been shown under Figure 4 whereas the sale of Plain Dahi was 25 MTs in 2002-03 which took a 17 times jump during 2008-09 as shown in Figure 7 and at the same time sale of Lassi also

PATNA DAIRY PROJECT

FIGURE 6

ICE-CREAM

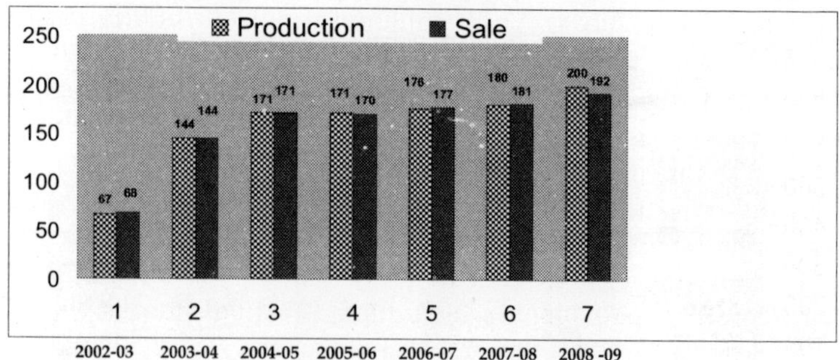

PATNA DAIRY PROJECT

FIGURE 7

PLAIN DAHI (In MTs)

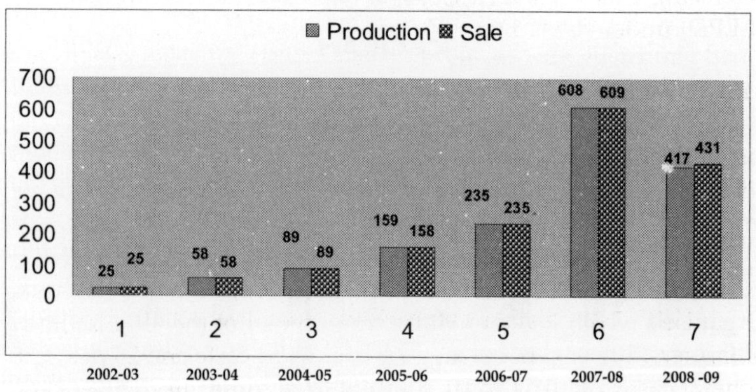

recorded a five times jump which was MTs. During 2003-04 that was increased to 605 MTs during 2008-09.

Hence, we find that the Patna Dairy Project is also performing at the best level which not only centers but milk and milk products heads of local people of Patna but also provides income and employment to the performs involved in the production of milk at village level and procurement of milk and

PATNA DAIRY PROJECT

FIGURE 8

LASSI (In MTs)

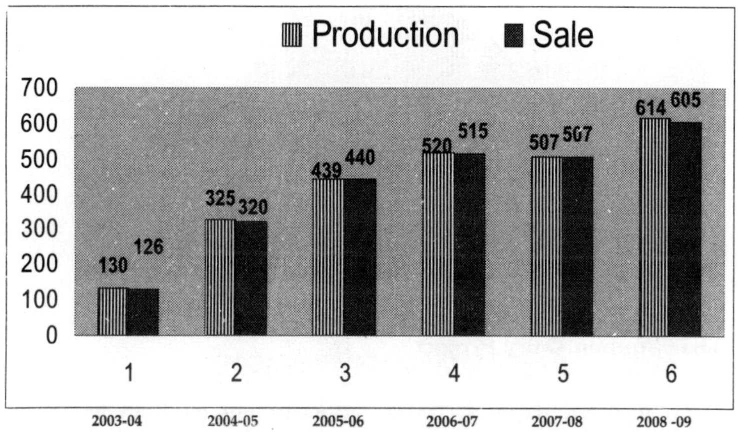

manufacturing of milk products at union level. The feeder Balancing Dairy has a capacity to handle 1.5 lakhs litre per day (LLPD) under Patna Dairy Project.

EMPOWERMENT OF WEAKER SECTION PEOPLE IN BIHAR

Dairy practices has empowered the people of weaker section including women in Bihar. COMFED has played an important role in empowering the rural economy of Bihar by linking members on large scale. By the month of October 2009, near about 7800 Dairy Co-operative Societies (DCS) have been Organised which link to 3.90 lac frames. Out of the total number of farmers, 50 per cent belongs to backward caste and 25 per cent general caste whereas women and SC/ST constitutes 15 per cent and 10 per cent respectively. Therefore, it may easily be concluded that dairying practice in Bihar provides an opportunity of economic empowerment among the people of rural Bihar and specially among the women and the same can be understood with help of figure on next page.

In addition to above, a number of steps have been taken by COMFED to empower people of rural Bihar which includes the followings:

Farmer Members (up 08-09)

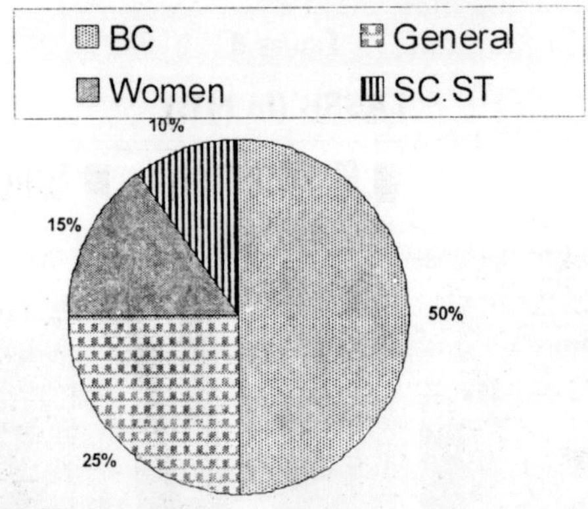

Source: COMFED, Patna.

Bihar Women Dairy Project

Bihar Women Dairy Project (BWDP), a project of women empowerment through dairy development exclusively for the rural women was implemented by COMFED with financial assistance from the department of women and child development. The project was launched in 1987. During its initial stage it was financially supported by Ford foundation also. Presently there are at least 550 Women Dairy Co-operatives Societies with a women membership of 43000. Apart from dairy activities women are being empowered by other activities also which constitutes training and skill enhancement, leadership development quality, awareness generation programme among women, legal rights of women through different training programmers are the major components. Child development as well as nutrition and knowledge regarding hygiene are also the important factors of women empowerment through COMFED. SHGs were also constituted which provides training to the women in the field of tailoring, vegetable production, saving programme as well as family planning, rural health mission programme and vaccination of children.

Rashtriya Krishi Vikas Yojanas

Under Rashtriya Krishi Vikas Yojans, a sum of Rs. 335.22 lakh was sanctioned by state government under financial year 2008-09. Under the same Yojanas (RKVYs) a sum of Rs. 26.97

crore was also sanctioned for Des Origination, establishment of a centre strengthening of dairy plants, capacity building of farmers, setting up of bulk milk cooler in the villages, etc. Apart from the above efforts, the State government has released Rs. 49.54 crore for ongoing Projects at Bihar Sharif, establishment of dairy plant at Dehri-on-sone and establishment of breeding units.

Distribution of Milk Animals to the Economically Weaker Members of Dairy Co-operatives

The Bihar state SC/ST/BC Finance and Development Corporations have sanctioned fund for the distribution of milch animals, especially the cross-breed cows for distribution to the Scheduled Caste/Backward Caste members in the dairy Co-operative Societies.

CONCLUSION

On the basis of above discussions we find that Dairy Practices in Bihar under the able management of COMFED in general and Patna Dairy Project in Particular performing very well at three fronts—Catering the needs of people, employment among rural people including women as well as income generation. Hence, the dairy practice deserves more expansion in Bihar State and for which government's initiative is essential with strong will power.

REFERENCES

Arora, V.P.S., Bhogal, T.S. and Biswas, P.G. (1998), "Milk Marketing in North-West U.P. and the role of Co-operative: A Temporal Analysis". Vol. XXXVI, No. 1, pp. 70-77.

Balaraman, Dr. N. "Need for Organized Production", The Hindu Survey of Indian Agriculture, 2005, pp. 141-42.

COMFED, Patna (Bihar) Status Report, 2008-09.

Singh, R.K.P. and Choudhary, A.K. (1999), 'Dairy Development through Co-operative, The Spell Bound Publishers Ltd., Rohtak, Haryana.

Singh, Virendra Rai, K.N. and Singh, V. (1998), "Economics of Production and Marketing of Buffalo Milk in Haryana", *Indian Journal of Agriculture Economics*, Vol. LIIV, No. 1, pp. 41-52.

Soveer and Singh, Pradesh (2004), *The Bihar Journal of Agricultural Markeing*, Vol. XII, January-March 2004, No. 1.

Review of Returns on Investment in Agro-Processing Units: A Case Study of Central Public Sector Agro-Processing Industries

RATNESH KUMAR

The growth of agro-processing industries in India which is proeminently an agricultural region endowed with abundant natural resources and a wealth of traditional skills for production of large variety of agricultural and horticultural crops is of paramount importance for rapid economic development of the nation. The region occupies a pre-eminent position in respect of several food and commercial crops, such as paddy, maize, groundnut, sugarcane, chillies, mangoes, several vegetables, cotton, tobacco, etc.

Apart from the possibility of setting up resource-based agro-industries, India has got a vast scope for the development of subsidiary industries related to and depending on agriculture in a large measure, such as dairying, livestock, meat and poultry industries.

Properly conceived, carefully planned and imaginatively

implemented, rural industries complexes can be set-up, which can be an answer to the problem of mass unemployment, backwardness and under development in rural areas, to regional imbalance in industrial development, and to congestion and pollution around cities.

The economic prosperity depends upon the development of agriculture as well as industry. Hence, their interdependence and integration is an adjunct for prosperity. The strategy of economic growth has to be such that it integrates rural and urban economics by reducing economic disparity and regional imbalances. Agro-industries are being used to promote employment opportunities to the surplus labourers and they also engage farmers in productive use during the off-season. Thus, further growth in agriculture is materially dependent on a swift increase in the production of agro-input industries. The endeavour of this paper is to measure the relative share of various cost items in the production of agro-processing industries and also to examine the feedback effect of agro-processing industries production on agriculture.

The hypothesis for the above objective is as follows: The relative importance or percentage share of raw material as compared to other factors like wages, fuels, power, etc. increases with the increase in agro-industrial production. Hence the demand for raw material increases and there takes place a shift of land resources from the low-value-yielding crops to high-value-yielding crops. Also the land productivity or yield per acre/ hectare increases and the quality of agricultural product is improved.

Over the period, the land productivity has increased in the case of both traditional (low-value-yielding) crops and commercial (high-value-yielding) crops. The reasons which may be attributed to the increase in productivity of rice, pulses, mustard, cotton and potato are manifold. Foremost is the adoption of modern agricultural practice by the farmers. It has been found that the quality improvement has taken place in the case of rice, oilseeds and pulses. The reason for this is the adoption of modern agricultural practices including the use of high-yielding varieties of seeds.

Though the Plan Documents and Industrial Policy Resolutions have laid stress on decentralisation of industries by the promotion of agro-processing small-scale Industrial units, rapid strides could not be made on this front. The large scale industrial units came to be concentrated in urban centres and even the modern small-scale industrial units (including ancilliary industries) that obviously depend upon the large units tended to concentrate in urban areas and metropolitan cities. One of the conceivable measures through which decentralisation of industrial activity can be achieved, is the promotion of agro-processing industrial units. The setting up of agro-processing industrial units is advocated by economists on more than one ground. The existing unemployed and underemployed rural population can be fully employed. The migration of rural population to urban centres can be prevented. The locally available resources—human and natural—can be utilised for the improvement of the income levels of the village economy. These are the virtues that merit the location of agro-processing industries in rural areas which, in course of time, make it self-sustaining with improved position of saving and investments.

The employment pattern of agro-processing industries reveals that the employment opportunities created by these industries differed from one industry to another, depending upon the nature of the agro-based industry. While some industries provide larger permanent employment, some other create seasonal employment. The composition of employment (i.e., white collar, skilled and unskilled) depended largely upon the nature of the agro-processing industry and the level of technology employed in it. A study reveals that while unskilled workers constituted a great majority in the Oil Mill (i.e., 78.89%), skilled and semi-skilled workers together accounted for highest per cent in Sugar Mill (i.e., 61.6%). The setting up of agro-processing industries brings about changes in the cropping pattern of the nearby villages where they are established.

The impact of agro-processing industries on rural employment may be studied in terms of—

(i) The direct employment created in the agro-processing industrial units;

(ii) The indirect employment generated in the farm sector in the wake of the setting up of the agro-processing industries.

It has been found that the nature of employment in agro-processing industries has been diverse, depending upon the nature of the agro-processing industries. Some of the agro-processing industries may develop following the availability of the irrigation facility and the changes in the cropping pattern. Generally speaking, the changes in the cropping pattern and the setting up of agro-processing industries go hand in hand. Given the supply of the necessary inputs (i.e., water, chemical fertilizers, pesticides, developed seeds, etc.) and the suitability of the soil, agro-processing industries can induce shifts in the cropping pattern.

The impact of agro-processing industries on rural wage structure has been significant. The setting up of agro-processing industries in or around rural areas influenced the wage levels and occupational structure of the workers in rural areas. The increase in wages is more pronounced in the case of female and children than in that of male workers. In other words, the decrease in the wage differentials among male, female and child workers has been spectacular in the agricultural sector.

The "harvesting and thrashing" operation is the highest paid in the villages associated with agro-processing industries. "Ploughing" takes the next position and "sowing, weeding and transplantation" are the lowest paid types of work. A comparison of the wages of agricultural workers with the wages of unskilled workers employed in agro-processing industries shows that the wages of unskilled workers, which are the lowest in agro-processing industries, are perceptibly higher than the highest wage in agriculture.

The impact of agro-processing industries on the rural wage structure has been two-fold—direct and indirect. First, the agro-processing industries employ agricultural workers for their unskilled operations and are paying much higher wages than the wages paid in agriculture. This has been the direct impact on the wage levels of agricultural workers and their earning capacity. Secondly, the agro-processing industries generate a pressure of demand for agricultural workers, because they create additional employment in the farm sector by the cultivation of agro-processing industrial crops on the one hand, and draw a considerable number of workers from the existing agricultural labour force of the villages on the other. Consequently, there has been a substantial increase in the wage rates for agricultural operations.

The setting up of agro-processing industries in rural areas will give impetus to the growth of tertiary sector, viz., banking, transport, communication, hotel business, etc. The setting up of agro-processing industries will result in the emergence of growth centres. Further, due to transportation required for raw materials to the industries, the tertiary sector, such as workshops, hotels, restaurants, cinema houses, etc. will develop. The development of the tertiary sector, in the places where the industrial units may be established will provide further employment opportunities for the rural population. It is no exaggeration to say that the growth of agro-processing industries will generate employment opportunities for the educated and skilled people in the secondary and tertiary sectors. The seasonal movement to other places for employment will almost cease after setting upon agro-processing industries.

Studies of household expenditure show that non-food items have an increasing share in the budget of rural households as rural incomes increase. A report of the International Labour Organization on the employment has observed: Studies in the district where improvements in rice production have taken place in the past five or six years, show that substantial proportions of farm households have improved their houses, built new ones, and purchased household furnishings and equipment. Change came not only in quantity but also in the quality of the items acquired. The expenditure on education, food, farm tools and equipment and transport also increased. The consumption potential in rural areas is sizable and easily stimulated when incomes rise.

Likewise, the demand for non-food goods and services increase when agricultural output increases. The demand stems from both backward and forward linkages with agriculture. The former includes demands for tools and equipment, repairs and supply services, buildings, and works; the latter includes processing, transport and the marketing of output. Besides the markets generated by agricultural development, external markets for manufactured goods and handicrafts from rural areas can be a source of employment. An adequate rural infrastructure offers manufacturers ready access to the rural labour market, materials and services. This indicates that agricultural development cannot be considered in isolation; it requires continual improvement in infrastructure. Moreover, it is a positive stimulus to the development and the growth and role of rural towns, the latter being the consequences of the development of agro-processing industries in rural areas.

1. As on 31.3.2008, there were 4 Central public sector enterprises in the agro-processing industries group. The names of these enterprises along with their year of incorporation in chronological order are given below.
2. The enterprises falling in this group are mainly engaged in producing and selling of Agro-processing Products including the activities such as forestry, growing of rubber plants, red palm trees, etc.
3. The consolidated financial position, the working results and the important management ratios of these enterprises are appended.

A & N Islands Forest and Plantation Dev. Corp. Ltd. (ANIFPDC): ANIFPDC was incorporated on 21st January, 1977 under the Companies Act, 1956 with the main objective of scientific harvesting, natural regeneration and development of forest resources on the principle of sustained yield. The company was established as per the recommendations of the National Commission on Agriculture 1972. ANIFPDC is a Schedule—'C' PSE in Agro-processing Industries sector under the administrative control of M/o Environment and Forests, Department of Forest with 100 per cent shareholding by the Government of India. Its Registered and Corporate offices are at Port Blair, Andaman and Nicobar.

ANIFPDC is engaged in forestry operation, cultivation and marketing of Red Oil Palm and Rubber Plantation. The company has four operating units viz. Forestry Divisions (one each at Little Andaman and North Andaman). Oil Palm Division at Hut Bay, Little Andaman and Rubber Division at Katchal.

The performance details of production of Crude Palm Oil and Rubber are mentioned below:

The performance of the company during 2007-08 remained unsatisfactory on both the fronts, i.e. physical and financial. The enterprise employed 1549 regular employees (executives 26, non-unionized supervisors 5, unionized supervisors 362 and workmen 1156) as on 31.3.2008. 0.65 per cent employees had professional qualifications. 44.22 per cent employees belonged to the age group of 51 and above years. The retirement age in the company is 60 years. It is following IDA 1997 and CDA 1996 patterns of pay scales. During 2007-08, 27 employees retired on attaining the age of superannuation and 2 skilled and 7 unskilled persons left the company in attrition.

ANIFPDC owns a gross area of 1593 hectares of Red Oil Palm estate at Little Andaman along with a processing unit with a capacity of 4 MT FFB per hour. The production capacity of Crude Palm Oil is around 1400 MT per annum. The gross area of Rubber estate at Katchal is 614 hectares. Expansion of these projects is constrained due to the restriction imposed under the National Forest Policy, 1988 on replacement of Natural Forest with monoculture man-made plantation.

The forestry operations at both the divisions of ANIFPDC have been completely stopped due to the ban imposed by the Supreme Court of India vide its order dated 10th October, 2001 on felling naturally grown trees from the forest of Andaman and Nicobar.

National Seeds Corporation Ltd. (NSC): NSC was incorporated on 19.3.1963 under the Companies Act, 1956 with the objective to promote and develop seed industry in the country and to contribute to the prosperity of farmers through supply of quality seeds and other agro-inputs/services as well as to enhance agricultural productivity. NSC is a Schedule – 'C' CPSE in Agro-processing Industries sector under the administrative control of M/o Agriculture, D/o Agriculture and Cooperation with 100 per cent shareholding by the Government of India. Its Registered and Corporate offices are at New Delhi.

NSC is involved in production and marketing of quality seeds, planting materials and sale of Biofertilizer through its three farms located at Bangalore (Karnataka), Nandikottur (Andhra Pradesh) and Kullu (Himachal Pradesh) and 12 Regional Offices and 76 Area offices spread all over India.

Advent of NSC was a logical result of the revolution that was taking place in plant breeding and genetics. At the time, when the nation was facing acute shortage of foodgrains, NSC became harbinger of Green Revolution. As a result, India became a foodgrain surplus country from one depending on wheat grain shipments from USA under PL–480 Scheme. Starting with production of 30-40 tonnes of Maize Foundation Seed, NSC today produces more than 80,000 tonnes of Certified/Quality seeds per year covering 800 varieties of 80 crops and Hybrids of cereals, millets, pulses, oilseeds, fodder, fiber and vegetables. The brief details of production of seeds are as follows:

During the year 2007-08, turnover and net profit increased by 44.6 per cent and 71.06 per cent as compared to 2006-07. Increase in turnover and profitability of NSC is attributed to decrease in human resources' cost increase in productivity (sale per employee), reduction in expenditure, technology change and ISO certification, etc. The market share of the company was 6.19 per cent during 2007-08 as compared to 5 per cent in the previous year. The earning per scheme (EPS) of the company, during 2007-08 was Rs. 1103 as against Rs. 633 in previous year.

The enterprise employed 664 regular employees (executives 239 and non-executives 425) as on 31.3.2008 as against 712 employees as on 31.3.2007. About 5.42 per cent employees were having professional qualifications and around 56 per cent employees come under the age bracket of 51 and above years. Average age of the employees was 51 years. Retirement age in the company is 60 years. It is following IDA 1997 and CDA 1996 pattern of remuneration. A total of 45 employees retired during the year and two employees joined the company. During the year, 203 employees were identified as surplus manpower, 37 employees availed of VRS and an amount of Rs. 0.65 crore was spent in this regard from internal resources. Since the introduction of VRS in 1992, total 925 employees have retired under the scheme. The total number of Directors in the company, as on 31.3.2008 was 4, out of which 2 were part-time Non-official Directors/professionals and one each full-time functional Director and Government/ Official Director.

The company is moving towards production and marketing of non-cereals, more hybrids, potato seed tubers and distribution of planting materials/plantlets. It has initiated establishment of tissue culture unit.

North-Eastern Regional Agricultural Marketing Corporation Limited (NERAMAC): NERAMAC was incorporated in the year 1982 under the Companies Act, 1956 with the main objective to manufacture, process, market, transport, distribute and promote the horticulture products and other related articles/ agro-products and to function as agents of the Government Cooperatives, Cooperations or any other agencies in the North-Eastern Region. NERAMAC is a Schedule "B"/BIFR referred CPSE in Agro-Processed Industries sector under the administrative control of Ministry of Development of North-Eastern Region with 100 per cent shareholding by the Government of India. Its Registered and Corporate Offices are at Guwahati, Assam, BIFR declared the company 'no longer sick' on its net-worth becoming positive.

NERAMAC is mainly involved in trading and marketing activities along with production of Agro-products like fruit juice, cashew nut, ginger, etc. through its 3 operating units at Nalkata, Agartala (Tripura) and Byrnihat (Meghalaya). Besides Registered/Head Office, it has 5 Zonal Offices in Assam, Tripura, Meghalaya, Nagaland and Sikkim, 2 sales outlets at Guwahati and Agartala and one Franchise outlet at Guwahati.

NERAMAC improved the production of Pineapple by about 74 per cent and that of Cashewnut by about 41 per cent during 2007-08 as compared to last year. The company turned to profit from loss in previous year and resulting in positive net worth during 2007-08, by improving its turnover by about 98 per cent and profitability by 102 per cent over the figures of last year.

The enterprise employed 120 regular employees (executives 7 and non-executives 113) as on 31.3.2008. Around 2.5 per cent employees were having professional qualifications and around 33.33 per cent employees were in the age bracket of 51 and above years. Average age of the employees in the company was 40 years. The retirement age in the company is 60 years. It is following both the IDA 1997 and The CDA 1996 patterns of remuneration. One employee retired during the year on attaining the age of superannuation and 10 employees availed of VRS during the year. Since introduction of VRS in 1994 total 29 employees have availed of the scheme.

The corporation owns 1.64 bighas of lands under Kailashahar sub-division, Tripura, 4000 sq. m. plot by Byrnihat, Meghalaya and 1.54 Bighas land under district Kamrup, Assam. These were allotted free of cost by the State Governments of

Tripura, Maghalaya and Assam respectively. The value of these properties has been taken as 'nil' in the books of the company. The company received plan assistance of Rs. 1.37 crore as loan during 2007-08.

State Farm Corporation of India Ltd. (SFCI): SFCI was incorporated in May, 1969 under the Companies Act, 1956 with the objective to maintain Central Government's Agriculture Farms in different states for production and distribution of quality seeds of different crops. SFCI is a Schedule 'C' CPSE in Agro-processed Industries sector under the administrative control of M/o Agriculture, D/o Agriculture and Co-operation with 100 per cent shareholding by the Government of India. Its Registered and Corporate offices are in New Delhi.

SFCI is maintaining 6 centre-state farms for production of Test stocks, Breeder, Foundation and certified seeds of different crops. The company also undertakes activities like plantation and maintenance of fruit crops, multiplication of quality seeding of Horticultural crops, production of vegetable seeds, cultivation of Bio-fuel and Medicinal plants and forestry plantations on wastelands. The land under possession at these 6 farms is 25736 hectares out of which cultivable land is 19616 hectares. Central Government owns 4 Farms at Suratgarh, Sardargarh and Jetsur in Rajasthan and one in Raichur, Karnataka; other 2 farms are in Hisar, Haryana and Bahraich in U.P. and on lease from respective State Government.

The product range of the company comprises of paddy, cotton, pulses, wheat, etc. The performance details of seed production for different crops are as follows:

Turnover of the company increased by 47.20 per cent during 2007-08 as compared to previous year. The company turned to profit-making during 2006-07 from loss incurring in the earlier years. The increase in turnover and profitability is attributed to effective control on product mix of crops, increase in cultivable area, improvement in productivity and cost control measures.

The enterprise employed 1965 regular employees (executives 293 and non-executives 1672) as on 31.3.2008 as against 1983 employees as on 31.3.2007. 1.27 per cent employees were having professional qualifications and around 32.16 per cent employees come under the age bracket of 51 and above years.

The retirement age in the company is 60 years. It is following IDA 1997 pattern of remuneration. A total of 12 employees retired during the year. In addition, 2 skilled employees also left the company in attrition. However, 6 new skilled employees joined. During the year, 7 employees availed of VRS and an amount of Rs. 0.19 crore was spent in this regard through internal resources. The total number of Directors in the company as on 31.3.2008 was 4, out of which 2 were part time Non-official Directors/ professionls and one each full time functional Director and Government/Official Director.

SFCI has been appointed by the Government of India (GoI) as a Nodal Agency to maintain the Foundation Seed Bank. It has also been assigned the job of popularizing new high yielding varieties of seeds for distributing the same among farmers. Growers Seed Production programme is being taken up in new areas of the country mainly where company's Farms are not located.

The company was referred to BRPSE which recommended a revival plan comprising capital investment of Rs. 37.63 crore and concessions like conversion of loan into equity and waiver of penal changes, etc. The revival plan was approved by the Government of India on 3.1.2008, and is under implementation.

In view of the impact of the selected agro-processing industries on the rural economy, the following suggestions and recommendations may be made for the policy-makers. The agro-processing industries are the cornerstone of development because they strike deep roots in indigenous economic environment. It is necessary therefore, that at least an important part of the developmental effort should bypass the big cities and be directly concerned with the creation of an 'agro-industrial structure' in rural and small town areas. For a poor man, the chance to work is one of two greater needs and even poorly paid and relatively unproductive work is better than idleness. Thus, the solution of unemployment by agro-processing industries can be made in rural areas.

Despite the fact that agro-processing industries occupied a predominant position in the industrial structure of the state, they did not keep pace with the all-industry average growth rate, whether in terms of employment, productive capital or value-added. In the context of the need for rapid industrialization and for balanced regional development, the role of State Government in development of agro-processing industries is pivotal.

As India is considered "industrially backward", the State should follow two broad objectives to ensure the development of the maximum number of industries based on agricultural products. First, all the agricultural products which are used as raw materials for the industries should be utilized to the maximum possible extent within the State, because agricultural raw materials are not only a strong factor for the location of these industries by reason of their bulky nature, they would create many indirect and secondary benefits through a chain of varied industries based on each product. Moreover, it is necessary to coordinate the plans and activities of agriculture and industry to take the maximum advantage of the State's strong agricultural base.

In this connection, it may be pointed out that the development of the agro-processing industries depends mostly on regular and adequate supplies of raw-materials of good quality and the agricultural sector should manage to supply the maximum amount of industrial raw materials, without disturbing the advantageous position which the whole country now enjoys in foodgrains. In this connection, it is imperative to note that the improvement in the quality of agricultural and agro-industrial crops depends upon various factors, viz., irrigation facilities, loan facilities and supply of modern agricultural equipment (such as tractors, H.Y.V. seeds, chemical fertilizers, etc.). So the Government should provide all sorts of infrastructural facilities to the farmers, particularly to those growing agro-industrial crops. To sum up, it can be argued that appropriate schemes should not only be made for crop diversification in order to develop more industries, but also efforts should be made for the development of industries which will strengthen agricultural base.

References

Aggarwal K.P. (1997), "Agriculture-Industry Inter-Relations", *Agriculture and Agro-Industries Journal*, Vol. 10, No. 3, March.

Arvind, M. Mafatlal (1975), What can Industry Do for Rural Development", *Kurukshetra*, June 1, p. 7.

Bala Subramanyam, R.C. and Potty, V.V.H. (1996), "Potential Areas for

Investment in Agro-based Industries", *Journal of Ministry of Trade*, Vol. 26, No. 9, September.

Basu, S.N. (1999), "Role of Forestry and Forest-Based Industries Linkage", *Indian Journal of Agricultural Economics*, Vol. XXXIV, No. 4, 21 October-December.

Bhargava, H.G. (1971), "Rural Development Through Agro-Industrial Centres", *Kurukshetra*, Vol. 19, No. 11, March 1.

Fronda, N.M. (2001), "India's Rural Development; In Assessment of Alternatives", *Economic and Political Weekly*, XVI, No. 142, January 3-10.

Gautam, M.S. (2002), "Some Aspects of Fruits and Vegetable Processing Industry in India", *Indian Journal of Agricultural Economics*, Annual Number.

Iqbal, A.B., "Agro-Industries Key to Economic Prosperity", *Khadi Gramodyog*, Vol. 21, No. 10.

Kamala, G.V. and Khot, S.M., "Policy Vacuum in Agro-Processing Industries", *Indian Journal of Agricultural Economics*, Vol. 27, No. 2.

Mitra, G.R., "Accelerated Technology and Reorientation of Our Agro-Industries", *Khadi Gramodyog*, Vol. 18, No. 10.

Ojha, G., "Agro_Industries and Planning for Economic Growth", *Khadi Gramodyog*, Vol. 18, No. 1

Pillai, K.M., "Proceedings of Technical Seminar: Development of Agro-Industries and Standardisation", *I.S.I. Bulletin*, Vol. 24, No. 6.

Sinha, P.N., "Scope for Agro-Based Industries", *Commerce*, Vol. 127, No. 3263.

Thakur, S.N. (1985), Rural Industrialisation in India: Strategy and Approach, Sterling Publishers, Jalandhar.

Economic Security against Rising Risks in Agriculture and Allied Sectors

Anjana Kumari

Agriculture contributes the biggest proportion to Indian National Income and rural areas account for the bulk of the country's population. Many economic problems, therefore, lie in agriculture and rural areas. For solving these problems various efforts have been made for several decades in the past and they have to be continued to be made for several decades in future. Provision of adequate, timely and cheap finance is an important problem for the development of agriculture and allied activities.

Agriculture is a productive occupation; as such one of the essentials of agricultural production is capital. This may be provided by the cultivator himself or like any other businessman, he may borrow it from some one else and repay it from the output of the field in which it has been invested. The problem of agricultural finance relates to (i) capital needs of the farmer, (ii) agencies of credit, and (iii) the repayment of loans. Thus the All India Rural Credit Survey Committee observed that Agricultural Credit is a problem when it cannot be obtained: it is also a problem when it can be had but in such a form that on the whole it does more harm than good. It may be said that, in India, it is this two-fold problem of inadequacy and unsuitability that is perennially presented by agricultural credit. Undoubtedly, an Indian farmer is not able to make the maximum use of his time, labour and productive capacity of his land because of the lack of adequate financial facilities.

Agriculture and allied sectors are considered to be the mainstay of the Indian economy. They contribute nearly 18 per cent to gross domestic product of India. About 65.70 per cent of the population is dependent on agriculture for their livelihood. The various components of allied agricultural activities are horticulture, dairy, poultry, fisheries, piggery, mushroom cultivation (agriculture), apiculture, sericulture, etc. Since these allied activities are more capital intensive so there is scope for increasing the credit in investment portfolio. All these are regarded as the essential ingredients of economic security.

'Horticulture and allied' sector is an integral element for food and nutritional security in the country. Horticulture is the main segment, while its various sub-segments are fruits, vegetables, aromatic and herbal plants, flowers, spices and plantation crops. Horticultural crops occupy around 10 per cent of the gross crop area of country producing 160.75 million tonnes. India is the second largest producer of fruits and vegetables in the world after China. It contributes about 22 per cent to the agricultural GDP.

Dairy

India is the top most milk producing country in the world. The livestock industry of India contributes to 8 per cent of the GDP, whereas 32 per cent of the GDP contribution from the agricultural industry comes from the livestock itself. A sustainable and financially viable livestock farming, which will generate wealth and self-employment through entrepreneurship, is the need of the day.

Poultry industry has been one of the key contributors within the livestock Sector. With annual production of 50.7 billion eggs, India become 5th largest egg producing country. It also produces 530 million broilers per year. This sector contributes 2.5 per cent to the GDP and provides employment to 1.5 million people.

Fishery is recognized as sunshine sector in Indian

agriculture. At present, India's total annual fish production is about 6.87 million tonnes. Major fish producing states are West Bengal, U.P., A.P., and Rajasthan. Constituting about 4.4 per cent of the global fish production, the sector contributes to 1.1 per cent of the GDP and 5.3 per cent of the agricultural GDP. It contributes to 3 per cent of the total export and 20 per cent of the agricultural exports of country.

Sericulture

Silk is a way of life in India. Sericulture refers to the mass scale rearing of silk producing organisms in order to obtain silk. India is ranked as the second major raw silk producer in the world. It contributes about 18 per cent to the total world raw silk production.

Mushroom cultivation is mushrooming in India now. The country's total output of cultivated mushroom was over 100,000 tonnes in 2007 from a mere 5000 tonnes in 1990. Major states which possess good potential for mushroom cultivation on small as well as industrial scale include Orissa, Andhra Pradesh, Karnataka, Haryana, Madhya Pradesh, Jammu and Kashmir and Uttar Pradesh.

Piggery

Among the various livestock species, piggery is most potential source of meat production and more efficient feed converters after the broiler. Apart from providing meat, it is also a source of bristles and manure. Pig farming will provide employment opportunities to seasonally employed rural farmers and supplementary income to improve their living standards. The major potential area is North Line—Eastern region. The contribution of pork products in terms of value works out to 0.80 per cent of total livestock products and 4.32 per cent of the meat and meat products.

Per cent share of agriculture and allied exports in national exports were 14.22 per cent in 2002 while it came down to 12.07 per cent in 2007.

Over the year, the gross capital formation in agriculture and allied sectors as a per cent of GDP has shown a fluctuating trend between 1999-2000 to 2007-08. It increased from 11.20 per cent in 1999-2000 to 12.68 per cent in 2002-03 and thereafter declined to 11.98 per cent in 2004-05. It again increased to 13.88 per cent in 2007-08.

For the purpose of providing economic security and to cover different rising risks in agriculture and other allied activities a new Company namely "Agricultural Insurance Company of India Limited" (AICIL) was registered under the Companies Act, 1956 with equity participation from NABARD, General Insurance Corporation of India and its four erstwhile subsidiary companies. It has a paid up share capital of Rs. 200 crores. It has been set-up with the objective to exclusively implement various crop insurance schemes (and products and other allied agricultural insurance business) in India. The assets and liabilities of Central Crop Insurance Department (CCID), Delhi were transferred to the new company with effect from 1.4.2003.

The company enjoys the distinction of being the largest crop insurance provider in the world in terms of the number of farmers insured annually. During 2007-08, the Scheme insured around 184 lakh farmers constituting 15 per cent of the total farm holdings in the country.

The main product, i.e. "National Agricultural Insurance Scheme" (NAIS) is presently implemented by 24 States and 2 Union Territories. Since the inception of the scheme and until rabi 2007-08 about 1155 lakh farmers have been covered. The coverage area is 184 million ha and the sum insured is Rs. 1,21,606 crore. Claims to the tune of about Rs. 11,607 crore have been reported against the premium income of about Rs. 3,626 crore benefiting nearly 302 lakh farmers. The Company is making efforts to bring the remaining States/UTs into the fold of NAIS.

The Honourable Union Finance Minister while presenting the Budget for 2007-08 announced Weather Based Crop Insurance Scheme (WBCIS) as a pilot scheme in a few States as an alternative to the NAIS. The Scheme operates on an actuarial basis with an element of subsidy from Union and State Governments.

AICL launched the pilot scheme on Weather Based Crop Insurance Scheme (WBCIS) during Kharif 2007 season in Karnataka for eight crops. About 50,000 hectares of crops were insured for a risk value of Rs. 53 crore with a premium of Rs. 7.03 crore under the scheme, out of which the farmers' share of premium was Rs. 1.42 crore. The remaining premium of Rs. 5.61 crore was subsidized by the Central and State Governments equally. Payouts amounting to Rs. 5.24 crore were settled promptly.

For Rabi 2007-08, AICL implemented this pilot scheme in 4 States, viz. Bihar, Chhattisgarh, Madhya Pradesh and Rajasthan. In all, the pilot scheme was implemented in about 120 Tehsils/Blocks of 22 Districts for the major crops and covered about 6.27 lakh farmers growing crops in over 9.84 lakh hectares against a sum insured of Rs. 1,705 crore, with a gross premium of Rs. 139 crore, of which the farmers' share of premium was Rs. 43 crore. The remaining premium of Rs. 96 crore was subsidized by the Central and State Governments equally. Total claims for this season has been worked out to Rs. 101 crores. The Gross Direct Premium of the Company is Rs. 835.00 crore which includes 150.74 crore from non-NAIS products.

The net worth of the company stood at Rs. 523 crore during 2007-08 while net incurred claims during the year was Rs. 530 crore. During the year 2007-08, the Company focused on developing its distribution channels through utilizing the services of NGOs, Self-Help Groups (SHGs) and Micro Insurance Agents to expand the Company's operations in rural areas.

Reaching out to the poorest and the remotest farmers has always been a challenge to the company. To this end, the Company has undertaken various intensive awareness and publicity activities, both direct and indirect. A number of awareness workshops were organized at the State and District levels where farmers, bank officials, district level government functionaries and others were briefed about the services on offer. A special effort was made to give wide publicity to the newly launched schemes. Publicity has been done through various media like newspaper, radio, TV, fairs and exhibitions, etc.

HURDLES IN ECONOMIC SECURITY THROUGH CREDIT FLOW

There are many obstacles to credit supply which hinder economic security. These are discussed below:

Lack of Technical Knowledge

As allied agricultural activities require technical knowledge for its better results, farmers who have become used to adopting traditional methods since ages, have lesser inclination to move towards new methods.

Regarding Bank Scheme

Farmers are not aware of different types of bank scheme regarding allied agricultural activities such as development of horticulture, sheep and goat rearing, piggery development, sericulture, etc.

Banks Branches in Rural Areas: Lesser number of bank branches particularly in rural areas of some states like Bihar, Orissa, Assam and North-Eastern region is one of the reasons for inhibiting credit flow to allied sectors. There are 10 villages per bank branches in India. High transaction cost for banks in servicing small loan accounts also causes hurdles for credit flow.

INADEQUATE MARKETING FACILITIES FOR THE PRODUCE

Due to lack of proper marketing facilities of the produce banks hesitate to take risk to finance in allied sectors. Also farmers don't get remunerative prices for their produce.

Inadequate Credit to Farmers

Due to the insufficient credit to farmers, there may not be the proper income generation from the activities.

Delay by Banks in Sanction of Schemes

Multiplicity of documents and procedural formalities of banks results into delay in sanctioning of credit amout due to which farmers suffer.

Diversion of Credit

Most part of the credit is diverted towards consumption purpose. It reduces performance of main allied activities.

Universal Schemes of Credit

Presently banks have products universally for whole of the region of the country which inhibits greater area for investment.

Avenues for Overcoming the Hurdles and Increasing Credit Flow in Order to have economic security is enumerated it infra.

Extension Services and Technology Transfer

Agriclinic, agribusiness centre, KVK or farmers club are to be encouraged for providing latest technical know-how for agriculture and allied activities to the farmers. These centers should be linked with banks for dissemination of knowledge and finance simultaneously to the farmers.

Information on Financial Literacy

Voluntarily focus should be made on opening Knowledge/ Credit counselling centres for education on financial services of the Bank, credit and repayment planning and facilitating interface between the poorer sections of the farmers specially focused on allied agricultural activities.

Micro-finance Concept

Self-help groups are more prominent in rural areas, where banks are still not able to meet the demand of the rural people. We should enhance formation, savings and credit linkage of SHG. Microfinance programmes should be extended in allied sectors so that they are able to meet the credit demand of the rural people. For example, Swarnima Scheme in Karnataka for Dairy.

Facility of Supply Chain, Value Addition and Export: Private sector (or, corporate) participation through contract farming and land leasing arrangements will allow accelerated technology transfer, capital inflow, processing and assured marketing of products like milk, poultry, fruits and vegetables. For example, Suguna poultry farm, Reliance fresh, Fritolay (for potato chips), etc. Some examples of region and crop specific models of contract farming are—Tomato cultivation in Pubjab, Haryana and Rajasthan, Mushroom in Haryana, Sunflower in AP and Karnataka, Gherkins in Karnataka, Fruits and vegetables in Tamil Nadu, AP and Maharashtra.

Revisiting of Scale of Finance

Revisiting of scale of finance and realigning the same to meet the realistic needs of farmers, especially capital intensive agricultural operations will increase credit flow.

Doorstep Availability of Credit to Farmers: There should be consideration to provide timely credit to farmers by simple processing and formalities.

Provision of Package

There should be provision of package in schemes for the consumption need of farmers aligned with credit.

Area Specific Credit Availability

Bank should have area specific schemes such as for irrigation in drought prone areas, enhancing rubber cultivation in Kerala, Litchi in Bihar, Emu farming in A.P., etc.

As is known that during 1950-60, the share of agriculture and allied activities in total GDP was about 50 per cent. Now it has decreased up to 17.1 per cent in 2008-09. The allied agriculture sector (mainly horticulture, dairy, poultry and fisheries) contributes about 60 per cent of the total agriculture GDP. Thus there is a great scope for increasing the credit. For this there is need to build an integrated team of specialists from agriculture, IT and Marketing who can work on this with dedicated effort. Corporate tie-ups, infrastructure building are some of the lucrative areas where efforts can be made.

The Central Government made a provision towards the debt relief scheme and committed to underwrite the entire burden of the relief which would be provided by commercial banks and RRBs. In addition, the Central Government was also committed to providing 50 per cent assistance for relief to be provided by the cooperative credit institutions. However, such scheme of loan waivers cannot be justified on economic grounds. It demoralises honest repayer of the debt and encourages misuse of funds.

In view of the above analysis, it can be concluded that private credit agencies may be allowed to play a supplementary role to the institutional credit for at least some sections of the cultivators and for certain types of needs but it cannot be accepted that the responsibility for meeting the credit needs of agricultural production programme may be left to be shouldered by private credit. The supply of institutional credit should be enough to meet the complete requirements of all types of cultivators for whole of agricultural production programmes in order to meet their economic security.

References

Rao, Aruna K. and Bhat, Ramchandea, An Evaluation of the Distribution of Rural Credit by the Primary Agricultural Credit Cooperative Societies.

Atibudhi, H.N. and Singh, J.P., Flow of Credit to Different Categories of Farmers.

Balishter, A.K., Yatendra Singh and Shiv Kumar, Overdues of Loans in Agriculture—A Study. Agricultural Banker.

Bhalerao, M.M., Malati and Singh, Ravindra, Regional Inequalities in Long-term Institutional Credit.

Chattopadhyay, Agricultural Capital Formation and Its Relation to Credit Facilities in India. *Indian Journal of Agricultural Economics*, 20(1): 188-192.

Credit Requirement of Agriculture, National Council of Applied Economic Research, New Delhi.

Dharmpalan, C., Personal Contact is Better than Legal Action, *National Bank News Review*, 8(7): 16-17.

Duhan, T.C. and Singh, C.B., Institutional Credit for Dairying in Haryana State, *Indian Journal of Agricultural Economics*, 43(3): 425.

Gadgil, M.V., Agricultural Credit in India: A Review of Performance and Policies, *Indian Journal of Agricultural Economics*, 41(3): 281-286.

Report of the Committee to Review Arrangement for Institutional Credit for Agriculture and Rural Development (CRAFICARD), Bombay.

An Analysis of Agro-Economic Condition in Jharkhand

RAJINI KUMARI AND VEENA KUMARI

The Constitution of India has provided enough ground for the livelihood of the people of India and that is why food sovereignty has become the people's fundamental right. It is the right to access and control of their means of production. It is the right to safe, culturally appropriate foods and sustainable food production.

Indian farmers normally give a prime place to the cereals in the cropping system. This cropping pattern is based on the consideration of food security, low risk and the easy market access to such farm produce. But this cropping pattern has not helped in increasing farmers' income the MSP system has so far favoured only three crops, namely sugarcane, paddy and wheat. This has encouraged mono-cropping and over-exploitation of natural resources in some areas. Therefore, now the thrust is on diversification of crop considering the Agro-climatic condition. Endowment of land and water resources and the market under the scheme of crop diversification. The emphasis is being given on horticulture crops such as fruits, vegetable, spice, medicinal and aromatic plants, plantation crops (like, coconut, cashew nut, etc.)

and floriculture. This kind of crop diversification would help in Generating Employment, improving economic condition of farmers, enhancing exports and providing nutritional security to the people.

While the country has been able to achieve the required household food security, Jharkhand has lagged behind. Jharkhand today produces around 23.67 lakh tonnes of foodgrains for a population of around 30 millions and average of 80 kg per capita per annum against 170 kg of minimum requirement. The implies that the shortage in foodgrains exceeds a little more than 50 per cent. The state is almost self-sufficient in vegetable production, but in regard to production of fruits, the shortage goes to the extent of 60 per cent per capita consumption of milk is also almost half of the minimum needs. The consumption level of fish, meat and egg is also very little in the rural areas, where the bulk of around 70 per cent population resides. According to a national family health survey, over 53 per cent of the children under the age of four are malnourished and under weight, 52 per cent of children in this age group are stunted and about 85 per cent of pregnant women are anaemic. In a nutshell, the level of food and nutrition security in Jharkhand is alarming, and requires immediate attention. Food security is the primary responsibility of the Government, a basic task that has direct relation to the welfare and quality of life of the people. Therefore, it is essential to outline and implement an effective food production programme, which is premised on the development of production of the farmers and other food produces. It is also necessary to see that the people are able to buy adequate food at affordable prices. It requires the Government to ensure that the people have sufficient wages or income to be able to buy food. Apart from this, the Governments responsibility also includes to ensure that the poor people belonging to disaster affected areas should have enough employment opportunities to generate wage income to buy enough food.

CURRENT STATUS OF FOOD SECURITY IN JHARKHAND

Jharkhand is a Tribal dominated state and there is enough natural resources in the state which include forest, mines and other natural resources. The state was carved out from undivided Bihar as the 28th separate state of the Indian Republic on 15th Nov.

2000. It presents a typical case of a rich state inhabited by poor people. Out of the total geographical area of 79.71 lakh hectares in Jharkhand, about 20.65 lakh hactare is net sown area (26%). Low land and medium land constitute about two-thirds area and the rest, about one-third, constitutes the uplands. About 24 lakh hactare is agricultural wastelands which can be reclaimed for agro-horticultural and silvicultural practices. The state has a total forest area of 23.33 lakh hactare (29%), which provides fuel, fodder and timber, besides various minor forest produce and stores a treasure of vast biodiversity. The state receives an average annual rainfall of 1500 mm but irrigation is available to hardly 10 per cent of the cropped area. The irrigation potential can be increased substantially through adoption of improved rainwater management practices. The state accounts for nearly 30 per cent of the total mineral production of the country except oil and natural gas and plays a vital role in the economic growth and industrial development of the nation. The state has a hard-working labour force, both men and women, for agricultural and industrial growth.

The major impediments to development of agriculture in Jharkhand are poor soil conditions due to soil erosion, causing loss of soil and plant nutrients, low level of irrigation accounting to rainfed agriculture in about 90 per cent of the cropped area, vast agricultural land lying waste, existence of a large number of small and marginal farmers, (about 75%) massive rural poverty (about 57% BPL families), vast deficit in minimum needed foodgrains, milk, meat, egg and fish, burgeoning population, indifference of youth to agriculture, declining public investment and weak linkage between research, extension and the farmer. Owing to these constraints the output per unit area of its crops is a bit lower than all India averages; milk yield per cattle is low and the value of its forest produce is one of the lowest in the country. All these factors have resulted in large incidence of poverty, unemployment, food insecurity, malnutrition, hunger and diease.

PRODUCTIVITY OF CROPS IN JHARKHAND AND NATIONAL AVERAGE

When the productivity of major crops is compared with those of all India averages, it is conspicuous that there are vast gaps, which if not bridged up, the question of ensuring food security in Jharkhand will remain a distant drem. The comparison has been depicted in Table 1.

TABLE I

Yield of Major Crops in Jharkhand as Compared to the All India Average in kg/ha

Crop	*Jharkhand*	*All India*
Rice	1226	1895
Wheat	1444	2470
Maize	0975	1721
All cereals	1116	1770
All pulses	0702	0570
All foodgrains	1091	1550

Source: Selected Plan Statistics of Jharkhand, Bihar and India at a Glance; 2001.

It is evident from Table 1 that the yield of rice in Jharkhand was over 35 per cent less than the national average and that of wheat was 43 per cent less. Similarly, the yield of maize was also substantially less than the national average. In ensuring food and nutrition security, apart from foodgrains, fruit, vegetable, milk, meat, egg and fish play an important role. Therefore, it is imperative that the position of demand and supply of these food items in the state be examined thoroughly. Data have been presented in Table 2 which indicate that except vegetable followed by fish, the production and productivity of fruit, milk, meat and egg will have to be raised substantially to meet the future requirements for food and nutraition security in the state

STRATEGY FOR ENSURING FOOD IN JHARKHAND

According to Prof. M.S. Swaminathan (2005), Chairman, National Commission on Farmer, Food insecurity in rural and urban areas has revealed that the major cause of malnutrition among children, women and men is the lack of adequate purchasing power to permit access to balanced diets and clean

TABLE 2

Year	Fruit			Vegetable			Milk			Meat			Egg			Fish		
	Demand	Production	Surplus (+) Deficit (?)	Demand	Production	Surplus (+) Deficit (?)	Demand	Production	Surplus (+) Deficit (?)	Demand	Production	Surplus (+) Deficit (?)	Demand	Production	Surplus (+) Deficit (?)	Demand	Production	Surplus (+) Deficit (?)
1995	8.73	2.88	-5.85 (-67.01)	19.81	14.57	-5.14 (-825.95)	1.96	1.02	-0.94 (-47.96)	2.18	1.53	-0.65 (-29.82)	2688	933	-1375 (-65.03)	0.88	0.67	0.21
2005	10.76	4.24	-6.47 (-60.13)	24.07	27.02	2.95 (-60.13)	2.37	1.35	-1.02 (-43.03)	2.66	1.70	-0.96 (-35.09)	3242	1030	-2212 (-68.23)	0.98	0.90	-0.0 (8.88)
2010	11.70	5.62	-6.08 (-51.96)	26.16	39.24	+13.08 (+50.00)	2.58	1.53	-1.05 (-40.70)	2.88	1.80	-1.08 (-37.50)	3520	1110	-2410 (68.46)	1.05	1.00	-0.05 (-5.00)
2020	13.92	7.02	-6.90 (-49.57)	31.09	68.25	+37.16 (+119.52)	3.06	2.09	-0.97 (-31.70)	3.43	2.00	-1.43 (-41.49)	4189	1583	-2906 (-69.37)	1.25	1.35	+0.10 (+7.40)

* Figure in Million numbers.
Figure in parentheses indicate percentages.

drinking water. He has advocated for this in the national perspective, where there is self-sufficiency in foodgrains and the problem lies with respect to its distribution as well as low purchasing power, particularly among rural poor. But in context of Jharkhand, the main reason for food insecurity is deficit in production of foodgrains. Dr. Swaminathan has suggested a three-pronged strategy to ensure economic well-being of and nutrition security for rural families. First, families possessing assets like land, live stock, fish ponds, will have to be assisted to enhance the productivity of their resource endowment on an environmentally and economically sustainable basis. Second, nearly a third of the rural population and a large proportion of women earn their livelihood through wage employment. They will have to be enabled to take to skilled non-farm employment through market driven micro-enterprises supported by micro-credit. And third, the skills of rural artisans working in the secondary and tertiary section of economy have to be mobilized to enhance the competitiveness of agriculture through value addition of primary products and diversification of livelihood opportunities.

CONCLUSION

Since Jharkhand is a forest and mines dominated states. we must begin the process of imparting dynamism and optimism in the farm sector through technology upgradation in state. Accelerated agricultural progress based on enhancement of productivity/profitability, stability, sustainability and equitability through farming system diversification, sustainable intensification, quality upgradation and value addition is vital not only for food security and sovereignty but also for poverty eradication in Jharkhand. The strategy for the technological upgradation of rural enterprises should be based on the principle of social inclusion. There is also a need to bridge the growing digital and genetic divides and technologies to promote labour diversification and not displacement.

Agricultural Diversification in North-Eastern Region in India

RAJNATH UPADHYAY AND SRIMAN PANDEY

I. INTRODUCTION

Indian Agriculture has made commendable progress since Independence and it has become lifestyle of more than 70 per cent people of India. Though green revolution has added much to the development of agriculture but enough has to be done in the field of agriculture. Keeping in view the growing population of India agriculture diversification has become the demand of the time. The aim of our planning process is to improve the quality of life of all citizens. Looking at the predominance of agriculture as the source of livelihood in the Eastern region, a breakthrough in the human development graph of the region can be achieved only by addressing the key issues of the agriculture and allied sectors.

The low levels of productivity and entrepreneurship contrast the huge potential of the Eastern region in the sphere of agriculture, horticulture, animal husbandry and fisheries. The time has come to fill the yield gaps and to capitalize on the opportunities offered by the region. In the context of globalization and opening up of the domestic agriculture sector to competition from outside, the highest priority must be accorded to exploiting available potential in the country and enhancing competitiveness. In this context the Eastern region provides possibly the widest and most lucrative prospects.

The Eastern region, which was one of the most developed and prosperous regions of the country prior to independence, is presently prone to a number of biophysical, institutional and socio-economic constraints. This has resulted in peculiar subsistence agriculture with low input, low yield, and low risk technology. Average farm size, irrigation coverage, average fertilizer consumption and power consumption in agriculture are all below the national average. Average fertilizer consumption in Orissa is lowest of any Indian state.

The cumulative result of these factors is low productivity and near stagnation or marginal growth in agriculture sector during the recent years.

Till the 'fifties, the Eastern Region was reputedly the most prosperous region in the country, maintaining a lead over the other regions with highest foodgrain yield of 644 kg/ha as against 608, 554 and 390 kg/ha in northern, southern and western regions, respectively. However, it lost its leading position thereafter, particularly with the advent of the Green Revolution, which ushered in the 'western' model based on large-scale adoption of HYV seeds, chemical fertilizers and supplemental irrigation along with plant protection measures. This model, most successful in North Western India, has not been widely replicated in the Eastern region because of a variety of constraints rooted to socio-economic features, fragmented and smaller land holdings as well as institutional, organizational, technological and developmental inadequacies. The Eastern Region comprising of Eastern UP (85,844 sq km), Bihar including Jharkhand (1,73,877 sq km), West Bengal (88,752 sq km), Assam (78,438 sq km), Orissa (1,55,707 sq km), and Chhattisgarh (1,44,422 sq km) occupies about 28 per cent of the country's geographical area with foodgrain production of 58 million tonnes (34.6% of the total), is inhabited by about 35 per cent of the country's population. The region has 1.24 times higher population density than the national average (318/sq km against 257/sq km national average: 1991 Census).

Agricultural development is much below its potential in

this region, with the result that employment in the agriculture sector is limited and a large proportion of the population still remains below the poverty line and suffers from malnutrition. For example, Bihar possessed about 3 per cent of the total cultivated area of the country and 8 per cent of the country's population, and produced about 6.9 per cent (14.56 million tonnes) of the total foodgrains in 1999-2000. The average yield of foodgrains in the state was 1620 kg/ha as against the national average of 1697 kg/ha. The yield of rice in Bihar was 15.40 q/ha as against national average of 19.90 q/ha. Similarly, the yield of wheat was 20.61 q/ha as against the national average of 27.55 q/ha.

II. PROBLEMS AHEAD

Most parts of the Eastern region lag behind the rest of India with respect to several social indicators. For instance, Bihar and Orissa rank lowest in poverty ratio and infant mortality is highest in Orissa among all major states of India. Development levels vary greatly within the Eastern region. Even within states like Orissa, the coastal and Northern regions have rural poverty head-count ratios of 45 to 46 per cent, but the Southern districts have 69 per cent of rural population below the poverty line making this the poorest area in rural India. Agriculture dominates the economy, accounting for 33 per cent, 32.8 per cent and 26.7 per cent of Gross State Domestic Product respectively in Assam, Uttar Pradesh and Bihar in 1990-2000 as compared to the all India average of 25.2 per cent (at 1993-94 prices).

Social Development Indicators: Selected States (mid-1990s)

Indicators	*Unit*	*All India*	*Best State*		*Worst State*	
Poverty ratio	Per cent	36.1	11.5	(Punjab)	55.2	(Bihar)
Infant mortality	Per '000	72.0	16.0	(Kerala)	105.0	(Orissa)
Overall literacy	Per cent	56.5	91.6	(Kerala)	42.0	(Bihar)
Female literacy	Per cent	43.9	88.5	(Kerala)	22.0	(Rajasthan)

Source: CMIE, Profile of States of various years.

In terms of average per capita Gross State Domestic Product, the Eastern region lags way behind the rest of India. For instance, in the mid-1990s, Orissa's per capita GSDP was only Rs. 1830 as compared to the national average of Rs. 3171. Average per capita income of Bihar and Orissa was the lowest among major Indian states. Growth in GSDP too in Eastern States has been below the national average for major States. For the overall period (1980-97), Bihar and Orissa recorded the slowest growth. The main reason for slow income growth in Eastern States has been slow agricultural growth in all time-periods as compared to the all India level, and indeed, at or below population growth rate.

III. CHARACTERISTICS AND BASIC RESOURCES OF THE EASTERN INDIA

The eastern region encompasses in itself certain physical features, which are distinct of them and have also developed certain resources, which add to the overall productivity of the region. However, a much greater degree of efforts and commitment is required to tap the existing resources and further improve other resources. A brief mention of the same is discussed for focused understanding.

III.1. Land Resource

Per capita availability of total land/net cultivated land in the Eastern Region is lowest in the country. In view of the highest percentage of net sown area to geographical area, there is hardly any scope of enlarging the area under cultivation in this region. Most of the farm holdings are marginal to small, and highly fragmented, hampering the adoption of high-tech agriculture. The need of the hour is tenurial reform and consolidation of holdings: the progress achieved in West Bengal in this direction is reflected in the significant growth in production in that State. The soils of the region are relatively fertile and still have many inherent limitations; however, efforts are required to build up and sustain soil productivity, particularly for intensified agriculture, which has to be practiced for faster economic growth.

In all the Eastern states more than 30 per cent of the total geographical area suffers from one or the other degradation problem. Among the different degradation problems, soil erosion is predominant in the states of Orissa, Chhattisgarh and Jharkhand. In Bihar and West Bengal drainage problems are a predominant concern. Salinity and sodicity problems occur to a considerable extent in West Bengal followed by Chhattisgarh, where soil acidity problems occur in as much as 15 per cent of the geographical area. Coastal soil salinity is a major problem in the states of West Bengal and Orissa. This renders the land less fertile and in an area, where agriculture is predominant, soil degradation reduces not only fertility and productivity, but also the means to livelihood.

III.2. Water Resources

Another natural resource is the Water Resource. The Eastern Region is rich in rain, surface and ground water resources. The average annual rainfall ranges from 1100 to 2000 mm, which is sufficient to meet the agricultural water requirement. There are, however, large spatial and temporal variations, which cause immense uncertainty and instability in agricultural productivity and production. While on the one hand, occurrence of long drought spells during crucial periods is quite common, on the other hand, heavy monsoon rains cause water congestion and flooding, making crop cultivation during the kharif season an uncertain venture. Annual surface water flow is abundant (117 million ha-m), but much less is utilizable (36 million ha-m) of which only about one-third has been actually utilized. Ground water potential is also high (30 million ha-m) of which less than 20 per cent is being utilized. The total overall utilizable surface water potential for irrigation is about 15 million ha-m while it is 12 million ha-m for ground water resource. The Eastern region is crisis crossed by large river systems. There are seven major rivers which have catchments area larger than 20,000 sq km and four medium rivers which have catchments area larger than 5000 sq km. The topography of the region renders it vulnerable to recurring floods and water logging. In the areas adjoining Nepal, floods are an annual feature during monsoon months, with all the rivers spilling over into adjacent areas. While the floods do cause considerable distress, to which the affected population has become rather accustomed, the floods facilitate beneficial rabi operations due to silt deposition. Efforts have been made in tapping this resource. The progress of creation of irrigation potential under major and medium irrigation systems is very slow in all the Eastern Indian states. The irrigation scenario in Bihar, Orissa and West Bengal is revealing. In the case of minor irrigation systems based on surface water, the rate of progress is higher in Orissa followed by West Bengal and Bihar. The percentage of irrigation potential created is satisfactory in Bihar (62%) and West Bengal (65%), but low in Orissa (33%). The major cause is meager exploitation of ground water in Orissa. The number of major and medium irrigation projects is highest in Jharkhand (117) followed by Bihar (98), Orissa (87) and West Bengal (37). The least number in West Bengal may be attributed to the plain topography.

Distribution of crops in irrigated areas shows that rice occupies the major chunk in all the States. While in Chhattisgarh rice occupies as much as 95 per cent, in Orissa it is 77 per cent. However in Eastern U.P., irrigated rice occupies less area than the national average. While water resources are inadequately developed, the developed resources are poorly utilized. Canal water for crop production is available in a relatively uncontrolled manner. It is excessive and uneven during the wet season, and too little during the dry season. In most cases, irrigation is practiced from field to field rather than through field channels which results in inefficient water use. Groundwater is developed to a smaller extent and that too is not fully utilized due to inadequate and erratic supply of electric power or non-availability of diesel and maintenance infrastructure.

III.3. Bio-Resources

The Eastern region of India possesses a distinct identity, not only because of its geography, history and culture but also because of the great diversity in its natural ecosystems. This part of India receives annual rainfall of 100-200 cm and climate varies from dry winter and hot summer to tropical Savannah. The dominating natural vegetation in the region is moist tropical evergreen and moist tropical deciduous. Physiographical, the entire eastern region could be divided into three regions with different geographical nature and distribution of flora and fauna: Plateau and Hills, Coastal Plains, and Gangetic plains. The plateau is mainly dominated by deciduous forests, of which timber trees such as Sal (*Shorea robusta*), Sishum (*Dalbergia sisso*) are important. Large areas in this region can be brought under crop diversification. The areas above 500-600 m above mean sea level are congenial for floriculture and cultivation of Orchids, where otherwise there is abundance of tropical deciduous forests.

III.4. Fish Resources

The region abounds in perennial and seasonal water bodies which hold high promise for the growth of fisheries. Adequate infrastructure is also a basic requirement for the development of fisheries. Strengthening of infrastructure development at the capture and culture phase, and also post-harvest infrastructure such as storage facilities, ice plants, cold chains, transportation, etc. as well as an effective marketing system are key requirements. The Eastern region is particularly handicapped in terms of supporting infrastructure for the fisheries sector. Indeed, despite excellent production potential of the region, large quantities of fish are imported from other parts of the country to the region. The marketing chain also is disorganized, on account of which the producer is denied remunerative returns. Lack of storage and preservation facilities has limited the scale of operations. Other requirements of the sector are provision of credit, manpower development, quality control arrangements, etc. In the absence of properly organized fishery production and marketing system, the fishery potential has also not been adequately developed and exploited.

III.5. Horticulture

Horticulture, which includes fruits, vegetables including root and tuber corps, mushroom, floriculture, medicinal and aromatic plants, plantation crops, spices and beekeeping has traditionally been an important activity in the Eastern region. Horticultural crops grown in these regions include mango, banana, pineapple, guava, litchi among fruits, potato, onion, tomato, cauliflower among vegetables, chrysanthemum, rose, orchids, etc. in flowers, ginger, turmeric large cardamom, coriander, cumin among spices and coconut, arecanut and tea among plantation crops. The productivity of many of the horticultural crops in this region is much below the National level.

III.6. Livestock Resources

Under conditions of relatively small land-human ratio and

low agricultural productivity in the Eastern region, animal husbandry forms a complementary source of employment and livelihood. Livestock production is an integral part of crop farming and contributes substantially to household nutritional security and poverty alleviation through increased household incomes. The returns from livestock especially dairying and mixed farming in small and medium holdings can be highly sustainable. Development of this sector, therefore, will result in more balanced development of the rural economy and improvement in the economic status of poor people associated with livestock. Its impact is however marginal due to the lack of quality breeds, feeds and fodder, and animal health care.

Contributions of Animal Husbandry to Growth of the Eastern Region

The Livestock and Fishery Sectors provide fish, milk, egg, wool and meat and much needed employment, especially of women, landless, small and marginal farmers, etc., and also cater to several needs of the economy, such as agricultural operations, transport, income generation, fuel and fertilizers, utilization of agricultural by-products and wastelands. India today ranks first in cattle and buffalo, second in goats, third in sheep and seventh in poultry population in the world. About 56 per cent of the world's buffalo population is in India.

The production of milk, egg and fish rose from 17.0 million tonnes, 1832 million nos., 0.75 million tonnes in 1950-51 to 74.7 million tonnes 30.2 billion nos., and 5.26 million tonnes respectively in 1998-99, is a major leap forward. The contribution of Livestock and Fishery sector to total GDP was 7.39 per cent (6.01% from Livestock and 1.39% from Fisheries) in 1998-99 at current prices. The value of output of livestock and fisheries sectors was estimated to be Rs. 1,48,954 crores during 1998-99 which is about 27 per cent of the total value of output of Rs. 5,53,175 crores from the Agricultural and Allied sector. This does not include Draught Animal Power which has been valued between Rs. 40 and 95 billion. The contribution of milk alone (Rs. 82,624 crores) was higher than paddy (Rs. 68,230 crores), wheat (Rs. 40,323 crores) and sugarcane (Rs. 23,314 crores).

The overall labour investment in livestock farming in small and medium holdings is high (around 73%) compared to crop farming (23%). Women constitute 71 per cent of the labour force in the livestock sector as against 33 per cent in crop farming. It is estimated that about 9.8 million people are directly involved in the livestock sector in principal status and another 8.6 million are involved in the subsidiary status.

IV. AGRICULTURAL DIVERSIFICATION IN EASTERN INDIA

Presently due to its high rainfall and waterlogged conditions, rice is the predominant *kharif* crop occupying 70-90 per cent of the entire region under irrigation/rainfed. At some places pulses and oilseeds are also grown as *kharif* crop. Wheat, potato, sugarcane, pulses and oilseeds are the major *rabi* crops while jute is also grown as pre-monsoon crop. The detailed agro-ecological sub-region-wise distribution of existing crops and cropping pattern is presented below.

Traditional Agriculture as Backbone

Sluggish growth of the agriculture sector in the Eastern region is mainly due to low irrigation coverage, erratic climate with deviations in rainfall of 20 per cent or more every third year for the last thirty years or so, and, most strikingly, a very high degree of dependence on a single crop, namely rice, which occupies 93.5 per cent of the foodgrains grown. Given the water intensive nature of rice, such reliance on it, where neither nature nor irrigation can be depended on for water, is risky indeed. Agricultural growth in the Eastern states averaged just over 1 per cent per annum over the last two decades.

Irrigation water management, excess water management, rain water management, watershed management and ground water management assume greater significance now than ever before for aiding future agricultural growth in the Eastern region while evolving agro-climatic region specific production and resource management technologies.

V. MAJOR ISSUES AND CONCERNS OF THE EASTERN REGION

V.1. Productivity

West Bengal is the leading producer of rice (13.95 million

tonnes) in the country, accounting for 15.59 per cent of total production. In the production of maize, Bihar is a close second to Karnataka, with 1.61 million tonnes and 14 per cent of overall production. In total production of foodgrains, West Bengal and Bihar stand fourth and fifth respectively in the country. In terms of productivity too, West Bengal had an average yield per hectare of 2192 kg. against the national average of 1697 kg. The other States, however, lagged below the national average yield: Bihar 1620 kg., Orissa 1022 kg., Assam 1427 kg. West Bengal has recorded remarkable success in raising productivity levels of rice to 2259 kg./ha., against the national average of 1990 kg./ha. However, this is still well below the productivity levels of Punjab, Tamil Nadu and even Karnataka. In Orissa and Bihar the yield gaps are wide in the case of most crops. The following tables give State-wise details relating to the major crops.

V.2. Post-Harvest Management: Promoting Marketing and Value Addition

These are critical areas that are essential to enhancing the income of producers and for revitalizing the rural economy. In view of the conditions prevailing in the Eastern regions and the long distances between production centers and the main market, post-harvest losses of the produce of this region is inordinately high and the shelf life of perishables is low. One of the major constraints in the way of agricultural development of the Eastern regions is the weak post-harvest and marketing infrastructure and the low level of value-added agro-food production. This has resulted in farming being largely uneconomical with major gains being cornered by a small group of traders. This sector constitutes the major weakness of the Eastern region. With regard to all commodities—agricultural, horticultural, livestock and fisheries—this is an area needing special attention.

Major emphasis should, therefore, provide special focus to strengthening marketing and value addition infrastructure in the region. A modern marketing system for agricultural and horticultural produce, animal products, fish and agro-forestry will have to be established based on post-harvest handling, grading, packaging, processing, storage and transport with adequate credit support. This aspect has to be assigned the top-most priority in order to meet the needs of each specific area. The strengthening of market structure will also entail review of existing legislation and removal of redundant restrictions on agricultural trade, creation of a comprehensive database use of information technology, ecommerce and development of a market intelligence system.

Horticultural commodities being perishable are vulnerable to high losses after harvest, till these reach the consumer. Depending upon crops and season of harvest, estimated losses range from 8.37 per cent, resulting in annual loss of more than Rs. 10,000 crores in the country. These losses are much higher in Eastern India owing to poor post-harvest handling, Infrastructural deficiency, unreliable transportation system and inadequate road network. Insufficient infrastructure, at the level of farms, unhygienic market conditions as also poor protection against sun and rain have considerably added to these losses. The type of infrastructure needed to ensure equitable returns to producers and which are essential for value addition like plastic crates, grading/packing centers, pre-cooling and cold storage facilities, auction platforms, transport systems and facilities at airport are yet to be established in the region.

It is suggested that establishment of alternative market systems having backward and forward linkages are essential in efforts to achieve higher productivity and ensure returns to growers, besides the system should have terminal markets with auction centers having modern facilities, backward linkages with farmers through collection centers, and forward linkages with consumers through retail sale centers. This system of market is viable and can be operated by cooperatives or companies. Government has to play the role of facilitator through policy reforms. APMC regulations have to be modified to facilitate free trade with minimal restrictions.

V.3. Inadequate Infrastructure

The Eastern region faces a serious constraint in terms of infrastructure. On most criteria, Eastern States lag behind the all India average. Orissa, for instance suffers from poor railway and telecommunication infrastructure. Orissa does well in terms of roads, but only for unpaved roads. With weak rural infrastructure, farmers concentrate overwhelmingly on rice cultivation, aided by canal irrigation-based supply-led cropping pattern further confounded by lack of adequate drainage network. Water management technologies in conjunction with rural infrastructure development would wean the farmers away from rice monocropping towards crop/farm diversification.

Reforms in the irrigation sector have been initiated only in Orissa within the Eastern region. Decentralization of the management of irrigation systems at various levels is happening now with the formation of water users' associations at minor, distributary and project level. Surface irrigation systems are getting rehabilitated and consolidated for facilitating the take over of system maintenance and water distribution responsibilities to the water users themselves

V.4. Marketing

Marketing is the key instrument in the development of the agriculture sector. The success story of dairy development in the country through the cooperatives, was largely due to an effective marketing network created by the National Dairy Development Board. Unfortunately, marketing seems to have taken the back seat in the context of Eastern States, though the States have been implementing programmes to increase agriculture, horticulture and livestock productivity, for the last several Five Year Plans. The reason why poultry products and milk is flowing into this region from outside points to the inadequacies of marketing infrastructure in the region. The region seems to be caught in a 'Catch-22' situation; though there is excellent demand for products of the region, the farmers are not able to produce and receive fair remuneration due to the high cost of input supplies and a non-existent marketing network.

Though the Eastern region has great potential in the animal husbandry sector, the same has not been exploited to the extent it should have been due to reasons of inaccessibility, lack of marketing network, poor infrastructure and delivery system. Though some infrastructure has been created by each of the States in the region, for instance, in terms of AI centers, breeding farms, liquid semen banks, hatcheries, liquid nitrogen plant, etc. in the livestock sector, most of these are lying in disuse due to sheer lack of budgetary support and unsupportable burden on the meager resources of the respective Governments. The reasons for the non-utilization of infrastructure are largely due to prohibitive cost of inputs, non-availability of effective transportation and delivery system.

V.5. Research and Transfer of Technology

Dissemination of information about new technologies and management practices is very weak in the region. There exists a wide knowledge gap which has to be bridged. The extension network needs to be strengthened significantly. The manpower available with state agencies needs to be trained to improve their knowledge and skills. Special attention is required towards imparting commercial orientation to the manpower engaged in development activities. Bihar and Jharkhand, Eastern Uttar Pradesh, Orissa, Chhattisgarh and West Bengal have one agricultural university each, besides Coordinated Centers for agricultural and horticultural crops located in these states.

V.6. Credit

The economy of the Eastern Region still persists on production for consumption rather than creation of marketable surplus. The banking industries, and banking habits in general, are yet to be fully developed and understood. The financial position and health of Regional Rural Banks and Cooperative Banks is precarious and the aggregate accumulative losses are very high. Primary Agricultural Credit Societies (PACS) are the vital link in the cooperative credit structure. The PACS system in the region, however, is financially and operationally weak and far from becoming self-reliant in respect of mobilization of resources through deposits.

These are some of the issues, which need to be dealt with in the right perspective. An attempt is made here to provide certain suggestions and recommendations.

VI. SUGGESTIONS AND RECOMMENDATIONS

1. As the region is marked by various deficits arising out of historical and other reasons, a special effort is required to reverse the trend towards alienation and distancing of the people from the mainstream. To this end, innovative participative planning, sensitive implementation and novel delivery systems are needed.

2. Providing multiple livelihood opportunities by increasing non-agricultural employment from utilization of local strengths and resources.
3. Sustainable agricultural development through Farming Systems Approach through an area specific farming systems approach, combining crop and animal husbandry, horticulture and agro-forestry.
4. Efficient National Resources Management through an integrated package aimed at environmental and economic sustainability.
5. Strengthening capital formation in the Agriculture Sector particularly in building essential infrastructure. Private sector investments should be encouraged in a conducive environment.
6. Stimulating new employment opportunities to make farming and other rural occupations intellectually stimulating and economically rewarded so that educated youth may be attracted and retained in rural areas.
7. *Decentralization and Micro-Planning*: For optimum delivery of services and programmes, a decentralized participatory system is required, based on micro-planning, local needs assessment, community empowerment and an enlarged role for women.
8. *Promoting Marketing and Value Addition*: This major lacuna in the Eastern region needs to be filled by developing modern marketing systems, based on post-harvest management, handling, grading, packing, processing, storage and transport, with adequate credit support and market intelligence.
9. *Eco-Regional Technology Missions*: This is based on the blending of traditional wisdom and practices with frontier technologies so as to promote employment generation, conservation and local initiative. A holistic approach should be adopted to integrate production and post-harvest technologies, on farm and off-farm employment, and to achieve vertical and horizontal linkage of different activities.

10. *Enhancing Availability of Institutional Credit*: The issue of increasing the availability of production and investment credit needs to be urgently addressed. Micro-credit, promotion of Self-Help Groups and provision of share capital assistance should be stepped up.
11. Synergizing the efforts of Governmental/Non-Governmental Agencies.
12. *Novel Systems of Extension Delivery*: The transfer of knowledge and innovation in the shortest time possible to users at the field level is essential for success of integrated intensive farming systems.
13. *Export Thrust*: The region offers enormous potential for exports. By building up marketing information and export orientation of production processes, promoting quality production and product diversification, and adopting targeted production and marketing strategies, huge gains may be obtained.
14. The WTO regime and the opening up of Indian agriculture have thrown up a range of opportunities for Indian agriculture while making it imperative to enhance the efficiency and competitiveness of agricultural operations. As seen above, the Eastern and North-Eastern region has huge potential for not only increasing productivity and efficiency but also for capitalizing on the opportunities offered by the new trade regime.

VII. CONCLUSION

On the basis of the studies and analysis so far, it has been concluded that the eastern region of the Indian economy has witnessed tremendous pressures both from the socio political and institutional set-up as well as the natural environment. The measures which have been suggested above if implemented in the right earnest will bear fruits and since the region is capable of performing it is hoped that policy planners both at the center and at the state level may work in this direction to reduce disparities in income, growth and development for over all performance.

References

Ahluwalia, Montek S. (2000), 'Economic Performance of States in Post-Reforms Period', *Economic and Political Weekly,* May.

Das, Arvind N. (1983), 'Agrarian unrest and Socio-economic Changes in Bihar, 1900-1980', Manohar, Delhi.

Datt, Gaurav (1998), 'Poverty in India and Indian States: A Update', *The Indian Journal of Labour Economics,* Vol 41, No. 2, April-June.

Jannuzi, F.T. (1974), 'Agrarian grisis in India: The Case of Bihar', Sangam Books, New Delhi.

'Land Reforms in Bihar: A Case Study', ANS Instutute of Social Studies, Patna (mimeo) (1986).

Prasad, Pradhan H., Gerry Rodgers, Alakh N. Sharma and S. Gupta (1986), 'Dynamics of Poverty and Employment in Bihar', ANS Institute of Social Studies, Patna (mimeo).

Sharma, Alakh N. (1995), 'Political Economy of Poverty in Bihar', *Economics and Political Weekly,* Vol. 30, Nos. 41 and 42, October.

Report of the Working Group TFYP Sr. No. 40/2001, Planning Commission, GoI, on Agricultural Development in Eastern and North-Eastern India for the Formulation of the Tenth Five Year Plan, August 2001.

Agriculture in Uttarakhand: Problems and Prospects

Devna Sharma and Rachna Dixit

Agricultural development for Uttarakhand was re-examined when the state was separated from Uttar Pradesh. Since the ecosystem of the hill regions is very different from the plains, it was essential to focus on the agriculture of the hill districts of Uttarakhand in a different manner. The Green Revolution of the 1960s benefited those areas that already had irrigation facilities, but this was not possible in the hills because of a lack of these resources. Uttarakhand is primarily an agricultural state although its share in the country's total area and production is very small. The contribution of agriculture to the state's domestic product is about 22.41 per cent and the population dependent on agriculture for their livelihood is about 75-85 per cent. The development of the hills is primarily linked to the development of agriculture and its allied activities. Since the hills are constrained in the development of large scale industralisation, and due to infrastructure constraints, the development of the service sector remains the prime focus. People in the hills have been primarily engaged in subsistence agriculture. The contribution of Uttarakhand to the country's total foodgrain and sugarcane production is negligence

(Tabel 1). Table 2 shows that the area under cultivation of foodgrains in Uttarakhand has increased between 2000-01 and 2005-06, but production and yields have declined.

TABLE I

Area, Production and Yield for Selected Commodity Group 2005-06

Commodity	*Uttarakhand*			*India*		
	Area (million ha)	*Production (million tonnes)*	*Yield (kg/ ha)*	*Area (million ha)*	*Production (million tonnes)*	*Yield (kg/ ha)*
Foodgrains	1.03	1.59	1548	121.60	208.60	1715
Coarse cereals	0.27	0.32	1188	29.04	34.07	1172
Pulses	-	-	-	22.39	13.39	598
Oilseeds	-	-	-	6.74	7.99	1187
Sugarcane	0.10	6.13	60733	4.20	281.17	66928

Source: Agriculture Statistics at a Glance, 2007.

TABLE 2

Area Production and Yield of Foodgrain

Commodity	*Uttarakhand*		*India*	
	Uttarakhand	*India*	*Uttarakhand*	*India*
Area (Million ha)	0.98 (0.80)	122.78	1.03 (0.85)	121.6
Production (million tonnes)	1.71 (0.80)	212.85	1.59 (0.76)	208.6
Yield (kg/ha)	1742	1734	1548	171.5

Source: Agriculture Statistics at a Glance, 2007.

The low agricultural yield reflects the small size and scattered land holdings, difficult terrain, unfavourable climatic conditions for some crops, lack of or inadequate availability of improved inputs and technology and credit and marketing facilities. The status of operational land holdings in Uttarakhand in Table 3 highlights the small fragmented land holdings in the state. As per the agricultural census, 2001, Uttarakhand's average land holding trends are similar to the national average. But the overall land holding average is lower than the national average because almost 70 per cent of the land holdings in Uttarakhand are marginal and 18 per cent are small.

TABLE 3

Operational Holdings, 2001

Operational	No. of Operational holdings (ha)		Area operated holdings (in '000 ha)		Average size of holdings (in '000 ha)	
	Uttarakhand	India	Uttarakhand	India	Uttarakhand	India
Marginal (< 1 ha)	628	76122	243	30088	0.39	0.40
Small (1-2)	158	22814	221	32259	1.40	1.41
Semi-medium (2-4 ha)	24	6568	132	38125	5.50	5.80
Large (> 10 ha)	1	1230	36	21124	36.00	17.17
All holdings	889	120822	844	159903	0.95	1.32

Source: Agricultural Statistics at a Glance, 2007.

With the state's limitations in land and water resources, yields need to be improved through scientific transformation and modernization of agriculture. Thus, the development policies for the agriculture sector of the state in particular have to be oriented towards marginal and small landholders. For sustainable development, additional investment is crucial. The prime objective of the development of the agriculture system is to increase sustainability of this sector in such a manner that it provides a better livelihood option and makes the population dependent on it move from subsistence farming to a well-knit higher-income farming system. In many countries, there is considerable scope for bringing new areas under cultivation, but in India the scope for extension of cultivation to new land is limited. Already, about 46.3 per cent of the total reported area is cultivated. Culturable land (culturable wastelands, other follows lands, permanent pastures, grazing lands, and miscellaneous

Uttarakhand, in contrast, has only 14.5 per cent of its area under cultivatiion and almost 60 per cent area under forest,

TABLE 4

Distribution of Agricultural Land by Type of use: 2004-05

Characteristics	*Uttarakhand*	*India*
Geographical area	5689	328725
Area for land utilization	5348	305233
Forest	3127	696872
	(58.5)	(22.8)

Not available for cultivation.

culturable wasteland is around 7.2 per cent. Most of this area is occupied by marginal and sub-marginal lands, and the extension of cultivation to this area will be expensive, since it requires extensive work for soil and water conservation, irrigation and reclamation.

CONCLUSION

The participation and interaction with data and study reflect the non-participation of the people in the development planning. The picture that emerges emphasizes the over-generation of problems in an area neglecting its diverse specified. It was found that often due to lack of proper planning and guidance the agricultural system deteriorate beyond repair due to many difficulties facing by Uttarakhand's farmers, some of these problems are:

- The state is geographically distributed among plains to hill and in hilly area the agricultural crops are mainly rain-fed. Therefore, productivity of the crops is less in comparison of irrigated crops.
- Due to deforestation in the state habitat of the animals are disturbed, therefore food chain is being disturbed and thus fraying away from forest into residential area in search of food animals are becoming man eater. Leopards of the state are mostly becoming man eater and so farmer are afraid to go out for work on agricultural fields.
- In the hills small agricultural holdings are also

affecting the economy of the state and the farmers are unable to introduce modern technology in their holdings and due to which production is badly affected. In search of better means of livelihood people of the state are migrating to other cities out of state. Due to lack of manpower agricultural production is badly affected.

- Globally urbanization is in increasing trend. Uttarakhand is fastly moving to the urbanization. Agricultural lands are badly affected due to expansion of urbanization. Resulting in reduction of agricultural land and thereby affecting reduction of crop production.
- Due to lack of proper roads and transportation, hilly farmers are unable to transport products to the markets and ultimately most of their raw products get damaged and thereby affecting the economy of the farmer.
- In the hills there are no proper credit banking facilities for boosting agricultural productivity.
- Several pests, diseases and weeds flourish due to rich humid climatic conditions of the state. Some pests like white-grub are threat to hill farmers especially in rainfed farming areas.

SUGGESTIONS

It is the urgent need of the time to take proper care regarding the optimum and extensive use of the available cultivated land of the region. To improve agricultural practices and better utilization of cultivated land following steps should be taken:

- To boost the agricultural productivity irrigation facilities should be provided in hilly area to reduce the dependency on rain-fed irrigation. Government should check that fund provided by them is properly used for construction of canal for irrigation because due to corruption most of the work is done is of very low quality or in paper only.

- To protect the farmers from man eating animals government should provide proper security, like fencing to the fields and providing crackers to the farmers.
- Rural and agro-based industries should be developed so that the pressure of population on agriculture may be minimized. Due to this migration of the farmers will be minimized.
- Urbanization is providing opportunities of jobs but reducing the agricultural lands due to which farmers are compiled to sell their farming lands. For this multistorey buildings construction and wasteland should be given for expansion of urbanization to protect agricultural land.
- Proper roads construction from villages to markets and better transportation facilities should be given priority to sell the crops.
- Research and development facilities should be developed and expanded. Keeping in mind to the topographical, geographical and climatically conditions of the state. Adequate arrangements should be launched to educate the farmers.
- Since size of the holdings for farming in hilly area are very small then collective farming should be emphasized by the government to increase production. By this collective farming modern technology can be easily used by farmers.
- There are no proper credit facilities in hilly areas so to boost the agricultural farming, proper credit facilities should be given which can provide easy and cheap credit to farmers in those areas. Rural bank should be set-up.
- There are some agricultural crops which need very less care and labour like Jaiyal, Jhangora, Burans, etc. So such types of crops should be cultivated in Uttarakhand to gain more profits.

Uttarakhand, the newly created state of India is going through transition phase. The government to find its place among the developing states of Indian economy should frame its plan and policies in such a way to give top priority to agricultural sector on which nearly half of its population depends.

References

Agricultural Economics and Rural Development—Tyagi, B.P.

Development Dilemma, Indian Scenario and Rural Himalayan Nehal—A. Farooquee, D.S. Rawat.

Development Strategy for the Hill, District of Uttarakhand—Surabhi Mittal, Gaurav Tripathi, Deepti Sethi.

Dimensions of Agriculture in the Himalaya—D.C. Pande.

Economic Developments in India—Montek Singh Ahluwalia.

Economy of Uttaranchal—P.C. Pandey, D.C. Pandey, P.S. Bisht, Rajnish Pandey.

Garhwal Himalaya (Nature, Culture and Society)—O.P. Kandari, O.P. Gusain.

Gazetteer of Garhwal Himalaya—H.G. Walton.

Glimpses of India Agriculture—R.S. Deshpande, Vijay Paul Sharma, R.P.S. Malik, Brajesh Jha, S.A. Ansari.

Glimpses of Indian agriculture—R.S.D. Deshpande, R.P.S. Malik.

Mountain Technology Agenda, Status, Graps and Possibilities—Anil P. Joshi, Sunil K. Agarwal, Rakesh.

Natural Resources of Himalaya—K.S. Gulia.

Poverty Planning and Development—Major D.S. Bisht (Retd.).

Pratiyogita Darpan (Extra Issue 2008).

Studies on Kumaun Himalaya—S.K. Sharma and N.C. Dhoondiyal.

The District Gazetteer of Uttaranchal—S.C. Bhatt.

Uttarakhand Today (1996)—K.S. Valdiya.

Uttaranchal environment and Development—S.C. Joshi.

Watershed Management in Himalaya (Concept and Strategy)—B.P. Pandey, Charup Pant, K.L. Arya and A.K. Sharma.

Growth and Transformations in Agricultural Output and Inputs in India: Need for Structural Adjustments

AMARJIT SINGH SETHI

In an agrarian economy like India, the pace and pattern of growth of agricultural output plays a pivotal role towards economic and social development. In such economies, agriculture draws its significance not merely from the point of view of providing livelihood to the rural masses, but also from the angle of forward and backward linkages with other sectors of the economy.

Beyond doubt, agriculture has continued to be one of major economic activities in the India. Its contribution in national income has temporally witnessed a consistent decline; the sector accounted for some 53.6 per cent in the country's income during 1950-51 (Sethi, 1997, p. 76) and has lately come down to a mere 18.5 per cent (CMIE, 2008). The phenomenon, of course, symbolizes healthy signs; with economic development, there is a general tendency of the share of agricultural sector to fall and that of secondary and tertiary sector to rise (Chenery *et al.*, 1974). However, in respect of employment, there have not been commensurate structural transformations. Dependence of the Indian population on agriculture was to the tune of 72.4 per cent way back during 1950-51 (Sethi, 1997, p. 83), which has lately come down (through nearly 10 per cent only) to 62.3 per cent (Kaur, 2008, p. 98), thus pointing towards structural distortions in the Indian economy. Furthermore, the pace of growth of agriculture has been at a variance with that of the other sectors; the growth in agricultural sector has declined from 3.7 per cent during early reforms period (1991-92 to 1996-97) to 2.5 per cent during Ninth and Tenth Plans (1997-98 to 2006-07; Government of India, 2008), presumably due to the declining real public investment in the sector. On the other hand, non-agriculture sector has witnessed growth at a rate of about 8 per cent per annum, primarily due to rapidly growing services sector.

Formulation of suitable structural adjustment programmes in agriculture may be facilitated through an examination of long-term growth paths and transformations in agricultural output. A few related studies (such as those due to Rao, 1968; Rao and Tharnarajakshi, 1978; Srinivasan, 1979; Rao and Deshpande, 1986; Dev, 1987; Rao *et al.*, 1988; Jeromi and Ramanathan, 1993; Kaushik, 1993; Rao, 1994; Rao and Gulati, 1994; Sawant and Achuthan, 1995; Bhide *et al.*, 1998; Behera and Mishra, 2007; Dev, 2008; Chand and Raju, 2009;, etc.) have been reported. Yet, the present study carried out to probe the pace and pattern of growth in India's agricultural output would add to the existing knowledge and would place in perspective the more recent trends.

The paper has been organized into four sections, including the present one on introduction. Database and analytical tools/ techniques adopted in the paper have been outlined in Section 2. Main findings from the study have been presented in Section 3.1 (on growth pattern) and Section 3.2 (on structural shifts). And, finally, concluding remarks and policy implications drawn from the paper have been given in Section 4.

DATABASE AND ANALYTICAL TECHNIQUES

Data used in the present study were compiled as time-series for 57 years' period (i.e., from 1950-51 through 2006-07) on

India's output from agriculture alone as well as from agriculture and allied activities. Compilation of the data were made (at both current and at 1999-2000 constant prices; at aggregated as well as at disaggregated levels) from various issues of National Accounts Statistics of the Central Statistical Organisation. The components in respect of output from agriculture were: Cereals (CRL), Pulses (PLS), Oil Seeds (OLS), Sugar (SGR), Fibers (FBR), Drugs and Narcotics (D&N), Condiments and Spices (C&S), Fruits and Vegetables (F&V), Other Crops (OTC, including Rubber, Guar Seeds, etc.)., By-Products (BPT), Kitchen Garden (KGN), and Overall Value of Output (VOA). It may, however, be mentioned that compilation was similarly made on sub-components of each of the major component as well, making it information on a totality of 52 items. Main heads under which the data were compiled on Agriculture and Allied Activities were: Value of Output (VAL), Agriculture (AGR), Livestock (LVS), Inputs (INP), Seed (SED), Organic Manure (ORM), Chemical Fertilisers (CFT), Current Repairs and Maintenance (CRM), Fixed Assets and Other Feed of Livestock (FLS), Irrigation Charges (IRC), Market Charges (MKC), Electricity (ELT), Pesticides and Insecticides (P&I), Diesel Oil (DSO), Financial Intermediation Services (FIS), Gross Domestic Product (GDP), Agriculture and Allied Activities (A&A), and Operation of Government Irrigation System (OGI).

For examining long-term behavioral growth paths, 14 different trend paths were estimated for each of the components of agricultural output (at constant prices) on which the time series were compiled. The paths were: Simple Linear (SLR), Parabolic (PRB), Cubic (CUB), Exponential (EXP), Exponential Parabolic (EPB), Exponential Cubic (ECB), Geometric (GEO), Hyperbolic (HYP), Log-Linear (LLR), Log-Parabolic (LPB), Log-Cubic (LCB), Modified Exponential (MEX), Gompertz (GOM), and Logistic (LGS). For a given component, equation of the best-fit was chosen on the basis of the Index I due to Sethi (2008). From such equations, relative growth rates (RGR_t) in time series $\{Y_t\}$ for an aggregate were computed at different points in time t (by following (Rudra, 1970 and Sethi, 2008) as

$RGR_t = \frac{\dot{Y}_t}{Y_t}$, where $\dot{Y}_t = \frac{dY}{dt}$ represents the time derivative of Y_t.

Temporal behaviour of duly portrayed in the form of diagrams, provided the basis to examine validity of alternative (acceleration, deceleration or constancy) hypotheses regarding growth pattern of the components. From these patterns, turning points, if any, were determined by following the methodology outlined in Sethi (2009). At the so-obtained turning points, *kinked growth rates* were estimated by following Boyce (1986). For instance, with one kink, growth rates in the two segments were computed through estimation of the equation involving dummies: $\ln Y_t = \alpha + \beta_1(D_1 t + D_2 k) + \beta_2(D_2 t - D_2 k) + u_t$ where k is the point in time where the kink (or the turning point) occurred. The OLS estimates of β_1 and β_2 then provided us with the kinked rates of growth, as $(\hat{\beta}_1 - 1) \times 100$ and $(\hat{\beta}_2 - 1) \times 100$ respectively.

Nature of structural changes was assessed through shifts in relative shares of different components in aggregated value of agricultural output. Speed of structural changes was measured in quantitative terms through two well-known indexes, viz., θ due to Moore (1997) and ξ due to Sethi (2003). Choice between the two indexes was made on the basis of their CV values.

Analysis in the present paper was carried out through computer software developed by the senior author.

MAIN FINDINGS

Main findings have been discussed in brief under the following sub-heads:

Growth Pattern

In this section, we have made an attempt to examine the most appropriate long-term trend paths traced by real output (at 1999-2000 constant prices) from various components of agriculture and allied activities. Regarding the long-term growth pattern of major crops, it was seen that the best-fit functions happened to be non-linear (i.e., either polynomials on logarithmic scale or the exponential ones) in nature (Table 1). The coefficient of predictability Φ was, in general, fairly high (≥ 0.82). The overall value of agricultural output (VOA) followed a pattern

TABLE 1

Equations of the Best-Fit in respect of Gross Value-added (at 1999-2000 Constant Prices) from Major Crops in India

Component	*Equation of the Best-Fit*	*Statistical Yardsticks*					*Values of the Unknowns*
		RMS	*Φ*	*D-W*	*I*	*Variation Explained (in %)*	
1. CRL	LPB	$5.109 \cdot 10^{5}$	0.975	1.673	1.169	97.4	b_0=1.003; b_1= 3.136; b_2= -7.979×10^{6}
2. PLS	LGS	0.027	0.715	1.609	0.845	70.4	b_0=1.150; b_1= -0.018; b_2=1.060
3. OLS	LPB	4.124×10^{4}	0.820	1.331	0.924	81.3	b_0=1.003; b_1=0.001; b_2=1.155×10^{5}
4. SGR	LCB	$1.547 \cdot 10^{4}$	0.939	1.095	1.023	93.5	b_0=0.994; b_1= 0.007; b_2 = -2.982×10^{4} b_3 = 4.052×10^{-6}
5. FBR	LCB	3.075×10^{4}	0.887	1.276	0.994	88.0	b_0=1.015; b_1= -0.004; b_2= -1.004×10^{4} b_3=1.390×10^{-6}
6. D&N	LLN	7.016×10^{5}	0.974	1.775	1.168	97.3	b_0=.996; b_1 = 0.003
7. C&S	LPB	1.287×10^{4}	0.947	1.303	1.076	94.4	b_0= 0.995; b_1= 0.003; b_2= 6.466×10^{6}
8. F&V	ECB	0.070	0.982	0.515	0.497	98.1	b_0= 0.971; b_1= 0.011; b_2= -4×10^{4}; b_3= 4.631×10^{6}
9. OTC	ECB	0.014	0.875	0.449	0.822	86.8	b_0= 0.859; b_1=1.035; b_2=0.998; b_3=1.000
10. BPT	LCB	$1.732 \cdot 10^{4}$	-0.921	0.374	0.856	91.6	b_0= 1.014; b_1= -0.002; b_2= 2.210×10^{4} b_3=2.702×10^{6}
11. KGN	ECB	7.633×10^{3}	0.899	0.628	0.879	89.3	b_0= 0.916; b_1=1.038; b_2= 0.998; b_3=1.000
12. VOA	LCB	$2.149 \cdot 10^{5}$	0.984	1.561	1.174	98.3	b_0= 0.998; b_1=0.002; b_2= -1.619×10^{5}; b_3=3.189×10^{7}

(cubic on logarithmic scale) associated with a very high (Φ = 0.98) degree of predictability. The other components associated with Φ-coefficient exceeding 0.95 were CRL, D&N and F&V. Pulses happened to be the only component (having grown in a logistic fashion) associated with a fairly low value (= 0.71) of the coefficient.

In comparative terms, the fit of long-term trend paths (as gauged through values of the Φ-coefficient) was more robust in respect of real value of output from the components of allied activities of agriculture. Except for FIS (with Φ = 0.75) and ORM (with Φ = 0.88), each of the remaining 16 components had the coefficient of predictability exceeding 0.95 (Table 2). As to what it implies is that the time series on real value from allied activities of agriculture have, in general, propagated in a closely predictable manner.

The so-identified equations of the best-fit provided us with the basis to estimate relative growth rates (RGR_t), which were then depicted diagrammatically; Figure 1 in respect of major crops and Figure 2 in respect of agriculture and allied activities.

TABLE 2

Equations of the Best-Fit in respect of Gross Value-added (at 1999-2000 Constant Price) from Agriculture and Allied Activities in India

Component	*Equation of the Best-Fit*	*Statistical Yardsticks*					*Values of the Unknowns*
		RMS	*Φ*	*D-W*	*I*	*Variation Explained (in %)*	
1. VAL	PRB	0.007	0.993	1.954	1.191	99.2	b_0 1.093; b_1 0.002; b_2 0.0009
1.1. AGR	PRB	0.012	0.987	2.120	1.184	98.6	b_0 1.069; b_1 0.0133; b_2 0.0007
1.2 LVS	PRB	0.004	0.997	0.200	0.919	99.7	b_0 1.170; b_1 -0.0031; b_2 0.0017
2 INP	CUB	0.012	0.988	0.623	0.992	98.7	b_0 1.119; b_1 -0.0189; b_2 -0.0019; b_3 -1.258×10^6
2.1 SED	ECB	0.006	0.948	0.891	0.995	94.6	b_0 1.036; b_1 1.006; b_2 1.000; b_3 0.999
2.2 ORM	LGS	0.002	0.880	0.486	0.829	87.5	b_0 1.005; b_1 -0.0315; b_2 1.044
2.3 CFT	EPB	42.952	0.983	0.999	1.060	98.2	b_0 0.515; b_1 1.213; b_2 0.998
2.4 CRM	ECB	0.293	0.989	0.469	0.963	98.9	b_0 0.9933; b_1 1.005; b_2 1.002; b_3 0.999
2.5 FLS	CUB	0.020	0.946	0.571	0.928	94.3	b_0 1.082; b_1 -0.0052; b_2 0.0015; b_3 -7.468×10^6
2.6 IRC	CUB	0.275	0.960	0.684	0.968	95.8	b_0 0.819; b_1 0.0199; b_2 0.005; b_3 -3.331×10^5
2.7 MKC	CUB	0.135	0.985	1.078	1.078	98.4	b_0 1.448; b_1 -0.1395; b_2 0.0107; b_3 -1.053×10^4
2.8 ELT	LCB	0.012	0.994	0.398	0.953	99.4	b_0 0.714; b_1 0.098; b_2 6.714×10^4; b_3 -1.923×10^6
2.9 P&I	LCB	0.018	0.977	0.834	1.019	97.6	b_0 .421; b_1 .217; b_2 -.004; b_3 0.03
2.10. DSO	LCB	0.013	0.978	0.818	1.019	97.7	b_0 .850; b_1 .071; b_2 -7.124×10^6; b_3 -7.313×10^6
2.11. FIS	LCB	0.039	0.755	0.606	0.693	74.2	b_0 .899; b_1 -.136; b_2 .004; b_3 -4.089×10^5
3 GDP	CUB	0.012	0.989	1.866	1.187	98.9	b_0 1.083; b_1 .009; b_2 5.629×10^4; b_3 5.766×10^6
3.1 A&A	CUB	0.011	0.989	1.967	1.187	98.9	b_0 1.067; b_1 .013; b_2 3.92×10^4; b_3 7.06×10^6
3.2 GI	CUB	3.217	0.978	0.462	0.947	97.6	b_0 4.052; b_1 -.960; b_2 .060; b_3 -6.124×10^4

FIGURE 1

Showing Patterns of Relative Growth Rates in respect of the Value of Output (at 1999-2000 Constant Prices) from Major Crops in India

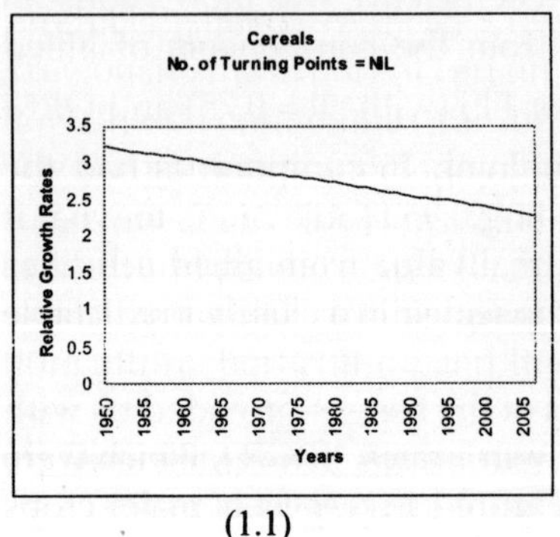

(1.1)

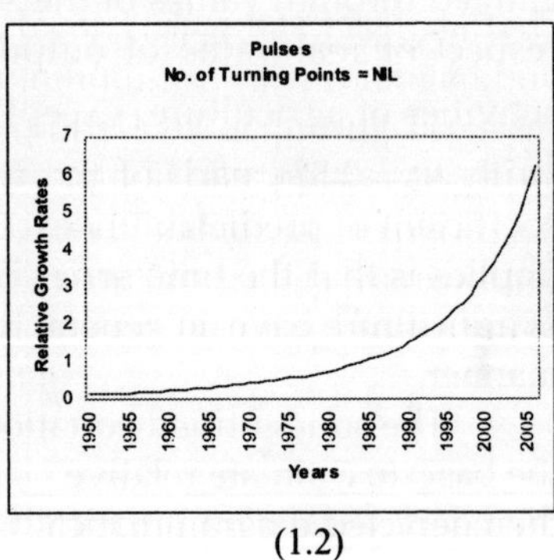

(1.2)

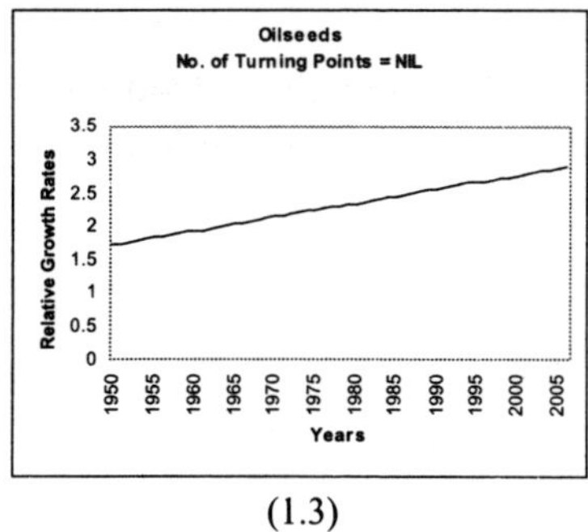

(1.3)

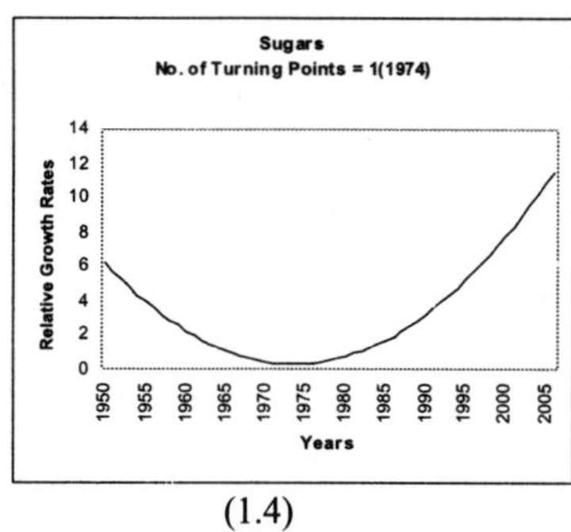

(1.4)

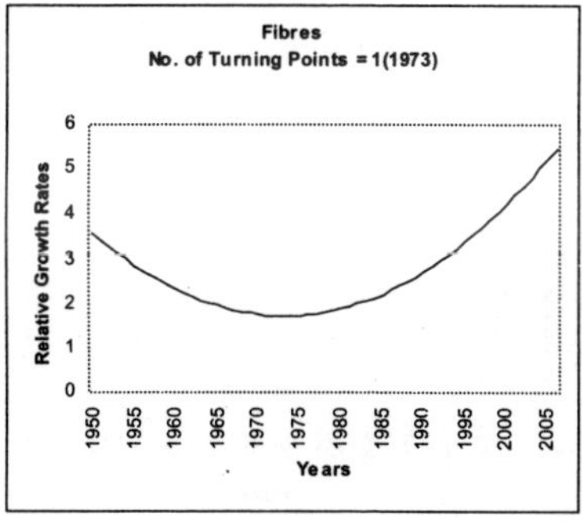

(1.5)

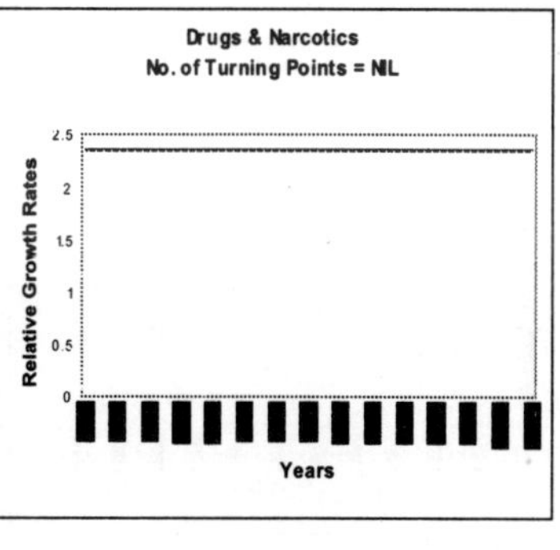

(1.6)

Condiments & Spices
No. of Turning Points = NIL

Relative Growth Rates

Years

(1.7)

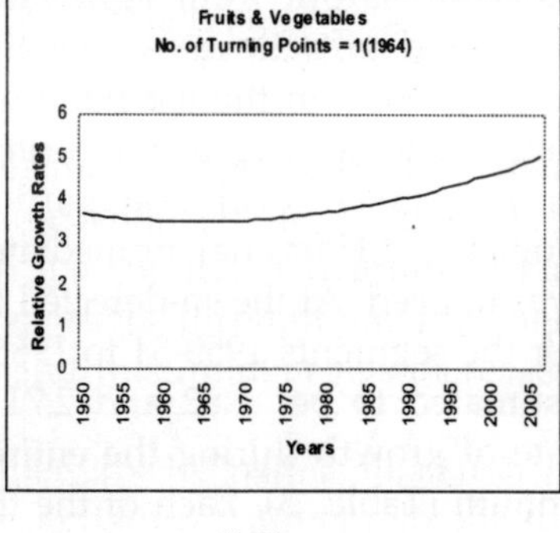

(1.8)

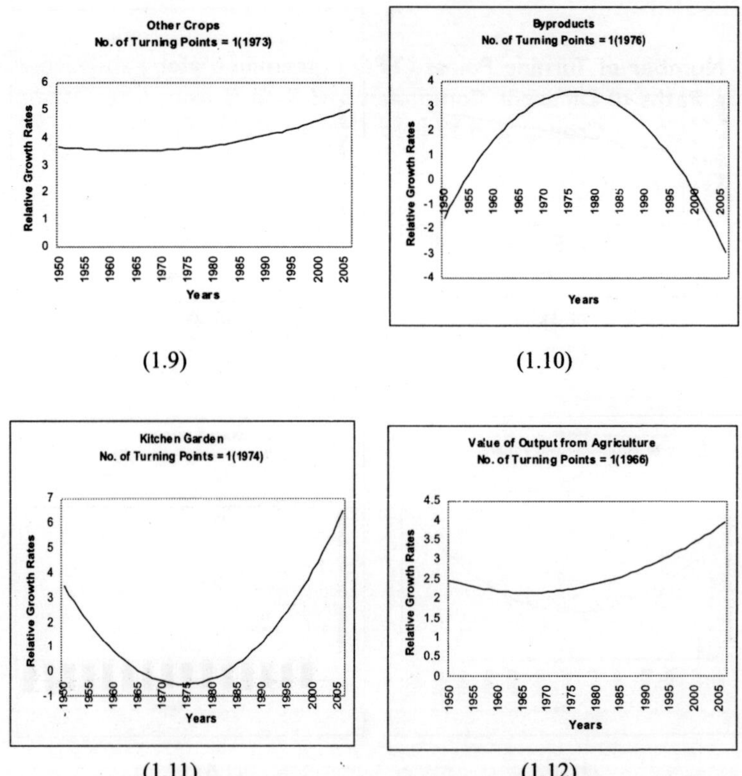

(1.9) (1.10)

(1.11) (1.12)

A glance at Figure 1 evinces that the time series on overall value of output from agriculture (part 1.12 of the figure) has registered growth rates changing in a parabolic manner. One turning point in the temporal path of relative growth rates was detected to have occurred during 1966-67 (the year typical of the onset of green revolution, particularly in the northern states like Punjab and Haryana), immediately beyond which an acceleration was noticed. At the so-detected turning point, *kinked growth rates* for the segments 1950-51 to 1965-66 and 1966-67 to 2006-07 were estimated to be 1.82 and 2.71 per cent respectively, with the rate of growth during the entire period being 2.53 per cent per annum (Table 3). Each of the three rates of growth were tested to be highly significantly different from zero.

TABLE 3

Number of Turning Points (TPs) determined along the Growth Paths of Different Components of Real Output from Major Crops, and Kinked Growth Rates therein

Component	*No. of TPs*	*Year of TPs*	*Kinked Growth Rates in Different Segments*	*Pooled Growth Rate*
CRL	0	-	-	2.799** (45.17)
PLS	0	-	-	0.885** (8.46)
OLS	0	-	-	2.338** (15.66)
SGR	1	1974	SG_1 =1.019* (2.53) ; SG_2=3.151** (10.93)	2.301** (14.19)
FBR	1	1973	SG_1 =1.751** (5.09); SG_2 =2.753** (12.21)	2.381** (19.05)
D&N	0	-	-	2.371** (45.30)
C&S	0	-	-	2.309** (30.86)
F&V	1	1964	SG_1 = 2.776* (6.54) ; SG_2 =4.242* (36.78)	4.00** (45.59)
OTC	1	1973	SG_1 = -0.32NS (0.93); SG_2 =1.556* (6.91)	0.864** (6.37)
BPT	1	1976	SG_1 = 2.520* (7.82) ; SG_2 =2.202* (8.11)	2.34** (17.90)
KGN	1	1974	SG_1 = 0.022NS (0.008); SG_2 =1.280* (7.10)	0.781** (7.672)
VOA	1	1966	SG_1 = 1.816** (8.74); SG_2 =2.707** (38.77)	2.526** (48.55)

NS: Non-significant; *: Significant at 5 per cent probability level; **: Significant at 1 per cent probability level.

FIGURE 2

Showing Patterns of Relative Growth Rates in respect of the Value of Output (at 1999-2000 Constant Prices) from Agriculture and Allied Activities in India

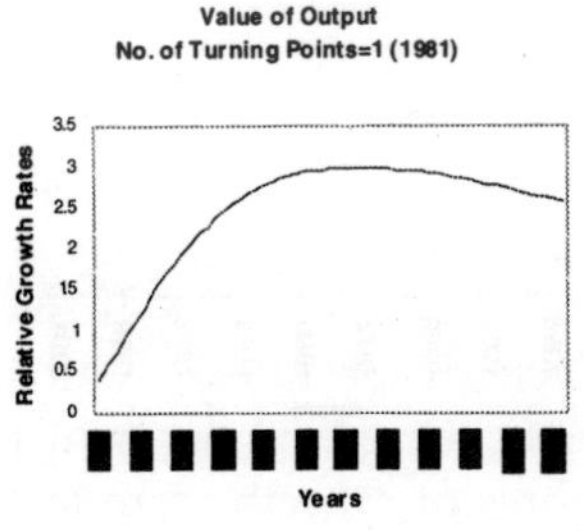

(2.1)

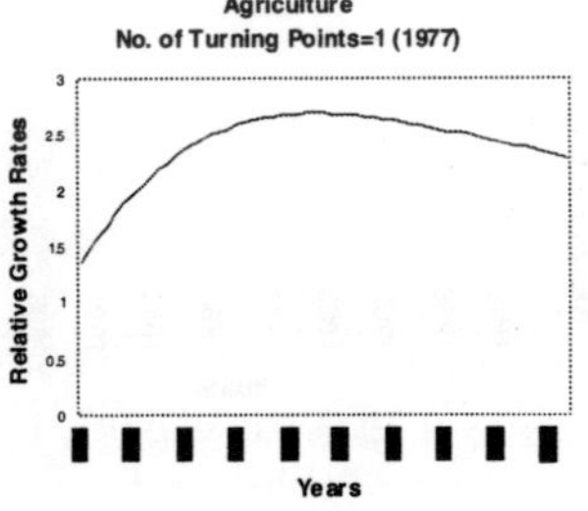

(2.2)

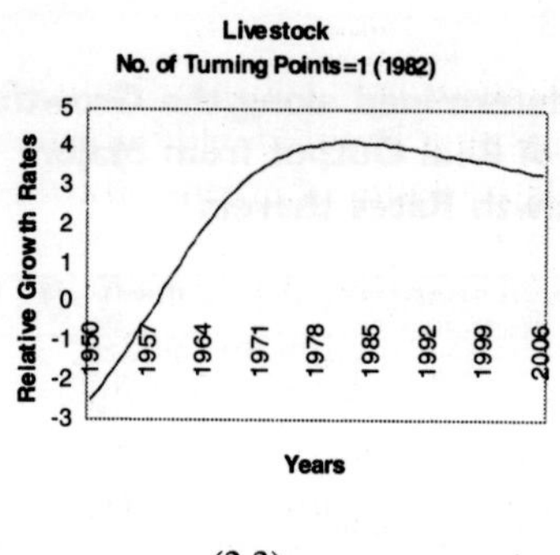

(2.3)

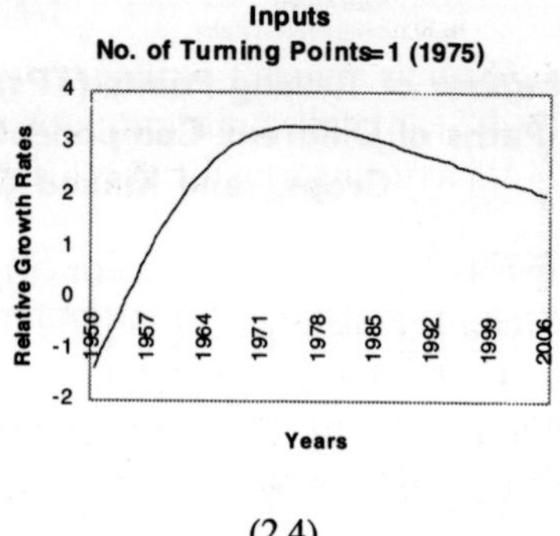

(2.4)

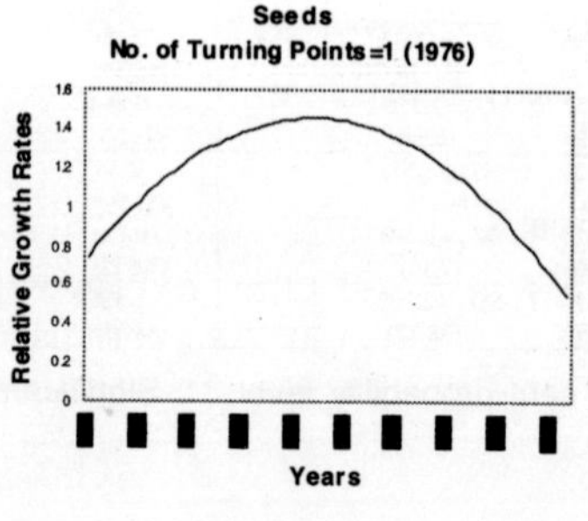

(2.5)

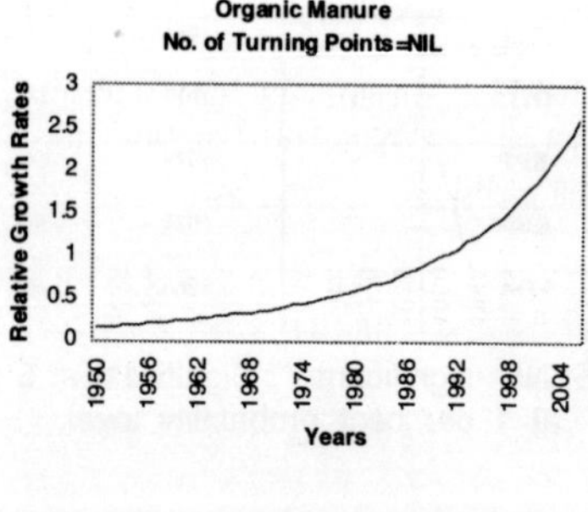

(2.6)

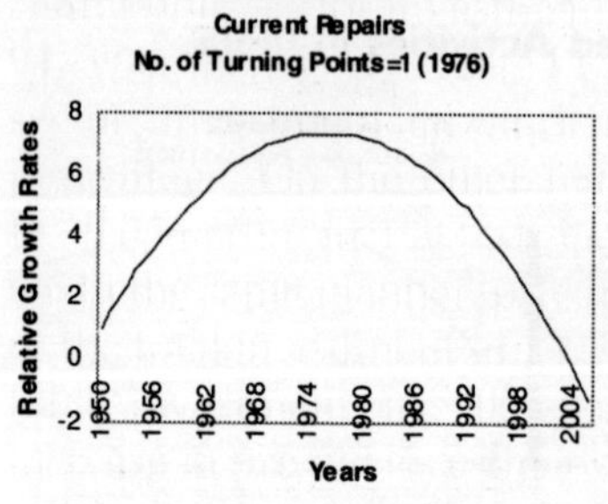

(2.7)

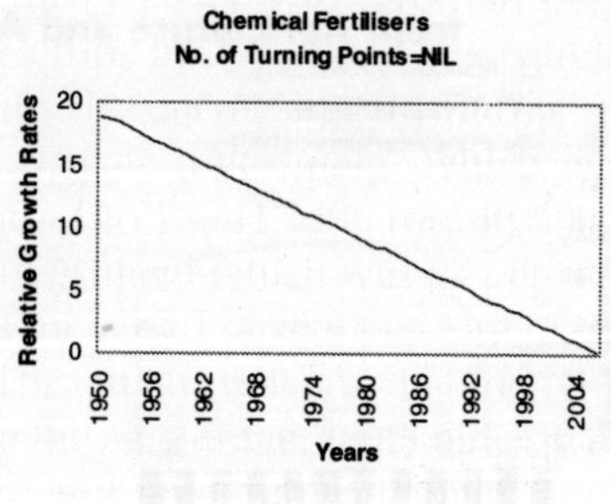

(2.8)

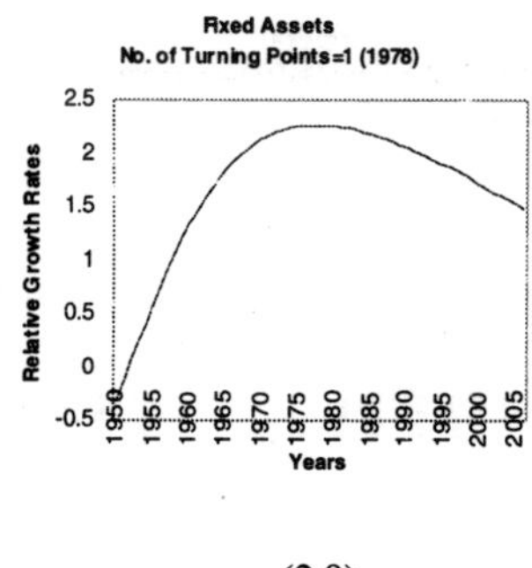

(2.9)

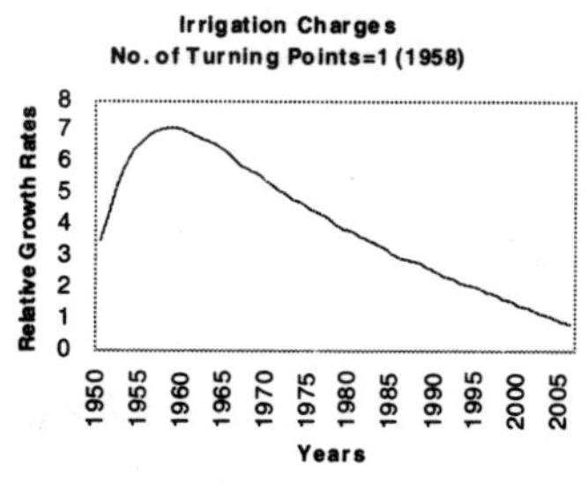

(2.10)

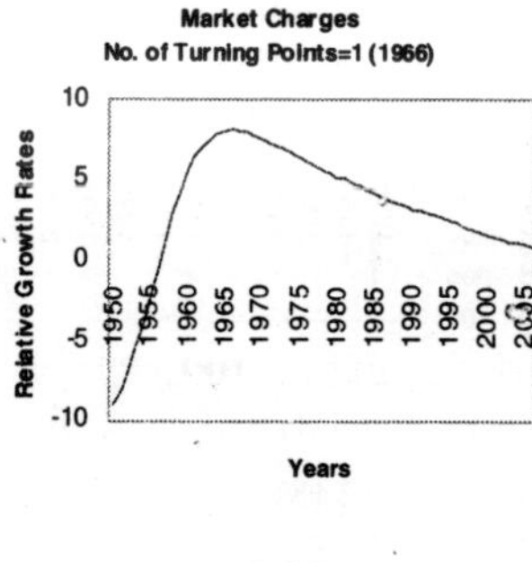

(2.11)

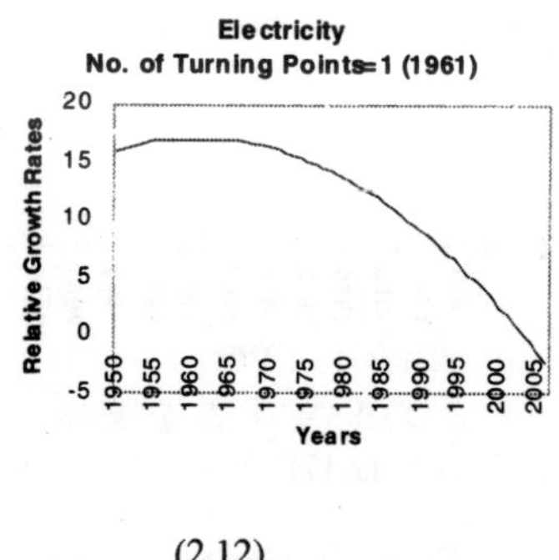

(2.12)

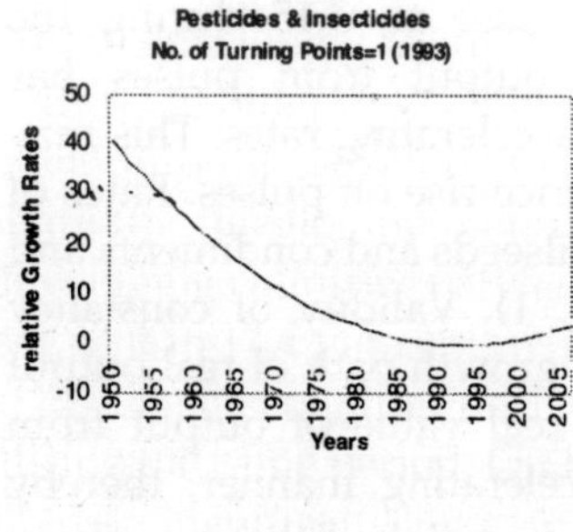

(2.13)

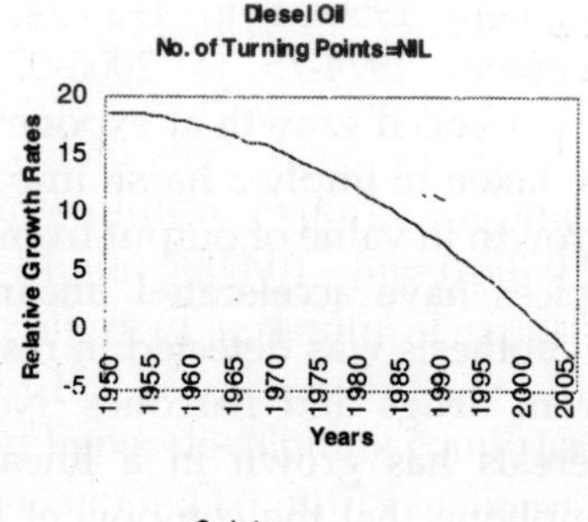

(2.14)

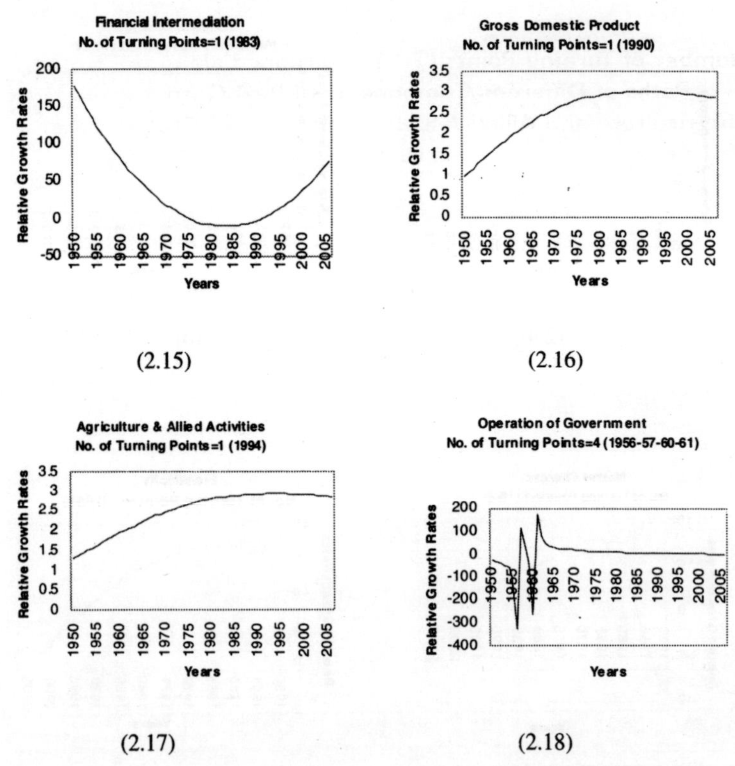

(2.15) (2.16)

(2.17) (2.18)

Quite a similar pattern of accelerating growth rates was experienced in respect of real value of output from each of sugar, fiber, kitchen garden, fruits and vegetable, and other crops. It is worth mentioning that in respect of sugar, the kinked growth rate (with one kink at 1974-75) was computed to be 1.02 during the segment 1950-51 to 1973-74, which rose to 3.15 during the segment 1974-75 to 2006-07. Real output from pulses has experienced growth at exponentially accelerating rates. This may be taken to imply a harsh impact of price-rise on pulses. Rates of growth in value of output from both oilseeds and condiments and spices have accelerated linearly (Fig. 1). Validity of constancy hypothesis was detected in respect of growth path of real output from drugs and narcotics. Notably, real value of output from cereals has grown in a linearly decelerating manner, thereby implying that the component has not been jolted that heavily in

TABLE 4

Number of Turning Points (TPs) determined along the Growth Paths of Different Components of Real Output from Agriculture and Allied Activities, and Kinked Growth Rates therein

Component	*No. of TPs*	*Year(s) of TPs*	*Kinked Growth Rates in Different Segments*	*Pooled Growth Rate*
VOO	1	1981	$SG_1 = 2.430^{**}$ (33.07) ; $SG_2 = 3.107^{**}$ (32.70)	2.714^{**} (63.27)
AGR	1	1977	$SG_1 = 2.445^{**}$ (25.31) ; $SG_2 = 2.666^{**}$ (30.00)	2.561 (61.42)
LVS	1	1982	$SG_1 = 2.315^{**}$ (19.72) ; $SG_2 = 4.606^{**}$ (27.62)	3.215^{**} (33.62)
INP	1	1975	$SG_1 = 2.175^{**}$ (16.82) ; $SG_2 = 3.155^{**}$ (31.30)	2.741^{**} (45.97)
SED	1	1976	$SG_1 = 1.24^{**}$ (13.29) ; $SG_2 = 1.345^{**}$ (17.6)	1.298^{**} (34.29)
ORM	0	-	-	6.676^{**} (14.75)
CFT	0	-	-	10.096^{**} (27.54)
CRM	1	1976	$SG_1 = 6.683^{**}$ (23.93) ; $SG_2 = 5.392^{**}$ (23.00)	5.968^{**} (49.50)
FLS	1	1978	$SG_1 = 1.648^{**}$ (27.84) ; $SG_2 = 2.245^{**}$ (10.92)	1.946^{**} (14.83)
IRC	1	1958	$SG_1 = 7.662^{**}$ (42.42) ; $SG_2 = 4.115^{**}$ (20.19)	4.324^{**} (24.91)
MKC	1	1966	$SG_1 = 4.197^{**}$ (6.13) ; $SG_2 = 4.957^{**}$ (21.46)	4.803^{**} (30.78)
ELT	1	1961	$SG_1 = 26.30^{**}$ (11.11) ; $SG_2 = 12.17^{**}$ (29.61)	13.59^{**} (35.14)
P&I	1	1983	$SG_1 = 16.412^{**}$ (20.25) ; $SG_2 = -3.17^{*}$ (2.80)	8.749^{**} (11.70)
DSO	0	-	-	12.579^{**} (26.57)
FIS	1	1993	$SG_1 = 17.59^{**}$ (37.18) ; $SG_2 = 4.514^{**}$ (6.61)	12.57^{**} (26.57)
GDP	1	1990	$SG_1 = 2.549^{**}$ (38.49) ; $SG_2 = 3.299^{**}$ (16.76)	2.701^{**} (56.03)
A&A	1	1994	$SG_1 = 2.529^{**}$ (40.82) ; $SG_2 = 3.394^{**}$ (11.52)	2.635^{**} (53.62)
OGI	4	1956; 1957; 1960; 1961	$SG_1 = 2.324^{NS}$ (0.35) ; $SG_2 = 7.725^{NS}$ (0.20) $SG_3 = -5.84$ (0.39) ; SG 106.18* (2.38 $SG_5 = 7.693^{**}$ (19.50)	8.036^{**} (27.43)

NS: Non-significant; *: Significant at 5 per cent probability level; **: Significant at 1 per cent probability level.

terms of its price rise. Rates of growth in agricultural by-products have undergone deceleration rather rapidly, thereby calling for the need to process the by-products (like *gur* jagary, straw of wheat, paddy, sugarcane, cotton, etc.) optimally, so as to induce value addition.

As per Figure 2, the time series on overall value of output from agriculture and allied activities has undergone growth in a parabolic manner. One turning point (during 1981-82) was detected along the path of the relative growth rates, immediately beyond which a deceleration was noticed. Again, treating the so-detected turning point as a kink, the kinked growth rates for the segments 1950-51 to 1980-81 and 1981-82 to 2006-07 were estimated to be 2.43 and 3.11 per cent respectively, with the rate of growth during the entire period being 2.71 per cent per annum (Table 4). Here also, each of the three rates of growth were tested to be highly significantly different from zero. Emphatically, the kinked rate of growth for the second segment (as a whole) being higher than that for the first segment (as a whole) may not be mistaken as an experience of acceleration phenomenon; rather the kink (1981-82 in the present case) has been detected to be the point beyond which the rates of growth have portrayed signs of deterioration.

Pattern of decelerating growth rates was similarly observed in respect of real value of output of each of agriculture and livestock. In respect of aggregated inputs as well, a deceleration in the growth rates was indicated, with one turning point having been occurred during 1975-76. Within components of inputs, deceleration was detected in respect of real value of (i) seeds, (ii) current repairs, (iii) fixed assets, (iv) irrigation charges, (vi) market charges, and (vii) electricity charges; each having shown one turning point. Further, diesel charges and chemical fertilizers, too, have shown a uniformly decelerating rates of growth (without experiencing any turning point). Such a deceleration may be the result of heavy subsidization, across the board, in agricultural inputs which, however, may not be viewed as a conducive sign from the point of view of overall development. Notably, the inputs which have undergone an acceleration, particularly after mid-90s were: (i) pesticides and insecticides, (ii) organic manure, and (iii) financial intermediation service.

NATURE AND PACE OF STRUCTURAL SHIFTS

During 1950-51, relative contribution of agriculture was as high as 83 per cent *vis-à-vis* 17 per cent of that of livestock. Over

TABLE. 5

Showing Distributive Shares (in %) of Different Crops in Value of Output (at Current Prices) of Agriculture in India

Year	GR	LVS	Total	Major Components of AGR											VOA
				CRL	PLS	OLS	SGR	FBR	D&N	C&S	F&V	OTC	BPT	KGN	
1950-51	[illegible].9	17.1	100.0	35.8	6.1	7.7	5.9	4.0	2.7	2.9	7.6	17.8	8.5	1.0	100.0
1955-55	[illegible]1.5	18.5	100.0	35.2	4.8	5.7	8.4	5.1	2.8	1.9	11.8	14.9	8.1	1.3	100.0
1960-61	83.5	16.5	100.0	40.5	6.1	7.6	7.5	5.2	2.5	2.6	10.3	9.4	7.3	1.0	100.0
1965-66	84.6	15.4	100.0	42.4	6.3	8.3	6.6	4.0	2.4	2.3	12.1	8.2	6.2	1.2	100.0
1970-71	85.0	15.0	100.0	42.3	5.3	9.2	5.9	4.8	2.1	2.4	14.4	6.9	5.5	1.0	100.0
1975-76	82.3	17.7	100.0	43.5	5.4	7.4	7.0	3.7	2.3	2.7	14.2	7.2	5.7	0.9	100.0
1980-81	82.5	17.5	100.0	38.0	6.4	8.0	6.1	4.2	2.0	1.5	15.7	6.7	10.5	0.9	100.0
1985-86	77.5	22.5	100.0	38.1	6.6	6.8	4.7	3.9	2.2	1.9	19.3	6.0	9.6	0.9	100.0
1990-91	76.6	23.4	100.0	35.9	6.9	11.4	5.3	4.4	2.2	1.9	17.2	5.5	8.6	0.7	100.0
1995-96	74.5	25.5	100.0	35.2	5.7	8.9	5.5	5.9	2.0	2.6	20.0	5.8	7.7	0.7	100.0
2000-01	72.9	27.1	100.0	35.2	4.3	5.9	6.9	3.0	1.9	3.1	25.1	6.8	7.2	0.6	100.0
2006-07	73.4	26.6	100.0	32.9	4.6	5.7	6.7	5.6	1.7	3.4	24.9	7.6	6.3	0.6	100.0

the long span of 57 years, agriculture has experienced a shedding of 10 per cent share (from 83% to 73%) to livestock (whose relative share has inflated from 17 to 27%; Table 5). So far as shifts in distributive shares of different crops in the real value of agricultural output is concerned (Table 5), relative contribution of cereals increased from about 36 per cent during 1950-51 to more than 43 per cent during 1975-76 (presumably due to impact of green revolution), but declined subsequently to nearly 33 per cent during 2006-07 (pointing towards stagnation in the output of cereal crops). Major shifts have been registered in respect of (i) fruits and vegetables (whose relative share has jumped from nearly 8 per cent during 1950-51 to 25 per cent during 2006-07), and (ii) other crops (whose relative share has regressed from nearly 18 per cent during 1950-51 to 8 per cent during 2006-07). Relative shares of rest of the crops have not portrayed any noticeable changes.

As regards structural transformations in the composition of inputs (Table 6), the major contributing components were observed to be (i) fixed assets and other feed of livestock (FLS), (ii) seed (SED), (iii) chemical fertilizers (CFT), (iv) organic manure (ORM), (v) market charges (MKC), and (vi) diesel oil (DSO). Over the study span (i.e., from 1960-61 to 2006-07), relative share of fixed assets has undergone a steep reduction (through nearly 25% points) from 64.1 to 39.3 per cent, implying thereby a

TABLE 6

Showing Distributive Shares (in %) of Value of Different Inputs (at Current Prices) of Agriculture and Allied Activities in India

Year	*Major Components of Inputs*											INP
	SED	ORM	CFT	CRM	FLS	IRC	MKC	ELT	P&I	DSO	FIS	
1960-61	16.3	8.5	3.4	0.8	64.1	1.3	4.1	0.4	0.3	0.6	0.3	100
1965-66	19.6	6.1	7.0	0.8	58.5	1.4	4.2	0.8	0.5	0.9	0.3	100
1970-71	15.6	4.3	11.3	0.9	58.5	1.2	4.5	1.6	0.9	0.7	0.5	100
1975-76	12.2	4.0	19.0	1.0	46.4	1.5	6.8	2.5	4.5	1.5	0.6	100
1980-81	9.4	3.4	18.7	0.8	54.2	0.7	6.9	1.8	1.4	2.0	0.7	100
1985-86	8.8	3.6	22.9	1.1	48.3	0.6	6.8	1.9	1.7	3.0	1.3	100
1990-91	9.4	4.3	20.5	1.3	47.7	0.7	7.5	1.8	1.1	3.4	2.3	100
1995-96	8.8	4.7	20.2	1.6	45.8	0.7	7.6	2.5	1.5	3.5	3.1	100
2000-01	7.6	5.7	17.9	1.7	45.6	0.7	7.6	2.9	0.9	6.7	2.7	100
2006-07	7.5	4.7	17.4	1.9	39.3	1.0	7.9	2.2	1.0	13.3	3.8	100

TABLE 7

Measures θ (due to Moore, 1978) and ξ (due to Sethi, 2003) of Structural Changes in Output from Major Crops, Output from Agriculture and Allied Activities, and Inputs in Agriculture

Time Span	*Output from Major Crops*		*Output from Agriculture & Allied Activities*		*Inputs in Agriculture*	
	θ	ξ	θ	ξ	θ	ξ
1950-1960	12.968	2.582	-	-	-	-
1960-1970	6.961	1.896	1.202	0.168	8.425	18.308
1970-1980	8.004	4.000	1.972	0.422	10.001	9.792
1980-1990	6.298	1.542	5.007	1.618	5.272	9.872
1990-2000	13.337	5.931	3.417	0.481	5.244	4.389
2000-2006	4.227	2.666	0.495	0.008	9.540	3.886
1950-1980	18.334	7.976	0.770	0.058	17.224	27.457
1980-1995	8.082	3.107	6.934	2.750	6.450	14.099
1995-2006	9.019	2.764	1.031	0.041	12.858	14.533
1950-2006	27.355	17.256	8.734	4.276	27.150	47.986
CV (%)	60.6	95.4	91.1	138.2	62.2	82.5

comparatively slower increase in their price (presumably due to subsidization). Relative share of expenditure on seeds (from 16.3 to 7.5%) as well as organic manure (from 8.5 to 4.7%) has also declined during the study span. However, the relative contribution of chemical fertilizers has shot from a mere

3.4 per cent during early 60s to as high as 22.9 per cent during mid-80s, but has marginally come down to 17.4 per cent as of late. Similarly, expenditure on diesel oil has jumped rather abruptly from a mere 0.6 per cent during 1960-61 to 13.7 per cent during 2006-07. And, again, relative share of market charges has increased over the study span from 4.1 to 7.9 per cent. Nevertheless, relative contributions of rest of the components of input have not undergone perceptible changes.

As regards speed of structural changes in each of the three characters, viz., (i) output from major crops, (ii) output from agriculture and allied activities, and (iii) inputs in agriculture (Table 7), the index ξ was invariably observed to be relatively more sensitive to structural changes. This was due to higher values of CV (95.4, 138.2 and 82.5%, respectively, for the three characters) associated with ξ as compared to those (60.6, 91.1 and 62.2%, respectively) associated with θ. The speed of structural changes during different periods/sub-periods might, therefore, be adjudged preferably through the index ξ.

As per Table 7, the speediest structural changes (ξ = 48.0) have occurred in inputs, followed by those (ξ = 17.3) in major crops and the slowest (ξ = 4.3) in agriculture and allied activities. In respect of each of inputs and output from major crops, changes have occurred grossly during 1950-80, whereas in agriculture and allied activities, such changes were experienced during 1980-95. Decade-wise, the fastest changes were recorded during 1960-70 (ξ =18.3) in inputs, during 1990-2000 (ξ = 5.9) in major crops, and during 1980-90 (ξ =1.6) in agriculture and allied activities.

POLICY IMPLICATIONS

In the light of rates of growth in real value of output from pulses, oilseeds, sugarcane, and spices at accelerated rates (presumably due to a severe impact of price rise on these crops), there is a need to go in for diversification in favour of such crops so as to bridge the gap between their demand and supply. Processing of agricultural by-products (like *gur* jagary, straw of wheat, paddy, sugarcane, cotton, etc.) needs be encouraged so as to induce value addition. Deceleration in real value of a large majority of agricultural inputs might be the result of heavy subsidization (across the board) in the inputs which, however, may not be a healthy practice from the angle of overall development. Keeping in view the observations on structural shifts, non-farming activities like dairying/livestock need be promoted so as to make available organic manure at cheaper rates and shed off, at least partly, heavy dependence on chemical fertilizers. In the light of sanitary and phyto-sanitary measures, policies need be framed so as to monitor and check indiscriminate use of insecticides and pesticides. Water-saving cropping pattern and techniques need be adopted so as to bring down input cost on diesel oil and, consequently, preserve water table.

References

Behera, B. and P. Mishra (2007), "Acceleration of Agricultural Growth in India: Suggestive Policy Framework", *Economic and Political Weekly*, 42(42): 4268-71.

Bhide, S., K.P. Kalirajan and R.T. Shand (1998), "India's Agriculture Dynamics: Weak Link in Development", *Economic and Political Weekly*, 33(39): A118-A127.

Boyce, J.K. (1986), "Kinked Exponential Models for Growth Rate Estimation", *Oxford Bulletin of Economics and Statistics*, 48(4): 385-91.

Centre for Monitoring Indian Economy (2008), "Highlights from CMIE's *Monthly Review of the Indian Economy* (July).

Chand, R. and S.S. Raju (2009), "Instability in Indian Agriculture during Different Phases of Technology and Policy", *Indian Journal of Agriculture Economics*, 64(2): 187-207.

Chenery, H., M.S. Ahluwalia, C.L.G. Bell, J.H. Duloy, and R. Jolly (1974), Redistribution with Growth: London, Oxford University Press.

Goldar, B. and V. Seth (1989), "Spatial Variations in Rate of Industrial Growth in India", *Economic and Political Weekly*, 24(22): 1237-40.

Government of India (2008), Economic Survey of India: 2007-08: New Delhi.

Jeromi, P.D. and A. Ramanathan (1993), "World Pepper Market and India: An Analysis of Growth and Instability", *Indian Journal of Agricultural Economics*, 48(1): 88-97.

Kaur, D. (2008), "Growth and Structural Changes in Labour Input in India—Evidence from Different Rounds of NSS", Unpublished M.Sc. Dissertation submitted to the Guru Nanak Dev University, Amritsar.

Kaushik, K.K. (1993), "Growth and Instability of Oil Seed Production", *Indian Journal of Agricultural Economics*, 48(3): 334-8.

Mahendradev, S. (1987), "Growth and Instability in Foodgrains Production: An Inter-State Analysis", *Economic and Political Weekly*, 22(39): A82-A92.

———(2008), "Agriculture: Absence of Big Push", *Economic and Political Weekly*, 43(15): 33-6.

Moore, J.H. (1978), "A Measure of Structural Change in Output", Review of Income and Wealth, 24(1): 105-18.

Narayana Reddy, M., J.C. Katyal, Y.V.R. Reddy and C.A. Rama Rao (1998), Estimating Agricultural Growth—A Piecewise Regression Approach", *Indian Journal of Agricultural Economics*, 53(2): 155-62.

Paramasivan, C. (2008), "Promoting Agricultural Sector in India", Third Concept, 21(251): 33-35.

Rao, C.H. Hanumantha (1968), "Fluctuations in Agricultural Growth: An Analysis of Unstable Increase in Productivity", *Economic and Political Weekly*, 3(1/2): 87-94.

———(1994), "Reforming Agriculture in New Context", *Economic and Political Weekly*, 29(16/17): 1005-10.

Rao, C.H. Hanumantha and A. Gulati (1994), "Indian Agriculture: Emerging Perspectives and Policy Issues", *Economic and Political Weekly*, 29(53): A158-A169.

Rao, C.H. Hanumantha, S.K. Ray and K. Subbarao (1988), Unstable Agriculture and Droughts: Implications for Policy: New Delhi, Vikas Publishing House Pvt. Ltd.

Rao, G.V.K. and R. Tharnarajakshi (1978), "Some Aspects of Growth of Indian Agriculture", *Economic and Political Weekly*, 13 (51-52).

Rao, V.M. and R.S. Deshpande (1986), "Agricultural Growth in India: A Review of Experiences and Prospects", *Economic and Political Weekly*, 21(38-39): A101-A112.

Rudra, A. (1970), "The Rate of Growth of the Indian Economy", in E.A.G. Robinson and M. Kidron (eds.), Economic Development in South Asia (London, McMillan).

Sawant, S.D. and C.V. Achuthan (1995), "Agricultural Growth Across Crops and Regions: Emerging Trends and Patterns, *Economic and Political Weekly*, 30(12): A2-A13.

Sethi, A.S. (1997), Dynamics of National Income: New Delhi, Deep & Deep Publications.

———(2003), "Inter-Sectoral Linkages in Haryana's Income ¾ A Temporal Analysis", *Artha Vijnana*, 45(3 and 4): 147-60.

———(2008), "Some Methodological Aspects of Rates of Growth Computations: Limitations and Alternatives", *South Asia Economic Journal*, 9(1): 195-209.

———(2009), "On Further Aspects of Estimating Rates of Growth and Turning Points along Growth Paths", *Journal of Income and Wealth* (Communicated).

Srinivasan, T.N. (1979), "Trends in Agriculture in India, 1949-50—1977-78", *Economic and Political Weekly*, 14(30/32): 1283-94.

Rural Credit: Trend, Issues and Challenges in India

Samir R. Samantara and B.B. Sahoo

Until 1969, the Commercial Banks were largely urban-oriented catering to the needs of trade and industry and agriculture was outside their domain of operation. With nationalisation of commercial banks in 1969 and interventions by the Government of India and the Reserve Bank of India in 1970s and 1980s, the functions of commercial banks were regulated and controlled. During 1990s, the financial sector reforms and prudential norms, i.e., income recognition, asset classification and provisioning norms, became instrumental in putting increased thrust on efficiency and viability of the banks through rationalization and consolidation, which resulted in relocation and closure of many rural branches. In response to the current agrarian crisis and farmers' suicides, a number of initiatives, i.e., doubling of credit in three years, revival of co-operative credit structure, policy response to farmer suicides and setting up committees have been put in place to look into sensitive issues

* The views expressed in the article are of the authors and not necessarily of the institution they belong to.

such as financial inclusion, farmers' indebtedness and farmers' suicides.

I. TREND IN RURAL CREDIT

Branch Expansion

Indian banking system has acquired a wide reach in terms of expansion of bank branches. The expansionary phase hit the highest point during the 80s. The number of rural branches of Commercial Banks increased 32.8 times during the period between 1969 and 1991 and there was a marginal increase of 1.3 times between 1991 and 2009. The annual growth in bank branches in rural, semi-urban, urban and metropolitan areas during the period between 1991 and 2009 was (-) 0.58 per cent, 2.87 per cent, 3.68 per cent and 5.08 per cent respectively. When rural and semi-urban areas are combined together to form 'rural areas' and urban and metropolitans are combined to form 'urban areas', during the period between 1991 and 2009, the annual growth of bank branches in rural areas and urban areas were 0.46 per cent and 4.30 per cent and the overall increase was 1.57 per cent. Diagram 1 presents the trend of bank branches in rural and urban areas from 1991 and 2009 and Diagram II presents the trend in bank branches in rural and semi-urban areas during the same period. Diagram I shows that the pace of growth in bank branches in rural areas has become slower than that in urban areas. It can be observed from Diagram II that during the period between 1991 and 2009, the number of bank branches in rural areas declined and that in semi-urban areas increased.

Diagram I: Growth of Bank Branches in Rural Areas and Urban Areas durind 1991 and 2009

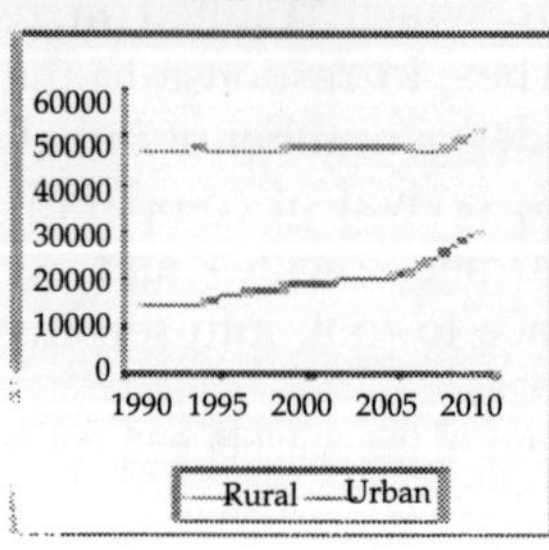

Diagram II: Growth of Bank Branches in Rural Areas and Semi-Urban Areas durind 1991 and 2009

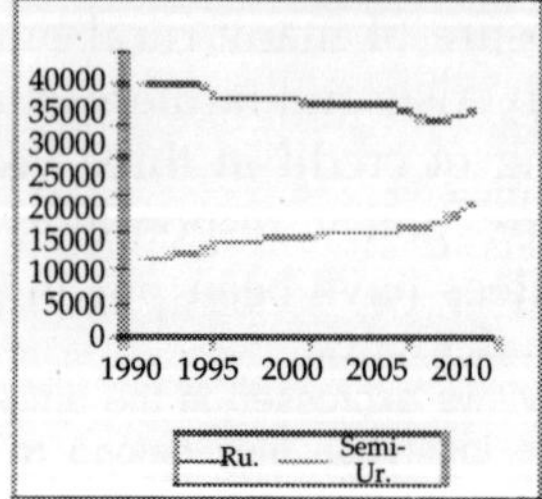

Net Bank Credit and Agricultural Advances

In 1969, the priority sector advances were Rs. 441 crore, which was 14.6 per cent of the net bank credit of Rs. 3,016 crore. Due to the implementation of various welfare measures for improving the situation of farmers, the priority sector advances increased to 40.7 per cent of the total net bank credit in 1991. Similarly, the shares of agricultural credit in total priority sector advances and agricultural credit in total net bank credit, which were 36.7 per cent and 5.4 per cent in 1969, increased to 40.7 per cent and 17.0 per cent in 1991. But agricultural credit in total priority sector advances and agricultural credit in total net bank credit were 41.4 per cent and 17.6 per cent in 2009. Thus, while there was a significant increase in priority sector advances and agricultural credit in 1991, they were nominal in 2009.

Further, when the increase in net bank credit, priority sector advances and agricultural credit were 18.31 per cent, 25.0 per cent and 24.37 per cent during the period between 1969 and 1991, they were 17.91 per cent, 18.02 per cent and 18.14 per cent respectively during 1991 and 2009. Table 1 presents the details of the growth in net bank credit, priority sector advances and agricultural advances of the Scheduled Commercial Banks in three selected years.

TABLE I

Details of the Growth in Net Bank Credit, Priority Sector Advances and Agricultural Advances of the Scheduled Commercial Banks in Three Selected Periods

(In percentage)

Particulars	*Between 1969 and 1991*	*Between 1991 and 2009*	*Between 1969 and 2009*
I. Agriculture	4.9	0.9	46.0
(i) Direct	18.4	0.7	134.8
(ii) Indirect	0.4	3.4	16.9
II. Others	4.1	0.9	37.8
III. Total priority sector advances	4.4	0.9	40.8
IV. Net bank credit	1.5	0.9	14.0

Source: Report on Trend and Progress of Banking in India, Various Issues.

Ground Level Credit Flow

During the period between 1969 and 2009, the ground level credit flow to agriculture and allied activities has expanded impressively. When the year 1999-2000 is taken as the base year, the total institutional credit to agriculture was Rs. 35.2 crore in 1990-91 and it increased to Rs. 707.7 crore in 2007-08. Thus, during the period between 1990-91 and 2007-08, the annual growth rate in the ground level credit flow was 20.63 per cent. Among the formal banks, the maximum growth in the credit flow was observed in Regional Rural Banks at 26.25 per cent followed by Commercial Banks at 24.34 per cent and Cooperative Banks at 13.45 per cent. It may be noted that there was a big leap in the credit flow for agriculture during the 3 years period of the Doubling of Credit, i.e., 2004-05 and 2006-07. But immediately after the end of the Doubling of Credit phase, the institutional credit to agriculture sector declined. In the case of Commercial Banks, the annual growth rate in the credit flow decreased by 5.8 per cent during the period between 2006-07 and 2007-08. However, the annual growth in credit flow in regional rural banks and cooperative banks were 21.4 per cent and 2.8 per cent during 2006-07 and 2007-08. However, the overall growth rate pulled down by 1.8 per cent due to the decline in the share of the ground level credit by the commercial banks. Table 2 presents the annual growth rate of institutional credit to agriculture sector in some selected periods between 1991-92 and 2007-08.

TABLE 2

Details of Annual Growth Rate of Institutional Credit to Agriculture Sector in Some Selected Periods between 1991-92 and 2007-08

Year	*Cooperative banks*	*Regional rural banks*	*Commercial banks*	*Total*
1991-92 to 2003-04	12.2	23.1	22.8	17.9
2004-05 to 2006-07	16.6	28.4	42.9	35.4
2006-07 to 2007-08	2.8	21.4	-5.8	-1.8
1991-92 to 2007-08	12.5	25.9	26.3	20.8

Diagrams III and IV present the supply of agricultural credit by the formal banks over the last 17 years during the period between 1991-92 and 2007-08. While Diagram III shows year-wise and bank wise agricultural credit, Diagram IV shows year-wise and bank-wise share of ground level credit flow for agriculture sector. It is evident from these diagrams that there was a steady rise in the credit flow for agriculture sector by the commercial banks during 2002-03 and 2006-07, but it was negative during 2006-07 and 2007-08. In the case of Regional Rural Banks and Cooperative Banks, the credit flows increased throughout the period between 1991-92 and 2007-08, but the pace of growth was very slow. Further, out of the total ground level credit flow of Rs. 11,202 crore in 1991-92, the share of Cooperative Banks was 51.8 per cent followed by Commercial Banks at 42.9 per cent. But over a period of the last 17 years, its supremacy in providing credit to agriculture had abysmally declined and in 2007-08, its share in the total ground level credit was only 19.4 per cent. However, in the same period the share of Commercial Banks in the total ground level credit for agriculture had increased from 42.9 per cent to 69.6 per cent. But there had been a steady growth in the share of the ground level credit in the case of Regional Rural Banks.

Diagram III: Year-wise and Bank-wise Institutional Credit to Agriculture

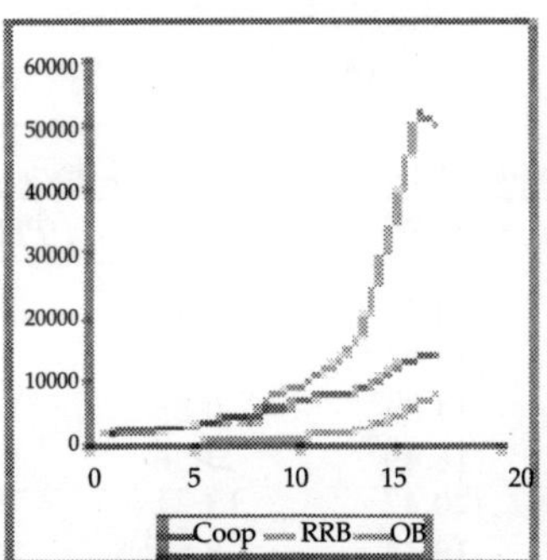

Diagram IV: Year-wise and Bank-wise Share in the Total Institutional Credit to Agriculture

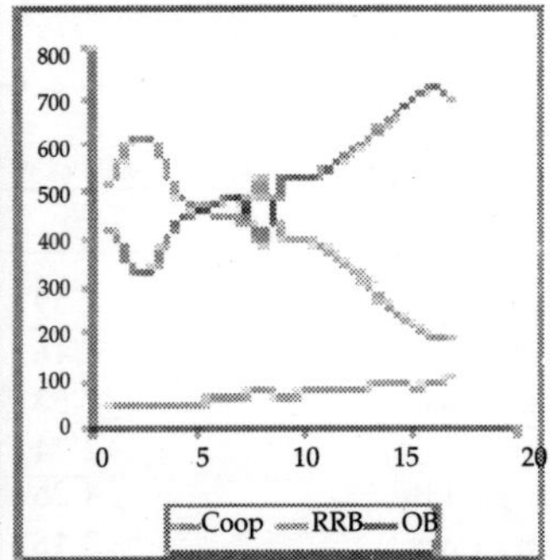

Priority Sector Lending

While the total credit flow of the scheduled Commercial Banks increased from Rs. 1,21,865 crore in 1991 to Rs. 23,61,914 crore at an annual rate of 19.05 per cent, that of advances to priority sector increased from Rs. 44,572 crore in 1991 to Rs. 8,24,773 crore at an annual rate of 18.73 per cent. The advances to priority sector, which was 36.6 per cent of the total credit in 1991, reduced to 34.9 per cent in 2008. During the last 17 years, no improvement has been observed in the share of advances to priority sector in the total credit flow. Between 1969 and 1991, the annual growth rates in net bank credit, total priority sector advances and advances to agriculture sector of the public sector banks were 18.3 per cent, 24.4 per cent and 25.0 per cent respectively. But between 1991 and 2009, the annual growth rates in net bank credit, total priority sector advances and advances to agriculture sector of the public sector banks were 17.9 per cent, 18.0 per cent and 18.1 per cent respectively.

Deposits and Credit

Table 3 presents the annual growth rate of area-wise number of accounts, deposits and credit of the Scheduled Commercial Banks during the period between 1991 and 2008. It is evident from the table that rural areas lag behind urban areas in each selected variable.

TABLE 3

Details of Area-wise Number of Accounts, Deposits, Credit of Scheduled Commercial Banks during 1991 and 2008

(Annual Growth Rate in %)

Area	*Deposit*		*Credit*	
	a/c	*Amount*	*a/c*	*Amount*
Rural	2.59	14.36	0.19	15.81
Semi-Urban	2.46	14.76	1.91	15.91
Rural areas	2.53	14.59	0.85	15.86
Urban	2.74	16.49	3.36	17.60
Metropolitan	4.28	20.42	13.71	21.78
Urban areas	3.48	19.14	8.65	20.54
Total	2.94	17.80	3.27	19.08

While per account deposit and credit had increased from Rs. 29.6 and Rs. 80.3 in 1991 to Rs. 195.9 and Rs. 849.8 in 2008 in rural areas, they increased from Rs.73 and Rs.537.6 in 1991 to Rs. 801.3 and Rs. 3141.3 in 2008 in urban areas. While credit was 2.7 times of the deposit in rural areas in 1991, it was 7.4 times in urban areas. By the year ending 2008, the gap between credit and deposit improved in favour of rural areas. In 2008, per account credit was 4.3 times of the deposit in rural areas and in urban areas, it was 3.9 times. Table 4 presents the details of per account deposit and credit in rural areas and urban areas during the period between 1991 and 2008.

TABLE 4

Details of Deposit and Credit in Rural and Urban Areas in Real Term

(Rs./Account, Base year = 1999)

Year	*Rural*		*Urban*		*Total*	
	Deposit	*Credit*	*Deposit*	*Credit*	*Deposit*	*Credit*
1991	29.6	80.3	73.0	537.6	47.7	169.4
1992	32.1	83.2	85.4	495.7	54.2	175.3
1993	36.2	94.6	96.8	730.0	61.4	221.0
1994	41.3	100.0	107.0	892.0	69.0	249.1
1995	47.8	119.3	125.7	1039.3	82.1	306.7
1996	54.9	142.7	140.2	1264.5	91.8	379.6
1997	64.0	158.4	163.6	1375.5	106.6	431.9
1998	74.1	191.1	185.7	1693.0	122.9	520.2
1999	85.8	235.9	227.1	1728.8	145.3	617.6
2000	99.5	262.7	263.4	1966.8	168.1	714.8
2001	110.9	323.5	292.9	2129.4	187.4	868.6
2002	126.3	373.8	333.7	2494.9	215.7	982.7
2003	139.0	433.2	377.8	2501.0	241.7	1073.5
2004	150.9	455.7	447.7	2240.4	279.3	1120.1
2005	160.9	538.5	523.7	2426.0	316.1	1261.9
2006	170.8	625.6	589.8	2757.9	364.2	1496.8
2007	182.5	713.1	708.9	3064.3	422.5	1741.6
2008	195.9	849.8	801.3	3141.3	472.0	1908.4

Credit to Farmers

In 1991-92, marginal farmers, small farmers and other farmers were 42.8 per cent, 31.3 per cent and 25.9 per cent of the total 1,41,710 farmers, who had loan outstanding (direct credit) with the Scheduled Commercial Banks, but the proportion slightly changed in favour of other farmers, followed by small farmers in 2006-07. Out of the total 2,44,870 farmers who had loan outstanding with the Scheduled Commercial Banks in the year 2006-07, the proportion of marginal, small and other farmers were 40.7 per cent, 30.8 per cent and 28.5 per cent respectively. During 1991-92 and 2006-07, the annual growth rate of other farmers who had loan outstanding with the Scheduled Commercial Banks at 4.71 per cent was higher than that of small farmers at 3.86 per cent and marginal farmers at 3.60 per cent.

Sectoral Distribution of Bank Credit

After the 1990s, the two important priority sectors, i.e., agriculture and small-scale industries, witnessed sharp reduction in their shares of the total bank credit. While the share of agriculture in the total deployment of non-food gross bank credit of the Scheduled Commercial Banks reduced from 15.6 in 1980-81 to 14.8 in 1990-91, for small-scale industries, it increased from 14 per cent in 1980-81 to 15.1 per cent in 1990-91. However, after 1991, there was a sharp decline in the share of both agriculture and small-scale industries in the total non-food gross bank credit. For instance, in 2008-09, the share of agriculture and small-scale industries were 13 per cent and 9.9 per cent respectively. Similar decline in medium and large industries were also observed. However, the share of bank credit in favour of other sectors, which was 23 per cent of the total non-food gross bank credit in 1990-91 increased to 26.1 per cent in 2000-01 and then to 34.2 per cent in 2008-09. The details of the sectoral deployment of non-food gross bank credit have been presented in Table 5.

Credit Deposit Ratio

The Credit Deposit Ratios (C-DRs), which were 37.6 per cent in rural areas and 74.2 per cent in urban areas in 1969, improved to 60 per cent in rural areas, but declined to 62.3 per cent in urban areas in 1991. These ratios in rural, semi-urban, urban and metropolitans had improved from 60 per cent, 49 per

TABLE 5

Details of the Sectoral Deployment of Non-Food Gross Bank Credit (Outstanding) of the Scheduled Commercial Banks in Some Selected Years

(In percentage)

Year	As % of the Priority Sector					
	Non-Food Gross Bank Credit	Priority sector	Agrl. and Allied	SSI	Industry (Medium and Large)	Others
1990-91	100.0	37.8	39.0	40.0	39.2	23.0
2000-01	100.0	36.0	33.6	36.3	37.9	26.1
2008-09	100.0	35.2	37.0	28.1	30.6	34.2

cent, 56.5 per cent and 72.8 per cent in 1991 to 60.3 per cent, 53.2 per cent, 58.4 per cent and 87.2 per cent in 2008. Thus, the overall C-D Ratio in rural and urban areas had improved from 61.9 per cent in 1991 to 74.4 per cent in 2008.

Non-Performing Assets

Considerable improvements in the asset quality of the banks have been witnessed in the post-reform period. Since the mid-1990s the non-performing loans as ratios of both total advances and assets declined substantially. A comparison of non-performing asset (NPA) levels in priority *versus* non-priority sectors of public sector banks since the mid-1990s shows that the share of the former has been falling while that of the latter has been rising. The NPAs from the priority sector fell from 50 per cent in 1995 to 45.4 per cent in 2001 and then increased to 55.2 per cent in 2009. When the composition of the NPAs in the priority sector lending in 2002 and 2009 were compared, it was found that the NPAs in agriculture as a proportion to the total priority sector lending of public sector banks declined from 31.1 per cent in 2002 to 23.5 per cent in 2009 and in private sector banks, it increased from 17.2 per cent to 39.6 per cent. However, in the case of small-scale industries, the NPAs declined from 42.1 per cent in 2002 to 28.7 per cent in 2009 in public sector banks and in private sector banks, they declined from 58.3 per cent to 18.4 per cent. In 2002, the priority sectors constituted 44.5 per cent of the total NPAs of the public sector banks and 21.8 per cent of the total NPAs of private sector banks. Table 6 presents sector-wise NPA position of the Commercial Banks.

TABLE 6

Details of the Sector-wise Non-Performing Assets of Public Sector Banks and Private Sector Banks in 2002 and 2009

(Rs. crore)

Particulars	*2002*		*2009*	
	Public Sector Banks	*Private Sector Banks*	*Public Sector Banks*	*Private Sector Banks*
Agriculture	7821.5	439.2	5708	1441
Small Scale Industries	10584	1485.3	6984	670
Others	6733.9	621.9	11626	1529
Priority Sector	25139.3	2546.4	24318	3640
Other Sectors*	31367	9121	19725	13247
Total	56506.3	11667.3	44043	16887

* It includes Non-Priority Sector and Public Sector.
PSB=Nationalised Banks+State Bank Group, PvSB=Old Private Sector Banks+New Private Sector Banks.
Source: Report on Trend and Progress of Banking in India.

II. ISSUES AND CONCERNS

Continuance of Informal Sources of Credit

The surveys conducted by National Sample Survey Organisation (NSSO) show that non-institutional sources still play a major role in providing credit to cultivator households. The share of non-institutional sources in the total credit of the cultivator households, which was 92.7 per cent in 1951, came down drastically to 30.6 per cent in 1991, but in 2002, it increased to 38.9 percent, which suggests that the dependence of cultivators on non-institutional sources has increased in post-reform period. Further, the major findings of the 59th Round Survey (NSSO, 2003) on indebtedness are the following:

- 45.9 million households (51.4%) of the total 89.3 million farmer households were non-indebted.
- Out of the total 43.4 million indebted households, 20.3 million households (46.8%) had availed financial services from informal sources.
- 49.8 per cent of the scheduled caste households, 63.7 per cent scheduled tribes households, 48.6 per cent of other backward class households and 50.7 per cent of other social group had not availed any financial services either from formal or informal sources.

Reduction in Bank Branches

The Narasimham Committee recognized the need for continuing with the expansion of banking infrastructure in rural areas. However, in the process of executing financial reforms, the importance of rural financial infrastructure got completely neglected and a great vacuum was created. While the number of rural branches of Scheduled Commercial Banks increased during the pre-reform period, it steadily declined in rural areas and increased in urban areas during the post-reform period and the financial system became increasingly urban-centric. Although in absolute terms, number of bank branches is the highest in rural areas, the share of rural branches in the total is witnessing a fall, while that of urban and metropolitan branches is witnessing a rise.

Disbursements Trends

While the share of Cooperative Banks in the total credit flow has come down from 51.8 per cent in 1991-92 to 19.4 per cent in 2007-8, the shares of Regional Rural Banks and Commercial Banks have increased from 5.3 per cent and 42.9 per cent in 1991-92 to 11.0 per cent and 69.6 per cent respectively in 2007-08. Further, although there is an increase in the C-D Ratio in rural areas, this is not sufficient to boost the agriculture sector. Therefore, effective steps are needed to increase the C-D Ratio in rural areas.

Neglect of Small and Marginal Farmers

In the post-reform period credit facilities to marginal and small farmers had declined. Although the number of farmers who had availed direct agricultural credit had increased from 141.71 lakh to 244.87 lakh at an annual rate of 3.71 per cent, the growth was quite uneven among different categories of farmers. For instance, during 1991-92 and 2006-07 the annual growth rate was 3.36 per cent for marginal farmers, 3.60 per cent for small farmers and 4.39 per cent for other farmers. Similarly, while the marginal farmers constituted 42.8 per cent of the total accounts in 1991-92, the small farmers and other farmers constituted 31.3 per cent and 25.9 per cent respectively of the total accounts. When the post-reform period is segregated into two periods, i.e., 1991-92 to 1998-99 and 1999-2000 to 2006-07, it was observed that in the first part, the number of accounts under direct agricultural credit declined at an annual rate of 2.93 per cent, and in the second part, it increased at an annual rate of 11.13 per cent.

III. CHALLENGES

There has been a long history of concern regarding rural credit. The increase in share of institutional credit has been rather slow. The dependence of small and marginal farmers is still very high on non-institutional sources. Lack of awareness, low income/assets and small-sized loan demand in the demand side and distance from the bank branch, branch timings, cumbersome documentation and procedures, unsuitable products, language and staff attitude in the supply side are the major constraints faced by the formal banking system in extending rural credit. Further, large number of villages (more than half a million villages), lack of infrastructure, vast geographical spread, high transaction costs and poor recovery are some other problems faced by banks. In the absence of any alternative, the poor and other weaker sections of the rural society depend on unorganized financial system, which utilizes local knowledge, offers credit for a wide variety of purposes and operates quite flexibly, though at a high cost. The other challenges that need careful attention are the following:

- Expanding financial inclusion and promoting economic growth;
- Integrating technology with bank operation to build up a reliable credit information system and database on customers;

- Reducing transaction cost, facilitate better pricing of risk and thereby increase the access of un-banked rural people;
- Ensuring easy flow of public information to rural citizens;
- Developing financial products and services that are adapted to the needs of the majority of people at affordable prices;
- Taking steps to reduce cost of funds, transaction costs and the risk costs; and
- Involving informal agencies such as Micro Finance Institutions (MFI), Non-Governmental Organisations (NGO) and Self-Help Groups (SHG) for increasing the banking outreach.

References

R.S. Sidhu and Sucheta Singh Gill (2006), Agricultural Credit and Indebtedness in India: Some Issues, *Indian Journal of Agricultural Economics*, Vol. 61, January-March.

Annual Report, NABARD, Various Issues.

Annual Report, RBI, Various Issues.

Economic Growth (2006), Financial Deepening and Financial Inclusion, Rakesh Mohan, Address at the Annual Bankers' Conference, 2006, at Hyderabad on November 3.

Rakesh Mohan (2005), Financial Sector Reforms in India, *Economic and Political Weekly*, Vol. XL, No. 12, March 19.

M.S. Sriram, Productivity of Rural Credit: A Review of Issues and Some Recent Literature, Working Paper No. 2007, Indian Institute of Management, Ahmedabad.

Report of the Expert Group on Agricultural Indebtedness, Banking Division, Department of Economic Affairs, Ministry of Finance, Government of India, 2007.

Report of the Sub-Group on Indebtedness of Farmers.

Balasaheb Vikhe Patil (2005), Rural Banking: Problems of Localised Banking Institutions, *Economic and Political Weekly*, Vol. XL, No.12, March 19.

S.K. Sinha (1998), Rural Credit and Co-operatives in India, Suneja Publishers, New Delhi.

Dinesh Chandra (1993), Rural Credit, Role of Informal Sector, Segment Books, New Delhi.

Rural Economy, An Intelligence Group Report, *The Economic Times*, 2002-03.

Surjit Singh and Vidya Sagar (2004), State of the Indian Farmer, A Millennium Study, Various Volumes, Department of Agriculture and Cooperation, Ministry of Agriculture, Government of India.

Agricultural Credit Flow in Bihar

Vinod Kumar and Ram Bharat Thakur

I. INTRODUCTION

Agriculture is still a major sector in Bihar's economy but the agricultural growth has been either stagnated or declined during last 15 years. Empirical evidences clearly indicates a declining trend in private and public investment in agriculture, particularly in Bihar. The small size of land holdings and declining profitability in crop production made the situation more alarming for investment in agriculture.

II. REVIEW OF LIERATURE

A large number of studies like Rajput and Singh (1977), Kurulkar (1978), RBI (1990), Singh and Tyagi (1995), Yadav and Singh (1996), Viswanath (1999), , Sangwan (2000), Vallabhan (2001), Uday and Thattil (2002), Pattararnarakha (2003), Mohanty (2003), Choudhary (2004), Shah (2004), Thomas (2005), Prasad and Phil (2006), and Mishra (2006) have been conducted to study the institutional crecit flow in rural areas but most of them were devoted to procedure of financing, utilization of loan and repayment of loan.

III. OBJECTIVES OF THE STUDY

The objectives of the study are to:

(a) Study the growth and instability in agricultural lending through different institutional sources.
(b) Identify the agro-economic and infrastructural factors affecting credit.

IV. GROWTH AND INSTABILITY IN AGRICULTURAL CREDIT

The main objective of this investigation is to study agricultural credit flow in Bihar. There are two types of credit flow, i.e., institutional and non-institutioanal. Institutional banks perform a gap filling function in Bihar whereas the situation is just reverse in other part of the country. Among major states in India, Bihar is on the lowest ladder in term of proportion of institutional loans to total loans, disbursed to farmers. (Table 1)

TABLE I

Incidence of Indebtedness to Institutional and Non-institutional Agencies in for Rural Area for Major States

States	*Institutional*		*Non-institutional*		*% of non-institutional to total indebtedness*	
	1991	*2003*	*1991*	*2003*	*1991*	*2003*
Bihar	9.4	5.7	7.1	16.7	43.03	74.55
M.P.	15.1	15.2	7	15	31.67	49.67
Orissa	18.5	17.9	6.2	10	25.10	35.84
T.N.	16.7	13.9	18.7	21.3	52.82	60.51
U.P.	12.5	10.2	7.7	14.5	38.12	58.70
West Bengal	20.6	12.1	7.6	11	26.95	47.62
India	15.6	13.4	9.8	15.5	38.58	53.63

Source: Household Indebtedness in India, NSS 59th Report, 2005 and Indebtedness of Rural Households, Debt and Investment Survey NSS 49th Report, 1992, National Sample Survey Organisation, Ministry of Statistics and Programme Implementation, Govt. of India.

Table 1 indicates that 74.55 per cent of loans obtained by farmers in Bihar is granted by non-institutional financing agencies against, 35.84 per cent in Orissa, 49.67 per cent in M.P., 58.70 per cent in U.P. and 53.63 per cent at national level in the year 2003.

Institutional credit expanded with slow growth rate during 2000-01 to 1006-07. (Table 2)

TABLE 2

Source-wise Institutional Credit Flow in Bihar during 2000-01 to 2006-07

(in Rs. Crores)

Year	Agricultural loan in Bihar					
	Inter-Commercial Banks	Gramin Banks	Co-oprative Banks	Total	India	% of agri-culture credit at national level
2000-01	325	77	146	548	5287	1.04
	(59.31)	(14.05)	(26.64)	(100.00)		
2001-02	462	75	83	620	62045	1.00
	(74.52)	(12.10)	(13.39)	(100.00)		
2002-03	605	154	102	861	69560	1.23
	(70.27)	(17.89)	(11.85)	(100.00)		
2003-04	794	232	561	1587	86981	1.82
	(50.03)	(14.62)	(35.35)	(100.00)		
2004-05	1325	431	274	2030	125399	1.62
	(65.27)	(21.23)	(13.50)	(100.00)		
2005-06	1489	450	235	2174	180486	1.20
	(68.49)	(20.70)	(10.81)	(100.00)		
2006-07	1916	797	172	2985	203297	1.47
	(64.19)	(26.70)	(9.11)	(100.00)		

* Figures in brackets are percentage to respective totals of Bihar.

Sources: 1. Department of Statistics and Evaluation, Govt. of Bihar, Patna.

2. Agriculture at a Glance, Ministry of Agriculture and Co-operative, Govt. of India, 2007.

Table 2 indicates that agricultural credit flow increased from Rs. 548 crore in 200-01 to Rs. 2985 crore in 2006-07. But the share of Agricultural Credit in Bihar to national level Agricultural Credit flow declined from 1.82 per cent in 2003-04 to 1.41 per cent in 2006-07. It clearly indicated that our institutional credit system failed to perform at par with their counterparts working in other parts of the country.

In Bihar, the performance of Commercial Bank in not only poor in granting loan to agriculture sector but their performance has been poor in granting loan to other sectors in Bihar. (Table 3)

TABLE 3

Credit-Deposit Ratio in Bihar during 2000 to 2006

Year	*Deposite*	*Credit*	*C-D ratio*
2000-01	27591	6396	23
2001-02	30482.02	6945.52	21
2002-03	338115	8089	25
2003-04	35824	9603.86	27
2004-05	40294.88	12031.2	30
2005-06 upto Dec. 2005	46134	14005	32.22
2006-07 Sept. 2006	4891312	5911367	32.53

Source: Department of statistics and Evaluation, Govt of Bihar, Patna.

Table 3 indicates that C-D ratio of commercial Banks increased from 23 per cent in 2000-01 to 32.53 per cent in 2006-07.

The Commercial Banks performed much better in other parts of the country. (Table 4)

Table 4 shows that C-D ratio reached 71 per cent at national level in 2006 and Tamil Nadu recorded C-D ratio of 104 per cent in 2006. C-D ratio of the majority of states are much higher than the norm prescribed by the govt of India. Backward states like Orissa and Madhya Pardesh also achived C-D ratio of more than 60 per cent. Thus, it means that the resource mobilised in Bihar are deployed in the other states and siphoned off instead of being ploughed back in this state. This, in fact, hampers the rural development and arrests the tempo of rural development programmer.

TABLE 4

Credit-Deposit Ratio of Public Sector Banks Major States of the Country (2006)

(in Rs. Crores)

States	Deposite	Credit	C-D ratio
Andhra Pardesh	94217	79433	84
Tamil Nadu	94051	97563	104
Bihar	39224	11763	30
Madhya Pardesh	47874	29342	61
Orissa	27809	18344	66
Uttar Pardesh	130178	54661	42
West Bengal	101229	58961	58
India	1550402	1093038	71

Source: Economic Survey, 2006-07, Ministry of Finance. Economic Division, Govt. of India, New Delhi.

V. INFRASTUCTURE FACTORS AFFECTING THE AGRICULTURAL CREDIT FLOW IN BIHAR

Infrastructure development is expected to exert influence on agricultural credit flow. The infrastructure like road, energy, irrigation, education and health have direct relationship with agricultural production which results in higher demand for loan. All these variables were infrastructure variables which may not have effective influence individually on the agricultural credit flow. But infrastructural variables may have combined effect on agricultural credit flow.

Number of districts on the basis of per hectare agricultural loan granted were computed for each of the specified categories presented in Table 5.

Tables 5 shows that more than 50 per cent of districts were under the category 'D', indicating that the majority of the districts could avail the quantum of per hectare agricultural loans of above Rs. 5000. There were only 6 districts in category 'A', which could avail per hectare loan facility of below Rs. 2500. These districts were either districts of Kosi region or agriculturally less devloped

TABLE 5

Districts Comes under Different Categories of Loan Disbursement in Bihar

Loan disbursement per hectare of net area sown (Rs.)	*Name of the districts*
A Below 2500	Arbal, Jamui, Lakhisarai, Madhepura, Shaikhpura, Sheohar.
B Between 2500-3500	Banka, Khagaria, Kishanganj, Munger, Supoul.
C Between 3500-5000	Araria, Bhojpur, Darbhanga, Jahanabad, Nawada, Saharsa, Sitamarhi.
D Above 5000	Aurangabad, Begusarai, Buxar, E. Champaran, Gaya, Gopalganj, Bhabhua, Katihar, Muzaffarpur, Nalanda, Patna, Purnea, Rohtash, Samastipur, Saran, Vaishali, W. Champaran, Bhagalpur, Siwan, Madubani.

Source: Department of Statistics and Evaluation, Govt. of Bihar, Patna.

districts. These two factors might have affected adversely the smooth flow of agricultural credit in these districts. There were 7 districts which could obtained agricultural credit between Rs. 3500-5000 per hectare. Indicator of different socio-economic variables were computed for all the 4 categories of districts classified on the basis of per hectare agricultural loan which are presented in Table 6.

Table 6 shows that the proportion of electrified villages, road length per 1000 kms of geographical area, literacy per cent, number of dairy co-operatives per 1000 villages, population per bank branch and per capita electricity consumption were comparatively high in districts of category 'D' than the category of districts 'A', indicating the association of these socio economic and infrastructural variables with agricultural credit flow in different districts of Bihar.

CONCLUSION AND SUGGESTIONS

Thus, the proportion of indebted farmers increased but the institutional indebtedness declined and non-institutional

TABLE 6

Socio-economic and Infrastructure Variables for Different Groups of Districts Categorised on the Basis of per Hectare Agricultural Loan

Agricl. loan per hect. Of net area sown (Rs.)	*Category-A (Below 2500)*	*Category-B (2500-3500)*	*Category-C (3500-5000)*	*Category-D (Above-5000)*
1. Villages electrified (%)	58	48	61	69
2. Road length per 1000 Km of geographical area	81	115	133	175
3. Literacy per cent	38	32	35	42
4. No. of dairy co-operative per 1000 villagers	-	4	22	502
5. Population per bank branch	18220	17112	21617	15295
6. Per capita electricity consumption (kwh)	132.57	139.86	146.83	152.26

indebtedness increased in Bihar. Due to inadequate saving and poor access to institutional credit institution, the majority of farmers rely on non-institutional credit in Bihar. The institutional financing agencies are more active around state capital and slack in advancing loan in remote area of the state namely; Purnea, Saharsa and Bhagalpur Divisions. Agriculturally developed districts namely; West Champaran, Patna, Begusarai, Samastipur, Nalanda, and Vaishali have larger credit flow than agriculturally less developed districts such as Madhepura, Banka, Supaul and Araria. Hence, there is an urgent need to increase agricultural credit flow to less developed and remotely placed districts in Bihar.

The performance of Commercial Banks is not only poor in granting loan to agriculture sector but their performance has been poor in granting loan to other sectors in Bihar. There is sufficient expansion of branches as well as big increase in deposit, but in comparison to deposit, the level of credit is very low. The credit-deposit ratio (C-D ratio) of the Commercial Banks in Bihar should be raised more. At least 60 per cent of the total advances to priority sector be lent to rural sector agriculture and allied activities.

The condition of co-operatives on Bihar are not satisfactory.

There is an urgent need to strengthen the co-operative structure through promotion of viable primary agricultural co-operative societies (PACS).

There has been association between social-economic and infrastructural variables with agricultural credit flow in Bihar. Institutional structure and infrastructure emerged as important determinats of agricultural credit flow in Bihar. Hence, the infrastructures like road, energy, irrigation, education and health should be taken care for positive influence on increasing agricultural credit flow in Bihar.

References

Deepak, Shah (2004), Measuring Viability of PACS During Reform Period in Maharashtra: A Case Study. *National Bank News Review*, Mumbai, 20(4).

Haque, T. and Mati, C.C. (1978), Structure and Flow of Agriculture Credit in India, *Indian Journal of Agricultural Ecomomics*, 33(4).

Jugale, VB and Pati, D.T. (1997), Distortion in PACS Credit: a case study of Miraj Taluka, *Indian Co-operative Review*, 43(4).

Rajeev, M. and Deb, S. (1998) Institutional and Non-institutional Credit in Agriculture case study of Hugli District of West Bengal, *Economic and Political Weekly*, xxxiii (47248).

Satish, P. (2006), Institutional Credit, Indebtedness and Sucides in Punjab, *Economic and Political Weekly*, 41(26).

Singh, R.K.P. and Nasir, S. (2003), Agricultural Credit Flow in Bihar an Economic Analysis, *Indian Journal of Agricultural Economics*, 58(1).

Takur, R.B. and Hassan, T. (2004), Institutional Finance and Socio-economic Development of Weaker Sections in Begusarai District; IVth Geographers Conference, RCS College, Manjhaul.

Agrarian Structure in India

BHARAT BHUSHAN AND KABITA KUMARI

Agricultural Sector not only plays an important role in improving the growth of rural economy but also the overall growth of the economy in India. Increased agricultural production always makes dent on the prices of agricultural commodities, which benefit millions of landless rural and urban consumers. It is proved beyond doubt that agricultural growth also significantly impacts on the reduction of rural poverty through increased employment opportunities and wage rates in India. Research also suggests that growth in agricultural sector also impacts substantially on the growth of industrial sector. However, the agricultural sector of India has been facing one of the worst crises ever since independence. While the overall growth of the economy has been in the range of 5 per cent to 9 per cent since the introduction of economic reforms, the agricultural growth is almost stagnant or decelerating over last one decade or so.

Two prominent features of the Indian economy have hardly changed over the last few decades.

(i) An overwhelming production of the Indian population lives in the rural areas, and

(ii) There is no significant diversification of the rural economy. According to the 2001 census 72.2 per cent of the population of the country lived in the rural areas. In 1951, this proportion was 82.7 per cent. Thus over the period of five decades, the share of the rural population in the total population was declining at the rate of hardly 2 per cent per decade. Figures of different states vary. However, the 2001 population census has revealed that out of 17 major states of the country only five states, Tamil Nadu, Maharashtra, Gujarat, Karnataka and Punjab have recorded more than one-third of their population as 'Urban' mainly because of the rapid growth of the population in their capital cities. Over the last few decades, for the country as a whole and for a large majority of the states, the composition of the population, in terms of 'rural' and 'urban' has not changed in any remarkable way.

An equal significant feature is the overwhelming dependence on agriculture for livelihood in the rural areas. According to the 2001 census out of the total rural workers in the country 73.3 per cent were employed in agriculture. In all major states, over one-half to over three fourths of the rural workforce was employed in agriculture, the only exception being Kerala (28.7%). However, the composition of the agricultural workforce in terms of cultivators and agricultural workers is changing; so also, the size distribution of agricultural holdings. This suggests the need for a closer look at the agrarian structure.

Till 1991, the proportion of agricultural workers, in the total agricultural workforce was increasing only at a slow pace. The picture has changed since then as the proportion of agricultural workers has increased significantly together with the increase in marginal farmers. More and more marginal farmers with small plots of land are opting for agricultural labour as their main occupation. This is reflected in the fact that more than half of the agricultural labour households possessed some land. (According to 60th Round of NSS Survey, 56 per cent of agricultural labour household had land between 0.4 and 1 hectare). Increase in the agricultural workforce has mainly been due faster growth of marginal holding, which could not provide adequate gainful employment to their operators. This process has accelerated in recent years. More and more agricultural households are coming into the category of marginal farmers. It is seen that during the course of the quarter century from 1970-71 to 1995-96, the number of marginal holdings as a proportion of the total holdings has increased from about half to over 60 per cent, while the areas cultivated in these holdings has increased from 8.97 per cent to 17 per cent of the total cultivated area. The major changes that have taken place in the agrarian structure are as follows:

(i) The proportion of agricultural workers in the agricultural workforce has increased. However, the proportion of landless labourers in the total agricultural workers has not increased.
(ii) The landholding structure in India is sliding downwards, with progressively greater concentration in the marginal holdings group.
(iii) Not only is the number of marginal holdings increasing, but the area cultivated is such holdings is also given.
(iv) The proportion of the area under medium and semi-medium holding accounts for nearly half of the agricultural area, and has remained more or less constant.
(v) There has from a significant decline in the number of large holdings as well as the area cultivated in them.
(vi) The area reported under tenancy is relatively small—around 8 per cent, although there is a large amount of cancelled tenancy.
(vii) All size groups of holdings participate as lesser as well as lessee.

Among the above salient features of the agrarian structure in India the most noteworthy is the increase in the number and the area under marginal holdings. It can be shown under Table 1.

From the Table 1 it is very much clear that a large number of cultivators in our country are marginal farmers. However, what is noteworthy is the fact that a progressively increasing share of

TABLE 1

Number and Area under Marginal Holdings from 1970-71 to 1995-96

Year	*Number*			*Area*		
	All groups	*No. of marginal holdings*	*% of marginal holdings*	*All groups*	*Area operated marginal holdings*	*% of area by marginal holdings*
1970-71	70490	35680	50.62	162120	14550	8.97
1976-77	81570	44520	54.58	163340	17510	10.72
1980-81	88880	50120	56.39	163800	19730	12.05
1985-86	97160	56150	57.79	164560	22040	13.39
1990-91	105290	62110	58.99	165600	24620	14.87
1995-96	115580	71179	61.58	163357	28121	17.21

cultivated land is farmed by marginal groups. It is very much clear from the Table 1 above that in the year 1970-71, 8.97 per cent of the land was cultivated in holdings of one hec. or less. A decade lesser the proportion of land cultivated in marginal holdings was 12.05 per cent of the total cultivated area. After one-and-half decade in their share in the total cultivated land rose to 17.21 per cent. If the same trend had continued, by now the marginal farmers must be cultivating nearly 20 per cent of cultivated land of India. By 1995-96 one-third or more than one third of total cultivated land are in five states—Kerala (53%), West Bengal (43%), Jammu and Kashmir (40%), Bihar (36%) and Uttar Pradesh (34%) was in marginal holdings and one more state Tamil Nadu was closed to joining their rank with (30.26%). Thus, it is very much clear that the marginal farmers not only constitute an overwhelming majority of the cultivators, but are becoming increasingly important as agricultural producers.

Nearly half (48%) of the total number of marginal farmers are located in three states. These states are Uttar Pradesh (23%), Bihar (16%) and Andhra Pradesh (9%). These three states together with Tamil Nadu (8%) and Kerala (8%), account for the third (64%) of the marginal farmers in the country. On the other hand, each of the following states Gujarat, Jammu and Kashmir, Punjab, Haryana and Himachal Pradesh have less than 1 per cent of the country's marginal farmers. In terms of area also, more or less the same position prevails. The largest area under marginal holdings is in U.P. (22.3%) of total area under Marginal holdings in India followed by Bihar (13.8%) and A.P. (10.3%), Himachal Pradesh and Punjab have less than 1 per cent of the India's cultivated area in this category. A major concentration of the marginal farmers, in terms of numbers as well as area, is in the three states of U.P., Bihar and Andhra Pradesh.

Significant changes have taken place in recent years in the agrarian structure in different states of India. Thus during the decade of 1985-86 to 1995-96 the number of marginal farmers in the total number of cultivators rose in the states of M.P., Orissa, Karnataka, Maharashtra and Gujarat. It may be noted that even a decade ago these were not states with high shares of marginal holdings. They seem to be progressing to attain that rank. On the other hand, there is a proportionate decline in the share of the marginal holdings in the total holdings in a few states, most notably in Kerala and Punjab, but also in West Bengal, U.P. and Tamil Nadu, while in Haryana, the share of marginal farmers in the total number of farmers has remained more or less stable. A similar picture is obtained in the share of area in the total cultivated area of the states. The area under marginal holdings has declined in Punjab, West Bengal and Kerala but has increased in Maharashtra, M.P. and Gujarat. If the gross value of agriculture per hectare of cultivated land is taken as an indicator of commercialization with the exception of U.P., all states, where there had been a proportionate decline in the share of marginal holdings had high value of agricultural produce per hectare, as compared to average value in India as a whole.

From the above analysis the following picture emerges:

(i) For the country as a whole, marginal farmers constitute the largest segment of agricultural holdings, with major concentrations in U.P., A.P., and Bihar.

(ii) Particularly in all states of India, marginal holdings accounted for an overwhelming majority of the total holdings in such states. The share of land cultivated under these holdings in a number of states was one-third, or more of the total cultivated area of the respective state.

(iii) In most of the Indian states and in the country as a whole the number of marginal cultivators and the area cultivated by them is increasing.

(iv) Only in a limited number of states is the number of the marginal farmers as well as the area cultivated by them decreasing. These are, with a few exceptions, the states with high value of gross produce per hectare.

STRUCTURAL TRANSFORMATION IN INDIAN STATES: SHARE OF EMPLOYMENT AND INCOME IN AGRICULTURE

Transferring labour from agriculture is desirable and is the classified route to structural transformation of the economy. What is not recognized is that such a transformation is already taking place in some of the states and it is not a countrywide problem but concentrated in about 13 states in our country in general but seven states in particular. By 2004 five states Kerala, Tamil Nadu, Tripura, West Bengal and Punjab have already achieved structural transformation in the sense of agriculture accounting for less than half of employment and income. Another ten have a share of employment between 50 and 60 per cent and at least half of them can be considered as candidates likely to achieve structural transformation by the end of the 11th Plan. On the bottom scale, there are at least seven states with an employment share in agricultur of more than 65 per cent. The rest have a share between 61 and 65 per cent concentration of workers in agriculture is thus essentially a problem confined to 13 states out of 28 major states accounting for 29 per cent of workers. This means that the rate of growth of non-agriculture has to be much higher that the projected 6 per cent for these states which is unlikely to be achieved. Note that the five top states, which have achieved structural transformation include three states not known for modern industrialization with large scale enterprises but quite possibly a high share of small scale and labour intensive industries and service activities. This can be shown in Table 2 below.

FACTORS AFFECTING CHANGES IN THE AGRARIAN STRUCTURE

There are some factors which are affecting the agrarian structure in our country in which these are very important:

TABLE 2

Structural Transformation in India, States 2004-05: Share of Employment and Income in Agriculture

Less than 50%	*51 to 60%*	*More than 60%*	*More than 65%*
1	2	3	4
Kerala (35.14)	Haryana (50.28	Orissa (61.28	Assam (66.29)
Tripura (37.24)	J & K (51.32)	Nagaland (61.35	M.P. (67.28)
Tamil Nadu (45.14)	Sikkim (53.21)	Karnataka (61.19)	Mizoram (68.17)
West Bengal (46.22)	Maharashtra (54.11)	Himachal P. (62.21)	Bihar (71.42)
Punjab (48.37)	Gujarat (56.17)	Manipur (63)	Meghalaya (71.22)
	U.P. (59.32)	Uttrakhand (64.25)	Arunachal P. (73.27
	Manipur (59.36)		Chhattisgarh (75.22)
	A.P. (60.24)		
	Rajasthan (60.27)		
	Jharkhand (60.22)		

(i) Land Market

In traditional societies, transaction in land are not very common because until a dire need arises a peasant does not like to sell his land. However, in the pre-independence era, large chunks of land had passed over to money lenders mainly for setting debts, or to the landlords because of faiiure to pay the rent, especially in draught years. These were not purely market induced transactions. During the post-independence period, the process of expropriation seems to have slowed down. Provisions of various legislations have also contributed to restrictions on land transfer. For example, a scheduled tribe land owner cannot sell his land to a non-scheduled tribe person. On the other hand, tenancy legislation enacted in a number of states, made it possible for the landless or marginal tenants to purchase the land which they had been cultivating on lease. This tendency was more prominent where the credit institutions, i.e. L.D.B. advanced credit to tenants for purchase of land in arts of the former Bombay and Saurastra states.

The situation has changed to certain extent, with large chunks of the land being acquired by the state, or by private entrepreneurs, with the active assistance of state, for non-farmer activities. That is why net cultivated area in our country has go down in recent years mainly because of such acquisitions.

(ii) Land Reforms

Land reforms legislation played much more important role influencing the ownership pattern. There were a large number of ejection of small tenants as there were numerous cases of acquisition of land by small farmers. However, in large part of our country, small land owners and landless tenants were the gainers due to land reform legislation.

(iii) Demographic Pressure

While the increase in the area under the marginal and small holding groups could be largely explained by the legislative measures supplemented by market process, the increase in their number is basically due to population increase in those households and lack of alternative employment opportunities in the country side. On extension of the household, or more commonly, the death of the head of the household leads to division of the holdings among the legal heirs. Unfortunately, there are no systematic studies of household dynamics in the rural areas of our country to enable us to arrive at a precise measure of sub-division of holdings due to demographic factors over a period of time. However, it is responsible to assume that the combined effect of the two factors, population growth and lack of non-farm employment opportunities, largely explaining the increase in the number of small and marginal holdings.

TOWARDS NEW AGRICULTURE

It is clear from the above discussion that Indian agriculture is essentially small farm-agriculture and this feature is likely to become more prominent in the coming years. Indeed, it can be seen that in the recent past, with the slow down in the public investment in agriculture, labour saving technological changes have become more prominent. But such technological changes are still not the only for of technological change occurring in agriculture. It is here the relevance of an alternative vision becomes important. The Assian experience suggests that agriculture can absorb additional labour if appropriate technological and organizational interventions are carried out. The thesis of "Economic Development in an Asian Perspective " suggests that the leading input in agriculture is water that could lead to more labour absorption with higher productivity. In India the net cropped area under irrigation is only around 39 per cent and there is vast potential for its increase. The entire gamut of efforts for the development of leading input in Indian agriculture can be summed up as land and water resource development and management. Creation and extension of such a leading input call for changing public investment in agriculture, which has witnessed an alarming decline during the last decade or so. To this should be added the availability of complementary inputs as credit, fertilizer, agricultural extension and so on. All these have witnessed discriminating trends during the last several years.

SPECIAL FOCUS ON DRY LAND AGRICULTURE

Indian agriculture can be broadly divided into irrigated and dry land agriculture. 53 per cent of the total cropped area are under dry land agriculture. The qualitative significance of the agreement includes the fact that 48 per cent of area under food crops and 68 per cent under non-food crops comes under dry land agriculture. It consist of vast part of the country from western Himalayas through most part of Rajasthan, Central high lands including Gujarat plains and Western M.P., Deccan Plateau including Maharashtra and Northern Karnataka, Telangana Region. Tamil Nadu uplanding and Western Karnataka and sub-humid eastern plateau covering Chhattisgarh, Jharkhand, Western Orissa and Northern Andhra Pradesh. The livelihood of a majority of rural population in these regions depend on dry land agriculture. That is why there is a need for a special focus on dry land agriculture.

From the above discussion it is very much clear that Indian agriculture is really facing a huge problems. So may suggestions are to prepare a road map for rapid rural transformation:

(i) Appropriate technological innovations for yield improvement and cost reduction in farming.
(ii) Appropriate policy and investment support.
(iii) Progressive land policy, trade policy, fiscal support are for diversified rural development.
(iv) Improving rural infrastructure.
(v) Improving governable and resources use efficiency at various levels.

(vi) Strengthening WTO permissible support services like (a) Research and extension, (b) Parts of diseases, (c) Marketing and Promotions services, (d) Infra-structure development, and (e) Agricultural insurance.

(vii) Identification of special products that are critical for food security, livelihood security and rural development to take advantage of flexibilities in terms of tariff cuts.

(viii) Awareness building and information system on challenges and opportunities of globalization.

(ix) Unfreezing the lease market.

(x) An active land market to enable small farmers to enlarge their holdings.

(xi) Financial support to small farmers to expand their holdings.

Reference

Aggrawal, A. (2006), "Special Economic Zones Revisiting the Policy Debate," *Economic and Political Weekly*, Nos. 43, 44, November 4.

Bhalla, Sheila (2005), "India's Rural Economy, Issue and Evidence," Working Paper Series 25; Institute of Human Development, New Delhi.

Khor, Martin (2006), Globalization, Liberalization and Protectionism: The Global Framework Affecting Rural Producers in Developing Countries, TWN—Third World Network, April.

Oxfarm (2005), Indian Agriculture in Crisis, New Delhi.

Sri Vastava Ravi and Richa Singh (2006), "Rural Wages during the 1990s: A Restimation", *Economic and Political Weekly*, Vol. XII, No. 38.

Vyas, V.S. (1996), "Diversification of Agriculture and Food Security in the Context of New Economic Policy", Concepts, Rationale and Approaches, *Indian Journal of Agricultural Economics*, Vol. 52, No. 4, October-December.

Vyas, V.S. (1991), "Agrarian Structure, Environment Concerns and Rural Poverty", Elm Hurst Memorial Lecture, XXIth International Conference of Agricultural Economists, Tokyo, Japan.

Policy for Land Acquisition for Non-Agriculture Uses and Compensation for Land: An Analysis

G. Savaraiah, G. Chandrasekhara Rao and M. Devarajulu

India lives in villages. Its geographical area is about 329 million hectares with an average population density of 325 persons per square kilometers. However, with population growth, per capita land availability declined from 0.89 hectares (ha) in 1951 to 0.3 hectares by 2001. More than 70 per cent of the population depends on land as their primary source of livelihood. The per capita agricultural land declined from 0.48 hectares in 1951 to 0.14 hectares by 2001. There is a heavier demand for agricultural land for meeting the needs of the growing population. With a projected population of 1581 million by 2050 the per capita land availability will go down further to 0.20 hectares. With a rise in population density and demand for new development projects, land acquisition for private and public purposes became imminent and has assumed greater importance. In fact, during the liberalization and globalization period, new growth opportunities have emerged in the Indian economy. This has increased the demand for the land that often entails the conversion of forest and agricultural areas for mining, infrastructure and urbanization projects. Mostly acquisition of lands was required for industrialization in many states. An attempt has been made here to review the policies of land acquisition and compensation for land.

METHODS OF LAND ACQUISITION IN INDIA

The entire land acquisition system in this country which is being run on much the same lines as in the days of the Raj is in more exploitative nature in the name of public purposes. Governments often used Land Acquisition Act (LAA), 1894 to acquire land for private business projects. Indiscriminate use of LAA 1894 by governments to facilitate private business projects in the guise of servicing public purpose has been severely contested by the local communities. In fact, farmers have been ruthlessly exploited ever since. Independence while their land has been taken away for variety of projects including the recent Special Economic Zones (SEZs). As the policy of land acquisition in many states aim at minimizing displacement, they first target common property resource, lands, because from the prevailing view point of the government, only acquisition of land belonging to households is considered alienation. This is because the LAA 1894 recognizes only the ownership rights and not usage rights such as grazing, gathering grass and branches of shrubs, collecting silt and sand, or merely squatting. On the other hand, the Indian Forest Act, 1860 recognised customery usage rights and permitted their continuation when a forest area was reserved. Since there are no usage rights in LAA, 1894, there is a serious adverse effect for those who are dependent on common property resources for sustenance in rural India.

Generally, before starting an industry or SEZ, the private entrepreneurs enter into a formal memorandum of agreement (MOA) with the appropriate State Government. After that the entrepreneur directly initiates a dialogue with key local stakeholders especially the land owners. The State Government plays a facilitator role only to the extent needed. But the State Governments are not becoming facilitators between the private Business and the land owners. Simply they issued notification and forcefully acquiring the fertile lands. Often private business and the States complicate the situation further by giving wrong and confusing signals through the media to other stakeholders.

PLIGHT OF THE STAKEHOLDERS

Land acquisition for industrial infrastructure and SEZs is considered as a predatory style of growth involving the loss of livelihood, land, forests, pasture and water sources for millions of rural families who earn their livelihood in agriculture and allied occupations. Rapid industrialization and development of SEZ displace the people, make them homeless, jobless and destitute. They pass through uncertainties struggling for their own existence. In fact, land acquisition has been branded as a dangerous weapon of willfully converting people into refugees by forcibly evicting or outing them from their own land which is treated as their mother for generations for the purpose of developmental projects like reservoirs, highways. SEZs, which are not only immediately disruptive, destructive and painful but also serious fraught with long-term risks and repercussions of making them still poorer than before displacement, more vulnerable economically, more disintegrated socially and even more shattered mentally and psychologically. The act of displacement with meager compensation has a terrible socio-economic and cultural disruptive impact on them. It naturally affects thousands of households who felt unsafe, insecure and deprived as they have lost their own land and ancestral property and would reduced to a state of penury, homeless and without a source of livelihood.

IMPACT OF LAND ACQUISITION ON WOMEN AND TRIBALS

Of those affected the indigenous groups of people, the elderly and women have been found to be more vulnerable to impoverishment. Scheduled Caste and Scheduled Tribe women are most adversely affected. The displacement of tribals in project areas has resulted in untold misery spelling disaster, distress and despair as the life supporting systems of tribes, i.e., common property resources land, forests are snatched away from tribals in the name of development projects. The displacement creates a situation that is most dismal for landless women who are dependent on the cultivable lands where they worked as agricultural laboureres or on forest resources. Women suffered from an increasing family disturbances including children's education as their productive activities in farm work, kitchen gardens and the collection and sale of minor forest produce and other cottage industries decreased or ceased entirely. The growth of micro-enterprises, SHGs, has also been stopped, women are no longer productive contributors to their households and lost social status within the community, where once held recognized roles.

IMPACT ON FOOD SECURITY

The per capita availability of agricultural land in India has been declining since 1951. This has a bearing on the food security. In fact, the transferring of agricultural land to non-agricultural use with stagnant agricultural productivity also may affect adversely the food security 10 million hectares agricultural land from 1950 to 1991 and of equal amount from 1991 to 2007 have already been converted into non-agricultural land. The food growing land is being displaced on a massive scale for corporate use. This displacement of agricultural farmers also deprive them from their means of livelihood. Many critics have called the policy for land acquisition for non-agricultural uses as misdirected and robbing of the land of poor farmers in the interest of corporate sector and call it a continued exploitation of land by capital, for example Krishna-Godavari basin has been destroying invaluable healable mangroves and natural resources along the seacoast in the name of development projects.

POOR COMPENSATION LEADS TO AGITATIONS AND PROTESTS

The land acquisition for the purpose of estabilishing any development projects normally deprives the large masses from their resource-base to which they are tied not only to their livelihoods but their sentiments, ethics, beliefs, cultures, etc. Some things relating to our sentiments, emotions and mental agony cannot be compensated for. Only physical assets like lands and houses are consider for compensation. Under the rehabilitation package the Government has given compensation of Rs. 1.00 lakh per acre for a barren land, Rs. 1.50 lakh per acre for a single crop un-irrigated land and Rs. 2.00 lakh for a double crop irrigated land. In case of the DKT *patta* land or government land cultivated by the weaker sections, only Rs. 50,000 and less amount has been given as compensation. In many cases the amount of compensation is always undervalued. In fact, this is an inadequate compensation without any rehabilitation plan. With regard to the jobs provided by corporate the security guards, peons and driver posts are given to the losers of the land under rehabilitation package. Payment of compensation, offer of jobs and house, etc., failed to assure them get their cooperation protests marches, agitations, bandhs and dharnas resorted to express the feelings of resentment by the people effected. In some cases, it lead to violence in West Bengal. But in many cases, those people had not been suitably rehabilitated and even if they had been alienated from the societal culture through which they had been groomed from their birth and which they had inherited. The existing policy appears to be more concerned with protecting the interests of big business men rather than the livelihood security of the displaced people.

VIOLATION OF HUMAN RIGHTS

Every year millions of persons are forcibly displaced in the name of development projects. The increasing role of the State as the promoter of corporate laid economic growth is underlined by the acquisition of land for development projects which are spelling the doom of displaced people. The State exercises its right of principal of eminent domain. Land acquisition by the Government is governed by LAA 1894. Unfortunately, this Act itself is violative of human rights. In the name of public purpose the Government grabs lands from poor and handover the land to corporates. But Government contemplates re-settlement and rehabilitation of the victims. Despite long promises, the record in this direction is really pathetic thereby proletarianizing displated persons more and more. The State Human Rights Commission has passed several interim orders against violation of human rights in the process of acquiring land for the people in Kakinada Special Economic Zone but the Government ignoring them in its apparent bid to promote real estate business. The National Alliance of People's Movement would not allow the Government to deprive the people of their rights to life and livelihood. The only silver lining that is visible is that the voices of these under-privileged sections of our society, often heard because of the rising activism of the human rights agencies, civil rights leaders, social activities, NGOs, ultran-left political and opposition parties, etc. The fallout of such development is the passing of the national rehabilitation and resettlement policy in 2007.

AMENDING THE LAND ACQUISITION ACT

It is now fairly clear that the State acquires land for no demonstrable public purpose. What it does is abrogate the right to property of one group of people to handover land to another group usually corporate or industrialists.

CONCLUSION

We want inclusive development or development with social justice. Most of the disadvantaged groups especially are the worst victims of these development projects. This kind of development uproots poor people from their age old places of residence and traditional profession. This is a clear violation of human rights. Land grabing for public purpose but through treachery and of proud by the deferent State Governments and afterwards championing the private corporate sector for 'private profit' is indefensible. Many State Governments have witnessed the wrath of the victims who resorted to hunger strikes, agitations and even violent forms of opposition and protests. Hence, there is a need for the community participation in the process of land acquisition and the rehabilitation packages. China has already imposed a ban on SEZs but Japan and South Korea have been provided shares to the victims in the corporate/industries. The Government should also provide jobs to the victims in addition to the cash and kind components of compensation. The aim of the Government should be to minimize large scale displacement as far as possible.

The Land Acquisition Bill proposed by the Government provided that if a private party could directly procure 70 per cent of the land he needed the Government would help compulsorily to acquire by paying remaining 30 per cent, which would lead to the exploitation of farmers who would otherwise be able to get a better price. In case where the farmer is willing to sell his land on the understanding that he will be relocated on another piece of land, the cost of this should be made part of the compensation package.

Land Reforms and its Impact on Agriculture in India

Dhiren Vandra

Structural reforms in Indian economy were introduced in a big way in 1991—which were followed by India, becoming founder-member of WTO after signing of GATT agreement in Dec. 1994. This structural reforms and obligation of WTO have affected Indian agriculture in a variety of ways. Major emphasis was given on Fiscal Management which led to cut the public investment in agriculture and squeeze on agricultural research and extension services.

A lot of importance was given to privatization of agriculture-related activities. In view of WTO obligations agricultural trade was liberalized. Number of restrictions were replaced and domestic intellectual property right were amended and extended the agricultural research. Agricultural Marketing Act was amended to allow private companies to trade in agriculture product. The banking sector reforms resulted in sector lending in order to ensure their profitability. This resulted decline in flow of agricultural credit. The scope of priority sector lending was enlarged to cover many activities including contribution of the rural infrastructural development and Khadi Village Industries Commission.

In recent times there has been a renewed interest in relationships between redistribution, growth and welfare. Land reforms in developing countries like India are often aimed at improving the Poor's access to land, although their effectiveness has often been hindered by political constraints on implementation. The large volume of legislated land reforms has had an appreciable impact on growth and poverty, so such land reforms have been associated with poverty reduction.

Pre-independent India had a feudal agrarian structure. A small group of large land owners including absence landlords had land rights. The vast majority of cultivators did not have any right or had limited rights as tenants or sub-tenants. The poor mostly leased in land for substance. If the tenants used improved seeds, manures or extra labour, they had to share half of the increased produce with the landlords. When the India became independent, policy-makers felt the system of cultivation by tenants had to be overhauled as it was highly exploitative.

The result was, tenancy reforms which aimed to either abolish tenancy or regulate tenancy to ensure fixed tenure, fair rent, etc. The whole point of tenancy reforms was to enable the poor tenants to cultivate their land were efficiently and improves their incomes. However, the impact of tenancy reforms varied from state to state and region to region. During the past two decades or so—the state of Karnataka in southern India tried to confer occupancy rights to tenants. Many state governments have banned agricultural tenancy but concealed tenancy exists. Many of the affluent states like Punjab and Haryana show a growing tendency towards "Reverse Tenancy" in which large farmers leave land from small and marginal ones.

The big land reform success story is "Operation Barga" in West Bengal. The operation which was launched in 1978 led to the emergency of 15,00,000 share croppers. West Bengal's tenancy law provides the record share croppers permanent and heritable rights.

Under the Indian constitution, land reform is the responsibility of individual states so while the federal government provides broad policy guidelines, the nature of land reform legislation the level of political will and institutional support for land reform and the degree of success in implementing land reform have varied considerably from state to state with the agenda remaining unfinished in most states. Indian official acknowledges its failures to implement land reforms.

Dr. K. Venkatasubramanian, member of India's Planning Commission, succinctly lists some of the key factors behind the tardy implementation of tenancy reforms in the country as under:

- Tenancy reforms have excluded the share croppers who form the bulk of the tenant cultivators.
- Ejection of tenants will takes place on several grounds.
- The right of resumption given in the legislation has led to land grabbing by the unscrupulous.
- Fair rents are not uniform and not implemented in various states because of the acute land hunger existing in the country.
- Ownership rights could not be conferred on a large body of tenants because of the high rates of compensation to be paid top the tenants.

Today, land reform in rural India is at the cross-roads. Despite the inequality, the constituency advocating land reforms is weakening day-by-day and the number of people pushing for a revocation of land ceiling is increasing. In the 90's as India embraced economic liberalization, a growing consensus emerged among the vocal opinion making class that ceiling on land have proved to be unofficial economic tool and hampered the development of agro-business. Increasingly, there is a demand for re-examination of the land reform issue. It is also being argued that liberalization of tenancy would not only increase the availability of land in the market but would also increase the poor people's access to land.

Dr. T. Haque (NIRD and NCAEPR) pointed out that, there is a danger that in the absence of adequate non-farm development, liberalization of tenancy may alienate the marginal farmers from land without an alternative source of income, particularly in the underdeveloped regions.

Haque's study makes it clear that tenants who have confirmed ownership right take more interest in farming. For instance, the survey results from Karnataka indicate that such people have interested in land improvement and raised their land productivity and socio-economic states.

Haque's finding have important policy implications, such as "Operation Barga" in West Bengal has contributed significantly to agricultural growth in other states like Kerala, A.P., Bihar, Himachal Pradesh, M.P., U.P. which have a ban on leasing out agricultural land, have failed to achieve the desired results because of concealed tenancy. Some agriculturally developed states like Punjab, Haryana, there is a growing tenancy toward reverse tenancy in which large and medium farm owners lease in land from marginal and small land owners, because,

- Non-availability of sufficient capital with marginal farmers for investment in modernization.
- Marginal farmer's desire to maximize income through leasing out and wage earning by hiring out employment both sides, i.e. within and outside agriculture.
- Large farmers' desire to maximize income by expanding the size of operational holding.
- The population pressure which forces all land owners to look for additional income.

Land reforms alone will not rid India of its poverty; you additionally need to spread the net of education, awareness and among those at the bottom of the ladder in the country.

You need a national consensus on the caste system and an end to the ritual discrimination of low casts.

You need credit reforms to enable the poor to get out of the clutches of the moneylenders.

But without the effective implementation of land reforms it is difficult to see change in rural poor. In the final analysis land reform is not a sufficient but a necessary condition for poverty eradication.

It was observed that many of the occupant tenants and informal tenants preferred to borrow money from local lenders at high rates of interest because of convenience and out of fear of harassment.

Actually this is a call for credit reform in the institutional sector, increasing the accessibility of the farmers the institutional credit which could help to improve their productivity and their economic condition.

THE LAND QUESTION IN INDIA

As the basic of all economic activity, land can either serve as essential assets for a country to achieve economic growth and social equity or it can be used as a tool in the hands of few people who hijacked a whole country's economic independence and effect of social processes. During the two centuries of British colonization, India's traditional land use and land ownership patterns were changed. The acquisition of land at low process by British entrepreneurs for mines, plantations and other enterprises. The introduction of the institutions of private property destroyed the community ownership systems of rural societies. Moreover with the introduction of the land tax under permanent settlement Act, 1793, the British popularized the Zamindari System.

Owning to these developments in a changing social and economic landscape, India at independence inherited semi-tendal agrarian system. The ownership and control of land was highly concentrated in the hands of a small group of landlords and intermediaries, whose main intention was to extract maximum rent, inform of cash or kind from tenants. Under this arrangement, the share cropper or the tenant farmer had little economic motivation to develop farm land to increase production with no security of tenure and a high rent, a tenant farmer was naturally less likely to invest in land improvements or use high yielding varieties and other expensive impacts that might yield higher returns.

At the same time the landlord was not particularly concerned about improving the economic conditions of the cultivators, consequence agricultural productivity suffered and the oppression of the tenants resulted in a progressive deterioration of their well-being.

In fact, the national objectives of poverty, abolition envisaged simultaneous progress on two fronts: High productivity and equitable distribution. Accordingly Land reformers were visualized as an important pillar of a strong and prosperous country. India's First Five Year Plans allocated substantial budgetary amounts for the implementation of land reforms. A degree of success was own registered in certain states especially with regards to issues. Such as the abolition of intermediaries, protection to tenants, rationalization of different tenure systems and the imposition of ceilings on land holdings. About sixty years down the line, number of problems remains far from solutions.

More than half of India's population is dependent on agriculture for livelihood. Yet more than half of these population own small holdings of less than 1 hectare and 10 hectares or more land are in the hands of less than 2 per cent of population. This absolute landless and really landless was 43 per cent of total per cent households.

The shift in agricultural production has been promoted most fervently since the 1980, by policy-makers and politicians, who concept like agriculture more than industry. The trend has been justified by the substantial increases in agricultural output promoted agricultural productivity through importation of fertilizers, seeds, pesticides and farm machinery.

A new seed policy that allowed multinational corporations to penetrate fully a market that previously had not been directly accessible: SANDOS, CONTINENTAL, MONSANTO, CARGILL, PIONEER, HOEGHST and CIBAGEIGY now are the multinational corporations with major investments in India's seed sector.

As a result of Green Revolution, India is transformed from importer to exporter for foodgrains, the factors responsible for this are politicize subsidies, facilitation to inputs, availability of agricultural credits, technology, improved seeds, use of fertilizers, irrigation facilities, plant protection measures and the steps taken for land reforms that is, rights of ownerships and Tenant laws.

The Green revolution had increased Indian food production by 5.4 per cent but new agricultural practices reduces nearly 8.5 million hectares of the crop base to water logging, salinity or excess alkalinity. Furthermore, although the amount of wheat production doubled over a period of 20 years and rice production increased by 50 per cent, so greater emphasis has been given on production of commercial crops, such as sugarcane and cotton instead of traditionally grown by the poor. But these changes have steadily eroded the self-sufficiency of the small farmers in foodgrain.

Agriculture is the largest portfolio of the World Bank in any country. 130 agricultural projects have been received in 1950. These projects have generally taken the forms of providing support to the fertilizer industry, exploiting ground water through electric pumps, introducing high yielding varieties and setting up banking institutes to finance the agricultural capitalists.

Most supporters of land reforms view that process as more than the mere redistribution of land to the landless; rather they place an equal importance on the availability of other inputs that can help to tern the piece of land into a productive asset. In the agricultural countries such as, India, where 2/3 of the agricultural production is dependent on irrigation, irrigation schemes that can enhance agricultural productivity assume special importance.

IMPORTANCE OF LAND REFORMS IN INDIA

From an economic perspective, the question of land is linked to critical issue of agricultural productivity, agrarian relation, industrial uses, infrastructure development, employment opportunities, housing and other related issues. Each one of these aspects is crucial for enhancing national security by ensuring consistence economic growth, food security, goods for export and soon which reinforce the country's economic strength by poverty reduction and empowerment of rural poor.

References

Anonymous (2009), Structural Reforms and Agriculture, *IEA Newsletter*, April 2009, pp. 34-35.

Bhatt, J. (2009), Tenancy reforms in India, www.legalservice India.com

Chatterjee, P. (2002), Land Reforms in India. Necessary, But not Sufficient to Fight Poverty, Development Cooperation, No. 2, March/April 2002, pp. 21-22.

Sethi, Manpreet, Land Reforms in India, Issues and Challenge, (en.wikipedia.org)

Timothy, B. and Robin, B. (2000), Land Reform, Poverty Reduction and Growth: Evidence from India, *Journal of Economics*, May 2000.

Achieving Food Security in India: Issues and Challenges

Dalip Kumar and Abha Mittal

INTRODUCTION

Achieving food security is an important issue for the developing countries like India, where millions of people are suffering from hunger and nutritional deficiency. Food availability and stability are considered good measures of food security. Dr. Amartya Sen, the eminent economist, in his work on the Great Bengal Famine, has attributed the death of millions to the inadequacy, or rather non-existence of an official policy, to cope with the food supply crisis. Poverty and the lack of purchasing power, therefore becomes the crucial consideration in attainment of food security. As most of the poor people in developing countries including India dwell in the country sides so the policies relating to rural development in its comprehensive form encompassing development of agriculture, health, nutrition, education literacy, etc. would alone lead to enduring solution to the problem of food insecurity, poverty, unemployment and social tension in the region (Ram, 1996). There are three goals of agricultural development. These are: (a) achieve 4 per cent growth in agriculture and raise incomes by increasing productivity (land, labour), diversification to high value agriculture and rural non-farm by maintaining food security; (b) sharing growth by focusing on small and marginal farmers, lagging regions, women etc.; (c) third is to maintain sustainability of agriculture by focusing on environmental concerns. (Mahendra Dev, 2009).

WHAT IS FOOD SECURITY?

In 1970s, food security was understood as the 'availability at all times of adequate supply of basic foodstuffs....' (UN, 1995). Food security is a concept emerged at the United Nations Food and Agriculture Organisation (FAO) World Food Conference in 1974. It is centered around two sub-concepts, food availability and food entitlement. Food availability refers to the supply of food available at local, national or International levels. The second food entitlement refers to the capability of individuals and households to obtaine food. In 1981 publication of Amartya Sen's Poverty and Famines: An Essay on Entitlement and Deprivation brought new concept of the problem of hunger or food security (Sen, 1981). Sen emphasized 'access' to food through what he called 'entitlements'—a combination of what one can produce, exchange in the market plus estate or other socially provided supplies. What Sen posited is that availability or supply of food does not itself create entitlements for food. In 1995, World Food Summit Declared "... food security, at the individual, household, national, regional and global levels ... exits when all people, at all times, have physical and economic access to sufficient, safe and nutritious food to meet their dietary needs and food preferences for an active and healthy life (FAO, 1996). World Bank used definition of food security—"Access by all people at all times to enough food for an active, healthy life. The term "access" here is inclusive of both the supply side (Availability) and demand side (entitlement).

Food security is related with the issues of availability, accessibility and affordability of food to all the people round the year. It implies sufficient stock of foodgrains either through domestic production or import, purchasing power of the people especially the marginalized people so that they can afford to purchase food in terms of adequate quantity and nutrition. In addition to that efficient distribution network to make the food accessible to all. The food deficient nation India achieved food security by 1970s due to green revolution which was the overall result of introduction of package programme. In the initial stage, use of chemical fertilizers, pesticides and irrigation had tremendous impact on soil fertility. But excessive use of these inputs led to decline of productivity causing several problems like soil degradation, salinization, water-logging, etc. Food production has also shown declining trend because of commercialization of agriculture as more importance is being attached to growing of cash crops for industrial purposes. Net sown area has not increased as more land is required for construction of homes and factories as a result of rapid urbanization. Agricultural scientists are concerned about the ill impacts of use of chemical fertilizers which increase productivity at the cost of soil fertility.

The need of the hour is to achieve the goal of food security in a country with more than 26 per cent population living below the poverty line and to promote sustainable agriculture. For this there is a need of giving importance to the organic farming which does not affect the quality of soil in the long-run. Food security is largely dependent on the distribution network rather than the total production. It has been observed that during the past few years, there is adequate food stock at the national level. However, if we observe the same at the household level, there is gross inadequacy and inequity. Rural-urban dichotomy is also observed. It is a very ridiculous that despite surplus foodgrain production there are chronic as well as seasonal hunger because of lack of affordability and accessibility.

Measurement of Food Security

There are a number of ways, by which food security can be measured. These levels include: continental, regional, sub-regional and household levels. At the continental and sub-regional levels, food security can be measured by comparing regional nutritional requirement with availability of dietary calories per head. The ultimate goal is to meet the food requirements of the population at all levels, the most widely used indicators are quantities of available food compared with need, as well as import requirements compared with the county's capacity to import.

At the household level, food security is measured by actual dietary intake of all household members using household income and expenditure surveys. It is important that changes in socio-economic and demographic variables be monitored continuously over time. Chen *et. al.* (1994), suggest measuring an individuals food security by food poverty indicators and by anthropological data.

Food indicator shows the number of individuals living in a household whose access to food is sufficient to provide a dietary intake adequate for growth, activity and good health. The anthropometric measure refers to nutritional status at individual level. Thus, individual food security implies an intake of food and absorption of nutrients sufficient to meet an individual's needs for activity, health, growth and development. The individual's age, gender, body size, health status and levels of physical activity determine the level of need.

The United Nations Development Program (UNDP), in its annual Human Development Reports, uses the following indicators to measure food security at national level: food production per head, agricultural production as a percent of gross domestic product, food consumption as a percent of total consumption, daily calorie supply per head, food supply from fish and seafood, food imports, cereal imports and food aid in cereals. Of course, UNDP data measuring food security at national level are estimated averages and do not reflect food security at household level.

FOOD AVAILABILITY

Food availability depends on the productivity of foodgrains. Foodgrains are considered to be of paramount significance for household food and nutritional security, the reason being that cereals and pulses are staple food and there are no perfect substitutes for them (Chand, 2007). Following important indicators of food availability—Per capita agricultural production, irrigation facilities, rural connectivity availability of forest areas. Irrigation has the greatest impact on food availability when it is labour-intensive, employs affordable and small scale techniques.

Availability of Foodgrains

In the early years after independence, India was a food-deficient country so far as the net per capita availability of foodgrains and other cereals are concerned. Intensive farming often leads to a vicious cycle of exhaustion of soil fertility and decline of agricultural yields. Approximately 40 per cent of the world's agricultural land is seriously degraded. In India, more of the population lives in rural areas. In that context, agricultural development among smallholder farmers and landless people provides a livelihood for people allowing them the opportunity to stay in their communities.

The per capita availability of foodgrains is presented in Table 1 and also in Graph 1. As per 1991 data, per capita availability of foodgrains was 186.2 kg per person per year. It was highest availability due to the good impact of green revolution. Chakarvarty (1987), points out that the main benefit of the green revolution has been confined to wheat, cotton, and to a much lesser extent rice. The situation with regard to edible oils, pulses and coarse grain has by and large deteriorated giving rise to what may be referred to as an unbalanced cropping pattern. The trend

TABLE I

Net Availability of Foodgrains in India

(Kg/person/year)

Years	*Rice*	*Wheat*	*Other Cereals*	*Cereals*	*Gram*	*Pulses*	*Food-grains*
1951	58.0	24.0	40.0	122.0	8.2	22.1	144.1
1961	73.4	28.9	43.6	145.9	11.0	25.2	171.1
1971	70.3	37.8	44.3	152.4	7.3	18.7	171.1
1981	72.2	47.3	32.8	152.3	4.9	13.7	166.0
1991	80.9	60.0	29.2	171.0	4.9	15.2	186.2
2001	69.5	49.6	20.5	141.0	2.9	10.9	151.9
2005	64.7	56.3	21.7	142.7	3.9	11.5	154.2
2007	71.8	57.0	20.8	149.6	4.3	10.7	160.4

Notes: (i) Cereals includes rice, wheat and other cereals.
(ii) Pulses includes all kharif and rabi pulses.
(iii) Foodgrains includes rice, wheat, other cereals and all pulses

Sources: Agriculture at a Glance, GoI.

of foodgrain production improved from 2.5 per cent during the 1960s to 2.9 per cent in the eighties. (Bhalla and Singh, 2001). In last five decades (1951-2007) per capita availability of the gram, pulses and other cereals is going to decline. Only net availability of rice and wheat is still going to increase.

GRAPH I

Net Availability of Foodgrains in India

(Kg/person/year)

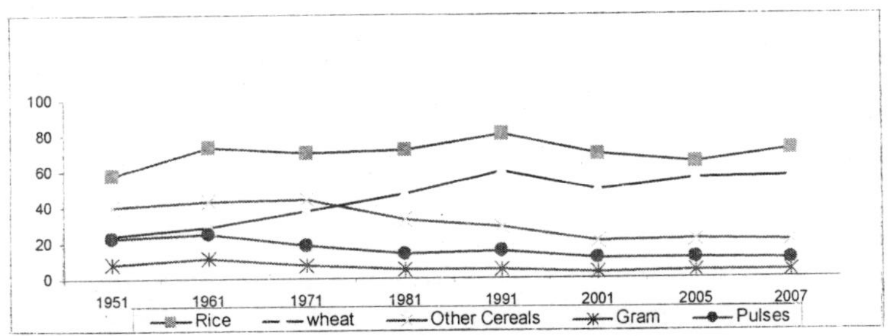

The poor agricultural productivity and production, and low level of foodgrain outputs resulting from the low level introduction of agricultural technologies; poor rural infrastructure; high vulnerability of crop production to natural disasters such as floods and droughts; and high rates of unemployment and poverty, are some of the reasons for the high degree of food insecurity. (Kumar, 2003). The total foodgrains production for the year 2008-09 was 233.88 million tonnes and stands out as record production. Production of Cotton increased from 99.97 lakh bales in 2000-01 to 258.84 lakh bales in 2007-08. Some of the lagging regions like Bihar, showed relatively high growth in recent years. Gujarat recorded high growth of 9 per cent per annum during 2001-02 to 2007-08 (Gulati, 2009).

Availability of Rice

In 1951 net rice availability was 158.9 grams per person per day. In the situation of such food scarcity our First Five Year Plan gave maximum priority to agriculture. As a result, the net availability increased to 201.1 grams in 1961 but again dipped

GRAPH 2

Net Availability of Foodgrains in India from 1951-2007

(Grams per day)

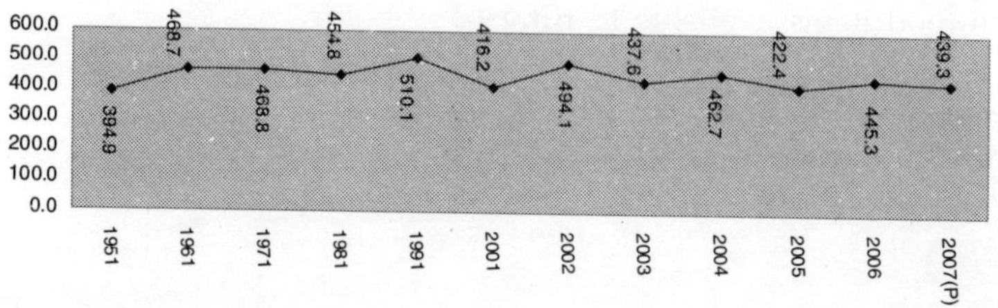

down to 161.9 grams in 1961. It was in 1960's that India had to pathetically go to the western world with the begging bowl. The period after 1961 the country continuously moved on in terms of foodgrain production. Thanks to the first green revolution which was initiated in the north-western parts, especially in the states of Haryana, Punjab and western U.P. The net rice availability reached to the highest (228.7 grams per person per day) in the year 2002. But again some sort of declining trend is being witnessed.

GRAPH 3

Net Availability of Rice in India from 1951-2007

(Grams per day)

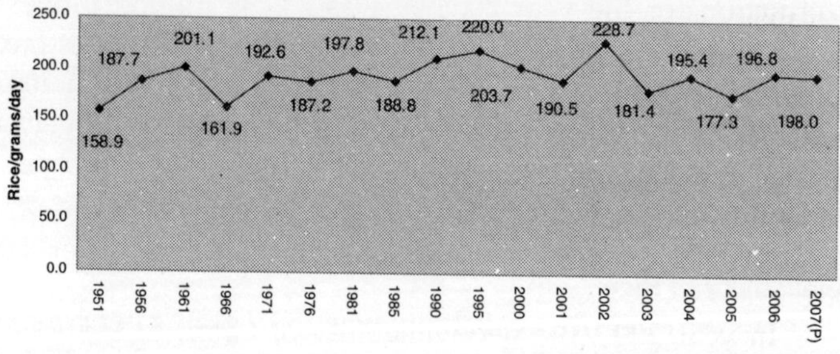

Availability of Cereals

According to NSS, per capita cereal consumption has been

declining since the early 1970's despite a significant rise in per capita cereal production. This can be attributed to changes in consumer tastes, from food to non-food items and, within food group, from coarse to fine cereals. The decline in cereal consumption has been greater in rural areas, where the improvement in rural infrastructure has made other food and non-food items available to rural households.

Cereals availability was 109.6 grams in 1951. It has declined to 58.9 grams by 2007. It was due to overemphasis on the production of rice and wheat neglecting other cereals. The net availability of cereals was highest at 121.4 grams in 1971 whereas it was at the lowest level of 46.7 grams in year 2003

GRAPH 4

Net Availability of other Cereals in India from 1951-2007

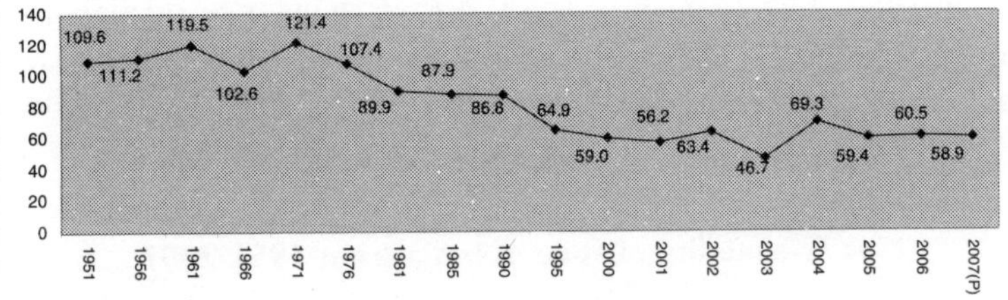

Availability of Gram

Gram is a major sources of protein, potassium, calcium and sodium. It is one of the most highly prized pulses of India. But the availability trends of gram is continuously going to decline. From the declining graph shown in No. 5, we can see the net availability of Gram in India. It was at the highest level of 30.2 grams in 1961 and the lowest at 8.0 grams per person per day in 2002.

In year 2007, the net availability of Gram in India is 10.7 gram per day per person. During the last fifty-five years population growth rate was high and rate of production of gram is low, so the net availability of gram is declining.

GRAPH 5

Net Availability of Gram in India from 1951-2007

(Grams per day)

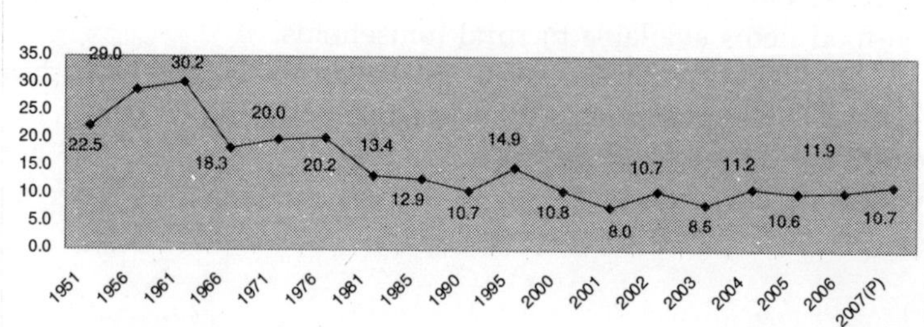

Availability of Pulses

In the case of availability of pulses which has declined from 60.7 grams in 1951 and 70.3 grams in 1956 to 29.4 grams in 2007. This anomaly could be noticed due to utter neglect of pulses production during the green revolution. It pushes the country towards nutrition deficiency as pulses are the major sources of protein in vegetarian diet.

GRAPH 6

Availability of Gram in India from 1951-2007

(Grams per day)

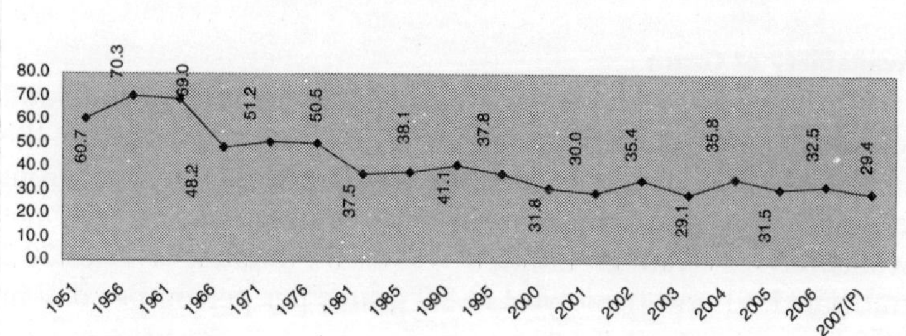

It also calls for the need of crop diversification. There is need to encourage pulse production as pulses are not only the major source of protein but also being the leguminous plants it helps in enriching the soil fertility due to nitrogen fixation.

TABLE 2

Percentage Distribution of Households by Food Availability Status in Various Rounds

Rounds	*% of Rural Households All India*		*% of Urban Households All India*	
	Getting enough food everyday through the year	*Not getting enough food every day*	*Getting enough food everyday through the year*	*Not getting enough food everyday*
NSS 61st Round (July 2004-June 2005)	97.4	2.6	99.4	0.6
NSS 55th Round (July 1999-June 2000)	96.2	3.8	98.6	1.4
NSS 50th Round (July 1993-June 1994)	94.5	5.5	98.1	1.9
NSS 38th Round (January-December 1983)	81.1	18.9	93.3	6.7

Source: Computed from NSSO various Rounds.

In Table 2 the urban-rural divide can be seen in terms of percentage distribution of households by food availability status in various rounds of survey conducted by NSS. In the First Round 97.4 percent rural households got enough food every day throughout the year whereas 2.6 percent did not get enough food everyday. The figures for urban areas are distinct with 99.4 percent getting enough food and only 0.6 percent urban households not getting enough food per day. The situations continued to worsen from the first round to 38th round of survey conducted in 1983. The gap increased both in rural and urban households. In the 38th round, 81.1 percent rural households and 93.3 percent urban households got enough food whereas 18.9 percent rural and 6.7 percent urban households had to sleep with empty bellies. This anomaly was not only due to lack of availability but also inability to access and to afford as a result of uneven distribution, ineffective channel of distribution and lack of purchasing power of the poverty stricken rural masses.

ACCESSIBILITY OF FOOD

Accessibility of food is the most important factor for determining the food security. Accessibility is highly related to the people's capacity to buy and also other socio-economic conditions. This depends on monthly consumption expenditure per person, structure of casual wages, nature of work, working age population, level of urbanization, literacy, etc. Per capita consumption expenditure is a good indicator of food security. State wise details can see in the Table 3. The NSS defines the casual wage worker as one who was casually engaged in others farm or non-farm enterprises and in return, received wages

TABLE 3

Various Factors for Accessibility of Food

States	*Monthly per capita Expenditure on Food (Rs.)*	*Rural Female Literacy in 2001*	*Proportion of Agri-cultural labourers in Workforce*	*Urbani-sation in 2001*	*Average Casual Rural Wage (Rs.)*
Andhra Pradesh	323.15	43.5	47.5	27.3	42.13
Assam	358.44	50.7	14.9	12.9	60.18
Bihar	270.26	29.6	51	10.5	43.95
Gujarat	345.46	47.8	33.2	37.4	49.72
Haryana	419.34	49.3	19	28.9	72.2
Jharkhand	263.22	29.9	32.8	22.2	48.07
Karnataka	283.04	48	34.5	34	41.32
Kerala	455.64	86.7	19.6	26	119.51
Madhya Pradesh	232.17	42.8	34.1	26.5	35.76
Maharashtra	293.29	58.4	37.8	42.4	38.58
Orissa	245.58	46.7	39.1	15	34.45
Punjab	416.45	57.7	21.9	33.9	73.12
Rajasthan	323.97	37.3	12.3	23.4	62.12
Tamil Nadu	315.49	55.3	42.9	44	56.48
Uttar Pradesh	345.88	36.9	28.9	20.8	51.25
West Bengal	329.93	53.2	33.1	28	48.38
All India	307.93	46.1	33.0	27.8	48.89

Source: NSS 2004-05, Census of India-2001.

according to terms of the daily work contract. The total number of agricultural workers in the country has been estimated at 259 million as of 2004-05. Of these, more than one-third are wage workers and almost all of these are casual labourers. Agricultural labourers are characterized by extremely poor physical and human capital and also the highest poverty levels (NCEUS, 2007). Female literacy is the most significant indicator contributing to increase in food insecurity and decline in malnutrition and mortality levels (Save the Children, 2008).

FOOD ABSORPTION

Food absorption is based on the health status of the peoples. Health status depends on Safe drinking water, sanitation, PHC facility, immunization, best nutritional status, etc. It has been estimated that in developing countries, one out of five people do not use safe drinking water, and around half are without adequate sanitation. (WHO-2007) Safe drinking water and sanitation are the two more important indicators for good health. Good health ensures effective absorption of food, and lastly improves the nutritional status. Sanitation status is discussed in terms of existence of toilet facility inside the house. State-wise details can be seen in Table 4.

The State of the World's Children-2008 suggests early and exclusive breastfeeding for the first six months, appropriate complementary feeding from six months to two years, skilled care at birth and special care for low-birth weight babies as key preventive measures to reduce child mortality. Thus, adequate food security of the child is necessary for their survival beyond the age of five. (UNICEF-2007)

IMPORTANT CHALLENGES TO ACHIEVE THE FOOD SECURITY

We see that the food security depends on availability of food and also access to it. Food security requires not only producing sufficient food to meet the market demand but also ensuring that all persons have the purchasing power to obtain food. India's population is going to increase and availability of foodgrains is going to gradually decrease. In this situation there

TABLE 4

Factors Determining Absorption/Utilisation

States	*Households having Safe Drinking Water (%)*	*Number of Villages Per PHC*	*Households having Toilet Facility*
Andhra Pradesh	80.1	18.9	18.1
Assam	58.8	43.1	59.6
Bihar	86.6	27.4	13.9
Gujarat	84.1	17.3	21.7
Haryana	86	17	28.7
Jharkhand	42.7	58.1	6.6
Karnataka	84.6	17.5	17.4
Kerala	23.4	1.5	81.3
Madhya Pradesh	68.4	46.4	8.9
Maharashtra	79.8	24.6	18.2
Orissa	64.2	40.1	7.7
Punjab	97.6	26.2	40.9
Rajasthan	68.3	24.7	14.6
Tamil Nadu	85.5	11.8	14.4
Uttar Pradesh	87.8	29.5	19.2
West Bengal	88.5	34.8	26.9
All India	78	27.6	21.9

Sources: Census of India, 2001 and Health Information of India, 2008.

is a big gap between demand and supply of the foodgrains. However, the challenges of achieving the food security for all people remain a real dream. We also know that around 40 per cent of farmers want to give up the farming if any option is available. Indian farmers have faced several problems during the last few years. Due to rising input price and falling output prices coupled with frequent crop failure because of unfavourable weather, real income of farmers have shown a declining trends. Now the Indian agriculture growth rate is likely to be stagnant. With due to sub-division and fragmentation of land, land holding is going to reduce. Per capita land availability is gradually going to decline. The number of hunger and malnutrition is going to increase day-by-day. As per report "Commonwealth or Common Hunger" released by NGO (Save the Children) around 43 per cent of Indian kids are underweight, and 7 million under five are severely malnourished. The report reveals 64 per cent of the world's underweight kids live in 54 Commonwealth countries, and India has both highest number and highest proportion of under weight children. (Himanshi Dhawan, 2010) Nutritional and Mortality Status of Children and Women of poor performing states can be seen in Table 5.

TABLE 5

Mortality and Nutritional Status of Children and Women

States	*Infant Mortality*	*Under-weight Children*	*Wasted Children*	*Stunted Children*	*Anemic Children*	*Thin Women*
UP	72.7	42.4	14.8	56.8	73.9	36
MP	69.5	60	35	50	74.1	41.7
Jharkhand	68.7	56.5	32.3	49.8	70.3	43
Orissa	64.7	40.7	19.5	45	65	41.4
Chhattisgrah	70.8	47.1	19.5	52.9	71.2	43.4
Rajasthan	65.3	39.9	20.4	43.7	69.7	36.7
Assam	66.1	36.4	13.7	46.5	69.6	36.5
Bihar	61.7	55.9	27.1	55.6	78	46.1
India	57	42.5	19.8	48	69.5	35.6

Sources: National Family Health Survey, 2005-06.

World Bank estimate around 35 per cent of the population is chronically undernourished in Bangladesh followed by 25 per cent in India, 20 per cent in Nepal and Pakistan and 25 per cent in Sri Lanka.

Food wastages is also important challenges for achieving the food security in India. Around 580 billion foodgrains got spoiled due to lack of proper storage facilities with the Food Corporation of India. Poor investment in agricultural research and education is also a challenge. The role of ICAR will be very useful to fight this challenge. Climate change and its impact on agriculture is also one issue, which is a great obstacle in achieving the food security. Year by year the temperature is going to rise, snow is going to melt, sea level is rising up, coastal sides are affected by the flood and cyclone. They directly affects the agricultural productivity. Glaciers aren't the only worry that the developing nations have, sea level is also reported to rise as climate changes progress, reducing the amount of land available for agriculture. And low crop yields is just one of the problems facing farmers in the low latitudes and tropical regions. The timing and length of the growing seasons, when farmers plant their crops, are going to be changing dramatically.

There is also a big challenge to achieving the food security, WTO Agreement on Agriculture. At the time of signature the Agreement on Agriculture it was hoped that the Indian farmers will be more benefited because of increasing the global market. But in the wake of WTO, the volatility of international prices has affected agricultural production adversely in the country. Except wheat and rice the agricultural commodities have shown declining trends. There have been substantial increase in the import of edible oils and pulses. Agreement on agriculture would be a big risk of livelihood insecurity of millions of farmers and agricultural workers in the country. Small farm economy like India's economy wants more output in agriculture sector but needs more input in technology, rural infrastructure, marketing and risk management. These inputs will definitely provide better output in agricultural sector.

Food security is a major cause of concern of agricultural scientists, and planners and its main challenges arise due to some factors like under developed agricultural sector, changing climate and declining agricultural productivity, rising foodgrain prices barriers in access to market, adverse impacts of globalization, inefficient PDS, rapid urbanization, climate changes and of course the lack of good governance. Increased agricultural productivity enables farmers to grow more food, which translates into better diets and, the market conditions that offer a level playing field into higher farm incomes. With more money, farmers are more likely to diversify production and grow higher-value crops, benefiting not only themselves but the economy as a whole. A large quantity of foodgrain are rotten or destroyed by rats and pests due to lack of proper storage facilities. The public distribution system has failed to address the problem thus, depriving the marginalized people to get access to foodgrain at affordable price regularly. The NREGA has to some extent brought some light in the lives of the rural poor who have achieved some strength to get access to food. But still much has to be done. More sustained efforts needs to be taken for sustainable agriculture by promoting organic farming, drip irrigation, efficient water management, storage facilities, and rural infrastructure, diversification of agriculture and non-farm activities and strengthening of the distribution network of PDS to make foodgrain available to the deprived. An evaluation study of the TPDS in Uttar Pradesh by Kriesel and Zaidi (1999) find that over half the population of Households in the lowest 5 per cent of the population did not get BPL cards. According to Swaminathan (2003), the TPDS has failed in the following ways, first improper targeting has meant that genuinely needy people have often been excluded. Second, targeting has also adversely affected the viability of public distribution and finally, targeting has undermined one of the main functions that it served in the past.

STRATEGIES FOR ACHIEVING FOOD SECURITY

Despite various schemes and programs, food security net has not covered all. For this some more proactive actions are needed. These may be population stabilization, boosting agricultural science and technology, securing property rights and access to finance, establishment of water security system, management of atmosphere and climate, diversification of farming system, demand and supply atlas of food, upgradation of traditional water harvesting system, water reuse and recycling system and improvement in agriculture and irrigation practices to achieve more crop per drop. Food availability must be improved to provide the irrigational facilities and lastly increase the agricultural productivity. Accessibility will improve by the policies for enhancing minimum agricultural wages and absorption of food by the better health facility. To provide safety nets to the teeming masses, the government has taken steps by making interventions through various programs. Steps are taken to revamp the PDS, and several poverty alleviation programs and schemes have been introduced from time to time. Some of these programs are Antodaya Anna Yojana (AAY), Annapurna scheme, Integrated Child Development Services (ICDS), mid-day meal, food for work and the most talked about recent programs of Mahatma Gandhi National Rural Employment Guarantee Act (MGNREGA). The newly introduced extension institutions and initiative such as Krishi Vigyan Kendra, Agri Clinics, Kisan Call Centres and Agricultural Technology Management Agency (ATMA) have not yet made their impact in large part of the country.

There is a need to focus more on poverty alleviation programmes and employment generation schemes. There is no denying the fact that even more than six decades after independence, food insecurity and starvation are big blots on the face of mother India which is moving on the path of achieving the goal of status of the developed country. This could be attributed to failure of our governance and developmental approach. It is contrary to the committed objective of welfare state and inclusive growth. The present UPA government has brought legislations to ensure Right to Information, Right to Work and is planning to ensure Right to Food to provide safety needs to the teeming millions. But recent study on the implementation of Right to Education reveals that despite this right large number of children are still out of school and the rate of drop-outs is high. If this is the outcome of such ambitious programmes then how can food security be achieved just by ensuring it as a right. Need of the hour is honest and sincere implementation of the right by strict monitoring and efficient governance otherwise the Right to Food will meet the same fate.

References

Bhalla, G.S. and Gurmail Singh (2001), Indian Agriculture: Four Decades of Development, Sage Publications, New Delhi.

Chakravarty, S. (1987), Development Planning: The Indian Experiences, Oxford University Press

Chand, Ramesh (2007), 'Demand for Foodgrains', *Economic and Political Weekly*, 42(52), December 29-January 4.

Chen, *et al.* (1994), "World Food Security: Prospects and Trends", *Food Policy*, 19(2), pp. 192-208.

Dhawan, Himansu (2010), India Leads Commonwealth Tally in Underweight Children, *The Times of India*, New Delhi, 14 October, 2010.

FAO (1996), Report of the World Food Summit, Rome, www.faro.org

Gulati, Ashok (2009), "Emerging Trends in Indian Agriculture: What can we learn from these?", 2nd Prof. Dayanath Jha Memorial Lecture, National Centre for Agricultural Economics and Policy Research, New Delhi.

Kriesel, S. and Zaidi, S. (1999), The Targeted Public Distribution System in UP: An Evaluation, Working Paper, The World Bank, Washington, DC, August.

Kumar, M. Dinesh (2003), "Food Security and Sustainable Agriculture in India: The Water Management Challenge", Working Paper No. 60, International Water Management Institute, Colombo, Sri Lanka.

Mahendra, Dev S. (2009), "Structural Reforms and Agriculture: Issues and Policies", Keynote paper presented in 92nd Annual Conference of Indian Economic Association, 27-29 December, 2009 at KIIT, Bhubaneswar, Orissa

NCEUS (2007), Report on Conditions of Work and Promotion of Livelihoods in Unorganised Sector, National Commission for Enterprises in the Unorganized Sector, New Delhi.

Ram, G.S. (1996), "Food Security System, Poverty and Rural Development", Presidential Address, *Agricultural Economics Research Review*, Vol. 9, No. 2, pp. 121-27.

Save the Children (2008), Saving Children's Lives: Why Equity Matters, Save the Children, London.

Sen, Amartya (1981), Poverty and Famines: An Essay on Entitlement and Deprivation, Oxford, Clarendon Press.

Swaminathan, M. (2003), "Strategies towards Food Security", *Social Scientist*, Vol. 31, Nos. 9-10, September-October 2003, p. 58.

UN (1975), Report of the World Food Conference, 5-16 November, 1975, Rome.

UNICEF (2007), The State of the World's Children 2008: Child Survival, United Nations Children Fund, New York, December.

WHO (2007), Health Status: Mortality, World Health Statistics, 2006, World Health Organisation, Geneva, pp. 29-31.

Environmental Resources and their Impact on Foodgrains Production and Productivity

Dastgir Alam, Firdos Ahmad and Jamil Ahmad

INTRODUCTION

After independence, Indian agriculture has passed through so many ups and downs. During the early decades of planning government made a lot of effort in form of land reforms and heavy investment over irrigation projects, etc. but Indian agriculture remain the gamble of monsoon for a longer period of time (Bhalla, G.S., 2000). In early 1960s when green revolution was introduced, farmers got a sign of relief when government supplied chemical fertilizers, high yielding varieties of seeds and even the assured irrigation facilities at subsidized prices (Dasgupta, M. Murthy, 1985). This improved not only the level of production but productivity also. This phase of Indian agriculture lasted for about thirty years. This period of Indian agriculture was very important because in this era we managed to reduce the dependency of agriculture over monsoon and natural environment in which agriculture was practiced (WCED, 1987).

When the Government of India decided to enter in the regime of openness via integrating the Indian economy with rest of the economies in 1991, agriculture became the worst affected sector since the new economic policies do not allow to continue the regime of subsidy and protectionism (Mathur and Sirkar, 2006). After this farmers are supposed to accumulate the resources for agricultural practices by themselves.

In addition to this rising prices of agricultural inputs created a great problem for small and marginal farmers who constitute a major part of Indian farmers (Shah, M., 2006). All these changes after 1991, once again brought the Indian agriculture in the same state from where we started after independence in terms of its dependency over nature and environment (Shah, A., 1997). In this present paper, we therefore analyse the production and productivity of Indian agriculture in its very natural environment. In this work we will try to analyse the level of production and productivity in terms of types of soil in a particular region and level of irrigated area assuming that other factors like chemical fertilizers, HYV seeds, genetically modified seeds are costlier and poor and marginal farmers are unable to purchase it. If they are purchasing, it may not be in appropriate amount because of high prices.

METHODOLOGY

For this present work statewise information is collected for area under foodgrain cultivation, net irrigated area of cultivation, production, productivity and type of soil. The study is divided into two sections. Firstly, we have analysed the impact of area under cultivation and net irrigated area on the level of production and productivity in different states. For this purpose following regression equation is prepared.

$P = f(A) = b_1A$

$P = f(I) = b_2I$

$P_i = f(I) = b_3I$

where

P = Production of foodgrains

A = Area under cultivation

b_1 = Degree of association between Production and area under cultivation

P_i = Productivity

$P = f(A, I) = b_4A + b'_4I$ I = Net irrigated area

b_2 = Degree of association between production and net irrigated area

$P = f(A, I, P_i) = b_5A + b'_5I + b''_5P_i$

b_3 = Degree of association between productivity and net irrigated area.

b_4 = Degree of association between production and area under cultivation when net irrigated area is also considered as a factor of production simultaneously.

b'_4 = Degree of association between production and net irrigated area when area under cultivation is treated as independent factor simultaneously.

b_5 = Degree of association between area under cultivation and production of foodgrains when net irrigated area and productivity are also considered as factors of production.

b'_5 = Degree of association between net irrigated area and level of production when area under cultivation and productivity are considered as other factors of production.

b''_5 = Degree of association between level of production and productivity assuming that area under cultivation and net irrigated area are other two factors of production.

Secondly, types of soil is considered as a factor which influences the level of production and productivity of land. For this purpose statewise data is collected for various types of soil and a comparative analysis is done, i.e. in which type of soil what is the productivity and level production.

When population of a country grows, the most important concern of the government is to take care of the availability of foodgrains. Since population grows by geometric progression and foodgrain production grows by arithmetic progression, there may be always some gap if growth rate for both are same. Malthus was the first person who looks into the matter and warned the world community about the food crisis that may be caused by the differences in the growth in population and growth in production of fodograins (R. Malthus, 1978). We may have a lower growth in foodgrains production in the long-run due to limited land area and capacity of land to produce food.

This problem of foodgrain production in appropriate

amount to meet with the rising demand for growing population may aggravated in the densely populated countries. India is one of those countries. To feed the population, a high proportion of land is used for subsistence agriculture. TERI (The Energy and Resources Institute) estimates that India will have 1.5 billion population in 2030 which requires a stock of food equal to 114 million tonnes of rice, 85 million tonnes of wheat, 13 million tonnes of maize, 104 million tonnes of fruits and 193 million tonnes of vegetables. This will put India in great trouble given the limited availability of land and water resource (TERI, 2005). This may force the Indians to expand the area of cultivation of sub-standard type of land including marginal and sub-marginal land area. But it will cost a lot as it require extensive work for soil and water conservation. The following table will give us an account of the level of production and productivity of foodgrains in relation to land area and irrigation net area.

TABLE I

Statistical Values

States	b_1	b_2	b_3	b_4	b'_4	b_5	b'_5	b''_5
Andhra Pradesh	0.59	0.462	0.174	0.501	0.138	0.471	0.016	0.811
Bihar	0.933	0.728	0.389	0.767	0.259	0.943	0.004	0.377
Haryana	0.291	0.354	0.821	0.127	0.278	0.048	0.116	0.255
Karnataka	0.837	0.098	0.002	0.862	-0.105	0.319	0.022	0.752
Madhya Pradesh	0.859	0.644	0.431	0.831	0.033	0.494	0.012	0.625
Maharashtra	0.616	-0.323	0.230	0.622	0.012	0.647	-0.006	0.133
Punjab	0.957	-0.178	-0.185	0.951	-0.039	0.440	-0.005	0.592
Rajasthan	0.792	-0.086	0.221	1.039	0.465	0.418	-0.023	0.719
Uttar Pradesh	0.736	0.680	0.305	0.607	0.533	0.626	0.478	0.165
West Bengal	-0.087	0.175	0.412	-0.061	0.165	-0.002	0.047	0.310
All India	-0.045	0.693	0.812	0.252	0.788	-0.026	-0.260	1.160

Source: Computed from the tables given in Appendix.

Production and Area

Above table reveals some important fact about the production of foodgrain in India which can help in formation of policies for agricultural development. When we keep area as an independent variable and production as dependent variable, we find that in case of India there is negative correlation between these variables, but states like Bihar, Punjab, Maharashtra, Karnataka, Madhya Pradesh, Andhra Pradesh, Rajasthan, Uttar Pradesh have strong correlation between these variables. On the other hand, West Bengal has weak correlation and Haryana has even negative relationship between these variable.

Production and Irrigation

Expansion of irrigation facilities along with consolidation of the existing system has been the main part of the strategy for increasing production of foodgrains. When we establish the correlation between production and net irrigated area we find that in the states like Bihar, Madhya Pradesh and Uttar Pradesh irrigation plays vital role in the production of foodgrain while in case of other mentioned states the correlation between these variables is very weak. At all India level irrigation plays an important role in the production of foodgrain.

Productivity and Irrigation

A comparison of productivity levels in Indian agriculture with the levels in other countries shows how low is the productivity of Indian agriculture. Therefore, here it becomes important to analyse the relationship between productivity and irrigation. Among the all above mention states only in Haryana, there is very strong correlation between productivity and irrigation and in the other states irrigation does not play significant role in the productivity of the foodgrain production but when we see the correlation between these variables at all India level, we find that there is very strong correlation, i.e. 0.812.

Production, Area and Irrigation

Now, we try to establish correlation between production, area and net irrigated area. We simply take production as a dependent variable and area and net irrigated area together as an independent variable, we find that states like Andhra Pradesh, Bihar, Karnataka, Madhya Pradesh, Maharashtra and Punjab area is playing vital role than irrigation in the production of foodgrains. Irrigation does not play any significant role in comparison to area in the production of foodgrain except in Uttar Pradesh, where the irrigation play an important role but at all

India level in compare to area, irrigation plays significant role in the production of foodgrain.

Production, Area, Irrigation and Productivity

Finally, we made a modest attempt to establish the correlation between production, area, irrigation and productivity. We take production as a dependent variable and area, irrigation and productivity together as independent variables. Only in Andhra Pradesh, production has a significant correlation with productivity. In Bihar among these variables only area plays a significant role in the production of foodgrain. In Haryana and West Bengal among these variables not a single variable play a significant role in the production of foodgrain. In Karnataka irrigation has a significant role in the production of foodgrain. In Madhya Pradesh, irrigation has a strong correlation with production and up to some extent area also plays considerable role in the production of foodgrain. In Rajasthan productivity has a strong correlation with production and also area has a comparatively significant correlation with production. In Uttar Pradesh area has a good correlation with production and irrigation has considerable correlation with production. At all India level among these independent variables only productivity has a strong correlation with production.

Soil and Foodgrains Production

Soil is the most important outer layer of the earth which is used for the production of food, fuel and other desired products. Hence an attempt has been made to analyse production and productivity levels of foodgrains in relation to the type of soil in different regions. The following Table 2 represents the information about the various types of soil, average production and productivity in some selected states.

The Table 2 reflects the impact of types of soil and net irrigated area on production and productivity of foodgrain in various states of India. In above mention states high production and productivity of foodgrain observed in Punjab, Haryana, West Bengal, Uttar Pradesh and Andhra Pradesh where the common soil is alluvial. Alluvial soil is the most important type of soil in India. It covers the vast valley areas of the Sutlez, Ganga and Brahmputra and the fringes of south peninsula. The alluvial soil

Table 2

Types of Soil, Production and Productivity

(kg/hectare)

	States	*Types of Soil*	*Average productivity of foodgrain 1991-92 to 2004-05 (kg/hectare)*	*Average production of foodgrain (000 tonnes)*	*Average irrigated area during 1991-92 to 2004-05 (%age)*
1.	Andhra Pradesh	Alluvial, Red, Black soil	1852.64	12914.74	39.10
2.	Bihar	Alluvial, Laterite soil	1519.09	7933.99	52.65
3.	Haryana	Alluvial, Desert soil	2858.77	20808.09	79.28
4.	Karnataka	Laterite, Red, Black soil	1193.00	8614.63	23.33
5.	Madhya Pradesh	Black, Red, Laterite soil	1088.07	12908.59	35.03
6.	Maharahstra	Black, Red soil	1562.08	11971.78	15.66
7.	Punjab	Alluvial, Desert soil	3755.31	22466.55	92.96
8.	Rajasthan	Red, Desert soil	924.77	11381.28	31.70
9.	Uttar Pradesh	Alluvial soil	1943.60	39475.46	71.55
10.	West Bengal	Alluvial, Laterite soil	2190.57	24254.26	44.19

Source: (i) CMIE Report 2002, Agriculture Issue, April, Mumbai.
(ii) CMIE Report 2007, Agriculture Issue, December, Mumbai.

occupy 64 million hectare of the most fertile land. The soil vary from loam to clay in texture and are rich in potash but deficient in nitrogen and organic matter. Generally the colour varies from grey to redish brown, being extremely productive, these soils are most important from the point of view of India. Almost all crops are grown in these soils. Among these states, Punjab and Haryana occupied first and second place in term of production and productivity of foodgrains. In these two states common soils are found, i.e. alluvial and desert soil. But there is a difference in productivity. In Punjab average production of foodgrain is 22466.55 thousand tonnes and productivity is 3755.31 kg/ha and in Haryana average production of foodgrain is 20888.09 thousand tonnes and production is 2858.77 kg/ha during the period 1991-92 to 2004-05. The simple reason of differences in productivity in these states is difference in net irrigated area. The average irrigated area in Punjab is 92.96 per cent while in Haryana it is 70.78 per cent during the same period. Another reason is availability of desert soil in both states. In desert soil moisture content is very low. It able to give more yield if water is adequately available.

On the other hand, low production and productivity of foodgrains is observed in the states like Rajasthan, Madhya Pradesh, Karnataka and Bihar, where laterite black and red soil are found. Laterite soil is a mixture of clay and red soil formed in the monsoon climatic region and having low fertility. Black soil formed due to the disintegration of lower rocks. These are highly fertile and moisture holding capacity is high. Lastly, red soil is formed due to the disintegration of metamorphic and igneous rocks, comparatively less fertile and presence of iron gives the red colour. Along the low quality of soil, inadequate irrigation facilities are also responsible of low productivity of foodgrains in these states. In these states average irrigated area vary from 52.65 per cent to 23.33 per cent during the period of 1991-92 to 2004-05. In Maharashtra the average production of foodgrains is 11971.78 thousand tonnes and the average productivity of foodgrain is 1562.08 kg/ha during 1991-92 to 2004-05 which is comparatively higher from low productivity states. In Maharashtra red and black soil are found which is comparatively less fertile soil and also get inadequate irrigation facilities that is only cover 15.66 per cent of area. It means other factor works for productivity in this state. We can therefore say that under Indian climatic condition alluvial is most fertile soil and black soil is another important soil for the production of certain agriculture product. Irrigation facilities is equally important for variation in productivity of foodgrain among the states.

CONCLUSION

The theoretical background on the basis of which we started the study seems to be inconclusive at state level. In some states net irrigated area plays important role in determining the level of production. These states are Bihar, Maharashtra and Uttar Pradesh. Other states have shown their discomfort in this connection but at all India level the relationship seems convincing. In case of relationship between productivity and net irrigated area, though we have a high degree of relationship at all India level but at state level Haryana is the single state where relationship is significant. More or less we get the same pattern when we take area and net irrigated area as independent variable simultaneously. Situation became more worse when we take area, net irrigated area and productivity as independent variable simultaneously. Contrary to this the types of soil has proved effective in determining the level of productivity in different states. The states with alluvial soil are more productive than others.

References

Bhalla, G.S. (2000), "The Nature of Agricultural Development in India", National Book Trust, New Delhi.

Dasgupta, A. and M. Murthy (1985), "Economic Evaluation of Water Pollution Abatement: A Case Study of Paper and Pulp Industry in India, *Indian Economic Review*, New Delhi.

Malthus, R. (1978), "Population: The First Essay", Ann Arbor: Ann Arbor Paperback, University of Michigan Press.

Mathur, A.S., Das, S. and Sirkar, S. (2006), "Status of Agriculture in India—Trends and Prospects", *EPW*, Vol. XLI, 30 Dec. 2006.

Shah, A. (1997), "Food Security and Access to Natural Resources – A Review of Recent Trends".

Shah, M. (2006), "Towards Reform – Watershed Programme", *Economic and Political Weekly*, Vol. XLI, 8 July, 2006.

The Energy and Resource Institute (2005), New Delhi.

World Commission on Environment and Development (WCED) 1987, Our Common Features, Oxford University Press, New York.

APPENDIX

State-wise Information about Foodgrains Production

Uttar Pradesh

Year	*Area (000 hec)*	*Production (000 tonnes)*	*Productivity (kg/hec)*	*Net Irrigated Area (%age)*
1991-92	18905.50	33819.50	1789.00	67.24
1992-93	19394.60	34612.20	1785.00	68.72
1993-94	19275.50	35542.00	1844.00	70.25
1994-95	19404.40	37588.00	1937.00	70.71
1995-96	19352.60	36672.30	1895.00	70.29
1996-97	19355.70	40695.20	2102.00	71.90
1997-98	19584.60	40020.70	2043.00	71.79
1998-99	19801.70	38823.70	1961.00	72.17
1999-00	20012.30	44261.10	2212.00	72.17
2000-01	20215.80	42496.60	1202.00	72.77
2001-02	20272.80	44048.00	2173.00	73.70
2002-03	17898.30	36316.70	2029.00	73.70
2003-04	20075.00	44177.00	2201.00	73.70
2004-05	19331.00	37564.00	1943.00	73.70
2005-06	19546.00	39839.00	2038.00	73.70
Average	19495.05	39475.46	1943.60	71.77

Sources: (i) CMIE Report, Dec. 2002, pp. 31 and 142.
(ii) CMIE Report, Apr. 2007, pp. 27 and 130.

West Bengal

Year	*Area (000 hec)*	*Production (000 tonnes)*	*Productivity (kg/hec)*	*Net Irrigated Area (%age)*
1991-92	6313.40	12856.00	2036.00	34.89
1992-93	6322.70	12388.00	1960.00	34.78
1993-94	6530.90	13100.60	2006.00	35.01
1994-95	6393.10	13278.60	2077.00	34.97
1995-96	6572.80	12884.80	1960.00	34.99
1996-97	6443.80	13756.30	2135.00	34.98
1997-98	6558.00	14354.30	2189.00	34.00
1998-99	6538.70	14367.50	2197.00	97.00
1999-00	6849.20	14915.60	2178.00	35.13
2000-01	6192.90	13815.20	2231.00	34.93
2001-02	6807.10	16501.20	2424.00	43.45
2002-03	6539.10	155225.00	2374.00	53.97
2003-04	6611.80	16009.20	2421.00	55.66
2004-05	6494.80	16107.30	2480.00	54.90
Average	51512.02	24254.26	2190.57	44.19

Sources: (i) CMIE Report, Dec. 2002, pp. 31 and 143.
(ii) CMIE Report, Apr. 2007, pp. 27 and 131.

Rajasthan

Year	*Area (000 hec)*	*Production (000 tonnes)*	*Productivity (kg/hec)*	*Net Irrigated Area (%age)*
1991-92	11288.20	7981.30	707.00	28.04
1992-93	12837.00	11479.10	894.00	26.40
1993-94	11628.90	7054.80	607.00	28.32
1994-95	12925.60	11710.40	906.00	28.54
1995-96	11902.30	9567.10	804.00	31.57
1996-97	12850.60	12821.50	990.00	33.28
1997-98	13750.90	14048.90	1022.00	31.75
1998-99	13475.80	12934.60	960.00	34.21
1999-00	10944.00	10800.00	987.00	36.18
2000-01	11372.10	10040.10	883.00	30.93
2001-02	12742.90	14001.90	1099.00	32.33
2002-03	8610.00	7532.00	875.00	40.46
2003-04	13963.00	17985.00	1288.00	30.12
Average	12176.25	11381.28	924.77	31.70

Sources: (i) CMIE Report, Dec. 2002, pp. 31 and 142.
(ii) CMIE Report, Apr. 2007, pp. 27 and 131.

Andhra Pradesh

Year	*Area (000 hec)*	*Production (000 tonnes)*	*Productivity (kg/hec)*	*Net Irrigated Area (%age)*
1991-92	7431.40	11705.50	1575.00	39.41
1992-93	7001.70	11685.10	1665.00	38.49
1993-94	6870.90	12253.50	1783.00	37.54
1994-95	6879.30	11783.40	1713.00	38.20
1995-96	6893.70	11666.70	1692.00	38.76
1996-97	7309.00	13681.60	1872.00	40.57
1997-98	6520.50	10822.10	1660.00	40.07
1998-99	7370.20	14905.40	2022.00	41.35
1999-00	7138.00	13692.20	1919.00	41.32
2000-01	7673.90	16027.80	2089.00	40.74
2001-02	7056.10	14836.60	2103.00	40.27
2002-03	6289.90	10655.50	1694.00	37.14
2003-04	6807.00	13697.00	2012.00	35.92
2004-05	6266.00	13394.00	2138.00	37.58
Average	6964.83	12914.74	1852.64	39.10

Sources: (i) CMIE Report, Dec. 2002, pp. 31 and 137.
(ii) CMIE Report, Apr. 2007, pp. 27 and 125.

Bihar

Year	*Area (000 hec)*	*Production (000 tonnes)*	*Productivity (kg/hec)*	*Net Irrigated Area (%age)*
1991-92	2372.20	3720.60	1568.00	43.45
1992-93	2406.70	3704.60	1539.00	58.53
1993-94	6556.00	10656.40	1625.00	56.18
1994-95	3233.20	4710.20	1457.00	47.52
1995-96	6280.80	6229.30	992.00	47.90
1996-97	N.A	N.A	N.A	50.27
1997-98	4230.00	6595.80	1559.00	49.39
1998-99	4080.20	6262.20	1535.00	47.34
1999-00	N.A	N.A	N.A	49.55
2000-01	7252.50	12055.10	1662.00	N.A
2001-02	7057.60	11849.70	1679.00	61.12
2002-03	6880.00	10270.00	1493.00	60.47
2003-04	7010.00	11220.00	1601.00	60.10
Average	5214.47	7933.99	1519.09	52.65

Sources: (i) CMIE Report, Dec. 2002, pp. 31 and 137.
(ii) CMIE Report, Apr. 2007, pp. 27 and 125.

Haryana

Year	*Area (000 hec)*	*Production (000 tonnes)*	*Productivity (kg/hec)*	*Net Irrigated Area (%age)*
1991-92	3585.00	9093.20	2536.00	76.00
1992-93	3967.10	10251.20	2584.00	75.63
1993-94	3893.30	10242.70	2631.00	75.80
1994-95	4011.90	11972.30	2984.00	76.40
1995-96	4020.50	10171.70	2530.00	76.99
1996-97	4025.80	11448.00	2844.00	76.21
1997-98	4187.10	11332.00	2706.00	76.84
1998-99	4129.00	12105.00	2932.00	78.34
1999-00	4287.40	13063.20	3047.00	81.31
2000-01	4343.50	13294.80	3061.00	83.89
2001-02	4253.50	133011.10	3127.00	83.39
2002-03	3980.00	12340.00	3100.00	85.80
2003-04	4290.00	13220.00	3082.00	84.01
Average	4074.93	20888.09	2858.77	79.28

Sources: (i) CMIE Report, Dec. 2002, pp. 31 and 138.
(ii) CMIE Report, Apr. 2007, pp. 27 and 136.

Karnataka

Year	*Area (000 hec)*	*Production (000 tonnes)*	*Productivity (kg/hec)*	*Net Irrigated Area (%age)*
1991-92	7189.50	7927.00	1103.00	21.55
1992-93	7351.40	8498.60	1156.00	21.09
1993-94	6983.60	8659.30	1240.00	21.57
1994-95	7039.30	8106.60	1152.00	22.32
1995-96	6855.90	8645.60	1261.00	22.09
1996-97	7371.50	9212.80	1250.00	21.91
1997-98	7060.10	8046.80	1140.00	23.45
1998-99	7416.00	9996.60	1348.00	23.76
1999-00	7665.50	9859.10	1286.00	24.83
2000-01	7803.80	10959.80	1404.00	25.39
2001-02	7175.20	8696.60	1212.00	25.57
2002-03	7024.20	6664.40	949.00	25.57
2003-04	6663.00	6717.00	1008.00	24.21
Average	7199.92	8614.63	1193.00	23.33

Sources: (i) CMIE Report, Dec. 2002, pp. 31 and 140.
(ii) CMIE Report, Apr. 2007, pp. 27 and 128.

Madhya Pradesh

Year	*Area (000 hec)*	*Production (000 tonnes)*	*Productivity (kg/hec)*	*Net Irrigated Area (%age)*
1991-92	11489.80	10346.20	900.00	31.78
1992-93	9744.00	10628.90	1091.00	24.44
1993-94	12273.70	13537.60	1103.00	27.08
1994-95	12873.20	13204.00	1026.00	38.98
1995-96	12192.00	12664.00	1039.00	39.46
1996-97	12326.00	14224.00	1154.00	42.47
1997-98	12562.00	13593.00	1082.00	41.74
1998-99	12177.50	14676.00	1205.00	43.36
1999-00	12515.60	15593.10	1246.00	37.56
2000-01	9845.80	8930.40	907.00	28.20
2001-02	11844.00	13608.00	1149.00	31.65
2002-03	10277.00	9739.00	948.00	30.95
2003-04	12677.00	15872.10	1252.00	37.68
2004-05	12473.00	14104.00	1131.00	N.A
Average	11805.04	12908.59	1088.07	35.03

Sources: (i) CMIE Report, Dec. 2002, pp. 31 and 140.
(ii) CMIE Report, Apr. 2007, pp. 27 and 128.

Punjab

Year	*Area (000 hec)*	*Production (000 tonnes)*	*Productivity (kg/hec)*	*Net Irrigated Area (%age)*
1991-92	5646.30	19634.80	3478.00	93.48
1992-93	5691.30	20006.70	3515.00	93.30
1993-94	5861.70	21577.00	3681.00	93.19
1994-95	5921.40	21816.80	3684.00	93.68
1995-96	5706.30	19806.20	3471.00	92.95
1996-97	5693.20	21553.30	3786.00	92.95
1997-98	5879.20	21143.20	3596.00	92.48
1998-99	6123.70	22906.90	3741.00	92.48
1999-00	6256.00	25201.40	4028.00	92.48
2000-01	6277.00	25318.00	4034.00	84.47
2001-02	6160.30	24886.90	4040.00	95.06
2002-03	6130.00	23490.00	3832.00	95.60
2003-04	6287.00	24724.00	3933.00	96.31
Average	5971.80	22466.55	3755.31	92.96

Sources: (i) CMIE Report, Dec. 2002, pp. 31 and 140.
(ii) CMIE Report, Apr. 2007, pp. 27 and 128.

Maharashtra

Year	*Area (000 hec)*	*Production (000 tonnes)*	*Productivity (kg/hec)*	*Net Irrigated Area (%age)*
1991-92	13071.40	8342.20	638.00	15.37
1992-93	13981.50	14143.80	1012.00	14.85
1993-94	14187.70	13544.40	955.00	14.87
1994-95	13530.90	11524.80	852.00	12.62
1995-96	13274.80	11646.00	877.00	14.01
1996-97	13792.50	14588.60	1058.00	14.26
1997-98	13174.30	9690.10	733.00	16.53
1998-99	13094.30	12752.00	974.00	16.61
1999-00	13636.60	12700.90	931.00	16.80
2000-01	13381.50	10133.40	757.00	16.78
2001-02	12797.80	11187.30	8874.00	16.77
2002-03	12790.00	10820.00	846.00	16.90
2003-04	12180.00	10930.00	876.00	16.89
Average	13318.49	11971.78	1562.08	15.66

Sources: (i) CMIE Report, Dec. 2002, pp. 31 and 141.
(ii) CMIE Report, Apr. 2007, pp. 27 and 121.

All India

Year	*Area (000 hec)*	*Production (000 tonnes)*	*Productivity (kg/hec)*	*Net Irrigated Area (%age)*
1991-92	121871.20	168380.00	1382.00	33.61
1992-93	123147.60	179480.00	1457.00	35.24
1993-94	122753.80	184260.00	1501.00	35.29
1994-95	123860.00	191494.00	1546.00	36.21
1995-96	121014.80	180414.00	1491.00	37.07
1996-97	123581.40	191494.00	1610.00	37.55
1997-98	123846.90	192260.00	1550.00	38.61
1998-99	125167.10	203606.90	1627.00	38.70
1999-00	123103.90	209801.50	1704.00	40.01
2000-01	11050.00	196810.00	1626.00	40.53
2001-02	121991.70	212850.00	1746.00	38.75
2002-03	113860.00	174770.00	1535.00	39.50
2003-04	123320.00	213900.00	1735.00	40.02
2004-05	120080.00	198360.00	1652.00	39.11
Average	114189.17	192705.74	1583.00	37.87

Sources: (i) CMIE Report, Dec. 2002, pp. 31 and 143.
(ii) CMIE Report, Apr. 2007, pp. 27 and 131.

WTO and Food Security in India

R. Raj Kumar and A. Gnanavelan

INTRODUCTION

Indian agriculture accounts for about one-fourth of the gross domestic product (GDP) In addition, it is a source of livelihood to two-third of population Indian agriculture has been facing serious challenges and opportunities under WTO. The argument for free trade in agricultural commodities is generally advocated on the ground that it is not necessary for nations to achieve self-sufficiency in the production of all crops. It is normally suggested that attention should be on crops with comparative advantage in domestic production compared to imports. The assumption of the theory of international trade like no single producer is large enough to influence world price, the supply function is infinitely elastic and perfectly competitive market structure is open to questions. Also there is little unanimity among researches about the consequences of trade liberalization for developing countries like India, particularly to the poor consumers who are net buyers of food due to growing pressures for liberalization and globalization of Indian agriculture.

The basic aims of new economic policy were: To correct macro-imbalances which had destabilized the economy such as foreign exchange shortage, high inflation, unsustainable fiscal deficit and mounting debts. As a matter of fact in 1991, when main features of economic reforms were announced, agriculture sector was not covered by these reforms. It was for the first time in 1995, that draft farm policy envisaging some structural change in agriculture was announced and it is also first time that GATT agreement brought agriculture sector and international trade of agriculture goods with in the purview of WTO thus integrating agriculture fully with global market.

Historically, during the course of development the share of agriculture in both output and labour falls. This has led some development experts to view agriculture as only ancillary to development. However, the fall in agricultural output and labour can be a result of biased domestic policies and international trade policies.

A well-integrated agricultural sector should enhance Food Security; reduce real food prices (especially beneficial to the poor who spend a disproportionate share of their income, of food), increase employment and income create important economic linkages in production chains, and have a positive impact on the environment.

Objectives of the Study

This present paper aims:

(1) To study International Food Security measures and WTO Functions.
(2) To study the types and indicators of food security.
(3) To analyses Indian Food Security Policies and WTO during the plan periods.

Food security is an issue normally associated with developing countries where food supplies are inadequate because of low production or inability to import and distribute adequate amounts.

Definition of Food Security

Food security can be defined as a situation in which "all

households have both physical and economic access to adequate food for all members, and where households are not at risk of losing such access." (FAO)

Who's Food Security?

Among all the Non-trade concerns, the issue of food security is by far the most frequently mentioned. This is especially true of developing countries; food security can be addressed at several levels; food security of the individual or family, national food security, and international food security.

Individual and Family Food Security

Although the issue is not often framed in this way, the most important level at which long-term structural food insecurity occurs is the household. Hundreds of millions of individuals, largely in developing countries, lack food security. The fundamental cause of this is poverty, that is, inadequacy of buying power. There are ample supplies of food in global markets to feed the poor, and a well established trading system to ensure that it gets to areas where there is demand. If the poor had sufficient incomes, this would translate into effective demand, and food insecurity would not be a problem except in certain transitory situations.

WTO rules on notification of existing subsidies by developing countries, and for promulgating rules that would prevent the unintended imposition of real limits on policies by domestic inflation and currency fluctuations, outside the sphere of agricultural policy. However, the major implication for negotiations of this view of structural food security—that it is mainly a household level issue—is that food security concerns are best addressed in the negotiations through a focus on ensuring that green box agricultural support measures and targeted poverty programs are not constrained.

Food Security and Agricultural Trade Policy Reform

The Uruguay Round Agreement on Agriculture (URAA), in its built-in agenda for future negotiations, and the Doha Ministerial Declaration explicitly confirm that Non-trade concerns will be taken into account in the current round of negotiations. Such concerns relate to non-food outputs including the environment, food security, rural amenities, and viable rural communities. Article 20 refers specifically to "Non-trade concerns, special and differential treatment to developing country members, and the objective to establish a fair and market-oriented agricultural trading system." Paragraph 13 of the Doha Declaration elaborates on these points and confirms all considerations and negotiations.

Food Security Indicators

Food security that are considered proxies for three measures of food security at the national level; Food availability, access, and utilization.

The indicators are summarized below:

(a) Food production per capita is a measure of a country's ability to feed its population.
(b) The ratio of total exports to food imports is a measure of a country's ability to finance its food imports from its total export revenues.
(c) Calories per capita and protein per capita are used to estimate consumption levels and therefore food availability at the national level.
(d) Non-agricultural population is used to analyze the nonagricultural sector in assessing how a country may be affected by changes in trade and agricultural policies.

International Food Security

International food security means that the aggregate supply of food produced in the world is adequate to provide sufficient calories to feed the world population at levels consistent with either demands. Periodically, not withstanding a secular downward trend. Whenever this occurs, there is concern about the ability of the world's agricultural producers and the resources they command to continue to meet world demand at constant or declining real prices. Land and water resources available for agricultural production are finite. However, the output from those resources has steadily increased with the development and adoption of new technology, greater investment, and improved human resources skills engaged in agricultural production.

Food Security fits rather uncomfortably with the other multifunctional benefits of agriculture, such as environmental goods for several reasons;

- Food Security is not a non-food item, which is what multifunctional outputs of agriculture are generally considered to be.
- It is questionable whether food security is a public good, with the properties of non-rivalry and non-excludability, given that a functioning market exists.
- Food security is not a joint product with production, as it can be attained through trade and storage

Global Food Security depends on the continued increase in the efficiency with which global agricultural resources are used, on continued market incentives to develop and adopt improved technology, and on continued public investment in the necessary institutions to supports sustained agricultural growth. Further reduction of the major distortions in agricultural markets can undoubtedly make a significant contribution to the continued achievement of global food security. First, it can encourage distribution of production among countries based on true comparative advantage. Second, trade barriers that inhibit the spread of new technologies that are embedded in agricultural inputs can significantly reduce global food security in the long-term, and these barriers to technology diffusion should be dismantled through successful negotiations.

Food Security in India during the Plan Periods

The Indian planners, right from the beginning, realized the need to attain self-sufficiency and food security as one of the important goals of planning. India is a country of its people, being the world's largest democracy. Indians have had freedom of speech, religion, and the press ever since their constitution was adopted on January 26, 1950. Within this democracy people still live everyday being food insecure. Food insecurity exists when all people, at all times, do not have physical and economic access to the sufficient, safe and nutritious food to meet their dietary needs and food preferences for an active and healthy life." Poverty easily coexists with food insecurity and is the main cause of hunger and malnutrition. In 1996, the Food and Agriculture Organization (FAO) defined food security as a situation which exists when all people, at all times, have physical and economic access to sufficient, safe and nutritious food to meet their dietary needs and food preferences for an active and health life. Indian adopts a broader definition of the concept and views food security from three different angles (1) the availability of food, which depends on production and distribution; (2) the access to food, which is determined by an individual's purchasing power, and in turn purchasing power is affected by livelihood access, access to housing, and caste and gender discrimination; and (3) the absorption of food. This is affected by sanitation, clean drinking water and health care. The report identifies 17 key indicators, which fall into six categories (food affordability and availability, livelihood access, access to housing, discrimination in livelihood access, access to sanitation, and health and nutritional outcome) that in turn can be grouped under the classifications of availability, access, and absorption of food. Indices and maps of food insecurity are created and food insecurity "hotspots" are identified from the 20 states studied. The average per capita income in India in 2001 was 450 dollars, but the average farming families make less than 300 dollars every year, while other families make no money and live off of their land. Eighty per cent of the population is earning less than two dollars a day. The average poor farmer produces from only about one acre, meaning on such a small place they produce crops for themselves and crops to sell. Rice is one of the most important crops because it is the staple food in most Indian's diets. Wheat, lentils, cotton, sugarcane, and tea are grown all over India. Tea is one of India's largest crops. Of the 1.5 billion pounds of tea picked each year, about 800,000 pounds are exported. Fishing is also a common job among Indians who live near the coastline. India exports 25 per cent of the marine fish production, and it is India's third largest export. Around 750,000 people are involved full-time in fishing, and about the same number is involved part time in fishing. In 2002, seafood exports earned about 1.4 billion dollars. For those working in the fishing industry, the amount that a fisher makes depends on the type of fish he catches and the industry that buys the fish. People working for the international industry with exports tend to make more money than those who are working for the domestic industry. Nonetheless, fishing communities are still very poor and the average fisherman usually makes less that one dollar everyday. Upper-class citizens are commonly those who are engineers and are very well educated and respected, and most of them do not live in poverty or food insecurity.

The Ninth Five Year Plan (1997-2002) states: *"One of the first efforts of the country was to build up a food security systems to ensure that the threat of famine no longer stalks the country. The fact that the country has not witnessed famine and acute starvation on a massive scale in the last five decades is the most eloquent testimony for the success of these efforts."* The Ninth Plan reviewing the situation underlines the stark reality; inspite of mounting food subsidies, evaluation studies indicate that supply of subsidies, foodgrains through PDS has not resulted in improvement in household level food security. Self-sufficiency of foodgrains at national level and availability of foodgrains at affordable cost at local level have not been translated into household level food security for the poor. The Tenth Plan has drawn attention to the changes in consumption pattern that have taken place in the post-Green Revolution period. Between 1971-73 and 1993-94, the food basket has become much more diversified with the share of cereals seeing a dramatic decline of ten percentage points in most regions. At decline from 15.3 kg per capita per month 1972-73 to 13.4 kg per capita per month in 1993-94. The corresponding decline in the urban areas was more modest—from 11.3 kg to 10.6 kg over the same period. At the same time, consumption of milk and meat products as well as vegetables and fruits have increased. Such changes are a natural outcome of economic development. Although India has the potential to be producing enough food to feed its entire population, there have been many setbacks in the past decade including droughts and natural disasters. The success or failure of crops is directly related to climate and weather. The 2004 tsunami caused many problems among the people who lived on the coasts that were affected. Not only were there food and water shortages for a period of time but also the long-term effects were devastating.

SUGGESTIONS AND CONCLUSION

Overall, the result of this study the policy-related impacts increased the gains from the URAA to most low-income and net food- importing countries. However, the impacts in any further liberalization will clearly depend on the specific nature of the agricultural policies used in the country. The overall conclusion from the above points, taken together, is that any substantial increase in international agricultural prices that could potentially result from the international agreements, (i) has not occurred yet, (ii) is probably a number of years away, and (iii) could well be offset by other economic factors at work in the meantime. Further more, any losses to net food-importing countries, and may be partial or completely offset in individual countries by other gains from the overall agreement.

In spite the efforts of government at national level and state level, the food security is not assured all common people. Though many committees and Commissions have recommended ways and means to improve the food available situation, Periodical media exposures of poverty and starvations death reminds us to that yet we have to pass many stages to achieve food security. In this connection the suggestions of Ramesh Chand and M.S. Swaminathan Committees are worth monetary.

- Continuation of the Policy of maintaining self-sufficiency in cereals.
- Continuation of the systems of minimum support prices and making it effective in all the states/areas of the country.
- Continuation of the policy of buffer stocking of cereals and their subsidized distribution for maintaining price stability.
- Retaining Food Corporation of India as the national foodgrain handling agency on behalf of the Government of India.
- Fixing the minimum support prices at a level 50 per cent higher than the cost of production.
- Dovetailing of domestic price policy with trade policy by renaming the CACP and redefining its terms of reference.
- Assigning statutory status to CACP.
- Phasing out of levy on rice millers and sugar factories.
- Switching over to universal PDS from the present system of targeted public distribution of cereals.

If the above policies are implements the food security can be effectively assured to all.

References

E. Gilbert (1988), Food and Poverty, p. 196.

Economic Survey (2002-2003), Government of India, Ministry of Finance.

FAO (Food and Agriculture Organization) (2000), "Agriculture towards 2015/2030. Technical Report", FAO, Rome.

International Perspective, p. 49.

Planning Commission, Ninth Five Year Plan (1997-2002), Vol. ii, p. 555.

Planning Commission, Tenth Five Year Plan (2002-2007), Vol. ii, p. 365.

Radhakrishna, R. *et. al.* (2003), "India's Public Distribution System.

Royal Society of Canada (2001), "Elements of Precaution; Recommendations for the Regulation of Food-Biotechnology in Canda", Royal Society of Canada. Ottawa.

Ruddr Datt and K.P.M. Sundaram, Indian Economy (2007), S. Chand & Company, New Delhi.

World Bank (2000), World Development Report, 2000/01, Attacking Poverty, New York, Oxford University Press.

WTO (World Trade Organaization) 2000, "Response of the Executive Secretary of the Convention on Biological Diversity", (CBD), June 8, Geneva.

Globalisation and Food Security in India

M. PANDIYAN

INTRODUCTION

India is the second most populated country in the World, with the total population enumerated in the 2001 census at about 102.7 crores. This form about 16 per cent of the world total population. It shows that every sixth person on the earth is an Indian.

Agricultural sector is the mainstay of the rural Indian economy. India has achieved a very speedy growth in the field of science and technology. Today we have attained self-sufficiency in agriculture.

Even though self-sufficiency of food production has been achieved, the population still lacks access to balanced food. It is a matter of concern that even though cereal production has kept pace with the increasing requirements and average per capita intakes of cereals have remained satisfactory, there have been a fall in the per capita consumption of pulses.

A nation may require self-sufficiency in food at a point of time, but the concept of food security necessities, that, timely, reliable and nutritionally adequate supply of food should be available on a long-term basis.

MEANING OF FOOD SECURITY

World Development Report (1986), defined food security as "access by all people at all times to enough food for an active, healthy life". Food and Agricultural Organizations (1983) defined food security as "ensuring that all people at all times have both physical and economic access to basic food they need".

Food security defined as the ability to assure on a long-term basis that the Food system provides the total population access to a timely, reliable and nutritionally adequate supply of food... Thus food security has four essential components.

1. Food availability,
2. Food accessibility,
3. Food utilization, and
4. Food security.

Food Availability

Food availability concern with the availability of sufficient quantities of food of appropriate qualities, supplied through domestic production or imports.

Food Accessibility

The access of food by individual requires adequate resources. These resources are primarily monitory. It depends on household incomes and individual wages, food prices, consumer credit, etc.

Food Utilization

The utilization of food through adequate diet, water, sanitation and health care brings forth the importance of non-food input in food security. Food security means minimizing the probability that in difficult times, food consumption might fall below requirements.

Component of Food Security

There are two aspects of the food situation in India;

Foodgrains security and food security. The physical and economic access to foodgrains implies 'Foodgrains' security, the food security would require the same for non-foodgrains items of food basket.

The Indian planners realized the need to attain self sufficiency in foodgrains as one of the important goal of Indian planning. India achieved self-sufficiency in foodgrains by the year 1976 – and since then Indian imports of cereals have remained negligible.

The Ninth plan (1997-2002) states, "one of the first efforts of the country was to build up a food security system to ensure that the threat of famine no larger stalks the country... In fact that the country has not witnessed famine and acute starvation on massive scale in the last five decades is the most eloquent testimony for the success of these efforts.

PROGRESS OF FOODGRAINS

Between 1950-51 and 2001-2002, foodgrains production had increased from 51 million tonnes to 198.4 million tonnes. It showed four fold increase in the production of foodgrains, however declined to 174.8 million tonnes in 2002-03.

The foodgrains production declined to 11.2 per cent in 2002-03. After that period the production has been increased continuously. It was increased to 198.4 million tonnes in 2004-05, which showed 13.5 per cent increase.

Cereals production accounted for 84 per cent in Foodgrains in 1950-51, their share has increased to 94 per cent in 2001-02 but as against them the share of pulses has declined from 16 per cent to just 6 per cent during the same period.

Between the period 1960-61 and 2004-05, cereal production was to 69.3 million tonnes 185.2 million tonnes. The pulse production was 12.7 million tonnes and 13.1 million tonnes during the same period.

Within cereals, the share of the two superior cereals, rice and wheat which was only 53 per cent in 1950-51 had improved to 78 per cent in 2001-02. During the same period the share of coarse cereals had declined from 30 per cent to 18 per cent. This indicates a substitution by the weaker sections in favour of rice and wheat and against coarse cereals consumed earlier.

TABLE 1

Production of Foodgrains

(In million tonnes)

Year	*Foodgrains*	*Cereals*	*Pulses*
1950 – 51	50.8	-	-
1960 – 61	82.0	69.3	12.7
1970 – 71	108.4	96.6	11.8
1980 – 81	129.6	119.0	10.6
1990 – 91	176.4	162.1	14.3
2000 – 01	196.8	185.7	11.0
2002 – 03	174.8	163.6	11.1
2004 – 05	198.4	185.2	13.1
2005 – 06 (P)	208.3	195.2	13.1

(P): Provisional Estimate.
Source: Economic Survey, 2006-07.

TABLE 2

Availability of Cereals and Pulses

(in million tonnes)

Year	*Population (Million)*	*Cereals in Million Tonnes*			*Pulses Net Availability (Million Tonnes)*	*Per capita net availability per day (grams)*		
		Net Production	*Net Imports*	*Net Availability*		*Cereals*	*Pulses*	*Total*
1950-51	363	40.1	4.1	44.3	8.0	334.2	60.7	394.9
1960-61	442	60.9	3.5	64.6	11.1	399.7	69.0	468.7
1970-71	551	84.5	2.0	84.0	10.3	417.6	51.2	468.8
1980-81	689	104.1	0.5	104.8	9.4	417.3	37.5	454.8
1990-91	852	141.9	0.6	145.7	12.9	468.5	41.6	510.1
2000-01	1033	162.5	4.5	145.6	11.3	366.2	30.0	416.2
2002-03	1068	143.7	7.1	159.3	11.4	408.5	29.1	436.3
2003-04	1086	173.5	7.7	169.1	14.2	426.9	35.8	462.7
2004-05 (P)	1103	162.1	7.2	157.4	12.7	390.9	31.5	422.4

(P): Provisional Estimate.
Source: Economic Survey, 2006-07.

NET AVAILABILITY OF CEREALS AND PULSES

Table 2 reveal that the annual net imports was 4.1 million tonnes during 1950-51, it increased to 10.3 million tonnes during 1965-66 and decreased to 0.5 million tonnes in 1980-81. After 1990-91, India become a net exporter of cereals. India's export of cereals during 2001-02 was a record of 8.5 million tonnes.

The data reveals an over all improvement in per capita availability of cereals and pulses. The per capita availability of foodgrains improved from 394.9 grams to 462.7 grams between 1950-51 and 2003-04. This indicate nearly 17.7 per cent over the period of 53 years (1950-51—2003-04). This has two component of cereals and pulses. The per capita availability of cereals increased from 334.2 gram per day to 426.9 grams. This is an increase in per capita availability of cereals by 27.7 during 53 years. But the per capita availability of pulses declined from 60.7 gram per day to 35.8 gram between 1950-51 to 2003-04. This indicate the decline of about 41 per cent in the per capita availability of pulses per day. While moving towards foodgrains security, India has succeeded in term of cereals, but has miserably failed to increase the production of pulses to feed the continuously increasing population.

Table 3 showed the net availability, procurement and public Distribution System of Foodgrains during the period between 1951 and 2004. It showed, the much improvement in net production of foodgrains production. It increased from 48.1 million tonnes to 186.5 million tonnes between 1951 and 2004. It increased 138.4 million tonnes over the period of 53 years. The same period, the net availability of foodgrains were also improved from 52.4 million tonnes to 170 million tonnes. Procurement of foodgrains showed the much improvement in the same period from 3.8 million tonnes to 41.1 million tonnes. Data showed that the procurement of foodgrains increased after the period of 1980. It increased from 11.2 million tonnes to 41.1 million tonnes during the period 1980 and 2004. It was due to the increase in the production of agriculture after the adaption of WTO agreement and globalization.

While India moving towards food security, Indian Government distribute the foodgrains through public distribution system at subsidized rates. The PDS supply increased from 8

TABLE 3

Net Availability Procurement and Public Distribution System

(Million Tonnes)

Year	*Net production Food Grains*	*Net Imports*	*Net availability of Food grains*	*Procurement*	*PDS*
1951	48.1	4.8	52.4	3.8	8.0
1960	67.5	5.1	71.2	1.3	4.9
1970	87.1	3.6	89.5	6.7	8.8
1980	96.0	-0.6	101.4	11.2	15.0
1990	147.9	1.3	144.8	24.0	16.0
2000	183.1	-1.4	168.3	35.6	13.0
2002	186.1	-6.7	189.5	40.3	18.1
2004	186.5	-6.5	183.3	41.1	NA
2005 (P)	173.6	-6.0	170.0	NA	NA

(P): Provisional Estimate.
Source: Economic Survey, 2006-07.

million tonnes in 1951 to 18.1 million tonnes in 2004. Because PDS conceived on a key mechanism in the Government Food Security System.

FOOD SECURITY AND NINTH PLAN

Ninth Plan (1997-2002) discussed the problem of food security at the national level and at the household level. The Planning Commission express "An approach to national security, which relies largely on domestic production of food needed for consumption as well as for building buffer stocks can be described as a strategy of self-sufficiency". It emphasized the extension of irrigation facilities and later in the sixties adopted green revolution. As a result, India was able to its goal of a balanced diet is still a district dream.

The Ninth Plan states "Even though self sufficiency of food production has been achieved the population still lacks access to balanced food. It is a matter of concern that the cereal production has kept pace with the increasing requirements and average per capita intakes of cereals have remained satisfactory, there have been a fall in the per capita consumption of pulses. It is important not only to improve pulse production but also make them available at affordable cost. The production and consumption of vegetables and fruits continue to remain low. Special efforts have to be made to improve production and improved access to vegetables especially green-leafy vegetables at affordable cost both in rural and urban areas".

At the household level, food security implies both physical and economic access to food that are adequate in terms of quantity and quality and affordability. To help the poor sections, the Government introduced the Public Distribution System (PDS) and adopted dual price mechanism. At the PDS outlet, the price of food was kept lower than the market price to enable the poor to purchase subsidized food. But due to political pressure, the government adopted a universal PDS. The result was non-poor also began to benefit from the PDS—and the poor were not able to enjoy the benefit of PDS. Ninth Plan reviewing the situation.

To achieve the household level food security the following efforts should be directed:

1. Development strategies and macro-economic policies that would create conditions for growth with equity.
2. Accelerating growth in food and agricultural sectors which provide direct sources for food and income with which to buy food.
3. Promoting rural development that focuses on the poor.
4. Improving access to land and other natural resources.
5. Providing cheap credit for poor households.
6. Increasing employment opportunities.
7. Introducing income transfer scheme including provision of PDS subsidized cheap food.
8. Stabilising food supplies and food prices.
9. Improving emergency preparedness planning for providing food aid during natural disasters.

FOOD SECURITY AND TENTH PLAN

Tenth Plan restructuring the PDS should make the system efficient.

1. Other than wheat and rice item should be excluded from the scope of food subsidies.
2. Sugar should be kept outside the purview of PDS.
3. The subsidy on kerosene should be phased out by raising its supply price for PDS shops.
4. The coverage of TDPS and food subsidy should be restricted to BPL population.
5. To reduce malpractices, food stamps should be issued to female member of the family who can be designated as heads of households for the purpose.
6. A food card system could be superior alternative to the prevalent Fair Price Shop (FPS) system and perhaps even a food stamp system.
7. A food coupon scheme was introduced in Andhra Pradesh in 1998-99 for distribution of rice and kerosene through PDS. This system has resulted in savings about 20,000 tonnes of rice, 71 lakhs litres of kerosene every month. This system may be replicated with suitable adaptation in other states as well.

MAIN COMPONENT OF THE FOOD SECURITY SYSTEM

1. Promoting domestic production to meet the demands of the growing population as also to reduce under-nutrition among quite a large sections of the population.
2. Provide minimum support prices for procurement and storage of food items.
3. Operating a public distribution system.
4. Maintaining buffer stocks so as to take care of natural calamities resulting in temporary shortage of food and to act on a countervailing mechanism against traders and businessmen who try to push up prices, especially during period of shortage of food.

CONCLUSION

India population was steadily rising, production of foodgrains rose equally. Net availability to cereals has gone up except in same years. But the government had to import large quantity of cereals from other countries to increase the net availability of cereals in the economy PDS should, therefore the reformed and made more efficient. The scheme of recentralized procurement of foodgrains should be encouraged and more states should be brought under its fold. All restriction on inter-state movement of foodgrains should be removed. The recommendation listed in the Tenth Plan for PDS should result in making the system more vibrant and efficient and capable of meeting the requirements of a liberalized economy.

References

Government of India, Economic Survey, 2006-07.

Internet.

Iswar C. Dhingra (2006), The Indian Economy Sultan Chand and Sons, New Delhi.

Planning Commission Ninth Five year plan (1997-2002) Vol. II.

Planning Commission Tenth Five year plan (2002-2007) Vol. II.

R.K. Uppal (2005), "Economic reforms in India" New Century Publication, New Delhi.

R.N. Soni (2000), Leading issues in Agricultural Economics, Shoban Lal Nagin Chand & Co. Jalandhar.

Ruddar Datt, (2006), "Indian Economy", S. Chand and Company, New Delhi.

Talwar Sabanna, (2005) "WTO and the Agriculture" serial publication, New Delhi.

Globalization, WTO and Food Security Availability, Access and Affordability of Food PDS and Food Subsidy

N.K. Thakur and Alpana Sharma

GLOBALIZATION

The economic globalization has been occurring for the last several thousand years, since the emergence of transnational trade. It has begun to occur at an incredible rate over the last 25-30 years.

The process of globalization has been an integral part of the recent economic process made by India. It played a major role in export led growth, leading to enlargement of job market in India.

Economic globalization can be defined as the process of increasing economic integration between two countries leading to the emergence of a global market place or a SINGLE WORLD which refers to free trade and increasing relations among member-countries in the different parts of the world.

Globalization means universalisation which is used in the

sense of being worldwide and it is a process of spreading various objects and experiences to people at all corners of the earth (like internet and television). To globalize means the worldwide scope of application "market and being increasingly globalized". The increasing integration of economies and societies around the world, transcending the boundaries of nation, state particularly through international trade. Globalization is a process where an increased portion of economic or other activities are carried out across national boundaries. The increasing worldwide integration of market for goods, services and capital to attract special attention; the economic integration of many formerly separated nation economies into ONE ECONOMY mainly through free trade and free movement of capital as by multinational companies but also by easy on uncontrolled migration. Globalization is frequently used to identify a trend toward increased flow of goods/services, money, ideas across the national borders and the subsequent integration of the global economy.

Globalization refers to the trend towards countries joining together economically, through education, society, politics and viewing themselves not only through their national identity but also as part of the world as a whole. It brings people of the world closer especially through a common medium like economy.

Globalization in its literal sense is the process of transformation of local or regional phenomena to global one. Globalization is the process by which events, activities and decision of one part of the country moves worldwide, i.e. across the border relation between countries, which describes the growth in international exchange and interdependence with growing flows of trade, capital, investment, manpower, etc.

Globalization is as liberalization refers to a process of removing government imposed restrictions on the movement between countries in order to create an open borderless WORLD ECONOMY.

Globalization is as deterritorial liberalization or reconfiguration of geography so that space is territorial borders. It is a process which embodies a transformation in the spatial organization of social relation and transactions assessed in terms of their extensity, intensity, velocity and impact generating transcontinental or interregional flows and net works of activities.

Globalization is westernized or modernization referred as dynamic, whereby social structure of modernity (capitalism, rationalism, industrialism, bureaucratism, etc.) spreads worldwide normally destroying pre-existence cultures and local self-determination in process.

Globalization is a complex series of economic, social transformation of ideas/activities world over.

In fact, globalization is a process that world's people and nation are more interdependence than even before and becoming more so.

Advantages of Globalization

(i) To globalize is to make worldwide scope of marketing and to make every thing global in scope, i.e. boundary-less.
(ii) It has reduced the boundaries among the country for free flow of trade, cultural, social, political, economical and environmental.
(iii) It has allowed access to technologies in developing countries.
(iv) It is helpful in reducing poverty worldwide.
(v) It promotes trade, peace, harmony worldwide.
(vi) It has benefited children, women for fundamental rights.
(vii) Goods and people are transported worldwide with more easiness and free trade has increased.

Disadvantages of Globalization

(i) Globalization is a real threat to the developing economies as other economies begin to rely more on the developed economies in free trade and economic relations which causes the threat to the developing economy (e.g. North Korean economy).
(ii) Globalization has its major threat on environmental effect which is a disastrous effect worldwide. Smaller countries development offer struggle with developed economy to keep up but these super power states (Developed economy) introduces the product of

intense harvesting of natural resources due to ample of investment, leaving the smaller countries' environment ravaged.

(iii) Free flow of talent often attract migration of these small countries causes a "TALENT CRUNCH" in the society.

(iv) Environmental misbalance is being created by excessive use of "green house production" and carbon/gas emissions ratio misbalances the entire climate worldwide.

No doubt globalization is a modernization which refers as dynamic whereby social structure of modernity (capital technology, etc.) spreads worldwide but normally it is destroying pre-existing cultures and local self-determination in process.

WORLD TRADE ORGANIZATION

World Trade Organization (WTO) was incorporated in January 1995, as a successor of GATT, after Uruguay Round, and is having 148 members worldwide. It is a multinational institution dealing with the rules of trade for the development of the world economy.

The main objectives of WTO are:

(i) To improve standard of living of people in its member countries.

(ii) To ensure full employment and broad increase in effective demand.

(iii) To improve and promote global trade, protection and security and making optimum use of world resources (natural/talent, etc.) for sustainable development among the member-countries.

(iv) To protect environment/security of free trade of goods/services worldwide.

WTO's Uruguay round was different from earlier rounds which determine its following provisions to promote agricultural products:

(i) All non-tariff barriers like quantitative restrictions (quota) would be covered into tariffs.
(ii) Reduction of tariff in agricultural products will be implemented over six years for developed countries and ten years for developing countries.
(iii) Countries with closed farm market will have to import 3 per cent of product of domestic consumption.
(iv) Trade distorting support for farmers will be reduced by 20 per cent over six years for the developed countries and 13.3 per cent for developing countries.
(v) The value of direct export subsidies will be reduced by 36 per cent and 21 per cent volume-wise over 6 years.
(vi) The poorest nations are exempted from all these provisions of farm products.

WTO has made some agreement among its member countries which has lend a distinct, a pro-capitalistic character to this global trade organization. These agreements are:

(i) Agreement On Agriculture (AOA).
(ii) General Agreement on Trade Services (GATS).
(iii) Trade Related Intellectual Property rights (TRIPS).
(iv) Antidumping and Subsidies Agreement (ADP).
(v) Agreement on Textile and Clothing (ATC).
(vi) Trade Related Investment Measures (TRIMS).
(vii) Dispute Settlement Mechanism (DSM).

WTO AND INDIAN AGRICULTURE

India, the most populous country in the world after China, having more than one billion population, the seventh largest geographical area, bears the pressure of 16.44 per cent of the world's population but only 1/4th of the world's land is available to maintain this population. More than 65 per cent population is spread in 6 lakh villages, dependent on agriculture and allied business directly or indirectly, contributes 18 per cent of GDP at present. As the planet's population continues to grow more and more food will be needed to be produced from less and less land which will not be possible by ignoring AGRICULTURE in overall development of economy.

Agriculture

Agriculture is the foundation of our economy which occupies the place of pride in the country's progress. It is the backbone of country's economy and provides employment directly/indirectly, prosperity, food security, livelihood, social justice and also works as anti-migratory force in balancing rural and urban population. Agriculture has been the "LIFELINE" of our economy and will remain so in the years to come also. Agriculture has potential to generate more and more employment per unit of investment and will be helpful in poverty alleviation of much larger population than that of any other sector in the country. The accelerating growth in agriculture has been more important today for narrowing the disparities between rural and urban populations.

Agricultural Growth

A robust growth in agriculture is also essential for food as nutritional security for growing population and it has been proved also that India has come out from "SIP TO MOUTH" situation to a "SELF-SUFFICIENCY" stage at present. The spectacular growth in agriculture is remarkable after Green Revolution (in 1960s) in getting rid of begging bowl to self-sufficiency level.

Fertilizers

Fertilizers contributes to more than 50 per cent alone in crop production apart from seed, irrigation and plant protection measures. Fertilizer consumption ($N_1 + P_2O_5 + K_2O$) has increased from 66000 MTs in 1950-51 to 225 lakh tonnes in 2007-08 or 0.49 kg/hect to 117 kg/hect at present, which really accelerated the agricultural production in the country.

Food Security

Food security is primarily a phenomenon relating to individual and determined by the sets of factors concerned with supply, access and guarantee to food. Food security was formerly considered essential in terms of production, i.e. adequate production of foodgrains would ensure the availability of food in the market as well as in the household.

Food security has been defined in many different ways at

TABLE 1

Food Production and Fertilizer Consumption (NPK) and Population

Year	*Foodgrain production (in million tonnes)*	*Fertilizer consumption (in 1000 MT)*	*Population (in millions)*
1950-51	50.8	66	363
1960-61	80.2*	293.8	432
1970-71	108	2256.3	684
1990-91	176	12,546	846
2001-02	211	17,360	1027
2004-05	204	18,398	-
2005-06	208	20,340	-
2006-07	217	21,651	1100
2007-08	233	22,570	1107

*means Green Revolution.
Source: Fertilizer Statistics, 2007-08.

TABLE 2

Compound Growth in Agriculture

Year	*Compound growth rate (in percentage)*
1951-61	2.62
1964-65	2.72
1971-81	1.70
1981-91	3.90
1996-97	1.50
2003-04	3.13
2005-06	1.80
2006-07	2.30
2007-08	1.86

Source: Economic Survey, GoI.

different times by different institutions. The most widely accepted definition of food security at individual level is that (defined by World Bank) "Secure access by all people at all times to enough food for healthy active life (IBRD 1986)". This includes the following elements:

TABLE 3

Projected Population, Foodgrain Production and Consumption, Input use by the end of the 11th Plan

Period	*2010-12*
Population (in millions)	1196.4
Per capita foodgrain consumption (in kg.)	223.4
Foodgrain requirement (in MT)	337.3
(a) Rice	128.2
(b) Wheat	130.4
(c) Pulses	29.8
(d) Course Cereals	48.9
(e) Oil Seeds	58.6
(f) Sugarcane	679.6
Gross area sown (million hect)	219.2
Net area sown (million hect)	142.0
Gross irrigation (million hect)	105.5

Source: FAI Statistics.

(a) Enough food for an active healthy life.
(b) Access to the food through adequate purchasing power.
(c) The guarantee of having access to it at any given time.
(d) Absorption of food in the body.

Food security is determined by:

(i) Production-based entitlements which will be influenced by policies that affect the demand and supply factors affecting production, some of which are related to international trade.
(ii) Trade-based entitlements which will be influenced by policies that affect the level of variability of food prices in relation to price of what individuals are able to exchange for food in case where these are substantial agricultural export trade-based entitlements affected by policies on both sides of the trade balance.
(iii) Transfer-based entitlement which may in turn be influenced by multilateral trade agreements.

(iv) Labour-based entitlements which are influenced by the level and location of employment, opportunity which may be influenced by trade policy.

Food security is influenced by availability of food. Increase in food availability in 1980's were driven by growth in the area under cultivation and growth in agricultural productivity.

Intensification of agricultural production and growth in crop yields will play a major role in India's future food production growth. Population density in India is much higher than rest of the world. Indian policy-makers operating through Food Corporation of India (FCI) are pursuing conflicting objectives of attempting to provide low price food for consumers while increasing the support price paid to farmers.

Government policies influence on entitlements such as to promote food production, market development, enhance the availability and to provide transfer in safety nets for food security.

India has made enormous progress in providing food security for its people. Per capita caloric consumption increased 20 per cent between early 1980s and 2000. However, a sizeable share of population still lacks access to sufficient quantities of food. Poverty remains a problem such that nearly a third of population still lives below the poverty line. In 1960, the rising price of staple foods was principal constraint to improve economic access to food. It is the duty of policy-makers to provide low price food to consumers while supporting producer's price. Government should subsidize both farmers and consumers through price policies, implying the need of policy alternatives to address the trade-off between the welfare of poorer consumers and that of producers.

Threats to Food Security

The food security problem in India is currently one of access, as a sizeable share of population lacks economic and physical access to sufficient food. Results from the ERS food security model indicate that 20 per cent of population is estimated to food insecure in 2002. Consumption for this segment of population is estimated to fall 10 per centbelow the nutritional requirement of 2100 calories/day.

The most important among internal threats to sustainable

food security is the damage to ecological foundations essential for sustained agricultural advances like lake, water, forest and biodiversities.

Secondly, in the area of farm economics resources flow to the agriculture sector is declining and indebtness of small and marginal farmer families are rising. Input cost (seeds, fertilizers, pesticides, etc.) are increasing whereas factor productivity is declining.

Thirdly, a technology fatigue has further aggravated farmer's problems since the smaller the farm the greater is the need for sustained marketable surplus in order to have cash income. "Lab to Land" linkage extension services, specific information are often not co-related resulting in distress.

Other threats includes trade bargain inherent in WTO agreement of 1994. Rapid expansion of proprietary science and potential adverse changes in temperature, precipitation and other environmental factors, legal threats/generic literary are also some threats to food security.

Food Availability

This is a function of both home production and imports of foods. There is no time to relax on production front. The present global surplus of foodgrains is the result of inadequate consumption on the part of poor and should not be mistaken as a sign of over-production.

The performance of domestic agricultural production has a major influence on food availability. Imports play major role but in India the food availability is there due to government's orientation toward self-sufficiency. Rice and wheat accounts about 80 per cent contribution in the food availability. Intensification of agricultural production and growth in crop yields will play a major role in India's future food production growth. Last two decades has historic performances in the country indicates strengthening the agricultural research extension is essential for achieving rapid and sustained growth in agricultural productivity. Various project of water management, surface irrigations infrastructure development are being invested through Government/State/Pvt.-Public partnership to secure food availability in future.

Food Access

Food access can be related to food availability through the behaviour of prices, i.e.,

(i) Open market farm retail price.
(ii) Price determined by Government which include support consumer price.

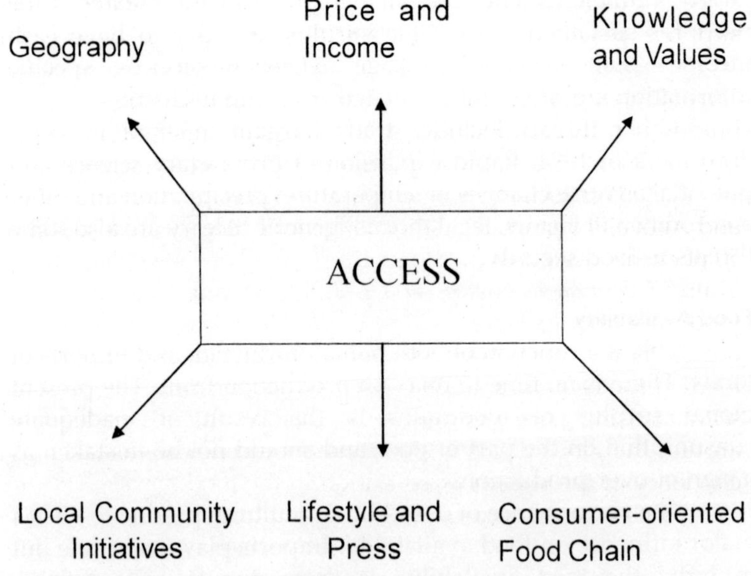

Food access is described as the transportation and food distribution system which gets food to where it is needed. Access is denoted as under.

Lack of purchasing power derives a person access to food even though enough food is available. More than 30 million tonnes of wheat/rice in FCI godowns at different locations is available but more than 200 people are affected by hunger. It is suggested that whenever poverty is pervasive, suitable measures to provide the needed entitlement to food like NAREGA, etc. is to be implemented on mass scale.

Food Availability

It refers to whether a person (or group of people) can reasonably find the means to pay something.

Public Distribution System (PDS)

Public Distribution System or PDS is commonly known as ration shop where wheat, rice, kerosene oil, sugar, etc. is available at lower price than that of market price which is a safety net for poor for food security. The PDS distributes these goods at fair price. Ministry of food and civil supplies, GOI controls over the supplies/price.

PDS ensures the distribution of essential items as selected cereals, kerosene oil and sugar at the subsidized price to the holder of ration card. These shops are operated throughout the country by joint assistance of central and state government.

PDS makes a distinction between Below Poverty Line (BPL) and Above Poverty Line (APL). BPL card holder get foodgrains at 50 per cent cost of FCI procurement price whereas APL gets foods grain at economic cost of FCI's. A BPL family will get 35 kg foodgrain/month at subsidized price. Government took special measures to release food for FCI at concessional rates and off loading foodgrains through tender sale at fair price shops. With scare of rising price and availability in food outlets being seen at around the globe, there is a renewal focus on sustainability and efficiency of the biggest intervention in the food market.

Subsidies related to PDS have two major issues:

(i) Whether targeted group receives sufficient subsidized foodgrain for PDS.

(ii) Whether these subsidies are provided efficiently.

In recent years the poor receives a meager benefit for PDS due to geographical coverage (NE/Hilly areas) having no purchasing capacity or ration provided once in a fortnight hence they are deprived of it due to income, and secondly due to long queue, inferior quality, uncertainty of opening/closing of shop and non-co-operation of operator/shopkeepers. In 1992 Govt. of India targeted to revamp PDS in backward region providing higher subsidies but it failed.

FCI supplies roughly 15 per cent of total foodgrains

TABLE 4

Distribution through PDS in Delhi

(All qty. in Quintals)

S. No.	*Item*	*2001-02*	*2002-03*	*2003-04*	*2004-05*	*2005-06*	*2006-07*
1.	No of cards (in '000)	3689	3838	3867	3990	2595	2814
2.	No. of cereal units (in '000)	33900	38400	39320	39100	25430	28968
3.	No. of sugar units (in '000)	15900*	2000	1900	2230	2201	1587
4.	Fair price shops (in number)	2975	2953	3131	3114	2731	2772
5.	No. of licensed shops of kerosene oil	2508	2521	2528	2475	2443	2443

* Sugar unit of targeted public distribution system (TPDS) cards, w.e.f. March.

Source: Economic Survey of Delhi, 2007-08.

consumption under scoring the importance of open retail market. PDS supplies subsidized food relatively modest. The role of PDS in restraining food price inflation is limited.

Working of a PDS (in Delhi)

There were 2772 PDS outlet in Delhi (May 2007). On an average, each fair price shop handles 1,000 ration cards. Table 4 shows the distribution through PDS.

For BPL purpose, families below 24,200/year income were identified. Above 22.93 lakh BPL families were found in 2004-05. In NCT of Delhi 3,79,512 BPL and 59,162 Antyodya Anna Yojana ration card and 113 Annapurna cards have been issued by March 2007. BPL families are entitled to get 25 kg wheat, 10 kg rice/ month/family at the price of Rs. 4.65/kg for wheat and Rs. 6.15 for rice. Government wanted to reform and make improvement in PDS distribution system by focusing on poor and needy section of society resulted in the launching TDPS (Targeted Public Distribution System) in 2001. The object is to identify the person/ families living below poverty line (BPL) and issue a distinct ration

TABLE 5

The Quantity of Cereals and Sugar Allotted to Delhi and its Distribution through the PDS during 2005-07

Description	*ITEM*					
	Rice		*Wheat*		*Sugar*	
	2005-06	*2006-07*	*2005-06*	*2006-07*	*2005-06*	*2006-07*
A QUANTITY ALLOTED						
1. Above Poverty Line (APL)	2934440	1127190	7030720	3017770	—	—
2. Below Poverty Line (BPL)	424200	445440	1060440	1039200	336360	336360
3. Antyodya Anna Yojna (AAY)	66600	66600	166560	166560	—	—
B QUANTITY LIFTED FOR DISTRIBUTION						
1. Above Poverty Line (APL	540471	954127	2406695	2818334	—	—
2. Below Poverty Line (BPL)	412536	433330	1035653	1022051	318895	315981
3. Antyodya Anna Yojna (AAY)	62099	66100	160439	160402	—	—
C PERCENTAGE DISTRIBUTED						
1. Above Poverty Line (APL)	18	84	34	93	—	—
2. Below Poverty Line (BPL)	97	97	98	98	95	94
3. Antyodya Anna Yojna (AAY)	93	99	96	100	—	—

Source: Economic Survey of Delhi, 2007-08.

card for selling specified cereals through PDS outlets at 50 per cent. Under PDS the scheme is for the poorest section of population having unable to get two square meal a day on sustained basis through out the year and their purchasing power is so low that they are not in a position to buy foodgrains round the year even at BPL rates. These families will be provided 35 kg. per family/month at the rate of Rs. 2 for wheat/rice which was limited to 15.33 per cent of the BPL families in Delhi. 59162 cards were issued to AAY families under this scheme. This scheme of 10 kg. food per head/month will be supplied free of cost to destitute people who are more than 65 yrs. of age and not receiving old age pension from the government (which is limited to 20 per cent only for national old age pension scheme).

Food Subsidy

In recent years an important agenda of economic reforms in India has been to reduce the scares of food and scale of food subsidy by means of targeting the system of PDS

The first budget presented on 28/2/1948 had a provision of 19.91 crores on food subsidy which was 1.6 per cent of total civilian budget.

Food subsidies in India compromise of:

- (i) Subsidies to farmers through minimum support price and purchase option of FCI.
- (ii) Consumer subsidy through PDS is a subsidy increased on foodgrain through PDS below the FCI economic cost.
- (iii) Cost of buffer operations: These costs are:
    - (a) Cost related to maintain the minimum level of buffer stocks as directed by national food security requirements.
    - (b) Cost of holding excess stocks for food security and PDS.
- (iv) The inefficiency of FCI, i.e. cost in excess of permissible limit in its various operations.

TABLE 6

Growth of Food Subsidies

Year	*Food subsidy (In Rs. Crores)*	*Annual Growth (in %)*	*% of GDP*
1991-92	2,850	16.33	0.44
1992-93	2,800	(-)1.75	0.37
1995-96	5,377	5.43	0.45
1999-2000	9,434	3.67	0.49
2000-01	12,060	27.84	0.58
2001-02	17,499	45.10	0.77
2002-03	24,176	38.16	0.98
2004-05	17,639	—	—
2008-09	32,667	—	—

Source: Economic Survey, 2008-09.

Food subsidy grew steeply at an annual rate of 28 to 45 per cent between 2001 to 2003.

The share of subsidy in GDI expenditure has gone up to 9.5 per cent, the highest since 1993. A sum of Rs. 32,667 crores is being prvided for food subsidy under PDS during 08-09. For FY 2009-10, the food/welfare subsidy is revised to 109.6 billion (Economic Survey, 2009)

All the food subsidies are targeted towards the relief of poorest in the society. As per report prepared by NIPFP suggested about food subsidies that minimum support price should be kept at C_2 level as recommended by CACP.

PD Share the safety net for poor for food security. Subsidy related to PD sharing has two major issues:

(a) Whether targeted group receive sufficient subsidies for PDS.

(b) Whether these subsidies are provided efficiently or not.

CONCLUSION

Globalization is a boundary less free trade which is to be used for well-being of people worldwide. The experiences/ technology transfers, capital flow, employment should spread worldwide through deterritorialization of geographical boundaries. It has reduced the distances and free flow of technology, trade, peace and harmony in the world.

Globalization is a fact and a process that world's people and nations are more interdependent than ever before and becoming more so in the years to come.

Globalization is a healthy process of development and boon for developing/under developed economies to match with the developed economies and this process must continue worldwide.

WTO is a regulatory body through which multinational institution dealing with the rules of trade for development of world economy. The global trade, protection, securities and optimum use of world resources for sustainable development among its member countries.

Food security is the availability of food and a household do not live in fear of starvations. Since first budget in 1948, it was stressed upon "Self-sufficiency in foodgrains must claim highest priority" and it is good that government is incurring expenditure for the fod security. The food security system in the country has the objective to provide minimum nutritional support to poor at affordable price stability in different parts of the country which involves a large amount in subsidies.

Food availability refers to the availability of food through own production as well as from import of foodgrain in the country. It is useful in maintenance of food buffer and to supply through PDS in the country.

Food access refers to transportation and food distribution system which gets food to where it is needed. All members of society should obtain sufficient food for the living.

PDS works to benefit basically BPL people in rural segments in India. PDS ensures the distribution of essential items, foodgrains, sugar, kerosene oil at subsidized price to cardholders and modulate in open market prices. PDS has more than 4.5 lakh opening throughout the nation. PDS is the joint responsibility of central and state governments to benefit below poverty line (BPL) people.

The greatest drawback in PDS is that it works on ration card system where there are mostly irregularities due to fair price shop owners attached to a certain political party and are biased in making ration cards/identification of BPL families. Secondly, the ration from buffer godowns does not reach to ration shops and are offloaded in open market. Number of BPL family cards are not matching with government figures. Inferior quality of items sold through PDS or closure of these shops at most of the time, BPL families do not get the benefit of these PDS.

It was aimed since first budget in 1948 to subsidize food and at that time 19.91 crores or 14.6 per cent of budget were kept for food subsidies. Since that time till date, food subsidy bills are incurring upto 32000 crores in 2008-09 and may more than 1 lakh crores in 2009-10.

Criss-cross movement by FCI, mishandling, pilferages in rail transport, storage in open godowns, unprotected foodgrains often incur cost which government has to subsidize. Non-cooperation of government authorities/local bodies also affects subsidy bills. Due to fake bills (without transportation of material) to PDS, huge money goes in the hands of middlemen/officials and enhance subsidies to the government.

RECOMMENDATIONS/SUGGESTIONS

Globalization is no doubt a universal process by which world has become a village and free flow of trade/opportunities/employment/talent, peace and prosperity is available worldwide.

The greatest threat is for developing countries. They begin to rely more on developed economies as free trade which causes a threat to the developing economy. Use of "Greenhouse technology" is a serious threat to global warming.

It is recommended that these developed economies should be regulated by use of anti-dumping, fixing of quota of export and protection to the undeveloped economy by regulation through WTO.

Heavy penalties should be imposed for the destruction of environment due to greenhouse discharges of gases so that world becomes free from global warming. Excessive use of agrochemicals/fertilizers also pollutes soil/water by these developed nations which should be limited on the basis of international standards.

Food subsidies are incurring more due to malfunction of PDS/FCI which is a great cause of concern for the government. The panchayati system should keep a watch on the working of PDS and time to time there should be verification of families/cards through the records of ration shops as well as buffers.

Suggestive measures for smooth working of PDS are:

(a) Thumb impression/signatures should be taken on issue register and to be verified by government official periodically. Simultaneously a village level committee should verify these entries, which should be represented by at least 10 members of different status of society (Women/SC/ST/OBC). This checking should be named as third party checking.

(b) Opening/closing time of shops, ration availability and rate should be displayed on board.

(c.) Bar coded tokens are to be issued so that the genuinity of the party at the time of issue of ration is to be judged.

(d) Villagers should keep watch on the working of PDS and report to BDO or DM nearby if there are irregularities in opening/closing of these shops.

(e) Biometric cards to be issued to be swiped in ration cards to minimize the fraud business.

(f) Quick disposal of pending cards/punishment to be awarded if found guilty and licenses should be cancelled under disobey of essential commodity act.

Government should encourage farmers to produce more by enhancing MSP of crops so that the interests of these farmers are to be kept for the welfare of society. Credit at low rates, increase in infrastructures like irrigation projects/roads/markets, godowns, co-operative/contract farming are the measures to enhance agricultural production through government/private participation for the development of agriculture. A robust growth in agriculture is needed for food and nutritional security for growing population and it has been proved that India became successful from "SIP to mouth" to self-sufficient in food production.

Let us join a campaign nationwide to enhance food production so that food security should be available as FOOD for ALL. Let us repeat the slogan given by our prime minister, Late Sh. Lal Bahadur Shastri and we have to keep in mind that we have to go miles away in making the country a self-sufficient in food reliance.

References

Ahluwalia, D., Public Distribution of Food in India.

Alagh, Y.K Globalization and Agricultural Crisis.

Bhalla, G.S.(1995), Globalization and Agricultural Policy in India.

Chadha, G.K., WTO and the Indian Economy.

Fertilizer Statistics, Various Issues (2000-09).

Food and Nutrition Bulletin—Various Issues.

Govt. of India, Draft Approach Paper to the 11th Five Year Plan.

Govt. of India, Economic Survey 2001-09.

Govt. of India, Ministry of Food and Agriculture. Farm Harvest Prices of Principal Crops in India Agricultural Prices in India—Various Issues.

Gulati, Ashok Mehta, Rajesh Narayan, Sudha, Indian Agriculture in a Globalizing World.

Indian Economic Association, Conference Volumes India—Various Issues.

Indian Journal of Agricultural Economics, Various Issues (2005-09).

Mishra, R.S. (2001), The WTO Agreement on Agriculture.

Panchmukhi, V.R., WTO and India—Challenges and Perspectives.

Radhakrishnan, R., Subbarao, K., Ravi, C., India's Public Distribution System (World Bank Discussion Paper No. 380, 1997).

Roscgrant, M.W.C. Ringlen and Gerpacio, R.V., Water and Land Resources and Global Food Supply.

Rosen, S. and Wicbc, K., Agricultural Productivity and Food Security in Developing Countries.

Sen, Aditya Sahai Suman, WTO and India's Response.

Shukla, S.P., WTO and India.

Surya Narayan, M.H., PDS, Beyond Implicit Subsidy and Urban Bias—The Indian Experience.

Swaminathan, M.S., Sustainable Agriculture: Towards an Evergreen Revolution.

World Bank, India's Foodgrain Marketing Policies.

Economic Reforms, Agriculture and Food Security in India

ASHWINI KANT JHA, BHAVNA JHA AND DILIP KUMAR

Basic tenets of the current economic reforms, liberalization and globalization are accepted by a large number of developing countries. In essence Indian government approach in this regard is not dissimilar to the policies pursued by a number of countries who have adopted for what has come to be known as structural adjustment. However, a distinguishing feature of our experience has been a sequential and a cautious approach to reforms. Accelerated of not triggered by the balance of payments crisis of 1991. It was natural to institute reforms in the foreign trade sector and in the first place such reforms also became necessary with our acceptance of world trade under the aegis of an international authority. Reforms in the foreign trade sector were followed by domestic reforms that is doing away with a large number of centralized controls and regulations as well as different forms of restrictive trade practices. In other words, dismantling Permit Quota Raj. These were followed by reforms in financial sector with more autonomy being extended to the financial institutions. The entry of foreign capital was liberalized and made less discriminatory. There was also pious resolution to curtail fiscal deficit. We all understand that what I described above is in some ways caricaturing the reforms process, which was much more blurred, with overlapping measures in different area. But the underlying sequence is clear. More importantly, the policy-makers in our country have so far resisted the so-called Comprehensive Approach to reforms engulfing all sectors in on one sweep.

The second distinguishing feature of Indian reform process is the slow and halting manner in which reforms were executed. The pressure exerted by some quarters to hasten the pace of reforms was resisted. Again, as in sequencing the slow pace of reforms was not a part of preplanned design. Several *ad-hoc* decisions were taken and as is expected in competitive politics, several compromises were made. But the dominant trends in the reforms process at least in retrospect, seen to be on the lines I have described above. The main reasons for following such sequential and cautious approach in my view have to be sought in the compulsion of a democratic multiparty polity where a measure of consequence building a imperative before any drastic step can be taken. One fact however is clear, i.e. India did not suffered from major dislocation as have been faced by several other countries in the initial phase of reforms. Example, sharp decline in GDP and employment ranging inflation and collapse of institutions. On all these counts, we have come out more or less un-scattered. If a different and a debatable issue whether due to these reforms the rate of growth has been accelerated whether the plight of vulnerable sections has become less serious. On those matters Jury is still out.

Now that we are entering into second phase of reforms which admittedly in a much more difficult phase we have to be careful about the future course of action. The first phase was relatively easy as the required changes in trade, finance and fiscal areas are well known. In the second phase issues of equity regional sectoral allocation, etc., will become more prominent. Hard decision of competition policy, labour policy, disinvestment and privatization will have to be taken. These sections of population who will adversely affected are numerically important, better-organized and articulate. They are capable to shift negative consequences of reforms on those who are poor, unrecognized and handicapped. The attempt in this is to suggest the imperatives for the next phase of reforms in agriculture, a sector with which I am slightly more familiar and iron understanding its features and characteristics. Edit by following Prof. Dantwala try to apply the touch stone of growth while examining contemplated measures of reforms in agriculture.

REFORMS IN AGRICULTURE

Even in the backdrop of the slow pace of reforms in the country policy changes in agriculture were still slower. There were sufficient reasons to take a more cautious approach to economic reforms in this sector. In the first place, there were no serious distorations in agriculture as were evidenced in industrial sector. Aggregate measure of support calculated by various scholars though yielding different results did not suggest any gross distortion either positive or in negative terms. A most sensitive indicator, inter-sectoral terms of trade, although, adverse to agriculture. Reforms in non-farm sectors and better alignment of Indian currency had a salutary impact on agriculture. Besides, it was recognized that non-price measures such as development of technology and creation of infrastructure were more important for agricultural growth than the market-oriented measures. In any case a large section of population in agriculture had very weak linkages with the markets both as producers and consumers those who had such linkages were firmly articulate and would not yield any advantages which they might be extracting from the system. Government was also extra careful as think could be done that might jeopardize food security. Finally, agriculture being a state object in foregoing and implementing policies for this sector, states had a larger say. Most of the states were dragging their feed in implementing reforms in the non-agricultural sector. There were more than lukewarm when it came to reforms in agriculture.

Mainly for this reasons no drastic policy changes could take place during the first phase reforms. Nevertheless certain irritants and obvious distortions were sought to be remove. The most important among these being the abolition of zonal restrictions on the movement of the agricultural commodities especially foodgrains even after the abolition of zones, occasionally state government did not impose movement restrictions. But the fact that India was a single market for agricultural commodities was by and large well established. The other direction in which economic reforms got a fillip was in the area of privatization. Private agencies were given of services and in agricultural extension.

Also, controls were released for a few commodities such as non-nitrogenous fertilizers in line with general trade reforms, there was liberalization of imports as well as exports of agricultural commodities to a certain extent.

Before we think of the second round of reforms in agricultural sector, we should bring some of the measures already initiated to their logical conclusion. For example, monopoly of cotton purchases in Maharashtra or food rationing in Calcutta are clearly anomalous in the present context. Irrational levied on sugar or rice milling have not served any useful purposes. They have added to price discrimination, clandestine trade risk and uncertainty. Use of Essential Commodities Act in most of the circumstances is a Panicky reaction rather than a part of a well thought out strategy. Some of the roadblocks have to be removed before we think about significant changes in the policies.

Now a time has come to make a comprehensive review of the government policies in agricultural sector. This is mainly because of the changes in the external environment especially after our joining WTO. There are also important changes in the internal environment. The country has been transformed from a deficit country to self-sufficient, in fact marginally surplus in the staple foodgrains. Yet dependence of work force on agriculture has not declined in any remarkable way nor the incidence of rural poverty is significantly reduced. Recent stagnation in agricultural productivity in the face of rising demand is another worrisome feature. The building up of foodgrains stocks to an uncertaintable level is another indicator which puts a question mark on the validity and efficacy of subsidies contributing to mounting fiscal imbalance and crowding put public investment in agriculture is another area of concern. These are basically symptoms of underlying a rot. A serious look at the agricultural policies is therefore urgently called for. In a meaningful way, success or failure of our economic reforms can be clearly judged as to what is happening in the sector on which largest number of people are dependent for their livelihood and which still has significant impact on other sectors of the economy.

Globalization, it is argued, will result in an efficient

allocation or world resources and enhance human welfare. Removal of the threat of hunger and provision of food security seems to be one of the major ways in which welfare can be enhanced. However, globalization is essentially an expansion of World Market. Market by its very nature, is sensitive only to the signals that are generated within its periphery. Since hungry people cannot put forward effective demand, market may remain completely intensive to them. In fact famine and hunger in large part of the world has been a direct impact of market force through fall in effective employment or income manifested in entitlement failure. Public action is required to correct these distortions in market so as to enable a world secured from hunger.

In this paper our focus is on India. After sixty-two years of independent, the government authority in India boats of self-sufficiency in foodgrains production. It is however ironic that though government godowns are flooded with excess foodgrains, tribal people in Orissa Survive on mango Kernel. These anomalies in the claim and reality have to be properly assessed. It is further more important since India is committed to GATT and WTO that seeks to open up our agrarian system to the competition from outside.

This paper heavily depends on secondary data. The present paper is organized as follows. In the next section, we concentrate on the supply factors that are important in studying the problem of food security. Section third, deals with entitlement failure that give to deprivation in food. Section fourth, complete the analysis with brief conclusion.

FOODGRAIN PRODUCTION

It is true that considerable under-nutrition may coexist with abundance of food. Nevertheless, supply of foodgrains is an important factor toward food security. A large number of studies exist that study foodgrains in India. These studies can be categorized into two groups. On the one hand, there are studies that lump up various types of foodgrains by their values (Bhalla and Singh, 1997). On the other, some studies focus on the individual crop pattern and foodgrains as a whole in terms of their physical quantity (Saha and Swaminathan, 1994). Both the methods have their relative merits and demerits. We, however, favour the latter method for the simple reason that valuation in agriculture is a really tricky issue. It raises a lot of questions that are unanswered as yet (Rudra, 1992). Hence, it would be worthwhile to consider foodgrains production in quantitive terms only.

Data on yearly production area and yield of principle crops can be obtained from various publications of the GoI. We have computed long-run linear growth of area production and yield for 15 selected states of India over the period 1950-51 to 2000-01. The result are presented in Table 1.

The figures in Table 1 have some clear indication. To begin with, it is obvious that in terms of both yield and production, North Western states dominate. However the picture is different for area expansion. In this case, Eastern states seem to take up upper hand. It implies that there is little scope for further expansion in area of foodgrains production in the lending states. Only way in which prodcution can be further improved in this zone is through improvement of yield rate. Unfortunately, however this depends on the availability and adoption of improved technology which have the usual limitations. Such technology adoption may enhance greater environment risks which may have adverse effects. Further, the Socio-economic fabric of the society can be seriously impaired through rising inequality and poverty as it is evidenced from the phases of the Green Revolution.

The onus now falls on the Eastern States. There is however serious apprehension as to the extent to which this region can be respond to the challenge. So far as the Central and Southern States are concerned, it seems they are more interested in the cash crops. Furthermore a large portion of these states face semi-arid conditions. Little advancement have been made toward sustainable development in the semi-arid region. Given the constraints in water supply, it is extremely difficult to enhance production in this area. Coupled with resources condition and the socio-economic structure, further improvement in foodgrains production along the traditional line seems extremely bleak.

In all, this calls for a radically new outlook towards food security. Harnessing local food habits and exploiting the possibilities of eco-friendly cultivation of high nutrient crops of local varieties may seem to be possible alternative. In fact, it is the

TABLE I

Linear Growth Rate of Foodgrains (1950-51—2000-01)

States	*Growth rates of*					
	Area	*Rank*	*Yield*	*Rank*	*Production*	*Rank*
North-West						
Haryana	0.43	6	4.07	2	4.52	1
Punjab	-0.12	11	4.26	1	4.14	2
UP	10.38	7	2.62	5	3.01	3
East						
Assam	1.07	1	0.73	15	1.83	12
Bihar	-0.1	10	2.23	7	2.09	10
Orissa	0.99	2	1.23	14	2.23	8
West Bengal	0.51	5	1.91	11	2.44	6
Central						
Gujarat	-0.51	13	2.74	3	2.22	9
MP	0.6	4	2.00	9	2.6	5
Maharashtra	0.002	9	1.73	12	1.73	13
Rajasthan	0.87	3	2.00	10	2.89	4
Southern						
AP	-0.54	14	2.63	4	2.07	11
Karnataka	0.07	8	2.29	6	2.37	7
Kerala	-1.1	15	1.45	13	0.34	15
Tamil Nadu	-0.41	12	2.03	8	1.61	14
Total	0.31		2.32		2.71	

Notes: 1. Figures in parentheses give the relative rank.
2. Figures for Haryana from 1957-58 and Gujarat from 1955-56.

dependence of the so-called HYV seeds that had led to a substantial decline in the bio-diversity of our traditional crop pattern. Globalization with its emphasis on profit with the exclusion of all other objectives have formed this process. Farmers are lured towards cultivation of HYV seeds that produce large monetary benefits. In the process, local varieties have been lost. These varieties have often proved to be better resistant to the natural calamities such as flood or drought. In short, emphasis should be move on local level supply and demand than on the nation-wide goal-seeking pursued so far.

ENTITLEMENT FAILURES

A significant way to deal with the problem is to concentrate on the so-called food requirement. Food requirement norms is based on 2250 calories daily per capita. This implies a per capita requirement of 186 kg. per year. This norm is set-up by AFO as well as the National Commission on Agriculture for the Developing Countries (2001) have calculated the additional food requirement. They have projected this figure upto the year 2020. We reproduce in Table 2 a brief summary of their findings.

TABLE 2

Additional Foodgrains Requirement in India

Year	*Additional Food Requirement (MT)*	
1991	-7.0	
1995	-6.1	*Indian Economic Survey* (1999-200)
2000	-8.8	
2005	-9.9	
2010	-9.1	*Projected Figure*
2020	-5.9	

Source: Mukhargee, Chattopadhyay and Neogi (2001).

Table 2 shows that no food deficit will occur after 2000. There appears to be little evidence that overall food supply have fallen short of the requirement, it is then a concern why under nourishment and malnourishment persists in a country where foodgrains supply is adequate. The answer clearly lies in the entitlement failures as suggested by Dreze and Sen (1989). Growth of the economy has been extremely uneven. This leaves a section of the people at precariously low level of existence. With extremely poor level of income and wealth, they cannot acquire enough entitlement over foodgrains that could save them from starvation and undernourishment.

Dreze and Sen (1984), argues that poverty can be used as an effective indicator of deprivation. We can compare the poverty figures across the states. Poverty measures are available for five years only (1973-74, 1977-78, 1983, 1987-88 and 1993-194). We represent the figure for only two years 1973-74 and 1993-94 in Table 3.

TABLE 3

Levels of Poverty in India by selected States

States	*1973-74*			*1993-94*		
	Rural	*Urban*	*Overall*	*Rural*	*Urban*	*Overall*
North-West						
Haryana	34.23	40.18	35.36	28.02	16.38	25.05
Punjab	28.21	27.96	28.15	11.95	11.35	11.77
UP	56.53	60.09	57.07	42.28	35.39	27.41
East						
Assam	52.67	36.92	51.21	45.1	07.73	40.86
Bihar	62.99	52.96	61.91	58.21	34.50	54.96
Orissa	67.28	55.62	66.18	49.72	41.64	48.56
West Bengal	73.16	34.67	63.43	40.82	22.41	35.66
Central						
Gujarat	46.35	53.97	48.15	22.18	27.89	24.21
MP	62.66	57.65	61.78	40.64	48.38	42.52
Maharashtra	57.71	43.87	53.24	37.93	35.15	36.86
Rajasthan	44.78	52.13	46.14	26.46	30.49	40.85
Southern						
AP	48.41	50.62	48.86	15.91	38.33	22.19
Karnataka	55.14	52.53	54.47	29.98	40.14	33.16
Kerala	59.19	62.74	59.97	25.76	24.55	25.43
Tamil Nadu	57.43	49.40	54.64	32.48	39.27	35.03
India	56.44	49.01	54.88	32.36	32.36	35.97

The figures in Table 3 have some clear indications. Firstly, relative position of the states have changed. Punjab was the state with lowest poverty both in 1973-74 and 1993-94. However in 1973-74, Orissa was the state with highest poverty. In 1993-94, the position was taken over by Bihar state such as AP and West Bengal have shown remarkable improvement in poverty redressal. This indicates towards proper public action for redressal of poverty. It may be noted that West Bengal is a laggard state in foodgrains production. Hence, the improvement is commendable.

An interesting feature of this table is lower rural poverty in several states. This indicate greater vulnerability of the weaker group in the urban sector to food security. In rural areas poor people may get food either in terms of wage or through loan. This somewhat helps them towards food entitlement. The finding indicates the view expressed by Dreze and Sen (1989) that the vulnerability of wage labourers can be particularly accrue in the intermediate phase in which class of workers have became large so that the traditional security measures proves inadequate while modern social security system has not yet developed.

It calls for a strong public action on the part of Government to remedy the situation. However, committed towards liberalization and globalization, the state does not seems to be interested in such matters of public choice.

CONCLUSION

We conclude above discussion on the direction of reforms in agriculture in the next round of economic reforms. The agricultural sector has multiple roles in developing countries, anchor rural development, provides resources for the livelihood and adequate incomes of a majority of people and to do this without destroying the environmental base. There are thus two inextricably linked components social and environmental to agricultural sustainability.

The erosion of the spirit and practices of international cooperation, especially on a north-south basis in having serious repercussions on agriculture and non-rural development in developing countries. This erosion is most noticeable in the decline in aid. However, the globalization process facilitated by structural adjustment, the Uruguay round and the WTO has even more serious implications. It is imperative that a change of mindset takes place, beginning at WSSD to review the present damaging framework and build a new paradigm of policies that can promote sustainable agriculture.

We should maintain ceiling on agricultural land holding till the pace of diversification in rural areas is accelerated and should not abandon the policy of food self-sufficiency till livelihood and consumption patterns change remarkably.

The main ingredient of a reform agenda in agriculture should be:

1. Acceleration of the process of liberalization in domestic markets.
2. Unfreezing the lease market.
3. Thoroughly revising agricultural prices support system.
   (a) Curtailing the scope of minimum support prices to aim at protecting variable costs for a few commodities in selected regions.
   (b) Giving greater emphasis on crop insurance and forward markets.
4. Carrying procurement operations on commercial lines.
5. Involving state and the lower tiers of Panchayati Raj in PDS.
6. Dovetailing price and trade policies in an effective manner.
7. Working out a long-term export strategy for commercial crops and other dynamic and high values crops.
8. Progressive decentralization of exports of agricultural commodities and removing other irritants.
9. Establishing the principle of cost recovery in agriculture inputs and phasing out subsidies by:
   (a) Placing a cap on existing subsidies.
   (b) Announcement of a time bound programme of phasing out input subsidies.

The paper tries to understand food security in the context of an under developed country like India which is committed towards liberalization and globalization. The analysis presented in the paper indicates that the foodgrains production scenario is far from satisfactory. However, even then India possess sufficient food stock to feed her people. Mass poverty and inequality resulting from uneven growth has led to massive entitlement failure. It calls for urgent public action to remedy the situation.

References

Bhaltia, B.M (1983), "Availability of Foodgrains" in *Population, Poverty and Hope,* edited by Centre for Policy Research, New Delhi.

Dreze, J. and Sen, A. (1989), "Hunger and Public Action", Oxford University Press, New Delhi.

Rudra, A. (1992), "Political Economy of Indian Agrticulture", K.P. Bagchi and Sons, Kolkata.

Subramanian Swamy, India's Economic Performs and Reforms, pp. 12-19.

Vijay Shankar Vyas, India's Agrarian Structure, in *Economic Policies and Sustainable Development*, pp. 1-30.

Index

Agrarian Structure;
  Factors Affecting Changes, 285
Agreements Related to Agriculture, 104
Agricultural Credit Flow in Bihar;
  Infrastructure Factors, 276
Agricultural Credit;
  Institutionalisation, 151
  Growth and Instability, 273
Agricultural Development;
  Growth Rates of Factors Affecting, 55
Agricultural Diversification and Economic Growth, 1
Agricultural Experts, 146, 155
Agricultural Export Liberalisation, 88
Agricultural Growth, 365
Agricultural Reforms, 120
Agriculture and Allied Sectors;
  Economic Security Against Rising Risks, 201
Agriculture and Research;
  Public Spending, 139
Agriculture;
  Composition of Investment, 118
  Structural Reforms, 144
  Trends of Investment, 150
  Flow of Imitational Credit, 128
  Gross Capital Formation, 136
  Structural Changes, 91
  Diversification, 146
Agriculture Development, 50
Agriculture in Developing Countries;
  Impact of Globalization, 153
Agro-processing Units;
  Review of Returns on Investment, 188
Ahmad, Firdos, 322
Ahmad, Jamil, 322
AICL (Agricultural Insurance Company of India Limited), 204
Alam, Dasgir, 322
Amending the Land Acquisition, 295
Animal Husbandry, 16, 41
Animal Husbandry to Growth of the Eastern Region, 223
AoA (Agreement on Agriculture), 102
Asean Countries;
  Development Experience, 67
Assam;
  Average Yield of Major Crops, 10
Availability of;
  Pulses, 312
  Gram, 311
  Rice, 309
  Milk in India, 35

Bank Credit;
  Sectoral Credit, 266
Bhardwaj, Sanjeev, 101
Bihar;
  Agricultural Credit Flow, 272
  Average Yield of Major Crops, 11
  Women Dairy Project, 186
Bio-Resources, 40, 221
Breeding of Animals, 166

CCID (Central Crop Insurance Department), 204
Climate Change;
Challenges, 98
Compound Growth in Agriculture, 365
Credit Constraints, 140
Credit;
Continuance of Informal Source, 268
Credit Deposit Ratio, 266
Credit to Farmers, 206
Crop Diversification, 85
Cropping Pattern and Crops, 8, 40
Productivity, 8
Horticulture, 8

Dairy Cattle Health, 168
Dairy Development, 18
Dairying Practice in Bihar, 174
Deposits and Credit, 264
Devarajulu, M., 290
Developing Milk Producing Units, 165
Development of;
Warehousing, 87
Rural Godowns, 87
Cold Storage, 87
Cargo Terminals, 87
Sea Ports, 87
Agricultural Output, 88
Poultry and Small Ruminants, 19
Agriculture in Backward Areas, 148
Disbursements Trends, 269
Diversion of Credit, 206
Dixit, Rachna, 232
Doha Round and Indian Agriculture, 4
Dry Land Agriculture, 288

Eastern India;
Agricultural Diversification, 224
Characteristics and Basic Resources, 219
Economic Liberalisation, 145
Economic Reforms, 380
Emerging Trade Order, 80
Employment in India;
Agriculture Still the Largest Provider, 70
Empowerment of Weaker Sections, 185
Environmental Resources, 322
E-Trading, 151

FAO (Food and Agriculture Organisation), 305
Farm Electrification, 84
Farming Systems Approach, 20
Farm Inputs;
Liberalisation, 87
FDI in Agriculture, 154
Food and Fodder Development, 167
Finance;
Revisiting, 207
Fish Resources, 222
Floriculture, 13
Food Absorption, 315
Food Accessibility, 352
Food Availability, 307, 352, 369
Food Processing, 147
Foodgrain Production, 384
Food PDS and Food Subsidy, 360
Food Security and Agricultural Trade Policy Reform, 344
Food Security;
Component, 352
Meaning, 352
Indicators, 345
Definition, 343
Measurement, 306
Food Security in Jharkhand;
Current Status, 211
Food Subsidy, 374
Food Utilization, 352
Free Trade, 145

GATT (General Agreement on Tariffs and Trade), 2, 101
Globalization, 360
Advantages, 362
Disadvantages, 361
Globalisation and Food Security, 351
Gnanavelan, A., 342

Good Quality Seeds, 86
Ground Level Credit Flow, 262
Growth in GSDP and Agriculture Sector, 26

Harnessing the Gains of Frontier Technologies, 20
High Rainfall and Humidity, 29
Horticulture, 41, 222
  Increase in the Production, 147
  Exports, 33
Hurdles in Economic Security, 205

Inadequate Credit to Farmers, 206
Inadequate Infrastructure, 28
Increase in Subsidies, 149
Index of Agriculture Production;
  Growth Rate, 135
Indian Agriculture;
  Enhancing Competitiveness, 83
  Priority Issues, 108
  Post-Reform, 132
  Trends in Investment, 116
Indian Economy;
  Basic Nature, 68
Indian States;
  Structural Transformation, 285
India;
  Structural Reforms, 48
  Structural Reforms at Global Level, 46
  Production and Export of Fish, 34
  Achieving Food Security, 304
  WTO and Food Security, 342
  Structural Changes and Agriculture, 44
  Growth and Transformations in Agricultural Output and Inputs, 239
  Agrarian Structure, 280
  Land Reforms and its Impact on Agriculture, 297
Individual and Family Food Security, 344
Information on Financial Literacy, 207
Institutional Finance, 120
International Food Security, 345
Investment in Agriculture, 111

Irrigation Facilities, 86
Irrigation Imperatives, 138

Jain, Deepak, 101
Jha, Ashwini Kant, 379
Jha, Bhavna, 380
Jharkhand;
  Productivity of Crops, 212
  Strategy for Ensuring Food, 213
  Agro-Economic Condition, 210

Kisan Credit Card Scheme, 130
Konar, Dhirendran Nath, 63
Kumar, Dalip, 304
Kumar, Dilip, 380
Kumar, Gaurav, 6, 120
Kumar, Ratnesh, 188
Kumar, R. Raj, 342
Kumar, Vinod, 272
Kumari, Anjana, 201
Kumari, Poonam, 144
Kumari, Rajini, 210
Kumari, Vena, 210

Land Acquisition in India;
  Methods, 291
Land Market, 286
Land Question in India, 301
Land Reforms, 287
Land Resources, 39, 219
Livestock Resources, 222

Major Crops Cropping Sequences, 9
  Agro-Ecological Sub-Regionwise, 9
Marketing of Milk, 168
Medicinal Aromatic Plants, 15
MGNREGA (Mahatma Gandhi National Rural Employment Guarantee Act), 320
Micro-finance Concept, 207
Micro-finance Institutions, 130
Milk Marketing by COMFED, 179
Milk Procurement and COMFED, 178
Misra, Pritibha, 101
Mishra, Pankaj Kumar, 111
Mittal, Abha, 304

Multi-Dimensional ASSAIL, 171

NABARD, 127
NAIS (National Agricultural Insurance Scheme), 204
National Cattle and Buffaloes Breeding Programme, 166
National Dairy Development Board, 165
National Policy for Farmers, 131
Neglect of Small Marginal Farmers, 269
NERAMA (North-Eastern Regional Agricultural Marketing Corporation Limited), 195
Ninth Plan and Food Security, 356
Non-performing Assets, 267
North-Eastern Region in India;
    Agricultural Diversification, 216
NSC (National Seeds Corporation Ltd.), 194

Operation Flood, 165
Organic Farming, 70, 85
Orissa;
    Average Yield of Major Crops, 11

Pandey, Bharti, 132
Pandey, Sriman, 216
Pandiyan, M., 351
Patna Dairy Project, 180
PDS (Public Distribution System), 371
Piggery, 203
Piggery Development, 19
Plantation Crops, 14
Plight of the Stakeholders, 292
Policy for Land Acquisition, 290
Poor Compensation, 293
Post-harvest Management, 29, 225
Potential for Fisheries, 21
Poverty Reduction, 157
Principal Horticulture Crops;
    Estimated Production, 33
Priority Sector Lending, 263
Production and Area, 325
    Irrigation, 326
Production of Floriculture, 147
Production of Foodgrains, 145
Productivity and Irrigation, 326
Progress of Foodgrains, 353
Providing Market Access, 102
Provision of Package, 208

Rain Water Harvesting, 86
Rao, C.H. Hanumantha, 140
Rao, G. Chandrasekhara, 290
Rashtriya Krishi Vikas Yojana, 186
Reducing Domestic Support, 103
Reduction in Bank Branches, 269
Reforms in Agriculture, 382
Rehabilitation Package, 129
Revival of;
    Cooperative Credit Structure, 127
RKVY;
    Basic Structure, 122
Rural Credit;
    Trend, 260
        Branch Expansion, 260
        Agricultural Advances, 261
Rural Poverty, 72

SAA (Service Area Approach), 129
Sahoo, B.B., 259
Sahu, Purushottam, 91
Samantara, Samir R., 259
Sanction of Schemes;
    Delay by Banks, 206
Savaraiah, G., 290
Scheme of Debt Waiver, 129
Sericulture, 203
Sethi, Amarjit, 239
Sharma, Alpana, 359
Sharma, Devna, 232
Shroff, Babilata, 91
Singh, Angrej, 80
Singh, B.V., 165
Singh, G.P., 165
Singh, Kuldeep, 44
Singh, N.P., 165
Singh, P.D., 174
Singh, Rajendra Prasad, 11
Singh, Ramakant Pd., 120
Singh, Satendra Narayan, 1
Social Development Indicators, 25
Soil and Foodgrains Production, 327

Somra, S.S., 44
Sources of Credit, 126
Special Thrust on;
Fruits and Vegetables, 21
Spices, 13
State Domestic Product;
Share of Agriculture, 36
Strategies for Achieving Food Security, 319
Structural Changes;
Theoretical Perspectives, 64
Subsistance Cultivation, 29
Sustainable Agro-Forestry Systems, 20

Tenth Plan and Food Security, 357
Thakur, N.K., 360
Thakur, Ram Bharat, 272
Thakur, Ram Naresh, 1
Threats to Food Security, 368
Towards New Agriculture, 287
Trade Barriers;
Agriculture, 158
Traditional Agriculture, 224
Dependence, 26

UNDP (United Nations Development Programme), 307
Unemployment and its Solution;
Increasing Trend, 148
Universal Schemes of Credit, 206
Upadhyay, Rajnath, 216
Uttarakhand;
Agriculture, 232

Vandra, Dhiren, 297
Vegetables, 12
Violation of Human Rights, 294

Water Resources, 39, 220
WBCIS (Weather-based Crop Insurance Scheme), 204
West Bengal;
Average Yield of Major Crops, 10
What is Food Security?, 305
Who's Food Security?, 344
Women and Tribals;
Impact of Land Acquisition, 292
Workers;
Occupational Classification, 66
Working of a PDS, 372
Work Programme of the Future, 105
WTO and Indian Agriculture, 364

Yadav, Krishna Nand, 174

Zamindari System, 301